Anatomy of
the Sacred

JAMES C. LIVINGSTON

THE COLLEGE OF WILLIAM AND MARY

Anatomy of the Sacred

An Introduction to Religion

MACMILLAN PUBLISHING COMPANY
NEW YORK

Macmillan Publishing Company
866 Third Avenue, New York, New York 10022

Collier Macmillan Canada, Inc.

Library of Congress Cataloging-in-Publication Data

Livingston, James C., 1930–
Anatomy of the sacred.

Includes index.
1. Religion. 2. Religions. I. Title.
BL48.L48 1989   200   87-38327
ISBN 0-02-371370-4

Printing: 5 6 7   Year: 1 2 3 4 5

*To My Students and Colleagues
in the Department of Religion at
The College of William and Mary*

Preface

Anatomy of the Sacred presents a comprehensive introduction to the nature and variety of religious belief and practice. Designed for those who have not had a previous course in religion, it provides the beginning student with an understanding of what religion is, of the universal forms of religious experience, and of the basic concepts that make up a religious world view. By employing a comparative analysis across a rich range of ancient and modern religious traditions, this introduction allows students to see the ways in which certain classic forms of religious life appear in different societies over time, as well as to recognize the incredible diversity of human religious expression and belief.

The book is divided into three parts. Part I is concerned with such questions as the problem of defining religion, why it is important to study religion, and how one goes about the task, including the several disciplines or methods used in the study of religion. Each method is illustrated with specific examples from the work of eminent scholars in the field, such as Rudolf Otto, Carl Jung, Evans-Pritchard, Levi-Strauss, Victor Turner, and Mircea Eliade.

Part II is an introduction to the universal forms of religious experience and expression and includes discussions of the sacred or holy, religious symbolism, myth and doctrine, sacred ritual, and the social and ethical dimensions of religion. Each chapter includes an analysis of influential scholarship on the subject, and each topic is fully illustrated with, for instance, examples of the variety of forms of religious ritual and types of religious community.

Part III, which constitutes more than half of the book, consists of a comparative analysis of six concepts, each one representing a fundamental structure or aspect of a religious world view. A religious perspective is holistic, that is, it sees nature, human life, and the divine as interrelated and as forming a comprehensive vision of the world. A religion, therefore, includes a conception of sacred power and of an exemplary natural and social order. It offers an analysis of the breakdown or corruption of that order and of the human problem, but it also provides an answer to the ever-present threat of evil and chaos. Finally, a religious world view affords a way of achieving liberation or enlightenment and an ideal vision of the goal or end of human life. Part III thus includes analyses of such concepts as deity, cosmogony, the human problem, theodicy, the ways to salvation or liberation, and the end or goal of salvation. Again, each theme is illustrated by examples drawn from a wide variety of religious belief and behavior, ranging from primitive and archaic cultures through the religions of the present.

Two concluding chapters introduce especially critical issues facing religion today: religious pluralism and the process of secularization. Each chapter of the book includes a preliminary overview which gives the student a clear preview of the the major themes that follow. Each chapter also includes photographs, review questions, and suggestions for further reading. An extensive glossary provides a ready explanation of important terms and names used in the book.

A number of persons have assisted me in the completion of this book, and I am much in their debt. My colleagues Vinson Sutlive, Jack Van Horn, James Tabor, Charles Adams, and Joanna Gillespie read portions of the text and offered helpful advice. Jack Van Horn also assisted in the search for appropriate Asian graphic materials. The criticisms and suggestions offered by several anonymous readers of early drafts were invaluable. The inclusion of a number of their recommendations has, I believe, greatly improved the text. I am immensely grateful to these scholars for their meticulous reading of the manuscript. A summer fellowship from The College of William and Mary afforded me an uninterrupted period during which I was able to complete four chapters—at a time when it was desperately needed. Marla Esten, Laura Dillard, and Suzanne Gibson, William and Mary undergraduates, gave me valuable help. My wife Jackie once again typed drafts of several chapters and assisted me in numerous editorial tasks. Debbie Jenkins prepared the final typescript of several chapters. I owe my editor, Helen McInnis, warm thanks for her encouragement and excellent advice and her assistants, Robin Roy and Judy Shapiro, appreciation for their valuable help with the graphic materials.

J. C. L.

Contents

CHAPTER 6

Society and the Sacred: Social and Ethical Dimensions of Religion

130

PART III

Classic Forms of Religious Belief and Practice

CHAPTER 7

Deity

163

CHAPTER 11
Ways to Liberation and Salvation   *285*

CHAPTER 12
Goals of Liberation and Salvation   *319*

PART I

The Study of Religion

CHAPTER 1

What Is Religion?

OVERVIEW

We begin our exploration of the anatomy of religion with the observation that religion is a universal and abiding dimension of human experience. This is followed, however, by a rather embarrassing admission, for when we attempt to define this pervasive phenomenon, we immediately run into difficulties. We look, then, at the problems connected with some of the influential definitions of religion. We will see that, while none of them is fully adequate, they do give us valuable insight into some essential aspects of religion.

The clue to the religious dimension of human life is likely to be found in those characteristics that set us apart from other living species. This leads us to a second question—"Why are we religious?"—and an attempt to answer the question by looking at some unique features of human self-consciousness, what is sometimes called our capacity for "self-transcendence," and what that means.

A further preliminary question explored in this opening chapter is why we should study religion, and why it is an important subject of study at this particular time in history. No doubt you will be able to come up with some additional reasons of your own.

This chapter concludes with a brief discussion of how we go about the study of religion; in this case, by looking at the question of whether a student of religion can or, indeed, should be a devout believer, a nonbeliever, or a neutral observer. The answer to this question may be more complex than we imagine. At any rate, it is a matter that we ought to think about as we begin our study of religion.

3

Defining Religion

Few aspects of experience reveal the wealth, variety, and complexity that we encounter in a study of the religions of humankind. The playwright George Bernard Shaw once remarked, "There is only one religion, though there are hundreds of versions of it." We wonder, however, what Shaw had in mind when he spoke of *one* religion cloaked in a hundred forms. St. Augustine was closer to the mark when he observed; "If you do not ask me what time is, I know; if you ask me, I do not know." Religion, like time, is something we take for granted. We never doubt that we know what it is—until, of course, we start thinking about it. Then we encounter some uncertainties. There are, however, some things about which we are certain. One is that religion is as old as humankind. The evidence of **Neanderthal*** and **Cro-Magnon** man—fellow members of our own species *Homo sapiens*—is clear. From as long as 100,000 to 25,000 years ago, these humans practiced burial rites that indicate a belief in an afterlife. They also apparently practiced rites of **propitiation**, that is, made efforts to appease or conciliate spirits or powers. All cultures and societies about which we possess reliable information clearly reveal some form of this behavior. There do not appear to be any modern *societies* without religious beliefs and practices; however, there are individuals in modern societies who do not exhibit conventional religious activity. Nevertheless, anthropologists would agree that religion is a universal human phenomenon—a pervasive and, as we shall see, permanent reality. A human being is rightly called *Homo religiosus*, a religious animal.

If I speak so assuredly of the fact that humanity has practiced religion everywhere and at all times, we would expect that I should be able to define the meaning of the term or at least to describe the range of phenomena to which the word *religion* applies. But here the difficulties already begin to appear. It is a strange quandary: Unless we can define religion substantively—that is, unless we can indicate its reference range—it does not seem possible that we can begin to inquire into its nature or history. It is the definition that designates or delimits the type of phenomenon to be investigated. If we do not know what constitute observations of *religious* phenomena as opposed to other phenomena—say, kinship, politics, or medicine—how can we begin our study?

Religion has been studied extensively, but those studies, by and large, have been based on rather intuitive and conventional notions

* Words in boldface type are defined in the Glossary.

A Japanese monk, sitting in silent meditation, reflects the often-solitary dimension of the religious quest. (*Source:* Courtesy of Magnum Photos, Inc.)

of what defines religion. To indicate something of the problem, we can look at several influential definitions or descriptions of religion. We will begin with two that assume some form of theism or belief in gods, but we shall see that, in light of other definitions, these are not capable of serving as inclusive definitions. Here are our examples:

A. *"Religion is the belief in an ever-living God, that is, in a Divine Mind and Will ruling the Universe and holding moral relations with mankind."*

—*James Martineau*

B. *"Religion is an institution consisting of culturally patterned interaction with culturally postulated superhuman beings."*

—*Melford E. Spiro*

C. *"The essence of religion consists in the feeling of an absolute dependence."*

—*Friedrich Schleiermacher*

D. *"Religion is that which grows out of, and gives expression to, experience of the holy in its various aspects."*

—*Rudolf Otto*

E. *"Religion is what an individual does with his solitariness."*

—*Alfred North Whitehead*

F. *"Religion is the recognition of all our duties as divine commands."*
                                                          —Immanuel Kant

G. *"The religious is any activity pursued in behalf of an ideal end against obstacles and in spite of threats of personal loss because of its general and enduring value."*
                                                          —John Dewey

H. *"Religion is the state of being grasped by an ultimate concern, a concern which qualifies all other concerns as preliminary and which itself contains the answer to the question of the meaning of our life."*
                                                          —Paul Tillich

I. *"Religion is comparable to a childhood neurosis."*
                                                          —Sigmund Freud

J. *"Religion is the sign of the oppressed creature. . . . It is the opium of the people. . . . Religion is only the illusory sun which revolves around man as long as he does not revolve around himself."*
                                                          —Karl Marx

Each of these definitions or theories of religion is informative and each has been influential. However, not one of them strikes us as fully adequate. Certainly, they are not all compatible; some appear to be too *limited* in terms of what we know about the variety of historical expressions of religion. Certainly, James Martineau would limit religion to **monotheism** and thus would exclude the **polytheism** of much Greek and Roman religion, and popular Hinduism, as well as Theravada Buddhism and Confucianism, which are nontheistic. This is hardly an adequate definition. The anthropologist Melford Spiro is careful to avoid such a narrow conception. Furthermore, Spiro associates religion with belief in "superhuman beings," but he does not equate such beings with the supernatural. That is, religions may believe in spirits, powers, and processes that transcend the human, but that does not mean these are wholly transcendent, occupying a world beyond this natural one. That is an important corrective. But Spiro's definition, while broad and encompassing, seems almost too vague in its generality to capture some important characteristics of religion.

The definitions of Schleiermacher and Otto focus on the *affective*, or emotional and feeling, dimension of religious experience that is so important. They point especially to the profoundly real and pervasive human experiences of finitude and dependence, awe, fear, and mystery as essential to religious life. They appear correct in what they affirm but again narrow in what they leave out. The critical place of belief and the socially and ethically active dimensions of religion are left in the shade. In their different ways, the definitions of Whitehead and Kant are too narrow in scope. Kant perceives the profound moral dimension of religion, but he essentially reduces religion to the function of moral regulation; thus he leaves out important affective, aes-

The ceremonial Jewish seder, focal point of the festival of Passover, reveals the important familial and ritual dimensions of religion. (*Source:* Courtesy of Merrim, Monkmeyer Press Photo Service, Inc.)

thetic, social, and ritualistic dimensions of religious life. Whitehead's definition, like Kant's, appears too individualistic; furthermore, it is so vague as not to be very helpful.

The difficulty that we encounter in the interesting definitions of Dewey and Tillich is that they may be *too* inclusive. Dewey says that "the religious" is a *quality* of experience, a quality that may be found in aesthetic, scientific, or political activity. For Tillich, the research scientist or the political zealot whose commitment represents a "state of being grasped by an ultimate concern" is, by his definition, religious. It was said of Dewey—not entirely in jest—that, for him, everything can be religious except religion! It does appear, however, that for Dewey and Tillich almost everything and anything is capable of being religious. But if everything human is religious, then it would seem to be synonymous with politics or artistic endeavor and not a very informative concept.

The definitions—or, rather, theories—of Freud and Marx suffer from different limitations. They are explanatory in intent; that is, they claim to explain why or how religion came into being or why it persists—in these instances, as a neurosis or as an illusory happiness. They are essentially reductive in that they seek to reduce religion to either psychological processes or socioeconomic factors. Such an approach can be guilty of the **genetic fallacy**, the confusing of the essence, value, or truth of religion with an explanation of its origin. They may also, of course, be considered prejudicial because they regard religion as something infantile and illusory that must be overcome.

This brief survey of influential definitions of religion has made us aware that any one definition will likely have its difficulties and that there are certain definitional characteristics that should be avoided. An adequate definition should, for example, avoid *narrowness* through the exclusion of certain essential features of religion. To say simply that "religion is the recognition of all our duties as divine commands" is a case in point. *Vagueness*, a problem encountered with Whitehead's definition, is also to be avoided. An adequate definition should include both *distinctiveness* and *generality*; it should be distinctive enough for us to be able to distinguish religious phenomena from other forms of cultural life and expression, and yet it should be general enough to avoid being provincial, that is, relevant to only one religion or to religious life in one cultural setting or one time period. Monotheism would be an example of a definition that lacks appropriate generality. It is also important that a definition of the nature or essence of religion not be confused with a *causal explanation* of why humans are religious, as we saw with the definitions of Marx and Freud. Finally, it should be evident that an adequate definition of religion should avoid being *reductive* or *prejudicial*.

It has been said that defining religion is reminiscent of the fable of the blind men attempting to describe an elephant. "One touches its trunk and describes it as a snake; another touches its ear and describes it as a winnowing fan; another touches its leg and describes it as a tree; another its tail and describes it as a broom."[1] A one-sided definition reveals only the author's failure to see or to acknowledge what does not conform to his or her conception.

Our exercise would appear to make it obvious that no one definition will easily cover all that we mean by religion. However, definitions such as those we have cited can complement one another. We may find that we are not quite in the difficulty faced by St. Augustine when he was asked, "What is time?" We can, at the least, offer several tentative definitions which together are capable of pointing to essential features of the phenomenon which we call religion.

Why Are Humans Religious?

If we are correct that religion is both universally common and unique to our species, then we might expect to find the clue to why human beings are religious in those characteristics that distinguish us from other species. Through the centuries, thinkers have attempted to suggest what is unique about humankind. We are called *Homo sapiens*, a Latin term indicating that we humans are essentially sapiential, that is, possessed of wisdom or rationality. Others have spoken of *Homo faber*, man the maker or creator; *Homo ludens*, man the player or actor; or *Homo viator*, man the hoper.

All these terms imply that humans possess a distinct form of self-consciousness. The human self is a unique form of life in that it can be an object to itself. We are not only conscious, like other animals, but also self-conscious. We can stand clear of ourselves, of our immediate environment, even of our entire world—and look at ourselves, our environs, and the cosmos and make judgments about them. We can contemplate and reflect not only about means but also about ends, about the meaning, value, and purpose of life. We can look about us and say, for example, "Vanity, vanity, all is vanity"; or we can come to a very different conclusion and rejoice, "God's in His Heaven and all's right with the world."

It is from this fact of self-consciousness, or "self-transcendence," that the pressing questions of life come flooding in on us: "Why am I here?" "Why do righteous people suffer?" "To whom or what do I owe my ultimate loyalty and devotion?" "Is death the end?" These are what philosophers call the **existential** questions of life; they are universal and perennial; they are part of what it means to be human. To deny such questions concerned with life's meaning—moral obligation, guilt, injustice, finitude, and what endures—is to be less than human. That is why much recent talk about secularization or the widespread rejection of religious belief and institutions is, at a fundamental level, merely superficial.

In the modern world, many political ideologies have taken the place of traditional religious belief and ritual, as this large audience paying homage to Mao Tse-tung attests. (*Source:* Courtesy of Camera Press, Jeannette Harris, agent.)

We as human beings need sets of coherent answers to our existential questions as well as **archetypal** patterns of behavior and frames of reference because our lives, unlike those of other animal species, are not definable solely in terms of the satisfaction of the basic biological needs of food, shelter, and sex. While a fully human life obviously includes the satisfaction of these drives, they are not sufficient to satisfy such a life. We have other moral, aesthetic, and religious needs that, strangely, have no limits and cannot easily be satisfied. We are a union of nature and spirit and our consciousness of the tension between our spiritual or religious aspirations and our finitude and creatureliness—that we are both free of nature and yet bound by nature—leads to our existential anxiety but also to our spiritual quests.

As humans, we are all too conscious of those things that challenge and threaten to destroy our deepest commitments and values—things such as moral failure, tragedy, inexplicable evil, and death itself. These realities can fill us with dread and terror, in part because they lie outside our ability to control. The sociologist Thomas O'Dea has spoken of religion as a response to three fundamental features of human existence: uncertainty, powerlessness, and scarcity. Religion is rooted, certainly, in a wider range of human experience and emotion than these, including such positive experiences as wonder, trust, love, and joy. But O'Dea is correct as far as he goes. The brute facts of our existence do bring us face to face with questions about which our normal practical techniques and scientific know-how are powerless to provide answers or solutions.

Unless these questions receive adequate answers—unless these "limit situations" of finitude, uncertainty, suffering, guilt, and failure are capable of being seen in some larger system of meaning or transcendent perspective—then morale may founder and cynicism and despair may begin to eat away at trust and hope. Religions are the vindicators of a holy and moral order in the face of the world's chaos and evil. If we ask, then, "Why are human beings religious?" the answer is that humans want to be delivered from the loss of meaning, from moral guilt, and from the threat of finitude and fatedness. Humans want to experience the joy and the moral animation accompanying the trust that we live in a spiritual world of moral meaning whose current leads not to death but to life and hope.

Why Study Religion?

We began this chapter by asking "What is religion?" We found that the question does not lend itself to a single, simple answer and that it will be wiser for us first to describe a rather wide range of religious belief and practice before we try to say more about what constitutes the essentials of religion. Why human beings are religious, we found, is more readily answerable, in view of our unique capacity for self-transcendence, which provokes those urgent and perennial existential questions about life, death, evil, and obligation.

Before we examine some of the classic forms of religious belief and expression as exhibited in diverse traditions, there are two additional questions that are important to consider. The first is *why* we should study religion and the second is *how* we should undertake the study of such a rich and manifold phenomenon. We will discuss the first question here and will explore the second both at the end of this chapter and more extensively in Chapter 2.

There are some very good reasons why it is especially important, even crucial, to study religion in our present situation in the latter years of the twentieth century.

1. *To understand* Homo religiosus. First, religion should be studied because we are *Homines religiosi*. As we have seen, part of what it means to be human is reflected in our capacity for spiritual self-transcendence. We ought, therefore, to study humans as religious beings just as we study humans as a biological species, as political creatures, or as beings possessed of aesthetic sensibility — if we are to understand human life in its fullness.

2. *To overcome our ignorance.* Despite the rather high standard of education in Europe and North America, most of us remain surprisingly ignorant of the history and current beliefs and practices of the world's great religious traditions — even of our own. In high school or in college, we may have done advanced work in mathematics or chemistry, English literature or American history, but most students have not been exposed to a rigorous study of religion in its various manifestations. If we have grown up in a religious tradition, we may have attended Sunday School or have taken instruction for our **Bar Mitzvah**, but very often this proved too elementary and did not progress beyond our early teen years — and, of course, had little to do with religious traditions other than our own. We often have a narrow, **ethnocentric** view because we naturally tend to identify religion with experience of our own tradition or with those conventional forms of religious behavior that we observe in our own communities. We are reminded of Parson Thwackum in Henry Fielding's novel, *Tom Jones:* "When I mention religion, I mean the Christian religion; and not only the Christian religion, but the Protestant religion; and not only the Protestant religion, but the Church of England." Needless to say, this can result in uninformed or poorly informed views, or, worse, in dangerously parochial or prejudicial attitudes.

3. *To comprehend our culture.* A third good reason for studying religion

is to understand better our own history and culture as well as others. The American experience is not fully comprehensible without understanding, for example, the effect of Puritanism on the early history of the nation, the spread of the **evangelical** "Protestant ethic" westward in the nineteenth century, or the role of the Bible in shaping the life and character of the American South. Similarly, it is not possible to comprehend European or South Asian culture without appreciating how, in each instance, Christian or Buddhist ideas have informed cultural beliefs about nature, self, family, government, and work. We can easily forget that it is only in recent times, and outside the Third World, that there has been a conscious effort to distinguish between a society's religion and its culture. Religious beliefs nevertheless continue, largely unconsciously, to shape the values and institutions of a society that may no longer hold a common religion or maintain an established church. We may be fairly certain that the complex yet ordered fabric of any culture is woven from the loom of fundamental religious assumptions, loyalties, and hopes.

4. *To achieve a global perspective.* Due to the modern scientific and technological revolution—particularly in mass communication and transportation—we find ourselves today living in a rapidly shrinking world. Space exploration has made us acutely conscious of the fact that we are traveling on a small globe called Earth and that we humans may be endangering life itself on this remarkable planet. Technology certainly has proved ambiguous. The knowledge explosion can liberate human lives, but it can also create resentment, distrust, and fear. Nuclear power can warm our homes, and it can destroy civilization as we know it. Technology has made us more conscious of our human interdependence, but that can be threatening. If we are to maintain peace and establish a stable world order among the nations, it is imperative that we achieve a knowledge and understanding of and an empathy for beliefs and ways of life that we now find very foreign to our own. We cannot possibly understand another people or culture without a thorough knowledge and appreciation of the role of religion in its life. The failure of the U.S. government to grasp fully the religious dimensions of the conflicts in Southeast Asia and Iran explains, in part, our serious miscalculations and errors of judgment in those regions in recent history. Many of the tragic conflicts in the world today are rooted in long-standing religious differences and animosities. We need only think of the conflicts between Arab and Israeli, Indian and Pakistani, and Protestant and Catholic in Northern Ireland.

It is paradoxical that our growing awareness of our proximity to, and dependence on, other peoples and nations has fueled disputes and wars at the same time that it has made us conscious we are now living in a genuinely ecumenical, that is, worldwide or global, age. For the first time in history, there is a real opportunity for contact and dialogue among the great religious traditions of the world.* True dialogue, however, demands a thorough knowledge of the other party and a genuine willingness to be open and receptive to what that party is saying. It requires that all those engaged in dialogue seek real understanding. The effort to achieve such interreligious communication and a more-global perspective on world affairs is not a mere luxury of a liberal-arts education. It is critically necessary to maintain world peace and to ensure human survival in the years ahead.

5. *To help us formulate our own religious belief or philosophy of life.* A final reason that can be suggested (this list is not exhaustive) for studying religion is that it can help us to reflect more systematically on some of the ultimate questions of life and death, and thereby it can help us to formulate our own religious beliefs or philosophy of life. Socrates was right in saying that "the unexamined life is not worth living," although Woody Allen pointed out that the examined life is not a bed of roses, either. As persons who claim to be educated, we should make every effort to see that our fundamental beliefs and convictions about life are brought to consciousness, are made explicit, and then are carefully examined and critically tested.

It is not easy to be reflective about our own beliefs since these beliefs are often so basic as to be taken for granted. What is required is to step back and to see ourselves from a different perspective—to see ourselves, perhaps, as others see us. Unless we look at our beliefs from a fresh and different perspective, we may not even notice them. They remain unconscious and uncritical guides and energizers of our actions. We can learn a great deal about the strengths and deficiencies of our own religious beliefs and behavior by looking at them from other points of view, especially those of an honest and friendly critic. The Protestant can learn much about his own religion from a Catholic, as can a Catholic from the experience of a Protestant. The Buddhist, for example, can awaken Christians to the rich resources of meditation in their own tradition.

We are often hesitant to look at other faiths or to examine our own critically because we feel that, in so doing, we are being disloyal to our own deeply felt convictions. That is a natural and healthy reaction. And yet our beliefs are not worth very much if they cannot stand up to any scrutiny. Also, without examining our be-

* Aspects of the new interreligious dialogue are discussed in detail in Chapter 13.

liefs, without looking at them from new and different perspectives and possibilities, we cannot expect our minds and spirits to grow, or to move on to deeper levels of insight, understanding, and sympathy. It would be foolhardy in any other field of human endeavor to think that our knowledge and understanding should remain frozen at a particular stage or level of maturity. It is, in fact, rather presumptuous to think that we have already plumbed the depths of even our own religious tradition.

To be self-conscious and reflective about our beliefs does not mean, of course, that we become so open that our minds begin to resemble the proverbial sieve that cannot retain anything and through which all beliefs pass as though equally true and valuable. That is spiritual promiscuity. Our temptation today appears to be to fall into either an uncritical and slothful relativism or an uncritical and slothful dogmatism. To remain both committed and yet open, to hold a *critical* faith, takes real courage.

The honest exploration of others' beliefs usually will lead to a deepening and broadening of our own, but this is not a foregone conclusion. Honest exploration of a variety of religious beliefs and practices not only may cause us to reconceive our own religion in new ways, but also *may* force us to a painful reevaluation of long-held and deeply felt convictions and perhaps to a change of allegiance. It is a risk, but it is the risk of being educated and of living in a dynamic world of competing beliefs and values. The philosopher Nietzsche was correct when he said that real courage is not the courage of our convictions but the courage to examine our convictions.

The Perspective of the Student— Commitment and Objectivity

We have looked at some of the difficulties in defining religion, why human beings are uniquely religious, and why it is important to study religion. A further question remains. Assuming the importance of the study of religion, how do we go about it? There are at least two possible ways of approaching the question. The first approach has to do with what, initially, may not seem obvious: the stance of the student or observer of religion. Should or could a student of religion be, for example, an ardent believer or a convinced nonbeliever?

There is a second possible approach. We can look at the study of religion in terms of the methods or academic disciplines that might appropriately be used to illuminate or to resolve a variety of questions a student might wish to bring to the study of a particular religion.

These could include questions such as the following: "When did a belief in an afterlife emerge in the history of ancient Israel?" "Are the Confucian *Analects* from the hand of Confucius, or are they the work of other authors and editors?" "How does the African Nuer religious ritual function in the larger life of the community?" "Is the statement, 'God is love' verifiable?" The methods most fruitful in dealing with these particular inquiries are, in their order, historiography, literary-textual criticism, sociology, and philosophical analysis. More will be said in Chapter 2 about these and other disciplines. It is important, however, that we look more closely at the way the study of religion is approached from the perspective of the student observer.

A basic question that must be faced in any inquiry involving the selection of data and interpretive judgment is the relation between the scholar's own intellectual commitments and values and scholarly objectivity. Some would argue that persons cannot truly understand a system of religious beliefs and practices unless they do so from *within* that religion—from the sympathetic perspective of a participant and believer. Others would say that ardent faith or belief is not compatible with genuine knowledge and understanding. Both the devout believer and the detached, uncommitted observer have charged that the perspective of the other distorts what they are capable of seeing and interpreting. Are commitment and scientific objectivity opposed to one another? We will attempt to show that they need not be—but that a very real tension does and should exist between them—and that this tension does not admit of any easy solution one way or another. We can analyze this tension between commitment and detachment by looking at the question of the student's perspective along a continuum from naïve, partisan religious belief at one extreme to a standpoint of conscious, uncommitted relativity at the other.[2]

At the first extreme, we can envision a person who is not only a believer and active participant in a particular religion but also is unaware that there are other religious options. This is often the position, for example, of a primitive* tribesman. The tribe's religious and cultural system is assumed to be the only "way things are." The possibility of adopting alternative beliefs or behavior is nonexistent. This could also be the position of a simple believer—for example, a young person who has not yet developed genuine individuality—in our own pluralistic culture today. The beliefs and moral norms of the family or the community are taken as self-evident. They are not yet open to reflection or to critical scrutiny. Such a person looks on or studies his religion as if none other existed. The sacred scriptures, the traditions, and the moral teachings of the individual's faith may be "studied,"

---

* The word *primitive* is used throughout this book in a nonpejorative sense, simply meaning preliterate human societies, either primordial or contemporary.

but only in the odd sense that these traditions and beliefs are learned
and accepted as unquestioned authorities. Here the tension between
commitment and objectivity does not exist.

In contemporary developed societies, it is much more difficult, if
not impossible, to evade the shocks of cultural pluralism and the
challenges of new and foreign ideas and values. Attempts on the part
of some religious groups—for example, the Amish people in rural
Pennsylvania or the Hasidic Jews in New York City—to isolate themselves and to keep outside influences at bay have proved only partially
successful. Even in the most homogeneous of communities, there is
the inevitable individual who will ask, "Why do we believe that?" or
"Why should we do this?" Someone is certain to question the accepted
way. When alternative beliefs and practices are proposed as reasonable
options, the self-evidence, and thus the simplicity, of our own belief
is gone. To become aware of another system of belief is, in a real
sense, to have a new perspective on our own.

I suspect that this is where most of us find ourselves today. While
we may identify ourselves as Jewish or Muslim, as Roman Catholic
or Methodist, or as a secular humanist or Marxist, we nevertheless
have some sense of seeing ourselves as others see us. We are more
self-conscious of our beliefs and aware that we might be called on to
give an account of them. While our religious or ideological beliefs
may still largely inform our system of values and our actions, we now
must take into account other truths—scientific, moral, or social—alternative beliefs that may require us somehow to adapt our long-held
beliefs to these newer insights. But how open and adaptable can a
system or belief be allowed to be and yet have it maintain a coherent,
recognizable shape? Here the tension between commitment to a set
of beliefs and values and disinterested openness to new truth is often
very great.

It sometimes happens—rather often these days—that a believer will
feel more and more obliged to measure and to interpret his or her
religious beliefs by norms or criteria taken from outside the religion
itself. Often this step is taken in an effort to defend a religion against
charges of being antiquated, to show, for example, that the religious
beliefs are not inconsistent with current scientific thinking. The person,
though remaining a believer, may—and perhaps not fully consciously—accept other standards of meaning or truth by which to
measure or to interpret his or her own religious belief. This might
be the case with a believer who also happens to be a philosopher or
a historian. A philosopher may, for example, feel obliged to judge
the credibility or adequacy of her religion based on some philosophical
criterion of what counts as justified or reasonable belief. The historian,
likewise, may reject certain teachings of his religion on the grounds
that, based on certain historiographical criteria, there is not sufficient

historical evidence to maintain them. The tension between commitment and objectivity may simply be slackening or, more likely, the tension between our religion and a new set of beliefs may be heightened. The passion or concern is just as real, although now it is divided between two possibly competing criteria of rationality or truth.

The final position on our hypothetical continuum is that of the completely detached and "objective" scholar who has no existential— that is, personal—interest in religion, including the religion under study. Often this is the position associated with the social scientist, the anthropologist or sociologist. Social scientists are not supposed to be interested in attempting to determine the truth of a religion or its general value. Rather, their aim is purely interpretive and explanatory, for example, to show how a religion functions in a certain social context in terms of the goals or ends it fulfills for that society. However, the "objective" observer can, often unconsciously, move from descriptive or interpretive statements of how a religion functions to normative judgments about standards of what is acceptable, good, or valuable. Notorious examples of this kind of false move in social science are the famous reports by Dr. Alfred Kinsey on the sexual behavior of American males and females. Kinsey purported simply to describe the actual sexual behavior of young Americans, but it was obvious to many astute critics that Kinsey's studies were not descriptively neutral. Rather, they gave the impression that certain sexual activity *ought* to be accepted as normative because it was widely practiced. The old maxim "Forty thousand Frenchmen can't be wrong" is sometimes hard to resist, but it is false. Simply because most people suffer from the common cold does not make it normative.

The question that needs to be explored, then, is whether a wholly disinterested neutrality is really possible. Can a person genuinely understand a foreign culture or another religion from the outside, from a perspective of complete detachment? Or is it even possible to speak of complete detachment and neutrality? Do we not bring to our observations and judgments certain preconceptions and unexamined assumptions about what is important, possible, or intelligible, or what constitutes evidence? Is not the gathering and organizing of data itself a process of selection? Are not some things overlooked or left in the shade? Do not the kinds or the forms of our questions set the boundaries and shape of the answers we can expect to receive?

The uncertain relationship between understanding and believing can be illustrated by looking at a work of the eminent anthropologist E. E. Evans-Pritchard. In his classic study, *Witchcraft, Oracles, and Magic* among the African Azande, Evans-Pritchard insists that if we are to understand the African Azande's religious beliefs and practices, we must seek to understand them in terms of how they are taken by the Azande themselves—according to *their* form of life. Evans-

Pritchard goes on, however, to maintain that the Azande belief in magic and witchcraft is, of course, illusory. He not only wants to urge that the Azande hold a different conception of reality than our Western scientific culture, but to go on "and to say, finally, that the scientific conception agrees with what reality actually is like, whereas the magical conception does not."[3] But why should we think that our concepts of rationality can provide the model by which to measure the truth of *all* other forms of belief? Critics of Evans-Pritchard argue that there is no *universal* norm of rationality. It follows that explanations or answers given to scientific questions require scientific answers, religious questions require religious answers. Religion, so the argument goes, can only be understood from within.[4]

A number of social scientists and philosophers have challenged the claim that a genuine understanding of a system of beliefs requires commitment to those beliefs. They point out, for example, that persons move from belief system A to a radically different belief system B and, having been a believer in system A, retain a "feel" for and a genuine understanding of that belief, although they are no longer committed to believing it. We might argue that, while it is imperative to begin a study of a religion from "within"—in terms of the way it understands itself—nevertheless, religious language and concepts are not wholly distinct or isolated from ordinary language and experience. A person might in turn reply, however, that this may be true of the way religious language and concepts function *within* a uniform cultural system, but that a witch doctor's concept of evidence or his test of what is real or true is, in fact, highly peculiar to many Western anthropologists. In other words, it is easy for the scholar studying another culture to assume the existence of some other, more universal, "norm of intelligibility" that transcends all particular cultures but, in fact, turns out to be the cultural norms with which he or she operates.

If we are really to appreciate different possibilities of making sense of human life, we may have to make a more-rigorous effort to stand outside our own preconceptions and to enter empathetically into the culture or religion we are studying. But this is easier said than done. It demands not only an initial "suspension of disbelief" but also a thorough knowledge of how these seemingly alien beliefs and behaviors fit into a larger form of life taken as a whole. Such an effort at understanding can be made, nevertheless, without demanding that we be naïve believers or completely neutral observers. Commitment and understanding are not antithetical. Neither involves a total absence of criticism or a pure neutrality.

Let us suppose that there is an ancient religion that tells how the earth was hatched from a giant bird's egg. Now, we can simply dismiss this out of hand as prescientific nonsense. On the other hand, we can make an effort to understand what might be conveyed by this marvelous tale. If we can do this, we probably possess the balance between empathy and objectivity required to study a complex variety of religious phenomena with both appreciation and critical understanding.

We covered some important ground in this opening chapter. We saw that the nature of religion is taken for granted—until, that is, we begin to analyze more carefully our assumptions and our definitions. We learned, however, that several of these influential definitions and theories, while inadequate when taken in isolation, can give us valuable clues to essential aspects and features of religion. We also learned something about why we humans are uniquely religious beings and why it is important, especially at this time in history, to study religion. Finally, we raised the question of how we go about the study of religion by briefly exploring the problem of scholarly perspective— that is, how our religious commitment or nonengagement may affect our ability to understand a religion genuinely. We concluded that religious commitment and objectivity, or the application of critical methods, are not incompatible; also, that we need not be a believer to understand a religion. We can turn now to how we study religion in terms of the methods or disciplines used by scholars in the field.

Notes

1. Eric Sharpe, *Understanding Religion* (New York, 1983), pp. 46–47.
2. For the general idea of this scheme, I am indebted to Winston King's *Introduction to Religion: A Phenomenological Approach* (New York, 1968).
3. For this discussion I am dependent on Peter Winch, "Understanding a Primitive Society," Bryan Wilson, ed., *Rationality* (Oxford, 1970).
4. Peter Winch, *The Idea of a Social Science* (London, 1958), pp. 87–88.

Review Questions

1. How would you have defined religion prior to reading this chapter? What factors do you think influenced your choice of this definition?
2. Try your hand at defining religion so that your definition is broad enough to encompass a wide range of religions yet specific enough to avoid confusing religion with other forms of cultural behavior.
3. What is distinctive about life that makes humans uniquely spiritual or religious beings?
4. Summarize some of the reasons why it is important to study religion, as presented in this chapter. Can you identify some additional reasons why religion is a valuable subject of study?
5. Where would you place yourself on the commitment–objectivity

spectrum with regard to your own religion or philosophy of life?
Do the problems associated with each position on the spectrum
seem real to you? If not, why not?

6. What is your position on the question of whether a religion can
truly be understood from outside? Why? Do you think it is
possible at once to be a believer—that is, an active participant
in a religion—and to be critically objective?

Suggestions for Further Reading

For good analyses of the problem of defining the elusive
phenomenon of religion, the following studies are
recommended:

BAIRD, ROBERT D., *Category Formation and the History of Religions* (The
Hague: Mouton, 1971).

CROSBY, DONALD, *Interpretive Theories of Religion* (The Hague: Mouton,
1981).

GEERTZ, CLIFFORD, "Religion as a Cultural System," in Banton, Michael
(ed.), *Anthropological Approaches to the Study of Religion* (London:
Tavistock Press, 1966). Reprinted in William A. Lessa and Evon Z.
Vogt (eds.), *Reader in Comparative Religion* (4th ed.) (New York:
Harper and Row, 1979).

SPIRO, MELFORD E., "Religion: Problems of Definition and Explanation,"
in Michael Banton (ed.), *Anthropological Approaches*.

For interesting accounts of religion as intrinsic to what it
means to be human, the following essays are
recommended:

BELL, DANIEL, "The Return of the Sacred," *The Winding Passage* (New
York: Basic Books, 1981).

TILLICH, PAUL, "Religion as a Dimension in Man's Spiritual Life," *Theology
of Culture* (New York: Oxford University Press, 1964).

For an interesting discussion of the problems involved in
understanding another culture or religion see the
following:

WILSON, BRYAN (ed.), *Rationality* (Oxford: Oxford University Press, 1970).

CHAPTER 2

Ways of Studying Religion

OVERVIEW

We shall begin examining the ways of studying religion by observing that religion is not a discipline in the sense that we can speak of the scientific method or of historiography as a discipline or a methodology. Religion constitutes *a field of study* that includes many disciplines or scholarly methodologies. Each discipline is used because of its appropriateness and its fruitfulness in answering certain kinds of questions. For example, if we want to find out if a sacred text is the work of one or of several authors, we need to apply the tools of literary–documentary criticism. If we want to find out how a ritual functions in the larger cultural life of an African tribe, we would best employ the methods used by the anthropologist. This chapter shall examine eight disciplines or methods widely used (our study cannot survey all the methodologies available) in the scholarly study of religion. Each method is illustrated with a concrete example or examples. But before we do this, we must say a word about the study of religion and theology.

Theology and Religious Studies

In our present culture, we often associate, even identify, religion with theology (from the Greek *logos*, "speech" or "inquiry," concerning *theos*, or the "gods"). In Chapter 1, we already encountered a difficulty in this equation since not all religions are theistic. Theology is, however, an accredited and respected academic pursuit in our society. A number of our universities have distinguished theological faculties or schools attached to them with renowned theologians engaged in teaching and writing. Is not theology, then, an appropriate subject within the broad academic field of religion? The answer, perhaps surprisingly, is a qualified "Yes." This requires some explanation.

For a subject to claim to be open to scholarly study, certain rules need to be agreed on. One critical scholarly rule is that persons studying a subject cannot appeal to criteria of analysis or evidence that are, in principle, unavailable to others who, though perhaps not believers, possess the requisite scholarly tools, empathy, and understanding. A second rule of academic scholarship is that a study should involve some form of critical analysis, that is, that it not consist merely of rote memorization, simple indoctrination, uncritical advocacy, or the effort to **proselytize**. Now, most departments or schools of theology are open to and employ those same academic tools and methods, such as literary and historical criticism, approved and used by scholars of religion; that is, theologians are, usually, engaged in a critical analysis of their religious tradition—despite the fact that they also stand inside a circle of faith or commitment. Just as a political scientist, who also happens to be a committed Republican or Democrat, is capable of carrying out a scholarly analysis of political history or of current political trends, so a theologian can be both committed and objective. As we discovered in Chapter 1, since all scholars are committed—either unconsciously or consciously—to certain convictions or presuppositions about what constitutes reality, rationality, or evidence, it is crucial that a scholar's preconceptions be undisguised. That way, the preconceptions can be recognized, analyzed, and criticized.

It would be perfectly legitimate, for example, to include in a department of religion a philosophical theologian—a person who, using beliefs and forms of experience drawn from his or her own religious tradition, applies to these materials the tools of philosophical analysis. The same would hold for a historical theologian who—a Catholic, for example—is an expert on the thought of Thomas Aquinas, or a Jew whose specialty happens to be nineteenth-century Jewish theology in Europe. What is crucial is that they be willing to apply to their own tradition the same critical tools and forms of analysis that they would apply to other, possibly quite alien traditions. The scholarly legitimacy of their work depends, then, not on whether they are, for example, an agnostic or a Lutheran, but on their commitment to those scholarly tools and methods widely agreed on by scholars who work in the field.

There are, to be sure, some Bible and theological schools that reject the application of those literary, historical, and social-scientific methods that have come to be accepted by the scholarly community. They see their task as the uncritical transmission of a tradition, or indoctrination and evangelization. While such organizations have the fullest freedom to carry out their pedagogical mission, this mission must not be identified or confused with the academic study of religion or with the critical study of theology.

Literary Criticism

Literary criticism plays an especially important role in the study of religion because the events that originally shape a religion and the record of its authoritative teachings are often found in a collection of sacred writings or scriptures. We think, for example, of such sacred texts as the *Tao Te Ching* and the *Analects* of Confucius in China, the *Vedas* and *Upanishads* in Hinduism, the Buddhist *Sutras*, the Muslim *Quran*, the Hebrew Bible, and the Christian Bible consisting of both the Old and the New Testaments. Since these sacred scriptures remain the authoritative norm of belief and practice, it is critically important that they be properly understood and interpreted. Here is where literary criticism plays a valuable role.

What kinds of questions can literary criticism help us to answer? Certain things obviously are important to understand if the original meaning and purpose of a sacred text is to be known. First, is the version or translation of the sacred text that lies before us the most original, authentic, and reliable text available? After all, we normally are reading a translation. Understanding the original intention and meaning of the writer will also be clarified if we can answer such questions as the following: Who was the author? When was the writing composed? Where was it written and to what audience? What was the author's specific purpose? And how was the work received, interpreted, and passed on? If we can determine the answers to these questions, we have come a long way toward understanding the text. These, then, are the kinds of questions that the literary critic can help to answer.

Textual Criticism

The work of the literary critic often is divided into two distinct critical tasks: *lower*, or *textual*, *criticism* and *higher*, or *documentary*, *criticism*. Textual criticism uses a number of methods and procedures to try to determine whether we are reading the original or the most authentic version of a particular text—or a later copy that may have been altered, revised, or edited.

The Christian Bible is an excellent example because sometimes we forget that the Bible was originally composed in Hebrew and in *koine*, or common Greek, not in English. What we presently have are translations. Furthermore, our English, French, or German translations are not based on the original copies—"autograph" copies—of the Hebrew and Greek manuscripts. The earliest, yet incomplete, texts of the entire

A vellum page of the *Codex Sinaiticus* from the fourth century C.E.
(*Source:* Courtesy of the British Library.)

Bible are *Codex Sinaiticus* and *Codex Vaticanus*, both in Greek script
from no earlier than the fourth century, C.E. *Sinaiticus* was discovered
in 1859. It contains the entire New Testament but only part of the
Old Testament. It was very influential in establishing the text of the
Revised Version of the New Testament in 1881. *Vaticanus* lacks 46
chapters of Genesis, 30 Psalms, and several minor epistles and the
Book of Revelation from the New Testament. Scholars do, of course,
have access to many papyri manuscripts and fragments of New Testament books dated before the fourth century, but nothing as early
as the first century, C.E.

The textual critic, therefore, has the formidable task of attempting
to establish a text that comes closest to the original so that it will
more completely reflect the author's words and enhance the reader's
understanding of early Christianity. Part of the textual critic's difficulty
is that an earlier manuscript is not necessarily the most original or

authentic. Copies were made by hand before the invention of the printing press. Since errors, deletions, and additions can be made in hand copying, they can occur early just as well as late in the transmission of a text. Comparison of the earliest available manuscripts demonstrates that this did in fact take place.[1] Most errors in copying were unintentional. Bad eyesight, coupled with poor light, was the likely cause of mistakes in spelling and punctuation, or in omissions. The scribe frequently found it difficult to distinguish between Greek letters that resemble one another.

Some changes in scriptural texts resulted from scribal errors of judgment. Words and notes standing in the margin of an older copy occasionally, due to uncertainty, were incorporated into the text. Zealous copyists often sought to improve spelling and grammar, and sometimes they even harmonized discordant parallels of important passages or attempted to clear up historical or geographical discrepancies. The shorter form of the Lord's Prayer in Luke 11:24, for example, was assimilated in many copies to agree with the familiar longer form in Matthew 6:9–13. Many intentional changes were made, of course, in good faith, the scribe believing he was improving or correcting the text. Changes of a doctrinal nature were less frequent but usually more serious. We know, for instance, that in the second century, Marcion, an early Christian heretic, removed from his copies of the Gospel according to Luke all references to the Jewish background of Jesus.

A striking illustration of the value of the textual critic is evident in the recent discovery regarding the early verses of Chapter 8 of the Gospel of John. The well-known story of the woman caught in adultery and forgiven by Jesus was present in the versions of John 8 common since the Middle Ages. More recently, however, textual scholars have discovered that not one manuscript of John 8 from before the end of the fourth century contains the story. Furthermore, none of the Johannine commentaries of the Church Fathers written up to the end of the fourth century includes any reference to this narrative. As a result of this discovery, scholars have determined that the first 11 verses of John 8 were not original to that gospel. In the Revised Standard Version of the New Testament and in the New English Bible, the eighth chapter of the Gospel of John begins at verse 12.

To underline, as we have, the possible errors involved in the transmission of the text of the New Testament is not meant to contest its spiritual authority or its historical reliability; nor is it meant to give the impression that the early scribes were inept or unreliable. On the contrary, their work was usually meticulous and faithful to the text. The biblical scholar is actually in a better position to re-create the Hebrew and Christian scriptures than are scholars working on the Buddhist **Tripitaka** or the earliest Muslim traditions about Moham-

med. The purpose here is simply to show the importance of establishing the most authorative text possible as the first step to genuine
interpretation and understanding of a sacred writing, whether it be
the Bible or the *Analects* of Confucius.

Documentary Criticism

In making a decision about the best document available, the textual
critic is dependent on the work of other scholars who may be able
to establish such important facts as the authorship and date of a
particular piece of literature. These latter scholars, often called
documentary critics, are in turn indebted to the textual critic; their
work is interdependent. Nevertheless, assuming a given text, the
documentary critic is concerned with establishing whether a writing is
a whole or a composite work of more than one author or editor,
when and where the work was composed, to whom it was addressed,
and for what purpose.

The valuable work of documentary critics can be seen in the contribution they have made to our understanding of the Book of Isaiah
in the Bible. For centuries, this book was thought to be the work of
one writer, Isaiah of Jerusalem, who received his prophetic call in
the year of King Uzziah's death (742 B.C.E.). Today, it is almost universally recognized that Isaiah is the work of at least two or three
distinct authors with different audiences and purposes in mind. Our
understanding of the book is, to say the least, much enhanced.

It is evident to the documentary critic that Chapters 1–39 of Isaiah
are addressed to a community resident in Palestine. The prophet
focuses on the dynasty of King David. Israel's neighbor, Assyria, is
given a position of prominence. The situation described in Chapters
40–55 is very different, both temporally and geographically. The most
striking feature of these chapters is the mention of Cyrus, the king
of Persia, as a victorious conqueror—a king and kingdom that did
not exist in the eighth century B.C.E. Jerusalem and Judah are now
assumed to be destroyed.

There now is scholarly agreement that the prophecies of Chapters
40–55 make no sense in the context of what we know of the period
of Isaiah of Jerusalem in the eighth century, but that they are highly
intelligible when seen as addressed to the Jewish community in exile
in Babylonia a century and a half later. The documentary evidence
that Isaiah is a composite work of at least two primary authors, separated by considerable geographical distance and periods of time and
addressed to distinct audiences in different circumstances, has greatly
advanced our understanding and appreciation of this complex and
otherwise puzzling book.

A scholar painstakingly working on fragments from one
of the Dead Sea Scrolls, discovered in 1947 in caves
overlooking the Dead Sea. The scrolls date from the
second century B.C.E. to the mid-first century C.E. and
present scholars with invaluable information about the
biblical text and sectarian Judaism at the time of the
emergence of Christianity. (*Source:* Courtesy of
John Allegro.)

Historiography

The history of religion, like the philosophy of religion, has its beginnings in antiquity. The scientific study of the history of religion is,
however, a product of the nineteenth century. The historian's task is
to establish the facts as the first step in reconstructing the historical
past or "what really happened." To state it so boldly is, of course, to
simplify the matter, for the "facts" that constitute the past are beyond
measure or full recall. Furthermore, the occurrences of the past can
never be experienced by the historian. The historian *selects* those accounts or evidences that are available to him through his sources and
does so based on some principle of selectivity. The choice of relevant
data will depend, in part, on the kinds of questions the historian puts
to the past.

What kinds of questions interest the historian of religion? They are interested in many of the same questions that occupy the documentary critic: who wrote what, when, why, and to whom? Like the documentary critic, the historian would like to establish what a writer borrowed and what was the writer's distinctive contribution, or how social and environmental factors influenced changes in the writer's language, ideas, and behavior.

The historian's sources extend, however, far beyond written texts and such disciplines as palaeography, the study of deciphering ancient manuscripts, and philology or linguistics, used by the literary critic. In reconstructing the religious past or in attempting to determine "what really happened," the historian calls on a vast range of non-textual sources, including archaeology; numismatics, the science of coins; geography; and, more recently, methods developed in anthropology, sociology, and psychology. Modern historical science has helped the student of religion to distinguish historical occurrence from such other genres as **myth**, **legend**, **saga**, and religious tradition, although all these obviously are significant in the ongoing historical life of religious communities.

It would appear obvious that the historical study of religion has to do with establishing what role religious experience and ideas play in the lives of individuals and communities and, in turn, how religion influences the development of larger societies, nations, and whole cultures. More recently, historians have been interested in looking at the question the other way around. They have asked what political, economic, social, or psychological factors are critical to an understanding of, say, the division of Islam into competing sects after the death of Mohammed, to the role of pilgrimage in the Middle Ages, or to the spread of Calvinism in Europe and North America since the sixteenth century.

Some modern historians, including Marxists, claim that the origin and development of religious movements can be adequately explained in terms of *only* material or economic conditions, rather than by appeal to the emergence of unique ideas or behavior. Other historians place far greater weight on political factors, while many continue to insist that the causes of the spread of Buddhism or the success of Martin Luther's Reformation must be attributed to the distinctly *religious* concerns or needs of the time or to the unique ideas and practical innovations of great religious geniuses. The causes of the Protestant Reformation have, for some time, been a topic of special contention among historians, and the debate illustrates both the importance of these historical studies in gaining a fuller understanding of that critical event in Western history and the difficulties in proposing any single causal explanation in history.

Some historians see the Protestant Reformation primarily as the response to economic factors. Other historians of the sixteenth century deny that economic factors were central, pointing out that northern Germany, where the Reformation originated, did not witness a significant transformation of economic life; it, in fact, remained traditionally agrarian. These historians do, though, see the powerful political and intellectual forces at work in the late Middle Ages and early modern period as more significant causes of the Reformation than the immediate religious events surrounding Luther's protest and theology.

Most historians today agree that the causes of the Reformation are multiple and complex and include political, economic, moral, and intellectual, as well as religious, factors. How to weigh these influences and apportion their significance remains a matter of considerable dispute. What is significant, however, is that we now can appreciate the many-sidedness of the Reformation and how it demonstrates the interdependence of religious and socioeconomic forces in history. The historian is able to help us see this complexity and interdependence and to observe religion from a new perspective.

Anthropology

Anthropology has to do with the study of humans who are viewed primarily as both the creators and the creations of culture. Since religious institutions and practices are found in every known culture, the religious life of societies is of great interest to anthropologists. This is especially true because social institutions and beliefs never operate in a vacuum. Religious sentiments, ideas, and behavior shape and, in turn, are shaped by family organization, the economic system, law, and politics. Anthropologists also recognize that religion is an especially powerful factor in any culture because a society shapes and defines its world by reference to sacred primordial models, sanctions, and patterns of behavior.

Anthropology is a relatively new science. The "father" of modern anthropology is Edward B. Tylor (1832–1917), and in his classic work, *Primitive Culture* (1871), he gave considerable attention to religion. This was also true of several other of the early anthropologists. However, it was the sociologist Emile Durkheim (1858–1917) who was most responsible for turning the interest of anthropologists to the study of the social functions of religion. **Functionalism** has been the method most widely used by these anthropologists. As the name would indicate, the anthropologist is interested in the question of what functions particular institutions or beliefs serve in the total life of a community.

Applied to religion, functionalism asks how the religious institutions and beliefs of a society elicit acceptance of or sanction certain behavior

Totems, like those found on these poles in British
Columbia, Canada, are of great interest to
anthropologists. Totems are images of animals or other
natural species that are associated with clans or tribes
and their kinship–religious relations and rituals.
(*Source:* Courtesy of The Bettman Archive.)

and how these factors assist in the integration and cohesion of that
society. Since religion is so critical to social integration and stability,
it is given a place of primacy in the studies of many anthropologists
today.

   To illustrate the work of an anthropologist, we will look at E. E.
Evans-Pritchard's celebrated study of the Nuer tribe of East Africa.
Evans-Pritchard describes how religion functions in a particularly critical way in maintaining Nuer society, which otherwise lacks real government. Feuds and breaks in Nuer social order are regulated to a
certain degree by the role of the "Leopard-skin Chief." In the case
of a serious social offense, such as the killing of a tribesman, the
offender can seek refuge with the chief while the latter makes efforts
to elicit proper compensation from the slayer's kin to pay the victim's
family—usually in the form of cattle. Compensation is obviously preferable to deadly feuding between near kinsmen. Evans-Pritchard has
shown, however, that the "Leopard-skin Chief" lacks real legal authority and power and that the success of his mediation is never assured.
He does not, for instance, stand in judgment in the case, and his
advice is not binding. If a settlement cannot be reached, vengeance
inevitably follows, and it can involve not only the immediate families
but also the wider tribal community. Such vengeful feuding is potentially very disruptive and even disastrous for the society. Vengeance
simply evokes counter-vengeance in an increasingly destructive spiral.

   Evans-Pritchard demonstrates how Nuer religion funtions both to
inhibit such social offenses as murder and incest and, when it occurs,

to sanction compensation to the injured party and atoning acts of sacrifice and purification. The Nuer believe that such serious crimes as murder are highly offensive to Spirit or God and, as Evans-Pritchard observes,

> ... the Nuer think that it is he who punished them. It is God's *cuong*, right, rather than, or as well as, man's that has been violated. The man who commits them, therefore, places himself, and possibly others too, in danger of having done something which brings Spirit into action in the affairs of men.[2]

Supernatural intervention usually takes the form of physical illness. The offending person literally is physically contaminated by his or her act. Moreover, it is believed that such pollution is contagious and may pass to others closely related to the offender. Thus, great social danger is connected with these antisocial crimes. Evans-Pritchard has shown how, in a society with no formal law or government, religion plays an indispensable role in maintaining sanctions against antisocial behavior and in insuring social order. As he concludes, "God is regarded as the guardian of the social order and his intervention a possible sanction for any rule of conduct."[3]

As we explore in future chapters the nature of religious symbolism, myth, and ritual, we will refer in some detail to the illuminating studies of other contemporary anthropologists.

Sociology

The sociology of religion also focuses on group social behavior and the way in which religion interacts with other dimensions of our social experience. In this respect, sociology is similar to anthropology, except that sociology is generally concerned with the religious life of contemporary, developed, literate societies.

Early in this century, there was a great flowering of interest in religion by sociologists who, even today, are regarded as the theoretical geniuses of the discipline. These included Emile Durkheim, Max Weber (1864–1920), George Simmel (1858–1918), and Ernst Troeltsch (1865–1923). These scholars perceived in religion an enduring human phenomenon. They were concerned to examine, among other things, the fundamental question of how the dynamics of social life and institutions effect changes in religious life and, in turn, how religious belief and behavior acts on and transforms social life. The latter interest is dominant in the work of Max Weber.

One of Weber's great contributions to the sociology of religion is his demonstration—reversing Karl Marx's analysis—that certain forms of social life and behavior deeply reflect the religious belief and practice of a society. In his most notable study, *The Protestant Ethic and the Spirit of Capitalism* (1905), Weber analyzed how the new Protestant ethic, which came with the Reformation of the sixteenth century, proved to be decisive in shaping the unique *spirit* of modern capitalist society. That ethic was embodied in the teachings of **Calvinism**, which emphasized the importance of serving God in a worldly, vocational calling. It further made virtues of hard work, frugality, and the wise use of material resources.

Weber was intrigued by this question: What were the unique circumstances that energized the modern capitalist spirit in Protestant America when compared with the seemingly more-favorable economic conditions in fifteenth-century Catholic Florence? What Weber brought to light was the fact that in Florence, the most highly capitalistic center in the world, the idea of serving God through the pursuit of capital was not only minimized but also actually considered unjustified. On the other hand, in the backwoods circumstances of eighteenth-century Pennsylvania, where business regularly threatened to fall back into simple barter, serving God through hard work and the pursuit of capital was commanded as a religious duty.

Contrary to Marx, Weber concluded that the religious life of Florence and of backwoods Pennsylvania were *not* reflections of the material conditions of the economy. On the contrary, the economic life of fifteenth-century Florence and eighteenth-century Pennsylvania were profoundly shaped by the peculiar religious ethos of each place. To the question "What could account for the sort of economic activity directed toward profit alone as a calling and ethical obligation?" Weber answers, "The spirit of Calvinist religion."[4] The difference between the capitalism that had existed in Florence and the *spirit* of modern capitalism is to be found in the new *sense of calling*, or ethical obligation to make money, marked by a quality of self-discipline distinctive of the personal and social ethics of Calvinistic Protestantism.

The period of Durkheim and Weber remains, in terms of theoretical genius, the high mark in the sociology of religion. From 1915 to World War II, there was a general falling off of interest in the study of religion among sociologists. In recent decades, however, sociologists have renewed an interest in religion, and important studies have appeared by a number of highly regarded scholars in the field. We will encounter the work of some of these scholars in later chapters.

Psychology

Psychology achieved the status of an established science only late in the nineteenth century. A number of the pioneers of psychological research, notably in America, took an interest in religion. The first

Psychology of Religion, written by E. D. Starbuck (1866–1947), appeared in the United States in 1899. Among the early workers in the field was William James (1842–1910), whose *The Varieties of Religious Experience* (1902) remains a classic. James explored the psychological dimensions of such phenomena as conversion, mysticism, and saintliness. The connection between psychology and religion is, in the popular mind, perhaps most closely associated with the great figures in the history of psychoanalysis, especially its founder, Sigmund Freud (1856–1939), and his pupil and associate, Carl Jung (1875–1961).

While psychoanalytic theories of religion have received wide attention, less-publicized but still-important experimental studies have been undertaken in recent decades. As an illustration of the work of an experimental psychologist, we have selected Gordon Allport's classic studies of the relationship between religion and prejudice. Allport

Geometric diagram known as a *yantra*, which is important in Hindu and Tantric Buddhist meditation. It represents the cosmic creative process, the various shapes corresponding to planes of psychic consciousness. The psychologist Carl Jung took a great interest in the *yantra* in his work on the archetypes of the unconscious.

posed this question: Are religious persons more prejudiced, more prone to hold irrational attitudes of ill-will toward others, than non-religious persons? It was an apparently well-established fact of social science that churchgoers in the United States were, ethnically and racially, more prejudiced than nonchurchgoers.[5]

Allport's studies have demonstrated that it is too simplistic to associate prejudice with churchgoing *per se*, "since it may reflect only formal behavior, not involvement or commitment to religious values."[6] Prejudice and churchgoing, according to Allport, simply are joined in certain psychological types and not because religion instills prejudice. Rather, he points out, "a large number of people, by virtue of their psychological makeup, require for their economy of living both prejudice and religion. . . . One does not cause the other; rather, both satisfy the same psychological needs."[7]

Allport discovered that there were very different correlations between prejudice and distinct types of being religious, what he calls *extrinsic* and *intrinsic* religion. Persons with an extrinsic orientation to religion "are disposed to use religion for their own ends. . . . [They] may find religion useful in a variety of ways—to provide security and solace, sociability and distraction, status and self-justification."[8] Persons with an intrinsic orientation, on the other hand, "find their master motive in religion. . . . Having embraced a creed the individual endeavors to internalize it and follow it fully. It is in this sense that he *lives* his religion."[9] Allport later discovered a third type, which he calls, "inconsistently pro-religious." These are people who accept both extrinsically *and* intrinsically worded items on questionnaires—they like religion, but their understanding and commitment appear contradictory and shallow.

Allport's research concludes that

> . . . prejudice, like tolerance, is often embedded deeply in personality structure and is reflected in a consistent cognitive style. Both states of mind are enmeshed with the individual's religious orientation. One definable style marks the individual who is bigoted in ethnic matters and extrinsic in his religious orientation. Equally apparent is the style of those who are bigoted and at the same time indiscriminately pro-religious. A relatively small number of people show an equally consistent cognitive style in their simultaneous commitment to religion as a dominant, intrinsic value and ethnic tolerance.[10]

Studies such as Allport's show the value of psychological studies in revealing the potential effect of forms of religion on social relations and behavior. Equally important, however, are studies, again like Allport's, that can warn us against making too-simple correlations between a phenomenon such as prejudice and religion or churchgoing as such.

Philosophy

The philosophical scrutiny of religion is one of the oldest and most instructive ways of examining religious experience and belief. At least since the time of Plato (427?–347? B.C.), philosophers have reflected on religious stories and beliefs and have sought, by various means of analysis, to establish the logical status, the meaning, and the truth of these narratives and doctrines.

The relationship between philosophy and religion has, however, varied significantly from century to century and from culture to culture. In India, philosophy emerged from and has remained intimately associated with historical developments in Hinduism. The same was true, at least until recently, in South and East Asia with regard to Buddhism and Confucianism. In the West, from the appearance of the Christian Platonist Origen in the second century C.E. to the time of Thomas Aquinas (1225–1274), philosophy played the role of handmaiden to religion. By this we mean that the claims of Jewish, Christian, and Islamic revelation were, in part, justified and defended by appeals to the doctrines of the ancient philosophers themselves. Thomas Aquinas, for example, used the language and concepts derived from Aristotle's philosophy to mount his proofs for the existence of God.

Since the seventeenth century, philosophy has, not infrequently, been put to a quite different but, nonetheless, powerful service of religion. It can be called **agnosticism** in the service of **fideism**, or to question knowledge so as to allow a place for faith. Immanuel Kant (1724–1804) expressed it in the celebrated preface to his *Critique of Pure Reason*. He remarked that his task was "to deny knowledge in order to make room for faith." Modern critical philosophy, in its uncompromising scrutiny of the nature of reason itself, often has demonstrated the limits of rationality; that is, reason pushed far enough reveals its own boundaries and contradictions.

In this century, philosophy's relation to religion has neither been that of handmaiden nor that of philosophical skeptic making room for faith. Today, the philosophical scrutiny of religion is more limited. Its role is to analyze the uses of religious language and, thereby, to test its logical status and meaning as well as its claims to knowledge and truth. To ask whether a particular religious expression has the status of a factual assertion, is simply performing an action ("I pronounce you husband and wife"), or is merely evoking the emotions. Philosophers believe that many problems and obscurities in religion are related to confusing these several distinct uses of language. Such a philosophical clarification of religious discourse aims to be neutral, although it obviously can challenge conventional religious belief if, for example, a certain purported religious assertion of fact fails to pass the analytical test.

To illustrate the way in which contemporary philosophy examines religion, we look at one philosopher's use of what is called the *falsification principle* to test the meaningfulness of certain forms of religious *assertion*. Antony Flew formulates the principle as follows:

> Suppose that we are in doubt as to what someone who gives vent to an utterance is asserting, or suppose that, more radically, we are sceptical as to whether he is really asserting anything at all, one way of trying to understand his utterance is to attempt to find what he would regard as counting against, or as being incompatible with, its truth.[11]

If *nothing* is incompatible with the truth of a statement, then, Flew argues, the statement does not assert anything. In other words, if there is nothing an assertion denies, then there is nothing that it asserts either. It really is not an *assertion* at all. Flew applies this principle to the claims or statements of theists who freely assert that "God has a plan" or that "God loves us." Flew inquires as to what would have to occur or have occurred to falsify such factual claims. Take the assertion "God loves us." Suppose someone

> . . . tells us that God loves us as a father loves his children. We are reassured. But then we see a child dying of inoperable cancer of the throat. His earthly father is driven frantic in his efforts to help, but his Heavenly Father reveals no obvious signs of concern. Some qualification is made—God's love is 'not a merely human love' or it is 'an inscrutable love'—and we realize that such sufferings are compatible with the truth of the assertion that 'God loves us as a father.' . . . We are reassured again. But then perhaps we ask: What is this assurance of God's love worth, what is this apparent guarantee really a guarantee against? Just what would have to happen not merely . . . to tempt but also . . . to entitle us to say 'God does not love us' or even 'God does not exist?'[12]

If "God loves us" is made compatible with *any* present or *any* possible state of affairs, then, Flew insists, since nothing is incompatible with the statement, that is, it does not deny anything, neither does it assert anything. The confident assertion "dies the death of a thousand qualifications." Because "God loves us" is not falsifiable, it cannot, claims Flew, be an assertion of fact.

A number of philosophers have accepted Flew's premises but disagree with his conclusion. Some, for example, agree that theological statements such as "God loves us" are genuine factual assertions and that they can be falsified, but that they can be falsified only in principle, *not in practice.* Eternal, irredeemable evil would, for example, falsify the assertion "God loves us." But we cannot design a crucial test because we finite humans never can see the entire picture.

Our purpose here is not to judge which philosopher is correct, but to show how contemporary philosophical analysis can raise important questions about the nature and meaning of religious language. Such an analysis can help the student of religion to be more alert to the rich variety but also to the peculiarities of religious language, a language that often must speak of suprasensible realities—for example, the nature of God—in the language of empirical or everyday experience. More will be said about this in Chapter 4 on religious symbolism and myth.

Phenomenology

One of the most recent and, in some respects, the most illuminating approaches to the study of religion is the phenomenological method. The word derives from the Greek *phainomenon,* meaning that which appears. Phenomenology originated in the philosophical movement associated with Edmund Husserl (1859–1938). Husserl sought to concentrate on the data of experience as it directly presents itself to human consciousness. He was concerned not with explaining experience, but with rigorous *description* only. He introduced the concept of *epoche* (from the Greek verb *epecho,* "I hold back"), or suspension of judgment, to indicate the "bracketing" from inquiry all attempts at explanation or all philosophical or theological questions of a phenomena's truth or value. For example, the question to be inquired of in phenomenology is not "Does God exist?" or "How does belief in monotheism arise?" but, rather, "How is God present to human consciousness? What forms or characteristics does the experience of God exhibit?"

The phenomenological study of religion had its beginnings mainly in Holland and Scandinavia, and among the most important and influential exponents of this method are Nathan Soderblom (1866–1931), W. Brete Kristensen (1867–1953), Gerardus van der Leeuw (1890–1953), Joachim Wach (1898–1955), and Mircea Eliade (1907–1986). These scholars have drawn on a rich store of data from the history of religion, especially from primitive and archaic religion, and have sought to isolate and describe the distinctive forms or structures of particular types of religious phenomena by means of comparison and contrast. Phenomenology is, then, a study of the *morphology* (the structures or forms) of religion as manifested in and across different cultures and temporal periods. The forms studied vary, depending on each scholar's particular interest; they might be creation myths, rites of sacrifice, prayers, or forms of religious leadership.

The goal of phenomenology is to portray religion in its own terms as a unique expression, a reality not to be reduced or explained in other—for example, psychological or sociological—terms. To avoid intruding judgments of value or truth into the descriptive task, the phenomenologist must remain detached and impartial. Yet insightful description and interpretation require a genuine feel for and empathy with religious experience. Phenomenology thus represents the effort to *reexperience* a certain religious phenomenon's essential character or structure.

Part III of this book undertakes a comparative typology of certain universal forms of religious belief and practice. Therefore, it is not necessary to exemplify this method here in detail. Brief mention of Mircea Eliade's study of the religious symbolism of water will suffice for our purpose.

Eliade has shown, through an impressive array of examples from the history of religion, how water serves as the religious symbol of potentiality, as the source of life. Drawing on examples from Indian, Babylonian, Brazilian, Semitic, and Oceanic creation mythology, Eliade describes the role of primeval waters as the source of life and growth. He shows how, as a symbol of creation, water serves as well as the supreme medicinal substance—healing, purifying, restoring youth, and conferring eternal life.

> Living water, the fountains of youth, the Water of Life, and the rest, are all mythological formulae for the same metaphysical and religious reality: life, strength, and eternity are contained in water. This water is not, of course, accessible to every body in every way. It is guarded by monsters. It is to be found in places which are hard to get to.... To reach the source of 'living water' and get possession of it involves a series of consecrations and 'testings,' just as does the search for the 'Tree of Life.'[13]

Eliade compares not only the **cosmological** symbolism of water and of the "water of life" but also the comparative symbolism of immersion and baptism, of miraculous rivers and springs, water **epiphanies**, and the pervasive symbolism of the deluge or Flood. In all these varied manifestations of water symbolism in the world's religions, Eliade perceives an essential, recurring theme at both the cosmic and the human level:

> To the creation of the universe from water there correspond—at the anthropological level—the beliefs according to which men were born of water. To the deluge or disappearance of continents into

the water—a cosmic phenomenon which must of necessity be repeated periodically—there correspond at the human level, the 'second death' of the soul and the ritual, initiatory death of baptism.
But, whether at the cosmic or the anthropological level, immersion
in water does not mean final extinction, but simply a temporary
reintegration into the formless, which will be followed by a new
creation, a new life or a new man, depending on whether the reintegration in question is cosmic, biological, or redemptive. In *form*
the 'deluge' is comparable to 'baptism.' ... In whatever religious
framework it appears, the function of water is shown to be the
same; it disintegrates, abolishes forms, 'washes away sins'—at once ·
purifying and giving new life.[14]

As we shall see, the comparative work of the phenomenologists
presents students of religion with a wealth of insights into those universal and pervasive forms of religious life that characterize humans
as uniquely religious beings.

The disciplines or methods that we have explored in this chapter
include some of the most important approaches used by scholars in
religious studies today. However, they by no means encompass all the
methods employed. Each of the disciplines calls on a number of aux-
iliary sciences. The historian, for example, is dependent on the work
of scholars in archaeology, palaeography, philology, geography, and
demography, or the study of population statistics, to name but a few.
The scholarly study of sacred texts no longer is confined to the traditional subdisciplines of literary criticism but increasingly consults
work in linguistics, the study of the structure of language; and semiology, the science of signs.

Structuralism

A methodological approach recently appropriated by scholars in the
field of religion is called **Structuralism.** The movement was born in
Europe between the world wars and is still developing, especially in
its application to the study of religion. How fruitful it will prove to
be is yet to be seen.

Structuralism traces its beginnings to the study of linguistics. Basically, what the structuralists contend is that the most profound meaning of language—indeed, of human communication generally—is not
to be found at the surface level of words or signs, for example, in
the plain meaning conveyed by an author or in a text's intended
purpose. The structuralist interpreter of a sacred myth or narrative
is interested, rather, in the *depth structure* of the text, in a structure
of which the author of the text is likely to be unaware. The language

used by the author is a system of signs, a system that—beneath the author's own manifest meaning—reveals a deeper structure of human life, of relationships and exchanges that can tell us some highly important things about the human mind and human activity. Religious myths and folklore are especially rich deposits that only recently have been mined by the structuralist critics.

The scholar who is most responsible for the application of structuralist interpretation to religion is the French anthropologist Claude Lévi-Strauss (1908–   ). In works such as *Structural Anthropology* and *The Savage Mind*, Lévi-Strauss has both established and popularized the structuralist method in the study of anthropology. His application of the method to the study of myth has been especially valuable in the exploration of religious texts. Since we will describe Lévi-Strauss's use of structuralist principles in Chapter 4 in a discussion of religious symbolism and myth, we need not pursue the methods of structuralism further here.

In the first two chapters we have explored such questions as the following: "What is religion?" "Why are humans uniquely religious?" "Why study religion?" and "How do we go about the study of religion?" We are now prepared to examine some of the universal forms of religious experience and expression.

Notes

1. For the following illustrations, I am dependent on Bruce Metzger's *The Text of the New Testament* (Oxford, 1968). This is a mine of information on the work of the New Testament critic.
2. E. E. Evans-Pritchard, *Nuer Religion* (Oxford, 1956), p. 190.
3. Evans-Pritchard, *Nuer Religion*, p. 192.
4. Max Weber, *The Protestant Ethic and the Spirit of Capitalism*, trans. Talcott Parsons (New York, 1958).
5. For example, see T. W. Adorno et al., *The Authoritarian Personality* (New York, 1950); M. Rokeach, *The Open and the Closed Mind* (New York, 1960); and R. M. Williams, Jr., *Strangers Next Door* (Englewood Cliffs, N.J., 1964).
6. Gordon W. Allport and J. Michael Ross, "Personal Religious Orientation and Prejudice," *Journal of Personality and Social Psychology* 5 (1967): 434.
7. Gordon W. Allport, "The Religious Context of Prejudice," *Journal for the Scientific Study of Religion* 5 (1966): 451.
8. Allport and Ross, "Personal Religious Orientation," p. 434.
9. Allport and Ross, "Personal Religious Orientation," p. 436.
10. Allport and Ross, "Personal Religious Orientation," p. 442.
11. Antony Flew and Alasdair McIntyre, *New Essays in Philosophical Theology* (London, 1955), p. 98.
12. Flew and McIntyre, *New Essays*, pp. 98–99.

13. Mircea Eliade, *Patterns in Comparative Religion*, trans. Rosemary Sheed (New York, 1963), p. 193.
14. Eliade, *Patterns in Comparative Religion*, p. 212.

Review Questions

1. What conditions are necessary for theology to be recognized as a scholarly field of study?
2. Indicate the difference in the work of the textual critic and the documentary critic. The literary critic and the historian seek answers to many of the same questions. In what ways does the work of the historian differ from that of the literary critic?
3. Describe functionalism as a method of investigation in the anthropological and sociological study of religion.
4. As an example of the application of experimental psychology to religious belief and practice, summarize Gordon Allport's conclusions regarding religion and ethnic and racial prejudice.
5. Characterize the phenomenological study of religion as a method. How does it differ from, say, the work of the anthropologist or the philosopher?

Suggestions for Further Reading

For an overview of various approaches among the scientific disciplines in the study of religion, see the following:

SHARPE, ERIC J., *Comparative Religion: A History* (New York; Scribner's, 1975).

WAARDENBURG, JACQUES, *Classical Approaches to the Study of Religion* I (The Hague: Mouton, 1973).

WHALING, FRANK (ed.), *Contemporary Approaches to the Study of Religion*, 2 vols. (Berlin, New York: Mouton, 1983).

For a detailed look at the work of textual criticism as applied to a particular sacred scripture, see the following:

METZGER, BRUCE M., *The Text of the New Testament: Its Transmission, Corruption and Restoration* (Oxford: Oxford University Press, 1968).

For brief accounts of other types of literary criticism as applied to sacred texts, see the following:

BEARDSLEE, WILLIAM, A., *Literary Criticism of the New Testament* (Philadelphia: Fortress Press, 1970).

McKNIGHT, EDGAR, *What Is Form Criticism?* (Philadelphia: Fortress Press, 1969).

PERRIN, NORMAN, *What Is Redaction Criticism?* (Philadelphia: Fortress Press, 1969).

> For a collection of essays by anthropologists and an analysis of themes in the anthropological study of religion, see the following:

LESSA, WILLIAM A., and VOGT, EVON Z., *Reader in Comparative Religion: An Anthropological Approach* (New York: Harper and Row, 1965).

DE WAAL MALEFIJT, ANNEMARIE, *Religion and Culture. An Introduction to the Anthropology of Religion* (New York: Macmillan, 1968).

> For a collection of essays on typical themes in the sociology of religion and works by both a classical and contemporary sociologist of religion, see the following:

ROBERTSON, ROLAND (ed.), *Sociology of Religion* (New York: Penguin, 1981).

WEBER, MAX, *The Sociology of Religion* (Boston: Beacon Press, 1963).

BERGER, PETER, *The Sacred Canopy* (New York: Doubleday, 1967).

> For an overview of recent work in the psychology of religion and a recent study that incorporates both classical theory and current empirical research, see the following:

DITTES, JAMES, "The Psychology of Religion," in Gardner Lindzey and Elliott Aronson (eds.), *The Handbook of Social Psychology* 2d. ed. (Reading, Mass.: Addison-Wesley, 1969).

BATSON, C. DANIEL, AND VENTIS, W. LARRY, *The Religious Experience: A Social-Psychological Perspective* (Oxford: Oxford University Press, 1982).

ALLPORT, GORDON, *The Individual and His Religion* (New York: Macmillan, 1950). An introduction to the stages and the patterns of religious development.

> For the philosophical scrutiny of religion, see the following:

CHARLESWORTH, M. J., *Philosophy of Religion: The Historic Approaches* (New York: Herder and Herder, 1972).

HICK, JOHN, *Philosophy of Religion* 3d. ed. (Englewood Cliffs, N.J.: Prentice-Hall, 1982).

_____, (ed.), *Classical and Contemporary Readings in the Philosophy of Religion*, 2d. ed. (Englewood Cliffs, N.J.: Prentice-Hall, 1970).

FLEW, ANTONY, AND MACINTYRE, ALASDAIR (eds.), *New Essays in Philosophical Theology* (London: SCM Press, 1958). Advanced contemporary discussion.

> For examples of the comparative-phenomenological method and approach to the study of religion, see the following:

ELIADE, MIRCEA, *Patterns in Comparative Religion* (New York: Sheed and Ward, 1958).

KRISTENSEN, W. BREDE, *The Meaning of Religion* (The Hague: Mouton, 1971).
VAN DER LEEUW, GERARDUS, *Religion in Essence and Manifestation* (London, 1938).
WACH, JOACHIM, *Types of Religious Experience* (Chicago, 1957).

For an account of Structuralism and its application to religious texts, see the following:

HAWKES, TERENCE. *Structuralism and Semiology* (New York, 1977).
LEACH, EDMUND, AND D. ALAN AYCOCK. *Structuralist Interpretation of Biblical Myth* (Cambridge, 1983).

PART 2

Universal Forms of Religious Experience and Expression

CHAPTER 3

The Sacred and the Holy

OVERVIEW

When the scientific study of religion was fully established in the latter decades of the nineteenth century, one of its principle concerns was to trace religion back to its earliest expression in history. A number of influential theories about the origin of religion were proposed by scholars. Because the often-scanty evidence did not go back very far into human origins and was not capable of being applied universally to very different cultures, the search for *the* origin of religion soon lost credibility and died out.

It is clear, however, that the search for origins was closely related to the question of religion's essence. For example, when scholars sought the origin of religion in **animism** or **totemism**, or when Sigmund Freud traced the source of religion to infantile projection, these scholars were, at the same time, concerned with what they thought they had discovered to be the root of religious experience. This interest in the root nature of religion—that is, what, if anything, is its common, universal essence—remains a concern of scholars today. In Chapter 1, we encountered some of the difficulties in attempting general definitions of religion. Despite this problem, most scholars today agree that religion is a system of activities and beliefs directed toward that which is perceived to be sacred or of ultimate value and power. Such things—be they spiritual beings, cosmic laws, natural places, persons, ideals, or ideologies—are thereby set apart as sacred or of ultimate significance.

Here we shall discuss the sacred or the holy as the root of religious experience and practice. We shall explore the nature of sacred power and the ambiguity of the sacred as **taboo** (from the Polynesian word *tapu*, meaning "to make holy"), that is, as the source of wonder and purity as well as of fear and danger. We shall also examine the psychological or personal experience uniquely associated with the encounter with the holy, and how the sacred, or holy, is manifested in special places and times. Finally, we shall explore a family resemblance between religion as the response to what is perceived as sacred and religion as commitment to what is held to be of ultimate meaning and value or as the source of ultimate transformation.

The Concept of Sacred Power

In his phenomenological description of religion in *Religion in Essence and Manifestation*, the Dutch scholar Gerardus van der Leeuw points to the preconceptual experience of *sacred power* as the root of all religion. "The first affirmation we can make about the Object of Religion," he writes, "is that it is a highly exceptional and extremely impressive 'Other.' . . . This Object is a departure from all that is usual and familiar; and this again is the consequence of the Power it generates."[1]

To the primitive, almost any natural object or human artifact can be the bearer of sacred power. "During an important expedition, for example, an African negro steps on a stone and cries out: 'Ha! are you there?' and takes it with him to bring him luck. The stone, as it were, gives a hint that it is powerful."[2] The important role that **fetishes**, amulets, totems, **icons**, idols, as well as sacred sanctuaries, temples, and sacraments play in the history of religion, point to them as special vehicles or bearers of sacred power. Certain persons—such as the king—and special times—such as the New Year's Festival—or specific activities—such as planting or sexual relations—are regarded as set apart and endowed with unique power, and therefore objects of awe, fear, and taboo. The distinction between such a uniquely effective power and that which is relatively powerless is, according to van der Leeuw, what characterizes the contrast between the sacred and the profane. It is *power* that creates for the sacred a special place and value all its own.

The Ambivalence of Sacred Power

A unique characteristic of sacred power is the fact that it evokes an ambivalent response. A person's impulse, in the face of the awesome and mysterious, is instinctively one of avoidance; and yet the sacred possesses a magnetic attraction as well. "In the human soul," van der Leeuw writes,

> ... power awakens a profound feeling of awe which manifests itself both as fear and as being attracted. There is no religion whatever without terror, but equally none without love. ... Physical shuddering, ghostly horror, fear, sudden terror, reverence, humility, adoration, profound apprehension, enthusiasm—all these lie *in nuce* within the awe experienced in the presence of Power.[3]

This ambivalent quality of sacred power especially needs to be underlined today, since modern life has tamed sacred power into something benign and benevolent. Modern society has little sense of the terror or dread of the sacred. In traditional societies, however, sacred power always shows itself ambiguously, simultaneously as awe and aversion, purity and danger. The sacred thus represents the two poles of a single dreadful domain: as both sanctity and defilement. The French sociologist Roger Caillois points out that the Greek word for "defilement" also means "the sacrifice which cleanses the defilement." So it is in primitive cultures that the taboo experienced as awe in the presence of sanctity is not distinguished from the fear inspired by defilement. The sacred both fascinates and repels, eliciting feelings of both awe and aversion.

Caillois suggests that religion (that is, the realm of the sacred) is rooted in a primordial dual motive: the acquisition of purity and the elimination of defilement.

> Purity is acquired by submitting to a set of ritualistic observances. The point above all is to become separated from the profane world in order to make possible the penetration of the sacred world without peril. The human [profane] must be abandoned before the divine can be reached. That is to say, rites of **catharsis** are to the highest degree negations or abstentions. They consist of temporary renunciations of the varied activities typical of the profane world. ... It is literally necessary to be purified in order to be worthy of approaching the domain of the Gods.[4]

A state of purity detached from the profane cannot, of course, be maintained for very long. Life requires a return to the profane, a world incompatible with sanctity. Hence, on leaving the sacred region, sacred vestments—for example, those of a priest—must be removed, or one must take a ritual bath, leaving the pure and consecrated life behind before emerging again into the region of the profane. This *must* be done, for contact with the sacred can also expose the profane community to the danger of supernatural defilement. Therefore, in many societies, holy persons such as kings, priests, or **shamans** must be kept from other members of the community lest the people be defiled. In Japan, for example, the utensils used in eating by the divine Emperor were destroyed, lest someone using them become infected.

Everything that is touched by a holy person is consecrated by this very act and can only be used by them. . . . Contact with it is fatal. The divine and the accursed, consecration and defilement, have exactly the same effects upon profane objects. They render them untouchable, withdraw them from circulation, and communicate to them their formidable qualities.[5]

The Holy as *Mysterium Tremendum* and *Fascinans*

The primal experience of sacred power with the accompanying feelings of awe, fear, purity, and danger, is pursued with great psychological insight by Rudolf Otto in his classic and influential study, *The Idea of the Holy*. Otto regards the holy as an experience peculiar to religion. He acknowledges that the holy often is associated with morality and that inevitably it does become conceptualized in the form of myths and doctrines. However, in Otto's view, the holy is fundamentally a nonrational and ineffable datum of human experience. In order to isolate the holy from either ethical or theological conceptions, Otto coined the word *numinous* to describe this uniquely religious phenomenon. The word comes from the Latin *numina* and refers to those powers or spirits that Latin farmers of ancient Italy associated with special places and functions.

Since Otto regards the numinous as unique, it is not reducible to any other more-primary experience. He points out that the history of religion is, from one perspective, simply the history of the ways in which the numinous experience has been expressed in myth, ritual, and doctrine.

Considered subjectively, a person's encounter with the numinous evokes a profound "creature-consciousness" or "creature-feeling." Otto describes it as the emotion of a creature "submerged and overwhelmed by its own nothingness in contrast to that which is supreme."[6] Considered as an objective reality, the numinous can be suggested only in terms of the way it grips and stirs the human mind and emotions. Otto attempts to describe the most fundamental of these affective or emotional responses by the words *mysterium tremendum* and *fascinans*. Each of these terms requires some comment.

The *mysterium* is the experience of a reality that, when encountered, is perceived as lying beyond our capacity to comprehend or conceptualize fully; it is extraordinary, unfamiliar, and therefore mysterious. It is beyond our comprehension "not only because our knowledge has certain irremovable limits, but because in it we come upon something inherently 'wholly other,' whose kind and character are incommensurable with our own. . . ."[7]

The experience of the numinous can be better understood, however, if we also grasp what Otto seeks to convey by the words *tremendum* and *fascinans*. *Tremor* denotes fear but the *tremendum* is more than fear proper. It is a feeling of peculiar dread and awe. Otto believes that religious dread lies at the root of the religious experience of the numinous. "It first begins to stir," Otto observes, "in the feeling of 'something canny,' 'eerie,' or 'weird.' It is this feeling which, emerging in the mind of primeval man, forms the starting-point for the entire religious development in history."[8] Religion has, of course, transcended the worship of spirits and "daemons," that is, has advanced beyond animism or the worship of nature. Nevertheless, the peculiar feeling of the "uncanny" and "aweful" tremendum survives in more sophisticated expressions of theistic religion, reflecting the transcendence, the "otherness" and sublimity of the numinous.

Otto describes two qualities of the *tremendum* in addition to the sense of awe or dread. One is the aspect of "might" or "overpoweringness," which he signifies by the term *majestas* (majesty). In the experience of "aweful majesty," the human consciousness of creature-feeling is especially vivid. Furthermore, the *tremendum* reveals itself as an "energy" that often is felt as holy "wrath." It is symbolized by such expressions as a deity's vitality, passion, might, or will.

Encounters with the numinous are experienced not only by emotions of dread, awe, majesty, and wrath. The numinous is also positively attractive, fascinating, and even intoxicating. The positive feelings accompanying this captivating side of the numinous include love, pity, mercy, joy, peace, and beatitude. While the forms of worship that issue from the experience of "awe" and "dread" would include **expiation** and propitiation, the *fascinans* provokes expressions of joyful thanksgiving, praise, and adoration.

Otto points to the universal character of the experience of the holy by citing examples from a wide range of religious traditions, as well as from art, music, and poetry. A classic example is the biblical prophet Isaiah's awesome vision of the Lord God in the Temple of Jerusalem.

1. . . . sitting upon a throne, high and lifted up, his train filled the temple.
2. Above it stood the seraphims: each one had six wings; with twain he covered his face, and with twain he covered his feet, and with twain he did fly.
3. And one cried unto another, and said, Holy, holy, holy, is the Lord of hosts: the whole earth is full of his glory.
4. And the posts of the door moved at the voice of him that cried, and the house was filled with smoke.

5. Then said I, Woe is me! for I am undone; because I am a man
of unclean lips, and I dwell in the midst of a people of unclean
lips: for mine eyes have seen the King, the Lord of hosts.

(Isaiah VI)

A similar numinous vision was experienced by Arjuna, the Hindu
warrior-hero, as recorded in the *Bhagavad-Gita*, a sacred text. The
Gita tells the story of Arjuna's request to Krishna—the God Vishnu
in human form—that he, Arjuna, be allowed to see the Supreme
Being Vishnu. Arjuna's wish is granted and the following terrible and
yet majestic revelation is described:

9. Thus speaking Vishnu, the great Lord of the Rule, then showed
to Pritha's son [Arjuna] his sovran form supreme . . .
12. If the light of a thousand suns should of a sudden rise in the
heavens, it would be like the light of that mighty being . . .
14. Thereupon [Arjuna], smitten with amazement, with hair standing
on end, bowed his head, and with clasped hands spoke to 'the
God . . .
17. I behold Thee bearing diadem, mace, and disc, massed in
radiance, on all sides glistening, hardly discernible, shining round
about as gleaming fire and sun, immeasurable . . .
20. . . . Seeing this Thy fearful and wonderful form, O great-hearted
one, the three-fold world quakes.

(Bhagavad-Gita, Ch. II)

The experience of the holy often takes place in encounters with
nature, especially in the silent presence of great mountains or the
sea. It is a theme found in the writings of many nature mystics, in
Romantic poetry, and in Chinese landscape painting. Otto cites the
English art critic, John Ruskin, who recounts the numinous experiences he had as a youth:

. . . Although there was no definite religious sentiment mingled with
it, there was a continual perception of Sanctity in the whole of
nature, from the slightest thing to the vastest; an instinctive awe,
mixed with delight; an indefinable thrill . . . . I could only feel this
perfectly when I was alone; and then it would often make me shiver
from head to foot with the joy and fear of it . . . when I first saw
the swell of distant land against the sunset, or the first low broken
wall, covered with mountain moss. I cannot in the least describe the
feeling; but I do not think this is my fault nor that of the English
language . . . . The joy in nature seemed to me to come of a sort
of heart-hunger, satisfied with the presence of a Great and Holy
Spirit. . . .[9]

From the first stirrings of primitive "daemonic dread" to the most
sophisticated revelations of saints and mystics, the experience of the

"Buddhist Monastery by Stream and
Mountains." The great landscape
painters of the Sung dynasty in
China evoked the presence of sacred
space and the infinite in their
paintings of mountains, water, and
mist.   (*Source:* Courtesy of The
Cleveland Museum of Art, gift of
Katherine Holden Thayer.)

numinous remains, Otto insists, a unique, original experience. Our sense experience supplies the occasion for numinous experience; the experience itself does not arise *out of* sense experience but only by its means. In the evolution of the world's religions there is, of course, a process by which the numinous is variously named and conceptualized. Yet even in the most sublime flights of spiritual vision, the element of the wholly other, the nonrational and mysterious, is retained. Indeed, it is intensified, as an Isaiah or a Ruskin testifies. Nevertheless, the growth of human rationality is accompanied by a "schematization" of the nonrational *mysterium*, as is seen in the development of theological and moral concepts and systems. Otto points out that the *tremendum*, for example, "is schematized by means of the rational ideas of justice, moral will, and the exclusion of what is opposed to morality; and schematized thus it becomes the holy 'wrath of God.'" Similarly, the alluring *fascinans* "is schematized by means of the ideas of goodness, mercy, love, and, so schematized, becomes all that we mean by Grace. . . ."[10]

Otto cites the doctrine of atonement, a theme found in numerous religions, as an especially good example of this rationalizing process. Atonement is simply a more-rational way of expressing the primal human feeling of the need for a shield or shelter from a sacred taboo.

As the human religious consciousness is filled out more and more with rational and moral elements, 'the nonrational primal experience of the holy may appear to be eclipsed, but it is never lost. If it were, according to Otto, the religious sense itself would be lost. Thus, Otto insists that the element of the nonrational numinous is always retained because it is the very essence of religion. "Revelation," he writes,

> does not mean a mere passing over into the intelligible and comprehensible. Something may be profoundly and intimately known in feeling for the bliss it brings or the agitation it produces, and yet the understanding may find no concept for it. To *know* and to *understand conceptually* are two different things.[11]

Sacred Space and Sacred Time

Mircea Eliade, the historian of religion and phenomenologist whom we discussed in Chapter 2, acknowledges Otto's contribution to an understanding of the numinous experience. However, he is critical of Otto's concentration on the psychological or emotional qualities of the numinous, such as the experience of the *tremendum*. Eliade wants to begin without any preconceptions about the qualities of the sacred and to explore how the sacred is manifested in the history of religions. He begins, therefore, with the simpler and more-neutral distinction popularized by Emile Durkheim: the fundamental contrast between the sacred and the profane.

According to Eliade, this contrast represents the two fundamental modes of being in the world assumed by mankind throughout its history. First, and most basically, the sacred always manifests itself as something nonordinary and thus wholly distinct from what is profane, common, or simply utilitarian. At the same time, Eliade points out that *anything*—a stone, a tree, or a building—can be set apart as disclosing the sacred. Both natural objects and human artifacts are capable of and have been transformed from a common use to a sacred presence. Eliade calls this *act of manifesting* the sacred a **hierophany** (from the Greek *hieros*, meaning sacred, and *phanein*, meaning to appear).

> It is a fitting term, because it does not imply anything further; it expresses no more than is implicit in its etymological content, i.e., *that something sacred shows itself to us*. It could be said that the history of religions—from the most primitive to the most highly developed— is constituted by a great number of hierophanies. . . .[12]

Eliade's extraordinary knowledge of the history of religions, including little-known primitive and archaic religions, has enabled him to compare a rich variety of spatial and temporal manifestations of the sacred and to comment on their significance. For the religious, space is not uniform; some places are qualitatively different from others. Eliade points to the experience of Moses on Mount Sinai and then comments on its significance:

> 'Draw not hither,' says the Lord to Moses; 'put off thy shoes from off thy feet, for the place whereon thou standest is holy ground' (Exodus 3:5). There is, then, a sacred space, and hence a strong, significant space; there are other spaces that are not sacred and so are without structure or consistency, amorphous. Nor is this all. For religious man, this . . . finds expression in the experience of an opposition between space that is sacred—the only *real* and *real-ly* existing space—and all other space, the formless expanse surrounding it.[13]

The break between sacred and profane space is what actually founds or establishes a world because sacred space reveals what T. S. Eliot called "the fixed point of the turning world," a central axis or pivot around which the human world revolves. The revelation or discovery of a fixed point of sacred space is equivalent, **ontologically** as well as psychologically, to founding or creating a world. Through it, an orientation is given in the chaos of ordinary, profane space. Eliade points out, however, that it is not possible to live in a completely profane, desacralized world. The setting apart and sacralizing of certain places is borne out in the behavior of modern, secular individuals as well as secular societies.

> There are, for example, privileged places, qualitatively different from all others—a man's birthplace, or the scenes of first love.... Even for the most frankly nonreligious man, all these places still retain an exceptional, a unique quality; they are the 'holy places' of his private universe, as if it were in such spots that he has received that revelation of a reality *other* than that in which he participates through his ordinary daily life.[14]

Sacred space implies a hierophany, an opening to the holy or divine, a place where communication with sacred power is made possible. Eliade refers to such space as an *axis mundi*, the center of the world. It is the point around which, symbolically speaking, the world rotates. The founding of sanctuaries, shrines, and temples are illustrations of such sacred openings. The biblical story of Jacob's dream at Haran is a classic example. In his dream, Jacob sees a ladder set on the earth and reaching up to heaven, with angels ascending and descending on it. The Lord then speaks to Jacob, saying, "I *am* the Lord God of Abraham thy father.... the land whereon thou liest, to thee will I give it, and to thy seed." When Jacob awakes, he is afraid and cries out "How dreadful is this place! This is none other but the house of God, this *is* the gate of heaven." Jacob then takes the stone that he had used as a pillow and sets it up as a pillar (monument) and pours oil on top of it. He then vows that the stone "shall be God's house" and "he called the name of that place Beth-el" (Genesis 28:12–22).

Consecrating a place is equivalent to founding a world, a cosmos out of chaos. Often, however, the sacred place, be it a simple altar or an elaborate temple, represents not only an "opening" to heaven but also a reproduction, on the human scale, of the cosmos or of Creation itself. It is an *imago mundi*, an image of the original world order. The symbolism of the altar or temple is often an explicit replica of the **cosmogony**—that is, a mirror of the original act of Creation, a prototype of the work of God or the gods. This is apparent in the symbolic construction of the ancient Hindu (Vedic) fire altar, consecrated to the god Agni. The ritual erection of the altar occurs, understandably, on the taking possession of a new territory.

> The water in which the clay is mixed is assimilated to the primordial water; the clay that forms the base of the altar symbolizes the earth; the lateral walls represent the atmosphere, and so on. And the building of the altar is accompanied by songs that proclaim which cosmic region has just been created. Hence the erection of a fire altar . . . is equivalent to a cosmogony.[15]

The Ka'ba, the House of Allah, in Mecca is the principal Islamic shrine
and is considered the geographic and religious center of the Muslim
world. (*Source:* Courtesy of Woodfin Camp & Associates, Inc.)

Every breakthrough to the sacred is effected by a hierophany, symbolized, for example, by a sacred pillar, tree, mountain, altar, temple,
or city, perceived as the center of the world. For Jews, such a center
is Mount Zion–Jerusalem; for Christians, it is the mount at Golgotha.
Islamic tradition holds that the highest place on earth is the holy
ka'ba, the small cubic building in the Great Mosque of Mecca that
houses the sacred Black Stone, because, it is claimed, the Pole star
bears witness that it faces the center of Heaven. The true world—sacred space—always lies at the Center, joining heaven and earth.

The Buddhist Stupa and Pagoda as Sacred Space

An excellent example of a sacred *axis mundi* is the Buddhist stupa
(India and Sri Lanka) or pagoda (Burma, China, and Japan). Stupas
first appear within Buddhism in India as places where the cremated
remains of the Buddha were interred as relics. They functioned as
reliquaries in homage to the Buddha and later to Buddhist holy
persons. Originally, they were simple mounds surrounded by railings
with four cardinal gateways. In time, they became elaborate structures

A typical dome-like stupa found in Sri Lanka.   (*Source:* Courtesy of Jack
Van Horn.)

and temples symbolizing, in rich variety, the Buddhist cosmos and
the path to enlightenment. Every aspect of the stupa plan conveys
symbolic meanings and powers.

The point on the ground selected for the center of the stupa is
symbolic, at the terrestrial level, of the transcendent sacred Center.
The stupa is the symbolic *omphalos*, that is, the navel and fulcrum of
the world. The axial point of the stupa thus represents the gateway
between the several planes of existence: the terrestrial, the celestial,
and the infernal realms. Furthermore, the orientation of the stupa
plan is determined by the movements of the sun; and it represents
a geometric diagram of the cyclical movements of the sun, the Center
of the cosmos.

Most strikingly, the stupa is planned as a **mandala**. The Buddhist
mandala is a circle, symbolizing the perfection of Buddhahood, in-
scribed within a square drawn in bright colors on the earth or as a
painting on cloth or paper. The square of the mandala is subdivided
into smaller squares, all expressing a paradigm model of the cosmic

pattern of the universe. The mandala is, then, a compressed image of the total cosmos. The mandala that is marked out on the ground where the stupa is to be erected is a symbolic representation of the spiritual or metaphysical meaning of the completed three-dimensional monument. Often the foundation of the stupa includes, for example, 9, 17, or 25 square holes arranged in appropriate rows. In the ancient stupas found in Sri Lanka (Ceylon), these holes "contain images of the *dikpālas*, the guardians of the ten regions of space (the cardinals, the ordinals, the zenith, and the nadir), the animals of the four directions (the bull, the lion, the horse, and the elephant), and images of the Hindu divinities connected with the directions of space and with the cycles of time."[16]

Above the stupa's foundation are terraced levels representing a variety of Buddhist faculties and powers, for example, the four types of Mindfulness and the four types of Renunciation. The terraces are topped by a hemispherical dome. The Buddhists speak of the dome as the "womb" or "embryo," or "egg." It is the "womb of the elements," that is, the creative source and power of the universe from whence all life flows. The dome is capped by a quadrangular *harmika* that symbolizes the eternal sacrificial altar and often contains relics.

THE PARTS OF THE STUPA

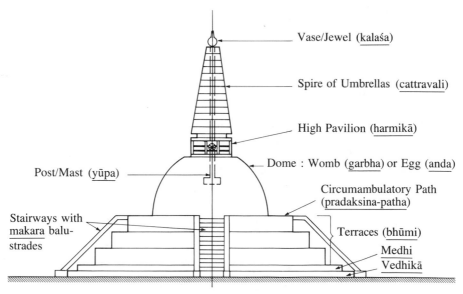

The parts of the stupa, each one representing an important Buddhist concept or psychic power. (*Source:* Courtesy of Cornell University Press. From Adrian Snodgrass, *The Symbolism of the Stupa* [Ithaca, N.Y.: Cornell Southeast Asia Program Studies on Southeast Asia, 1985], p. 162.)

It later became associated with the Buddhist Eightfold Path (see Chapter 11). The stupa is crowned by a vertical cone-shaped spire or tower. This elongated cone is often marked with several rings or umbrella-like notches that progressively diminish toward the apex. The stupa's spire represents the tree of life or tree of enlightenment on the summit of the sacred Mount Meru inhabited by the gods. The various notches of the cone-tree correspond to certain psychic faculties or stages of consciousness on the way to enlightenment. "Just as the Phoenix rises from the ashes, so the tree of life and enlightenment grow out of the ashes of the sacrificial altar [the harmikā] which crowns the dome, the monumental world-egg and womb of a new world."[17]

In the Buddhist countries of South and East Asia, the stupa appears in a variety of regional forms. The principal feature of the stupas of Sri Lanka is the beautiful bell-shaped dome. The terrace stupas of Tibet and Nepal do not feature the dome but appear rather like terraced pyramids. Tower-shaped pagodas are common in China and Japan. Their distinctive feature is the multiple stories set off by clearly articulated roofs. But whatever their form, the stupas and pagodas of Buddhist Asia represent the *axis mundi*, the sacred tree or cosmic mountain, that Center that joins earth and the realm of the transcendent and the real.

Mount Zion as Sacred Space

In part through the stimulus of Eliade's work, scholars are now especially aware of the religious significance of geography, of space. The great geographically focused religions—such as the Egyptian, Babylonian, Indian, and Chinese—developed their mythic and ritual symbolism around the constants of their geographic space, around their sacred rivers, mountains, and cities. But sacred space also has played a formative role in the Western historical or "diasporic" religions—that is, those dispersed throughout the world—as testified to by the role of Jerusalem, Mecca, Golgotha, and Rome. Sacred mountains are especially common in the symbolism of the three Western biblical religions—Judaism, Christianity, and Islam—particularly the mountains and hills of Palestine and Arabia. It is noteworthy that the Hebrew word for mountain, *har*, appears 520 times in the Bible.

The pervasive symbolism of the cosmic mountain in Israelite and later Jewish religion can serve to illustrate the importance of geography on the religious imagination. Mountains are, of course, the nearest things to the sky and are obvious symbols of those transcendent powers "on high," that is, the gods and the dwelling place of the gods—such as the Greek Mount Olympus, the Japanese Mount Fuji, or the Indian Mount Meru. Since mountains are the abode of the gods, they are the natural places of worship. The Israelite tribes

Buddhist monks paying homage to Mount Fuji. Every year, thousands of Japanese pilgrims climb the sacred mountain, where it is believed the shades of ancestors dwell. (*Source:* Courtesy of Burt Glinn, Magnum Photos, Inc.)

each had their shrine or sanctuary on a mountain—Dan in the north; Schechem, Gibeon, Gilgal, and Bethel in the center of Palestine; and Hebron and Beersheba in the south. Mount Sinai, where Moses received the Law and sealed the Covenant with Israel's God, Yahweh, and Jerusalem (Mount Zion), the site of the monarchy of the great King David and the Temple, became especially sacred to Israel and to later Judaism.

The sacred mountain served the Israelites, first, as an image of security. There the people hid from their enemies, protected by Yahweh. As the Psalmist writes, "I will lift my eyes to the hills, from where my help comes" (Ps. 121:1). But the mountains were a bulwark not only against the human enemy but also against the desolation and waste of the desert wilderness, against chaos. The mountain also symbolized authority. The Law was given to Moses on Mount Sinai and it was on the mountains that Yahweh's spokesmen, the prophets, delivered the "Word of the Lord," God's warnings, blessings, and judgments. The antiquity, security, and authority of the mountain are joined in the image of the mountain as *axis mundi*, as the meeting place of heaven and earth and thus the sacred center, or navel, of the world. Moses goes up Mount Sinai to find God; there he receives the divine Law, which in turn creates Israel into a people bound by shared values and responsibilities.

Later, when King David brought the ark of the Covenant to Mount Zion–Jerusalem, it became *the* "holy mountain," a second Sinai—the *axis mundi* and center of security, authority, fertility, and blessing. Yahweh's dwelling in Jerusalem (Mount Zion) protected Israel against the encroaching powers of chaos:

> Great is YHWH and much to be praised
> In the city of our God is his holy mountain;
> The most beautiful peak, the joy of all the earth.
> Mount Zion is the heart [that is, the navel] of Zaphon
> The city of the great King.
> God is her citadel, has shown himself her bulwark. . . .
> God will make her secure forever.[18]
>
> *(Ps. 48)*

The image of Mount Zion–Jerusalem as the Center of space is especially pronounced in later **rabbinic** literature and Jewish folklore. A famous rabbinic text maintains that

> . . . just as the navel is found in the center of the human being, so the land of Israel is found at the center of the world . . . and it is the foundation of the world. Jerusalem is at the center of the land of Israel, the Temple is at the center of Jerusalem, the Holy of Holies is at the center of the Temple, the Ark is at the center of

the Holy of Holies and the Foundation Stone is in front of the Ark, which spot is the foundation of the world.[19]

Because Mount Zion, and especially its Temple, served as their *axis mundi*, pious Jews regarded them as essential to the maintenance of the cosmos. As long as the services in the Temple were performed, there were blessings in the world, the crops were plentiful, and man and beast ate and were satisfied. When the Jerusalem Temple was destroyed, God's blessings departed from the world. The Temple and its ritual were the two cosmic pillars—the sacred poles—that support the world.

The destruction of Jerusalem and the Temple and the exile of the Jews to Babylonia in the sixth century B.C.E. destroyed Israel's center and broke the link between heaven and earth. Disaster and chaos ensued. For orthodox Jews, the land of Israel, the city of Jerusalem, and Yahweh are inseparable. This fact points to the full tragedy of the 1900 years of Jewish exile from their Holy Land. For Jews, the overcoming of exile and chaos is traditionally accomplished through the commemorative rituals of the Sabbath and the high holy days during which there is a renewal of original, sacred time. However, the Zionist restoration of the land and the nation of Israel in 1947 represents the actual recovery of the Jewish center, of sacred space itself.

To summarize this theme, we can say that sacred space establishes a world, a cosmos, a fixed point in profane or chaotic space. Communication and passage is thereby opened between heaven and earth; a passage from one mode of being to another. Such a break in ordinary space creates a Center that makes orientation, hence meaning, possible. For the religious person, neither space nor *time* is ordinary. There are times as well as places set apart for festivals and holidays that break the unvarying and meaningless time of ordinary temporal duration. Through ritual, a person passes from ordinary, profane time into sacred time.

> One essential difference between these two qualities of time strikes us immediately: *by its very nature sacred time is reversible* in the sense that, properly speaking, it is a *primordial mythical time made present.* Every religious festival, any liturgical time, represents the reactualization of a sacred event that took place in the mythical past, 'in the beginning.'[20]

Since sacred time is mythical or primordial time, it is intimately connected with origins. In many primitive and archaic religions, the cosmos is ritually re-created or reborn annually on New Year's Day by returning to and reenacting the mythical time of the Creation "in the beginning" (see Chapter 8). Sacred space, the "house of god" or

the "gate of heaven," represents not only the cosmos but also the
year. This is again evident in the construction of the Hindu altar to
the fire god Agni, referred to earlier. As Eliade explains it,

> The 360 bricks of the enclosure correspond to the 360 nights of
> the year, and the 360 *yajusmati* bricks to the 360 days. This is as
> much as to say that, with the building of each fire altar, not only
> is the world remade but the year is built too; in other words *time
> is regenerated by being created anew.*[21]

The mythic time portrayed in the original cosmogony is the prototype or paradigm model for all other times. Therefore, the ritual
reenactment of the Creation renews the cycle of the seasons and
thereby restores time and preserves the temporal process from passage
into chaos and death. Since the world does periodically retrogress
toward stagnation and chaos, it must be ritually renewed. The New
Year's ritual is just such an act of purification and restoration. The
impurities and sins of the past year are purged away and the threat
of returning to the chaos of nonbeing is forestalled.

Through the periodic ritual repetition of the cosmogony, time is
regenerated and temporal existence is restored and revitalized. Life
can be renewed only by the regular ritual repetition of the originating
events. In a similar way, the Christian, through participating periodically in the Eucharist or Holy Communion—which for the Christian
reenacts an original yet eternal act of redemption through Christ—
perceives that "old things are passed away," that sin is forgiven, life
is renewed, and eternal life conferred.

We can conclude this topic by saying that Otto and Eliade are
certainly correct that humankind has always lived in a sacred world
of space and time. It is a world made real and sanctified by a break
with ordinary time and space, making it possible to found a world
and to model life after a sacred prototype, as it was "in the beginning."
Eliade is right that the essence of religion is the desire to live in
relation to a sacred order that is expressed in a prescribed pattern
of behavior and belief. Such a sacred order, as we have seen, is
distinct from the common or profane and is the source not only of
meaning (value) but also of life-giving power. Such a sacred order,
it should be pointed out, does not necessarily involve a division of
the world into the "natural" and the "supernatural." Such a separation
is common in some theistic religions that perceive reality as constituted
by two distinct worlds, one a physical world governed by natural laws
and the other a supernatural world of spiritual beings and powers.
However, a sacred world need not be an order distinct from the
natural world; rather, it can be seen as the natural world consecrated
and made holy by special times and places.

Religion as Ultimate Concern

Analysis of the sacred as the essence of religion can appropriately conclude with a few comments on a resemblance between Durkheim's and Eliade's contrast between the sacred and the profane and Paul Tillich's (1886–1965) more-philosophical concept of religion as *ultimate concern*. Tillich does not conceive of religion in terms of a division between the natural and the supernatural nor as a distinct *a priori* faculty similar, for example, to our moral sense. Rather, he sees religion as the "depth dimension" of all human experience. By the use of the metaphor "depth," Tillich is pointing to what is ultimate in an individual's or a society's life—what gives that life meaning and what sustains it in being. There is, then, a certain equivalence in the role that the sacred plays in Durkheim's thought and the role of ultimate concern in Tillich's writings. According to Tillich,

> man is ultimately concerned about his being and meaning. 'To be or not to be,' in *this* sense is a matter of ultimate, unconditional, total and infinite concern. . . . Man is unconditionally concerned about that which conditions his being beyond all the conditions in him and around him. Man is ultimately concerned about what determines his ultimate destiny beyond all preliminary necessities and accidents.[22]

This quotation obviously betrays a more reflective, philosophical stage of religion than those that engage the interest of Durkheim and Eliade. Nevertheless, it shares a common concern for an order of meaning and a power of being that is set apart from what is of merely secondary or profane interest. Humans have sought ultimate security and meaning in a great variety of things, from totemic animals—such as the monkey in north India (the staple of life)—to divine kings, and to such sublime concepts as that of the Chinese Tao, the Indian Brahman, the Buddhist Nirvana, and the God of Western monotheism. But in each instance what is sacred is ultimate and what is ultimate is sacred, in that it does possess the power to threaten and to save our being, to empower life and give it a meaning which the vicissitudes of temporal existence cannot destroy.

It is appropriate, then, to speak of the object of religion as the holy or the sacred, or as an object of ultimate concern. But that object can only be pointed to, addressed, or communicated in the language and gestures of our own social and historical experience. We turn, therefore, in Chapters 4 and 5 to a discussion of the distinct modes of religious expression and communication—to symbol, myth, and ritual.

Notes

1. G. van der Leeuw, *Religion in Essence and Manifestation* I (New York, 1963), p. 23.
2. van der Leeuw, *Religion in Essence*, p. 37.
3. van der Leeuw, *Religion in Essence*, p. 48.
4. Roger Caillois, *Man and the Sacred* (Glencoe, Ill., 1959), pp. 38–39.
5. Caillois, *Man and the Sacred*, p. 42.
6. R. Otto, *The Idea of the Holy* (New York, 1958), p. 10.
7. Otto, *The Idea of the Holy*, p. 28.
8. Otto, *The Idea of the Holy*, p. 14.
9. Otto, *The Idea of the Holy*, p. 215.
10. Otto, *The Idea of the Holy*, p. 140.
11. Otto, *The Idea of the Holy*, p. 135.
12. Mircea Eliade, *The Sacred and the Profane*, trans. W. R. Trask (New York, 1961), p. 11.
13. Eliade, *The Sacred*, p. 20.
14. Eliade, *The Sacred*, p. 24.
15. Eliade, *The Sacred*, pp. 30–31.
16. Adrian Snodgrass, *The Symbolism of the Stupa* (Ithaca, N.Y., 1985), p. 129.
17. Lama Anagarika Govinda, *Psycho-cosmic Symbolism of the Buddhist Stupa*, (1976), pp. 30–31.
18. Translation of M. Dahood, *Psalms* (Garden City, N.Y., 1966) p. 288.
19. *Midrash Tanhuma*, Kedoshim 10, quoted in A. Hertzberg, *Judaism* (New York, 1963), p. 143. For this and other citations on Mount Zion as Center, I am indebted to J. Z. Smith's excellent essay, "Earth and Gods," *The Journal of Religion* 49 (1969): 103–127.
20. Eliade, *The Sacred*, pp. 68–69.
21. Eliade, *The Sacred*, p. 74.
22. Paul Tillich, *Theology of Culture* (New York, 1959), pp. 7–8.

Review Questions

1. Scholars such as Roger Caillois and Rudolf Otto have analyzed a number of important characteristics of the primal experience of the sacred or holy. What are some of the important characteristics associated with the experience of sacred power and what Otto calls the numinous?
2. In Mircea Eliade's discussion of sacred space, what does he mean by a hierophany, an *axis mundi*, and an *imago mundi*?
3. Describe some of the symbolic meanings or associations connected with such sacred places as the Buddhist stupa or the Jewish Mount Zion. Can you point to other sacred places in other world religions? Are there places in the United States that are, for Americans, sacred space?

4. Indicate some times that represent—for some of the world's religions—periods of purification, renewal, or rebirth.
5. Describe what Paul Tillich means by religion as an "ultimate concern." Can you think of examples of some *nontraditional* objects of "ultimate concern," that is, things or persons or ideologies that give individuals a sense of meaning, purpose, and hope?

Suggestions for Further Reading

CAILLOIS, ROGER, *Man and the Sacred* (New York: The Free Press, 1959).

DURKHEIM, EMILE, *The Elementary Forms of the Religious Life* (New York: The Free Press, 1965).

ELIADE, MIRCEA, *The Sacred and the Profane* (New York: Harper and Row, 1961).

NISBET, ROBERT, "The Sacred," in *The Sociological Tradition* (London: Heinemann, 1966).

OTTO, RUDOLF, *The Idea of the Holy* (New York: Oxford University Press, 1958).

TILLICH, PAUL, *Systematic Theology* I. (Chicago: University of Chicago Press, 1951).

———, "Religion as a Dimension of Man's Spiritual Life," in *Theology of Culture* (New York: Oxford University Press, 1964).

VAN DER LEEUW, GERARDUS, *Religion in Essence and Manifestation*, 2 vols. (New York: Harper and Row, 1963).

CHAPTER 4

Sacred Symbol, Myth, and Doctrine

OVERVIEW

This chapter begins with a discussion of the uniquely human capacity for symbolic expression and then proceeds to explain different kinds of symbolic communication. This is followed by a number of illustrations of the ways in which religious symbols can bridge or "bring together," for example, the profane and the sacred, or varieties of religious meanings or concepts, or even entire religious communities around shared values and associations.

The chapter then explores several forms of symbolic communication—such as metaphor, parable, and story—and the unique ways in which they strike insight and communicate unexpected meanings. This is followed by an extended discussion of religious myth and its characteristics, and why it is considered an indispensable form of human expression. The study of religious myth is of great interest to anthropologists, psychologists, and literary critics, as well as to historians of religion. Special attention is given to the various ways in which these scholars interpret the meaning and significance of myth.

The chapter concludes with a discussion of religious doctrine, that is, with the need to translate the symbolic and mythic language of religious narrative into concepts and propositions. The purpose of doctrines is to achieve conceptual clarity, coherence, and comprehensiveness. In this regard, religious doctrine is compared to scientific models that seek to interpret experience in certain ways or according to certain patterns.

Symbolic Communication

Every living creature feels and, through feeling, responds to the stimulus of the external world by means of gestures or sounds. A primal form of such response is the simple utterance. But, as Erich Kahler points out, "even the cry of a hunted animal, the groan of a suffering or starving creature is a *symptom* of something, it is a *sign* of some motivated feeling." It is, however, only a sign of something, "not or not necessarily, a sign made *to* and intended *for* somebody."[1]

We should attend to Kahler's qualification, "or not necessarily." The lower animals not only *express* their responses to stimuli but also *communicate* through their piercing barks, repetitive songs, and anxious gestures. Kahler refers to animal communication as a form of *signaling*. The communication is immediate, specific, and practical. In the case of human beings, communication takes on a new dimension because it is capable of *abstracting* from the immediate situation, forming judgments and concepts, generalizing, imagining, and fantasizing. The qualitative difference between animal and human communication lies in what students of language call our *symbolic* capacity—the distinction between mere signaling and human symbolizing.

Signs and symbols are both forms of expressing meaning. They point beyond themselves to something else. Animals are most susceptible to signs. A dog is alert to all kinds of signals from his master that denote "food" or "time for a walk." Susanne K. Langer, who has done more than any other philosopher to make us aware of the nature and role of symbolism, points out the pervasive character of *natural* signs:

> A sign indicates the existence—past, present, or future—of a thing, event, or condition. Wet streets are a sign that it has rained. A patter on the roof is a sign that it is raining. A fall of the barometer or a ring round the moon is a sign that it is going to rain. . . . A natural sign is part of a greater event. . . . It is a *symptom* of a state of affairs.[2]

The words *sign* and *symbol* are often used interchangeably, but they must be distinguished in terms of the relationship between the sign or symbol and the thing symbolized. We have spoken of signs as symptoms or natural reminders. Symbols are special kinds of signs. "We use certain 'signs' among ourselves," writes Langer,

> that do not point to anything in our actual surroundings. Most of our words are not signs in the sense of signals. They are used to talk *about* things, not to direct our eyes or ears or noses toward

them. They serve to let us develop a characteristic attitude toward objects *in absentia*, which is called 'thinking of' or 'referring to' what is not here. 'Signs' used in this capacity are not *symptoms* of things, but *symbols*.[3]

Symbols are also sometimes distinguished as *representational* or *presentational*. Representational symbols tie together things that are distinct even when there may not be any natural or symptomatic connection between the symbol and the thing symbolized. The connection is due to custom or habitual practice. For example, the color green on the traffic light denotes "proceed." Why not the color blue? It would do as well, but conventional usage has come to associate green with "proceed." The point is that the meaning of representational symbols is determined by their cultural context and use. The image of an elephant may bring to the mind of an American businessperson thoughts of his or her political party or ideology; to a piously educated Indian, it represents a complex of meanings associated with a popular Hindu god. Many of our most common religious symbols—the eight-spoked wheel in Buddhism or the Jewish Star of David—are representational symbols. Their power to communicate meaning is clearly dependent on learned associations.

Presentational symbols are another important type of symbolization, one that often takes the form of an image or icon. Presentational symbols are more than signs or natural symptoms, and more than representative in a purely conventional sense. *They participate in, or are similar to, the thing they symbolize.* A secular example would be a map that resembles the geographical reality it depicts. Presentational symbols are especially powerful conveyors of religious meaning since they are more than reminders. They genuinely "participate in," manifest, or "make present" the holy or sacred. For this reason, presentational

Common Buddhist *mudras* symbolizing (1) fearlessness, (2) appeasement, (3) worship, and (4) concentration. (*Source:* From E. Dale Saunders, *Mudra: A Study of Symbolic Features in Japanese Sculpture*, Bollingen Series 58. Copyright © 1960 by Princeton University Press. [Figures from Pictorial Index drawn by Mark Hasselriis.] Reprinted with permission of Princeton University Press.)

symbols cannot easily be changed or removed. Water and blood, for example, have qualities that are intrinsically associated with cleansing and new life, or with death and sacrifice. In the Eastern Orthodox Church, certain images or pictures called icons are believed not only to represent but also to "make present" the divine. They are similar to the sacramental actions of the priest in the Roman Catholic Church, actions through which the sacred is made present. In Buddhism, certain gestures—called **mudras**—disclose aspects of the Buddha spirit. Likewise, through certain sounds—called **mantras**—such as the Hindu chanting of OM, and the chant of the devotees of Hare Krishna, the sacred is actually, palpably present.

Religious Symbols

Many symbols, including religious symbols, are objects or sounds that stand for something but are not intended to give us information about what they symbolize because we already have direct knowledge of the symbol's referent. Rather, the symbol functions as a kind of shorthand reminder or signal of some information or mode of action already known. The flag hoisted on holidays, such as on the Fourth of July, reminds us in one image of all that is involved in patriotic pride and duty, but the flag itself does not inform us, it does not give us that information. In religious rituals, bells, incense, bodily gestures, and colors *remind* us of other things—meanings and values—already known, or they prompt us to some action.

Other symbols convey knowledge of the thing they symbolize, about which we would otherwise remain ignorant. To do this, the symbol must be *presentational*, it must in some manner *resemble* the thing symbolized. The way this is traditionally put is to say that there must be a genuine **analogy** between the symbol and that to which it points.

In Chapter 1, we spoke of the human capacity for self-transcendence, the fact that we live continuously on the threshold of something more. This is uniquely true of the human religious quest. Religiously, we stand on a threshold beyond which we can speak only by analogy, by symbol. The object of the religious quest is the Holy, the "Wholly Other" that, while immanent in the world of sense, at the same time transcends the visible and imaginative signs and images by which we seek to glimpse and conceptualize it. Religious expression and communication is, then, preeminently symbolic, because it points to and addresses a reality that is essentially transcendent, mysterious, and never fully plumbed. *We can speak of it, even depict it, but only symbolically and by analogy.* Religious language is then fundamentally poetic language—

Several key symbols from some of the great world religions. Each one serves as a "condensed" symbol reminding believers of crucial religious doctrines or teachings.

although, as we shall see, it is not *merely* poetic. To say "All flesh is grass" is both poetic and religious. It speaks by the use of a metaphor—it is not literally true—and yet it conveys a profound truth about the human condition. We shall, however, return to a discussion of the logical status of religious symbolic language later in the chapter.

We have said that religious language is, at bottom, symbolic. Moreover, it is essentially the language of poetry, parable, story, and myth. And it is so necessarily, for it not only *evokes* feelings and affections but also *invokes* that which is Holy, Ultimate, transcendent of the world of profane things. The religious symbol is a bridge erected between the finite and "the Something More."

The image of the bridge is especially apt because the word *symbol* is derived from the Greek verb *symballein*, meaning "to throw or bring together." We have already spoken of the way in which the symbol analogically bridges, or "brings together," the image, gesture, or sound, taken from our ordinary experience, and the Holy, which remains elusive, mysterious, and ineffable. But a living symbol "brings together" in other important ways as well. A religious symbol, and especially certain *master-symbols* or *root-metaphors*, can "bring together" in the sense of literally creating communities. For example, the Christian crucifix and the image of the reclining Buddha serve as master symbols, bringing together a rich complex of spiritual meanings for these two communities. The anthropologist Mary Douglas points to the way in which the eating of fish on Fridays by Irish Catholics and the abstinence from the eating of pork for Jews have served as "condensed symbols" for a complex pattern of meanings and associations that bind members of these religious communities.

A third way in which the religious symbol "brings together" is the fascinating manner in which it can join in one, often simple, image a variety of events and meanings. A single example will suffice. The historian Cyril Richardson has shown that the sacred fish, a common symbol in the ancient pagan world, was also a pervasive image in the earliest Christian catacombs. The simple image ⋈ brings together symbolically a number of cardinal Christian meanings: Baptism,

Matthias Grünewald's famous painting of the Crucifixion from the Isenheim Altar symbolizes the Passion and sacrifice as well as the anguish and ardor that we associate with Christianity. (*Source:* Courtesy of O. Zimmeman, Musée d'Unterlinden—Colmar.)

Holy Communion, Resurrection, and the **eschatological** Messianic Banquet in the Kingdom of God. How did the fish represent these multiple meanings? Richardson explains it as follows:

> When we consider the high significance of adult baptism in the Early Church, and the role that the baptism of Jesus played in the imagination of the early Christian, we can find a ready clue. . . . Jesus was the God revealed in the water. In the earliest strata of the Gospel the baptism of Jesus is the event which determines His mission, gives Him the awareness of the Kingdom as now present in some sense in Himself. . . . Indeed, the feast of Epiphany originally celebrated the baptism and certainly antedated the feast of Christmas. What connection would be more obvious than this: Jesus is the God revealed in the water, hence the sacred fish?
>
> But the fish is also food. The same God . . . descending again into the water at Christian baptism, is the heavenly food of the Eucharist [that is, Holy Communion]. Hence the consecration of the bread and wine is often depicted by the consecration of the sacred fish. . . .
>
> Yet the fish, as the sacrificial food, is also the food of the Heavenly Banquet. There is an eschatological note in the symbol. It looks

The Paranirvana of the Buddha from Gal Vihara, Sri Lanka. This giant statue, portraying the Buddha in "complete nirvana," represents Buddhist deathlessness—perfect enlightenment, free of craving and delusion. (*Source*: Courtesy of Jack Van Horn.)

Primitive contemporary Mexican pottery depicting the Last Supper and featuring a huge fish that, since early Christianity, has symbolized numerous basic teachings. (*Source*: Courtesy of the collection of John and Scottie Austin.)

> toward the final consummation of the Kingdom in the Heavenly Banquet.... For the sacred fish is Leviathan of Jewish apocalyptic; and Leviathan is the main course at the Heavenly Banquet....
>
> But we are not yet done. The fish is the symbol of Resurrection. The sign of Jonah, which perpetually recurs in the Catacombs, is the sign of Christ's resurrection, and of our own.[4]

Thus, it is that this simple image   ⋈   , which could be swiftly stroked in the sand as a means of identification, is capable of "bringing together" in one coherent symbol the central beliefs of the Christian faith.

Metaphor, Parable, and Story

Before turning to a more-extensive discussion of the role of myth in the life of religious communities, a few words must be said about other important symbolic forms.

Metaphor is a distinctive form of symbolic communication. A metaphor—"Time is a river"—is not a literal statement. It is, nevertheless, a basic form of our ordinary discourse. When we want to know the nature of something, we often ask "What is it like?" We live and speak through pointing out resemblances. Metaphor is then a basic means of communication.

What are characteristics of the symbolic form of metaphor? "The Lord is my shepherd" is, like other symbolic discourse, nonliteral; it also involves a comparison, it is like an analogy. But while analogy moves from the known ("shepherd") to the unknown ("The Lord") in a positive and proportional sense, a metaphor strikes insight by creating something entirely new, something both similar and dissimilar. The poetic metaphor "All flesh is grass" holds two different things together and thereby creates a novel meaning, a new insight.

In metaphorical speech, it is important that the tension between "the is and the is not" (the similarity in the difference) be retained in order to avoid slipping into literalism. Metaphor, by making us conscious of the symbolic and tentative character of our religious speech, protects against a mistaken literalism and idolatry, that is, a confusion of the sacred with the finite. Yet metaphor is not simply a "useful fiction." "All flesh is grass" reveals a genuine truth of our experience.

Parable is another distinctive form of religious discourse. It is essentially an *extended metaphor*, and it reveals the same surprise and openness to new insight that we have observed in a true metaphor. These qualities of the parable are present in the definition given by C. H. Dodd:

> At its simplest, the parable is a metaphor or simile, drawn from nature or common life, arresting the hearer by its vividness or strangeness, and leaving the mind in sufficient doubt about its precise application to tease it into active thought.[5]

Because parables draw from the ordinary things of everyday experience, they have a homely way of communicating truth. But the surprise and vividness of the communication derives from the unexpected use, the difference, to which the commonplace image is put. The revelation of the story comes through the presence of the extraordinary in the ordinary. Jesus and Buddha, for example, made use of such ordinary images as rafts, lost coins, weddings, monkeys, elephants, mustard seeds, workmen in the field, and fire—but in unexpected and therefore illuminating ways. The Kingdom of God is like a mustard seed; the search for metaphysical answers is likened to blind men feeling an elephant. The impact of the parable lies in the simplicity and authenticity of the mundane event translated into a moral or spiritual truth.

Another feature of parable is its unity of content and form. Its reality and power lie in the fact that it is not an abstract discourse; like a story, it is vividly narrative in character. Furthermore, the hearer is addressed in his or her wholeness, since the feelings, emotions, and the human will are all engaged as forcefully as the conscious mind.

Many profoundly human experiences—such as death, suffering,

guilt, and hatred—as well as "peak experiences" of a more positive nature—joy, peace, beatitude—require a language that is capable of illuminating them. Parable is such a language because it uses the ordinary to disclose the extraordinary.

We have spoken of the general features of parable; it is time to illustrate what has been said with specific examples. We select one parable from the Buddhist tradition and another from the New Testament. Both are interesting, though baffling, stories; they can be viewed as "root metaphors," symbols of the central truths of these two great religions. The Buddhist parable, entitled "Visakha's Sorrow," is one of many that bring home powerfully the Buddha's teaching regarding the extinction of craving (tanha):

> Thus have I heard: Once upon a time the Exalted One was in residence at Savatthi, in Eastern Grove, in Visakha Mother of Migara's mansion. Now at that time Visakha Mother of Migara's granddaughter had died, and she was Visakha's darling and delight. And Visakha Mother of Migara, garments wet, hair wet, at an untimely hour approached the Exalted One. And having approached, she saluted the Exalted One and sat down on one side. And as she sat there on one side, the Exalted One said this to Visakha Mother of Migara: "Well, Visakha, how is it that you come here at such an untimely hour, approaching with garments wet, with hair wet?" "Reverend Sir, my granddaughter has died, and she was my darling and delight. That is why I approach at such an untimely hour, with garments wet, with hair wet." Should you like, Visakha, to have as many children and grandchildren as there are human beings in Savatthi?" "I should like, Reverend Sir, to have as many children and grandchildren as there are human beings in Savatthi." "But, Visakha, how many human beings die every day in Savatthi?" "Reverend Sir, ten human beings die every day in Savatthi. . . . My granddaughter, Reverend Sir, is in no class by herself, apart from the other human beings who die in Savatthi." "What think you, Visakha? Should you ever, at any time, be without garments wet, without hair wet?" "No indeed, Reverend Sir."
> "Verily, Visakha, they that hold a hundred dear, have a hundred sorrows; . . . ninety dear, have ninety sorrows . . . eighty . . . seventy . . . sixty . . . fifty . . . forty . . . thirty . . . twenty . . . ten . . . nine . . . eight . . . seven . . . six . . . five . . . four . . . three . . . two . . . one dear, have one sorrow. They that hold nothing dear, have no sorrow. Free from grief are they—free from passion, free from despair. So say I."[6]

We may not "like" the Buddha's parabolic message since it does assault our ordinary sense of social sympathy. It points, nevertheless, to the Buddha's hard teaching about the relation of desire and suffering.

In the New Testament parable of the workers in the vineyard, Jesus tells a story that also shocks a deep-seated human conviction, our sense of the necessity of justice. The parable makes nonsense of our notion of merit; it accentuates the scandal of grace:

> And Jesus said to his disciples. . . . For the kingdom of heaven is like a householder who went out early in the morning to hire laborers for his vineyard. After agreeing with the laborers for a denarius a day, he sent them into his vineyard. And going out about the third hour he saw others standing idle in the market place; and to them he said, "You go into the vineyard too, and whatever is right I will give you." So they went. Going out again about the sixth hour and the ninth hour, he did the same. And about the eleventh hour he went out and found others standing; and he said to them, "Why do you stand here idle all day?" They said to him, "Because no one has hired us." He said to them, "You go into the vineyard too." And when evening came, the owner of the vineyard said to his steward, "Call the laborers and pay them their wages, beginning with the last, up to the first." And when those hired about the eleventh hour came, each of them received a denarius. Now when the first came, they thought they would receive more; but each of them also received a denarius. And on receiving it they grumbled at the householder, saying, "These last worked only one hour, and you made them equal to us who have borne the burden of the day and the scorching heat." But he replied to one of them, "Friend, I am doing no wrong; did you not agree with me for a denarius? Take what belongs to you, and go; I choose to give to this last as I give to you. Am I not allowed to do what I choose with what belongs to me? Or do you begrudge my generosity?" So the last will be first, and the first last.
>
> *(Matthew 20:1–16)*

Why do parables strike us as subversive, and yet as so real and authentically human? The answer lies, to a considerable degree, in their form as stories. A number of scholars have pointed to the fact that human life naturally takes he form of what can be called "the narrative quality of experience."[7] It has to do with our unique human experience of a past, present, and future. It is worth noting that what we call "the humanities" are not concerned with modes of abstraction and quantification, as in science, but with narrative forms of human experience: parable, epic, legend, myth, drama, and history. And this is because human life is inherently temporal. The forms that unify our experience are memory and anticipation. Our memory of the past and our anticipation of the future unite our experience into a narrative form—a sequence of before and after, that is, a story.

The stories that we hear and the ritual dramas in which we participate shape our own inner story, our own sense of place, and our own pilgrimage through time. There is nothing that pleases us, nothing that emotionally satisfies us more than a good story. The reason is that it corresponds with the narrative structure of our experience. The story moves us because it resonates in the depths of our own being; it rings true. Art imitates life, and the truly great stories are so true to life as to effect a shock of recognition, an emotional catharsis, and a spur to action. Most of the time, we are unconscious of the profound impression that the great archetypal stories and myths have in shaping our own sense of self, where we have come from, who we are, and where we are going. They also link us with others who share a common story—the American story, or the Jewish story, or woman's story. That is why genuine conversion is both so agonizing and yet so liberating an experience. In religious conversion, we literally repudiate one story of our life and embrace another.

Religious Myth

Another important religious form of symbolic narrative is myth. The word *myth* has long been open to ambiguity and confusion. In our common usage today, myth has come to mean what is not true. If we are told something that we have reason to doubt, we say "Oh, that's just a myth." One reason for this skepticism is that traditional education in the West has long associated myth with the stories of the exploits of the Greek and Roman gods. In classical Greece and Rome, these mythic tales already were criticized as fictional "tall tales." However, in this century numerous scholars have rejected the view that myth is to be understood simply as prescientific error and have concentrated on its complex nature and functions. Myth now is seen as a multileveled form of symbolic communication.

Like parable, myth tells a story. However, unlike parable, which discloses a moral or a singular meaning, myth can serve as a community's charter for its whole life-world, that is, it can explain or legitimize the natural order or a community's institutions and behavior. Many comparable definitions of myth are current; Alan Watts presents a brief and highly serviceable one:

> Myth is to be defined as a complex of stories—some no doubt fact, and some fancy—which, for various reasons, human beings regard as demonstrations of the inner meaning of the universe and of human life.[8]

This definition points to the symbolic, narrative character of myth and to its service as a model or paradigm of the natural and human order, but the definition also expressly avoids the assumption that myth is untrue, "a mere tale." This is important because one of the concerns of recent students of myth has been to challenge any theory of myth that reduces it either to idle play or to crude philosophic speculation. These scholars see myth, along with art and science, as basic, though distinct, forms of symbolic communication. Each has its own logic and intelligibility; neither is "truer" or "better."

Myth, however, does several things that science does not do, unless science itself takes on the form of a mythic vision—which, of course, sometimes happens. First, myths provide grids or models by which we can envision an entire world. The world is perceived as ordered, as having a meaning and purpose that often is portrayed mythically in a story of the original act of Creation itself or of certain archetypal events, such as Prometheus stealing the fire from the gods. Myth also shapes our sense of self, of who we are. The lives of certain exemplary persons—sages, saints, prophets, heroes—serve as root metaphors, as archetypes of what it means to be genuinely real and truly human. Myths therefore disclose and sanction models of behavior and moral norms, often for each stage in the human life cycle. Finally, myths portray why evil and chaos erupt and threaten our world and our own personal being—and what we must do to be saved, liberated, or renewed. We need not illustrate here the rich variety of myths about the creation and maintenance of cosmic order, human nature and destiny, or salvation since we will explore these in detail in Chapters 8, 9, and 12.

Myth is such a pervasive cultural form that many consider it to be indispensable as long as we continue to seek to make sense out of the deeply human questions that lie outside the province of technology or science. The anthropologist Malinowski speaks to this point. "A myth," he writes,

> is an indispensable ingredient of all culture. It is . . . a constant by-product of living faith, which is in need of miracles; of sociological status, which demands precedent; of moral rule, which requires sanction.[9]

The fact that myth, as well as science, is a primary and unique way of apprehending reality and charting the natural and human order suggests its indispensability. Evidence of the pervasiveness and inevitability of myth as a form of cultural life, even today, is apparent in the role it plays in modern literature and social thought, as well as in expressions of popular culture. We need not look only to the great classic works of Dante, Shakespeare, Milton, Goethe, or Melville for confirmation. André Gide makes use of the Theseus myth; the Nobel Prize–winning novelists John Steinbeck, Albert Camus, and William Golding all have recast mythic themes from Genesis: the Fall, the story of Cain and Abel, and the Tower of Babel; and T. S. Eliot has used Parsifal and the myth of the dying and rising God-King. James

Joyce has employed the myths of Moses and Odysseus. It is also instructive that the two giants of modern psychotherapy, Freud and Jung, found it necessary to appeal to mythic figures and archetypal images—Oedipus, Eros, Thanatos, the Earth-Mother, the Divine Child, and so forth—in their attempts to express and to illustrate their theories.

Raphael Patai has called attention to the reappearance of numerous archaic mythic patterns in contemporary popular culture, in science-fiction novels, in television commercials, and, of course, in movies. Today, we see in the Indiana Jones movies and in the James Bond books (over 10 million copies) and films examples of the deeds, sufferings, and testings of the archetypal mythical hero's journey in an age of technology:

> The Bond hero's journey involves a descent into Hades, the domain of evil, inhabited by the modern counterparts of malevolent magicians, sorcerers, witches, and warlocks whose guile and technological sophistication are many times greater than those of 007. Moreover, while he is alone almost all of the time, his enemies are many, organized into well-trained and blindly obedient corps of corruption. Yet James Bond willingly enters these labyrinths and seeks out their Minotaur-like ruler, as Theseus did in the famous Greek myth. He is willing to face torture and even death, never because of any personal reason or ambition, but simply because he is willing to suffer, to experience unspeakable agony in order to save the rest of us from disaster.... The greater the dangers he faces, the sufferings he undergoes for our sake ... the more we will identify with him.[10]

Myth is indeed a perennial cultural form. But what is its function? How are we to interpret it? On this matter, there is considerable dispute. A number of distinct—though not necessarily mutually exclusive—theories currently attract significant followings among philosophers, anthropologists, psychologists, and theologians. Among the influential current theories are (1) the *ritual theory of myth*, which will be discussed in Chapter 5 on religious ritual; (2) the *functionalist* theory of Bronislaw Malinowski and his followers; (3) the *psychoanalytic* theory of Freud and especially Carl Jung; (4) the *structuralist* theory of Claude Lévi-Strauss and the anthropologists and literary critics who have followed his lead; and (5) the *phenomenological* theory of Mircea Eliade, which we will treat briefly in view of our earlier discussion of Eliade's general theory.

Functionalist Theory

Bronislaw Malinowski offers the clearest treatment of the functionalist approach in his book *Myth in Primitive Psychology*. We have remarked that Malinowski considers myth as an indispensable ingredient in all culture. Furthermore, he insists that myth or sacred tale is unique and must be distinguished from legend and fairy tale. Myth, he asserts, is regarded "not merely as true, but as venerable and sacred." "These stories live," he continues, "not by idle interest, nor as fictitious or even as true narratives; but are to the natives a statement of a primeval, greater, and more relevant reality, by which the present life, fates, and activities of mankind are determined."[11] To the primitive, myth is as much a reality as the biblical stories of Creation, the Fall, the Redemption by Christ's Sacrifice on the Cross are to Christians. It governs faith and shapes conduct.

Malinowski not only rejects a "tall-tale" view of myth but also denies that it serves primarily as an explanation satisfying a scientific interest; rather, its meaning is to be understood in terms of its social function within a particular culture. This is stated explicitly in the following passage. "Myth," he writes, is

> but a narrative resurrection of a primeval reality, told in satisfaction of deep religious wants, moral cravings, social submissions, assertions, even practical requirements. It expresses, enhances, and codifies belief; it safeguards and enforces morality; it vouches for the efficiency of ritual and contains practical rules for the guidance of man. . . . It is not an intellectual explanation or an artistic imagery, but a pragmatic charter of primitive faith and moral wisdom.[12]

Malinowski gives numerous examples of myths of origin, death and life, and magical power that reveal their profoundly practical, psychological, and social functions. A myth of the origin of death is representative:

> Once upon a time there lived in the village of Bwadela an old woman who dwelt with her daughter and grand-daughter. . . . The grandmother and grand-daughter went out one day to bathe in the tidal creek. The girl remained on the shore, while the old woman went away some distance out of sight. She took off her skin which, carried by the tidal current, floated along the creek until it stuck on a bush. Transformed into a young girl, she came back to her grand-daughter. The latter did not recognize her; she was afraid of her and bade her begone. The old woman, mortified and angry, went back to her bathing place, searched for her old skin, put it on again, and returned to her grand-daughter. This time she was recognized and thus greeted: 'A young girl came here; I was afraid; I chased her away.' Said the grandmother: 'No, you didn't want to recognize me. Well, you will become old—I shall die.' . . . I shall not slough my skin. We shall all become old. We shall all die. . . . After that men lost the power of changing their skin and of remaining youthful.[13]

Malinowski points out that this myth is but a dramatization of the human loss of the power of rejuvenation and the reality of death, but its social function is

> to transform an emotionally overwhelming foreboding, behind which, even for a native, there lurks the idea of an inevitable and ruthless fatality. Myth presents, first of all, a clear realization of this idea. In the second place, it brings down a vague but great apprehension to the compass of a trivial, domestic reality. . . . Elements of fate, of destiny, and of the inevitable are brought down to the dimension of human mistakes.[14]

In this myth of the origin of death, we can see what Malinowski means by a sacred story "told in satisfaction of . . . social submissions . . . even practical requirements."

The Psychotherapeutic Theory of Carl Jung

Carl Jung's contribution to the scientific study of religion is centered on his theory of the archetypes of the collective unconscious, that is, on those firmly established symbolic and mythic images that reappear in a variety of cultures and historical periods. In these archetypes, Jung finds great significance for religious symbolism, myth, and psychic healing.

According to Jung, the human psyche consists of three layers—the conscious mind, the personal unconscious, and what he calls the "collective unconscious." The personal unconscious consists of all those contents "forgotten" or repressed from the conscious mind that are associated with the individual's own history. This level of the unconscious is not, however, the deepest layer. That belongs to the collective unconscious, which is the focus of Jung's attention.

The term *collective unconscious* has been generally misunderstood. Jung does not mean by it a collective inheritance of images and myths that are a joint possession of the human race; rather, he means that the unconscious includes materials that are psychically real prior to their personal appropriation. They are inherent potentials in the psychic structure of all individuals. These unconscious psychic contents are archetypal in character; what Jung calls "forms or images of a collective nature which occur practically all over the earth as constituents of myths. . . ."[15] They are "primordial images" that can be seen to recur throughout human history. They are not, however, inherited conscious ideas. "The archetype is," Jung writes,

> on the contrary, an inherited *tendency* of the human mind to form representations of mythological motifs—representations that vary a great deal without losing their basic pattern. . . . The inherited ten-

dency is instinctive, like the specific impulse of nest-building, migration, etc. in birds. One finds these *representations collectives* practically
everywhere, characterized by the same or similar motifs. They cannot
be assigned to any particular time or region or race. They are
without known origin, and they can reproduce themselves even when
transmission through migration must be ruled out.[16]

The motifs studied by Jung include the Divine Child, Mother Earth,
the Hero, the number four, and the mandala. Jung sees Christ, for
example, as exemplifying the ancient hero motif:

> The idea of Christ the Redeemer belongs to the world-wide and
> pre-Christian motif of the hero and rescuer who, although devoured
> by the monster, appears again in a miraculous way, having overcome
> the dragon or whale or whatever it was that swallowed him. How,
> when, and where such a motif originated nobody knows. . . . Our
> only certainty is that every generation, so far as we can see, has
> found it as an old tradition. . . . The hero figure is a typical image,
> and archetype, which has existed since time immemorial.[17]

For Jung, the importance of an archetype, such as the hero, lies in
its psychic efficacy or therapy. The universal hero myth, for example,

> shows the picture of a powerful man or god-man who vanquishes
> evil in the form of dragons, serpents, monsters, demons, and enemies
> of all kinds, and who liberated his people from destruction and
> death. The narration or ritual repetition of sacred texts and cere-
> monies, and the worship of such a figure . . . grip the audience with
> numinous emotions and exalt the participants to identification with
> the hero. If we contemplate such a situation with the eyes of a
> believer, we can understand how the ordinary man is gripped, freed
> from his impotence and misery, and raised to an almost super-
> human status.[18]

Jung points out that participation in the ritualization of the hero
myth can shape and create whole communities around the life-world
of the hero. However, Jung is interested not only in the archetype's
social function but also in its power of individual psychic healing,
which he calls *individuation* or "self-realization." According to Jung,
the development of genuine selfhood is not the same as what we
mean by individuality. The latter "means deliberately stressing and
giving prominence to some supposed peculiarity, rather than to collective considerations and obligations." Individuation, on the other hand,
"means precisely the better and more complete fulfillment of the collective qualities of the human being."[19] Individuation is neither the
loss of the self in favor of some social role or persona nor the giving
of oneself over to some primordial image. It is, rather, the develop-

ment of a self that involves the integration of the personal ego *with* archetypes of the unconscious. An example of what Jung means by individuation is a believer's identification with the archetypal Christ-hero in the Catholic Mass.

> Looked at from the psychological standpoint, Christ, as the Original Man (Son of Man, second Adam) represents a totality which surpasses and includes the ordinary man, and which corresponds to the total personality that transcends consciousness. . . . So the mystery of the Eucharist transforms the soul of the empirical man, who is only a part of himself, into a totality, symbolically expressed by Christ. In this sense, therefore, we can speak of the Mass as the *rite of the individuation process*.[20]

Jung perceives myth as vitally significant for *it represents the deepest level of the psychic life of mankind*. To refuse to take myth seriously is to imperil the soul, to court neurotic and even psychotic disorders. Jung concludes that "The mythology of a tribe is its living religion, whose loss is always and everywhere, even in the case of a civilized man, a moral catastrophe."[21]

Structural Interpretation

The structural study of myth, the most recent approach to gain a significant following, can be viewed from one perspective as a reaction against functionalism. The latter studies myth in its immediate, practical context. Structuralism, on the contrary, has more in common with Jung's theory since it seeks to discover in myth more universal principles or "structures" of the human mind and psyche and is therefore interested, once again, in exploring crosscultural comparisons. In pursuing structural analysis, the anthropologist Claude Lévi-Strauss and others draw heavily on the science of semiotics—that is, on the study of "systems of signification"—and on the work of mathematicians and computer scientists. What the structuralists find illuminating in these sciences is a common interest in inbuilt patterns of relationship or structures of the mind.

Lévi-Strauss, for example, sees in myth and folktale a nonrational logic and meaning that he regards as humanly universal but that *is not apparent in the manifest mythical story itself*. The obvious differences in character portrayal and narrative incident that we observe in the world's great myths is belied, Lévi-Strauss insists, "by the astounding similarity between myths collected in widely different regions. Therefore the problem: If the content of a myth is contingent, how are we going to explain the fact that myths throughout the world are so similar?"[22]

According to Lévi-Strauss, the answer is not to be found in the culturally particular mythic contents themselves but *in the relationships of the constituent parts of the myth* that, because they are not apparent, need to be decoded. Structural interpretation begins, therefore, by breaking down the myth into its several components and then exploring these component relationships since the depth-meaning is *not* to be found in the distinctive incidents or characters per se. In this regard, structuralism is analogous to the science of linguistics that discovered meaning is not *in* the particular sound because the same sound has different meanings in different languages. Meaning is found, rather, in the structural relations of sounds.

What Lévi-Strauss discovers in the relations between the several segments of a myth is a certain *binary structure* that he and his followers regard as constituative of human thought itself. Edmund Leach, an anthropologist who has applied Lévi-Strauss's structural analysis, writes:

> Binary oppositions are intrinsic to the process of human thought. Any description of the world must discriminate categories in the form 'p is what not-p is not.' An object is alive or not alive and one could not formulate the concept 'alive' except as the converse of its partner 'dead.' So human beings are male or not male, and persons of the opposite sex are either available as sexual partners or not available. . . . In every myth system we will find a persistent sequence of binary discriminations as between human/superhuman, mortal/immortal, male/female, legitimate/illegitimate, good/bad . . . followed by a 'mediation' of the paired categories thus distinguished.[23]

Following Lévi-Strauss's employment of structural linguistics and computer systems, Leach outlines the basic concepts as they apply to an analysis of myth. First, there is the binary structure of both language and myth, which can be compared to the unit of information, the "bit" or "binary digit," basic to communication theory. Second, he calls attention to the function of *redundancy* in both communication theory and myth. Redundancy results from the fact that the messages we transmit to a human receiver always encounter the competition of interference (noise) as well as the freedom of the receiver to interpret what he or she receives. Myth is a form of communication that is especially susceptible to interference. Hence, redundancy is necessary so "the believer can feel that even when the details vary, each alternative version of a myth confirms his understanding and reinforces the essential meaning of all others."[24]

Third, *mythic* communication is *mediation*, or the introduction of the category of the abnormal, the holy and nonnatural. Mediation seeks to deny the binary antinomies between, for example, life and death or man and God. It serves as a bridge. Thus, the "other world" would be the mediation between the opposites of life and death, as virgin

I	II	III	IV
1. Cadmos seeks his sister, Europa, ravished by Zeus.			
		2. Cadmos kills the dragon.	
	3. The Spartai kill one another.		
	4. Oedipus kills his father, Laios.		
		5. Oedipus kills the Sphinx.	
6. Oedipus marries his mother, Jocasta.			9. Labdacos (Laios' father) = *lame* (?)
	7. Eteocles kills his brother, Polynices.		10. Laios (Oedipus' father) = left-sided (?)
8. Antigone buries her brother, Polynices, despite prohibition.			11. Oedipus = swollen foot (?)

birth or incarnation would mediate or reestablish a bridge between man and God.

Equipped with these theoretical tools, we can look at a rather simple, abbreviated example of how Lévi-Strauss goes about structural analysis. Our illustration is taken from his interpretation of the well-known Oedipus myth. He first breaks the myth into what he perceives as its several components or incidents, each of which has to do with *relations* between the individual characters or their status in the narrative. This is indicated in the preceding chart, where he arranges the 11 segments into 4 columns. Other incidents could be selected, but Lévi-Strauss argues that they would simply be variations of similar relations. The particular characters and incidents would be shown to be interchangeable.

To understand the myth, we must *not* read it diachronically, that is, in narrative sequence, but must read each column as a unit. The relations in each column exhibit a common feature. In the first column, they "have to do with blood relations which are overemphasized, that is, are more intimate than they should be. Let us say, then, that the first column has as its common feature the *overrating of blood relations*."[25]

The second column, which records incidents of fratricide and paracide, are just the opposite: They feature *the underrating of blood relations*. The third column refers to the destruction of monsters, abnormal or anomalous creatures. The fourth column refers to men whose names all, hypothetically, "refer to difficulties in walking straight and standing upright." The feature of the third column is that the monsters are half-man–half-animal, the point being that they stand in the way of thoroughly human life. They represent, according to Lévi-Strauss, the *denial of the autochthonous* (sprung from the earth) origin of humankind. The chief feature of the characters in the fourth column, namely, difficulty in walking is, according to Lévi-Strauss, "a universal (mythic) characteristic of men born from the Earth."[26] The fourth column therefore signifies *the persistence of the autochthonous origin of man*. We can observe, then, that IV is the reverse of III just as II is the reverse of I. But what do these redundant, binary relations tell us about the meaning of the Oedipus myth? According to Lévi-Strauss, the real meaning of the story has to do with the difficulty that a culture holding autochthonous beliefs (about humankind's earthly origin) has in squaring that belief with the knowledge that human beings are actually born from the union of man and woman. While the problem cannot be solved, "the Oedipus myth provides a logical means by which to relate this original problem—born from earth or born from man and woman?—to the derivative problem: born from different (II) or born from same (I)?" Lévi-Strauss concludes that "by a correlation of this type, the overrating of blood relations is to the underrating of blood relations as the attempt to escape autochthony is to the impossibility to succeed in it."[27] In other words, these contradictions or tensions are "resolved," a kind of resignation or acceptance is made of the tension concerning the origin of life, blood relations, life and death, and so on.

Scholars do not respond to Lévi-Strauss's approach dispassionately. Many social anthropologists are hostile, claiming that his crosscultural comparisons are forced, highly speculative, and lacking in necessary ethnographic detail. Other scholars believe Lévi-Strauss underestimates the significance of the explicit narrative meaning and overrates the meaning that he finds in the method itself, that is, the binary contradictions. The meaning of a myth is not, these scholars would argue, exhausted by its binary structure. It would also appear that his concept of "resolution" is, in fact, a type of functionalism. Perhaps most telling, however, is Lévi-Strauss's identification of myth with *natural* myths or those found in preliterate cultures in which we find a union or interplay of animal and human characters. It is interesting that, by and large, he does not draw on the great Semitic and Indo-European myths for his examples. Lévi-Strauss has, despite these limitations, shed important new light on one way in which myth both communicates fundamental, unconscious human messages and resolves critical human limit situations concerning—for example, the origin of life, the question of death, and the rules of sexuality.

Eliade's Phenomenological Interpretation

In Chapter 3, we discussed Eliade's distinction between the sacred and the profane. That theme relates directly to his theory of myth because myth is an account of a sacred history, a primordial time in which reality as we now know it came into being. Eliade describes myth as follows:

> Myth narrates a sacred history; it relates an event that took place in primordial time, the fabled time of the 'beginnings.' In other words, myth tells how, through the deeds of Supernatural Beings, a reality came into existence, be it the whole of reality, the Cosmos, or only a fragment of reality—an island, a species of plant, a particular kind of human behavior, an institution. Myth, then, is always an account of a 'creation'; it relates how something was produced, began to *be*. . . . The actors in myths are Supernatural Beings. They are known primarily by what they did in the transcendent times of the 'beginnings'. . . . It is this sudden breakthrough of the sacred that really *establishes* the World and makes it what it is today.[28]

From this description, only a few points need to be stressed. First, religious myth has to do with the acts of the gods or supernatural beings. Second, myth is, for Eliade, always an account of origins; it tells us how something came into existence. Myths are thus the exemplary models of all natural and human life and activity. This relates to the third, or existential, role of myth. "Myth," Eliade insists, "constitutes the paradigms for all significant human acts."[29] "Myth teaches (mankind) the primordial 'stories' that have constituted him existentially . . . his legitimate mode of existence. . . ."[30] Myth thus answers our most urgent questions about existence. It gives us a sense of orientation and meaning in face of the threat of chaos and **anomie**, hence it serves a unique and universal role.

Since myth is the universal response to humankind's experience of limit situations such as finitude and moral guilt, it is possible to carry out a crosscultural phenomenological comparison of the myths of many cultures. Finally, myth is "true" because it is concerned with reality; that is, it effectively answers such existential questions as why we are mortal, why there are social relations of hierarchy and subordination, or why there is suffering. By knowing the myth, we know the origin and nature of things — a knowledge not abstract but "living," for it is constantly reexperienced through ritual reenactment.

It is interesting to note that the four theories we have outlined — those of Malinowski, Jung, Lévi-Strauss, and Eliade — all perceive myth as not simply a vestige of the prelogical mind but as in some sense universal, indispensable, and displaying its own distinctive logic. They all wish to defend the idea that myth is in some sense "true." To this, we shall return after a brief analysis of models and religious doctrines.

Models and Doctrines

"The symbol gives rise to thought."[31] This is the philosopher Paul Ricoeur's striking way of indicating that in literate societies the symbolic and mythic language of religion naturally calls for interpretation, for conceptual clarification and translation into propositional language. The product of this interpretive process is what we call doctrines and dogmas. The move toward conceptual clarification and generalization is a necessary one because a myth can "tell many little lies in the service of a great truth."[32] The lie would be, for example, a literal or scientific reading of the accounts of Adam and Eve in the Garden of Eden. On the other hand, the truth of that myth would be the experienced fact of human dependence, finitude, and the inordinate human desire to be like God. Because we live in a literal, scientific age, the symbolic language of the Genesis myth of the Creation and the Fall must, therefore, be *interpreted*; it must be "demythologized," that is, reinterpreted to bring out the universal and existential meanings that lie within the mythopoetic story. Conceptual language can facilitate such an understanding. However, religious language is fundamentally symbolic and analogical since it speaks about that which eludes literal statement. The translation from symbolic to conceptual and propositional language (doctrine) can, therefore, actually hinder understanding if it results in a literalness that denies the intrinsically metaphoric, analogical nature of religious expression and communication. Ricoeur states both the interpretive problem and its goal: "Between the concept which kills the symbol and pure conceptual silence, there must be room for a *conceptual* language which preserves the character of symbolic language."[33]

It is appropriate to speak of religious language as *metaphysical poetry*. Like metaphysics, it does make factual assertions; it therefore must meet the demands for coherence, comprehensiveness, and criteria by which its truth-claims can be tested. On the other hand, religious language is *poetic*, symbolic, and analogical. A way of seeking both conceptual clarity and comprehensiveness, while protecting religious language against a mistaken literalism, is to conceive of master symbols, root metaphors, and myths as *models*, functioning in a manner similar to scientific models.

As employed in science, a model seeks to construe certain patterns in observable data. It is an image that attempts to organize or restructure our interpretation of the world. While not literal, a scientific model does lead to theories that can be tested by observations. Similarly, religious models (symbols and myths) lead to conceptual beliefs or doctrines that construe or interpret experience in certain ways, according to certain patterns or exemplary paradigms. Ian Barbour characterizes the role of religious models as follows:

> Models can represent the enduring structures of the cosmic order which myths dramatize in narrative form. Images which originated in religious experience and key historical events are extended to interpret other areas of individual and corporate experience. As models of an unobservable gas molecule are later used to interpret other patterns of observation in the laboratory, so models of an unobservable God are used to interpret new patterns of experience in human life. Ultimate interpretive models . . . are organizing images which restructure one's perception of the world. One may notice features which might otherwise have been ignored.[34]

A religious model is able to take account of a wide range of experience or phenomena; it is therefore, authenticated in experience. A model might be likened to an especially illuminating sentence in an otherwise turgid, complex book. We can make no sense of the narrative until we come on the sentence or image that enlightens everything that has come before and that will follow later.

Models are ways of experiencing what is not observable straightoff and so are symbolic representations. But, as many philosophers of science would also insist, there simply are no bare uninterpreted data, even in science. All data assume some implicit theory. We do not simply experience; we "experience as": "In the act of perception, the irreducible 'data' are not isolated patches of color or fragmentary sensations, but total patterns in which interpretation has already entered. Our experience is organized in the light of particular interests"[35]—or in the light of a certain grid, pattern, or model.

Where religious models differ most from scientific ones is in the fact that they serve numerous noncognitive functions—such as deeply felt social and psychological needs. They also provide norms and motivations for ethical action. In other words, religious models engage our deepest human concerns. This does not mean, however, that religious models lack cognitive significance. The religious beliefs and doctrines that we derive from our models and paradigms also must "give a faithful rendition" of those areas of our experience that are humanly significant, especially our "religious and moral experience and key historical events."[36] Thus, *extensibility* of application (comprehensiveness) and *fruitfulness* are, according to Barbour, essential criteria for the truth or adequacy of any religious doctrine or assertion.

The symbols, myths, and models that serve as the source of religious doctrine and belief are, however, never verifiable in the same sense that scientific theories are testable. But that does not mean that religious doctrines are not communicable and therefore testable to a degree. If various religious or ideological communities shared no language, concepts, or experience in common, then, indeed, their several claims would be incommensurable and untestable. There are, in fact, widely shared human experiences and profound symbolic and conceptual similarities to be found in the world's religions. Therefore, Barbour would appear to be correct that "persons in diverse traditions can appeal to facets of each other's experience and can discuss together their interpretive frameworks. Intelligible reasons can be offered, rather than arbitrary 'leaps of faith.'"[37]

Two things can be said by way of conclusion: (1) Religious language is unique and resists scientific modes of verification and (2) all religious communities take for granted that their religious language makes assertions, that is, it refers to what is most true and real. Religious discourse is, then, fundamentally mythopoetic—but with a difference. W. M. Urban rightly remarks that the mythopoetic "is present in all genuine religious language, only . . . it is heightened and deepened in a peculiar way. It is, so to speak, poetry transposed to another scale."[38] The crucial point here is the phrase "transposed to another scale." This is what distinguishes religious language from either aesthetic or emotive discourse. Rather than disengaging from the question of fact and truth and settling for a world of fairy tale and imagination, religion, in the words of Clifford Geertz,

> deepens the concern with fact and seeks to create an aura of utter actuality. It is this sense of the 'really real' upon which the religious perspective rests and which the symbolic activities of religion as a cultural system are devoted to producing, intensifying, and, so far as possible, rendering inviolable.[39]

The "transposition to another scale" means that religious language not only symbolizes (for that it must) but also *asserts* nonsymbolic truth—it makes doctrinal claims that are not *merely* poetic. What makes mythopoetic discourse uniquely *sacred* or religious is, then, the fact that it is believed to be true. It is this alone that gives religious communication its power. Religious symbol, parable, and myth all assert, implicitly if not explicitly, that human values are grounded in what is ultimately real.

We have attended in some detail to the symbolic nature of religious communication, especially to its verbal, narrative forms in parable, story, and myth. In the past century, equal—if not more—attention has been given to the study of ritual action as a primary form of religious expression and communication. To that subject we now must turn.

Notes

1. Erich Kahler, "The Nature of the Symbol," in Rollo May (ed.), *Symbolism in Religion and Literature* (New York, 1960), p. 50.
2. Susanne K. Langer, *Philosophy in a New Key* (New York, 1951), pp. 45–46.
3. Langer, *Philosophy*, p. 24.
4. C. Richardson, "The Foundations of Christian Symbolism," in F. Ernest Johnson (ed.), *Religious Symbolism* (New York, 1955), pp. 6–8.
5. C. H. Dodd, *The Parables of the Kingdom* (London, 1935), p. 16.
6. *Udana* VIII, 8:91–92, in *Buddhist Parables*, trans. E. W. Burlingame (New Haven, 1922), pp. 107–108.
7. For what follows I am especially dependent on the seminal essay by Stephen Crites, "The Narrative Quality of Experience," *Journal of the American Academy of Religion* 39 (Sept. 1971).
8. Alan Watts, *Myth and Ritual in Christianity* (London, 1953), p. 7.
9. B. Malinowski, *Myth in Primitive Psychology* (London, 1926), p. 125.
10. Raphael Patai, *Myth and Modern Man* (Englewood Cliffs, N.J., 1972), pp. 292–293.
11. Malinowski, *Myth*, p. 39.
12. Malinowski, *Myth*, pp. 81–83.
13. Malinowski, *Myth*, pp. 104–105.
14. Malinowski, *Myth*, p. 76–77.
15. C. G. Jung, *Psychology and Religion* (New Haven, 1938), p. 63.
16. C. G. Jung, "Symbols and the Interpretation of Dreams," *The Collected Works of C. G. Jung* 18 (Princeton, 1977):228.
17. Jung, "Symbols," pp. 231–232.
18. Jung, "Symbols," p. 238.
19. C. G. Jung, "Two Essays in Analytical Psychology," *The Collected Works of C. G. Jung* 6 (Princeton, 1977): 171–172.
20. C. G. Jung, "Transformation Symbolism in the Mass," *The Collected Works of C. G. Jung* 11 (Princeton, 1977):273.
21. C. G. Jung, *Essays on a Science of Mythology* (New York). Patai, *Myth and Modern Man*, p. 23.
22. Claude Lévi-Strauss, *Structural Anthropology*, trans. C. Jacobson and B. C. Schoepf (New York, 1967), p. 125.
23. Edmund Leach, *Genesis as Myth* (London, 1969), pp. 9–11.
24. Leach, *Genesis as Myth*, p. 9.
25. Lévi-Strauss, *Structural Anthropology*, p. 215.
26. Lévi-Strauss, *Structural Anthropology*, p. 215.
27. Lévi-Strauss, *Structural Anthropology*, p. 216.

28. Mircea Eliade, *Myth and Reality* (London, 1964), pp. 5–6.
29. Eliade, *Myth and Reality*, p. 18.
30. Eliade, *Myth and Reality*, p. 12.
31. Paul Ricoeur, *The Symbolism of Evil* (Boston, 1969), p. 348.
32. Reinhold Niebuhr, "The Truth in Myths," in Eugene Bewkes (ed.), *The Nature of Religious Experience* (New York, 1937), p. 129.
33. Paul Ricoeur, "Biblical Hermeneutics," *Semeia* 4 (1975):36.
34. Ian G. Barbour, *Myths, Models, and Paradigms* (New York, 1974), p. 49.
35. Barbour, *Myths*, p. 120.
36. Barbour, *Myths*, p. 143.
37. Barbour, *Myths*, pp. 145–146.
38. W. M. Urban, *Language and Reality* (London, 1939), p. 572.
39. Clifford Geertz, "Religion as a Cultural System," in William A. Lessa and Evan Z. Vogt (eds.), *Reader in Comparative Religion*, 2nd ed. (New York, 1965), p. 213.

Review Questions

1. Describe the characteristics of a natural sign, a representational symbol, and a presentational symbol.
2. In what different ways can a religious symbol serve to "bring together"?
3. Characterize the special features of a metaphor and a parable. How do the Buddha's parable, "Visakha's Sorrow" and Jesus's parable of the workers in the vineyard illustrate the nature of parable? What is meant by the "narrative quality of experience," and how are narratives (stories) expressive of a religious consciousness?
4. How would you characterize myth as a form of religiosymbolic expression and communication? How would you distinguish the main features of Malinowski's, Jung's, and Lévi-Strauss's theory of myth?
5. Describe the use of a religious model (as one uses models in science) to achieve conceptual clarity and comprehensiveness.
6. If religious discourse (parable, myth, and so forth) is fundamentally symbolic and analogical and cannot be tested by scientific modes of verification, by what criteria, if any, can religious claims (doctrines) be tested for their truth or adequacy?

Suggestions for Further Reading

For the study of symbolism, see the following:

BEVIN, EDWYN, *Symbolism and Belief* (London: Macmillan, 1938).
CASSIRER, ERNST, *Essay on Man* (New Haven: Yale University Press, 1962).

_____, *The Philosophy of Symbolic Forms*, 3 vols. (New Haven: Yale University Press, 1954–1957).

GEERTZ, CLIFFORD, "Religion as a Cultural System," in Michael Banton (ed.), *Anthropological Approaches to the Study of Religion* (London: Tavistock Publications, 1966).

LANGER, SUSANNE, *Philosophy in a New Key* (New York: New American Library, 1954).

WHEELWRIGHT, PHILIP, *The Burning Fountain: A Study in the Language of Symbolism* (Bloomington: Indiana University Press, 1964).

For discussions of metaphor, parable, and models, see the following:

BLACK, MAX, *Models and Metaphors* (Ithaca: Cornell University Press, 1962).

BARBOUR, IAN, *Myths, Models, and Paradigms: A Comparative Study in Science and Religion* (New York: Harper and Row, 1974).

CRITES, STEPHEN, "The Narrative Quality of Experience," *The Journal of the American Academy of Religion* 39 (Sept. 1971).

McFAGUE, SALLIE, *Metaphorical Theology* (Philadelphia: Fortress Press, 1982). This book and Barbour's include references to the best current literature on the subject of the use of metaphor, parable, and models in religious discourse.

RICOEUR, PAUL, *Interpretation Theory: Discourse and the Surplus of Meaning* (Fort Worth: Texas Christian University Press, 1976).

_____, "Biblical Hermeneutics," *Semeia* 4 (1975).

_____, *The Rule of Metaphor* (Toronto: Toronto University Press, 1977).

TeSELLE, SALLIE, *Speaking in Parables* (Philadelphia: Fortress Press, 1975).

For the study of myth, see the following:

CAMPBELL, JOSEPH, *The Masks of God: Primitive Mythology* (New York: Viking Press, 1959).

DUNDES, ALAN, *Sacred Narrative: Readings in the Theory of Myth* (Berkeley: University of California Press, 1984).

ELIADE, MIRCEA, *Cosmos and History: The Myth of the Eternal Return* (New York: Harper Torchbooks, 1959).

_____, *Myth and Reality* (New York: Harper and Row, 1963).

KIRK, G. S., *Myth: Its Meaning and Function in Ancient and Other Cultures* (Cambridge: Cambridge University Press, 1970).

_____, *The Nature of Greek Myths* (New York: Penguin Books, 1974). Chapter 3, "Five Monolithic Theories," raises critical questions about universal theories.

JUNG, CARL G., and C. KERENYI, *Essays on a Science of Mythology* (New York: Harper and Row, 1963).

_____, *Psychology and Religion* (New Haven: Yale University Press, 1938). See also *The Collected Works*, vols. 7, 11, 18.

LÉVI-STRAUSS, CLAUDE, *Structural Anthropology* (New York: Basic Books, 1963).

_____, "The Story of Asdiwal," in Edmund Leach (ed.), *The Structural Study of Myth and Totemism* (London: Tavistock Publications, 1967).

MALINOWSKI, BRONISLAW, *Myth in Primitive Society* (New York: Norton,

1926). Reprinted in *Magic, Science and Religion* (Garden City, N.Y.: Doubleday, 1954).

NIEBUHR, REINHOLD, "The Truth in Myths," in Eugene Bewkes (ed.), *The Nature of Religious Experience* (New York): Harpers, 1937).

SEBEOK, THOMAS (ed.), *Myth: A Symposium* (Bloomington: Indiana University Press, 1955).

On the cognitive status of religious language: Most of the books cited deal with this problem directly or indirectly, but for a more philosophical analysis the following are recommended as introductions:

FERRE, FREDERICK, *Language, Logic, and God* (New York: Harper and Row, 1961). This book surveys a number of positions and is a good introduction to the issues.

RAMSEY, IAN, *Religious Language* (New York: Macmillan, 1967).

FLEW, ANTONY, and ALAISDAIR MACINTYRE (eds.), *New Essays in Philosophical Theology* (London: SCM Press, 1955).

CHAPTER 5

Sacred Ritual

OVERVIEW

This chapter explores the nature of sacred ritual as a universal form of religious expression and communication. We begin with a definition of religious ritual and the reasons why ritual has played such an essential role in religious life. This is followed by a discussion of several approaches to the study of religious ritual, including the relationship between ritual and myth, the social functions of ritual, and the connections and resemblances between ritual and human drama and play.

The discussion then turns to an analysis of two classic types of sacred rituals. First, rites that are connected to the human life cycle—such as birth, marriage, and death—and to human crises—such as illness. These rituals often reflect a distinctive structure that is analyzed and illustrated in rites associated with birth, puberty, and initiation into a religious vocation.

A second classic type of sacred rite is associated with fixed points in the yearly calendar and is connected either with the changing of the seasons or with the commemoration and rehearsal of a momentous historical event, for example, the Passion of Christ. Here, again, a distinct ritual pattern often can be discerned, and it is illustrated in an analysis of the ancient Babylonian New Year festival and in the Roman Catholic Mass.

A striking feature of many sacred rites is the offering of a sacrifice. The various purposes of sacrifice are discussed and particular attention is given to rituals of atonement for defilement, transgression—or sin— and the critical role played by the sacrificial representative—or scapegoat—as sin remover. This theme is illustrated from the earliest account of the Jewish Day of Atonement that is found in the Book of Leviticus. According to some recent scholars, rites of sacrifice, which go back to the Palaeolithic age, are at the root of all religion and

are an outlet or a means of escaping violence by transferring human aggression outside the community, thereby maintaining peace
and solidarity.

The chapter concludes with a discussion of rituals as sacraments
and how sacraments reflect some of the most characteristic features
of sacred ritual.

Ritual Action

Rituals are found in every human community and are a primary
means of social communication and cohesion. The English word *rite*
derives from a Greek word, *dromenon,* meaning "a thing done" to
achieve a specific end. If a symbol is a meaningful sign, a ritual can
be called a significant *action.* Rituals range from simple gestures, such
as bowing or shaking hands, to elaborate ceremonial dramas, such as
the Eastern Orthodox liturgy or a British royal coronation. The Confucianist sage Hsün Tzu spoke of the significant role of ritual in the
following memorable words:

> When rites are performed in the highest manner, then both the
> emotions and the forms embodying them are fully realized.
> . . . Through rites Heaven and earth join in harmony, the sun and
> the moon shine, the four seasons proceed in order . . . and all things
> flourish; men's likes and dislikes are regulated and their joys and
> hates are made appropriate. Those below are obedient, those above
> are enlightened, all things change but do not become disordered;
> only he who turns his back upon rites will be destroyed. Are they
> not wonderful indeed?[1]

A religious ritual can be defined as *an agreed-on and formalized pattern
of ceremonial movements and verbal expressions carried out in a sacred context.*
One of the interesting things about religious rituals is that they can
serve as "condensed symbols." Friday abstinence, until recently, was
such a symbol of the Christian life for Roman Catholics, just as certain
dietary practices remain for observant Jews a condensed symbol of
their faith. Rituals are capable of expressing and communicating several levels of meaning, in a fashion similar to our description of the
fish symbolism in Chapter 4. Moreover, the meanings or functions of
a ritual may not be "manifest" or obvious, but only "latent," or hidden
to the participants themselves.

Many scholars would concur that ritual is the very heart and soul
of religion and that ritual must be viewed as both prior to and more
fundamental than either myth or doctrine. W. Robertson Smith (1846–
1894) was among the first to hold this view and to insist that myth
is merely an explanation of ritual and, therefore, of secondary impor-

tance. This perception of ritual as constituting the essence of religion was reinforced by Durkheim, and it remains a fundamental conviction of his followers at the present time. It is a view that was dominant in the early decades of this century, largely through the influence of the Myth and Ritual school.

Robertson Smith, Durkheim, and their contemporary followers may be quite wrong in their effort to derive myth from ritual. However, they are unquestionably right in emphasizing the central role of ritual in the life of religion. It is critical to point this out in our present context, since persons brought up in a Western, secularized culture are likely to approach religion intellectually—that is, see it as a system of beliefs—and to undervalue the bodily and behavioral aspects of religious life. Ritual is primordial and universal because it appeals to the whole person, weaving together bodily gesture, speech, and the senses—the sight of colors and shapes, the sounds of chants or mantras, the tactile feel of water and fabric, and the smell of incense or the aroma of symbolic foods. Through its appeal to bodily movement, verbal chants and responses, and our multiple senses, ritual is symbolic in the most profound sense, for it "brings together" the mind, the body, and the emotions and, at the same time, binds us to a community of shared values.

Approaches to the Study of Ritual

Our primary interest in this chapter is in understanding the nature and principal types of religious ritual. However, we will turn briefly to some of the approaches to religious ritual that recently have engaged the interest of scholars in the field.

One issue concerns the relationship between ritual and myth. Have rituals developed in order to enact myths? Or are myths a later narrative justification of rituals? Because both myths and rituals are fundamental to religious life and because they are very often closely associated, the nature of their relationship has interested scholars for some time. Largely through the influence of Robertson Smith, Frazer, and Durkheim, the Myth and Ritual school advanced the claim that ritual precedes myth and that myth is simply the narrative interpretation of ritual. Drawing on the work of anthropologists, the classical scholar Jane Harrison noted that the Greek word for drama is derived from *rite*, or "things done." In a series of important studies, she traced classical art and drama to their origins in ritual.[2]

According to Harrison, "primitive man . . . tends to re-enact whatever makes him feel strongly; any one of his manifold occupations, hunting, fighting, later plowing and sowing, provided it be of sufficient interest and importance, is material for a *dromenon* or rite."[3] These rites were public, magical dramatizations that in later secular drama become essentially restatements of these primal religious rites. In *Themis: A Study of the Social Origins of Greek Religion,* Harrison made two important claims: that myth arises only out of ritual and that it is "the spoken correlative of the acted rite," the thing said *over* a ritual act. Harrison's thesis about the ritual basis of myth was supported in the work of others, but despite some excellent studies, the ritual theory of myth has its difficulties. It would be stretching the evidence considerably to claim that *all* myths have a ritual basis. On the contrary, it would appear quite evident that some rituals are based on myth or sacred story. The Christian Mass would be a good example.

Anthropologists today are understandably skeptical about any claim concerning the priority of either ritual or myth. No period in history gives us evidence of either one existing entirely alone. Clyde Kluckholn's conclusion is therefore widely shared by scholars today:

> To a considerable degree the whole question of the primacy of ceremonial or mythology is as meaningless as all questions of 'the hen or the egg' form. . . . In sum, the facts do not permit any universal generalizations as to ritual being the 'cause' of myth or vice versa. Their relationship is rather that of intricate mutual interdependence, differently structured in different cultures and probably at different times in the same culture.[4]

It should be pointed out, however, that religious myths do have a capacity to live on in secular guise. This is evident in popular folktales and even in the archetypal motifs found in modern literature, for example, the James Bond novels. Sacred ritual, on the other hand, tends to fade away once it loses its religious context. Nevertheless, it is a simplification to overstress the idea that religion was originally "not so much thought out as danced out." The fact is that all ritual has an intellectual dimension. On this point, Melford Spiro argues that neither ritual nor myth is intelligible without the presence of certain *doctrinal* assumptions that underlie the religious system and the behavior of its devotees. It is important to keep in mind that, no matter how elemental ritual is to religious life, its performance assumes that it is undertaken to achieve some specific goal or goals. This leads directly to a second contemporary approach to the study of ritual: the attention given to its social and psychological functions.

In the early decades of this century, scholarly interest in religion shifted from a focus on religious origins and development to the question of the function of religion in human society. Malinowski and A. R. Radcliffe-Brown (1881–1945) were early leaders in functional theory and analysis. The latter pointed out that society is like an organism, for example, like a human body. In a body, all the organs function together to maintain the whole organism. So it is with society: All parts of the system work together to insure the continuity of the social organism. According to the functionalists, religious myth and ritual are critical to this task. Furthermore, ritual actions may be continued in a society for reasons not wholly consistent with their apparent purpose. For example, rituals may be enacted to dispel forms of anxiety or to strengthen the social order, even if these functions are not apparent to the participants themselves.

Radcliffe-Brown points out that the common tendency to look for the explanation of a ritual in its manifest purpose is due to a false assimilation of rituals to merely technical acts. "In any technical activity an adequate statement of the purpose of any particular act or series of acts constitutes by itself a sufficient explanation. But ritual acts differ from technical acts in having in all instances some expressive or symbolic element in them."[5]

In his study of the Andaman island natives, Radcliffe-Brown describes how certain objects or activities, such as the taboos associated with childbirth and food, have a special *ritual value* for the Andamanese because they serve socially important functions. Take the example of food.

> The social importance of food is not that it satisfies hunger, but that in such a community as the Andamanese camp or village an enormously large proportion of the activities are concerned with the getting and consuming of food, and that in these activities, with their daily instances of collaboration and mutual aid, there continuously occur those interrelations of interests which bind the individual men, women, and children into a society.[6]

Concerning his functional theory of ritual, Radcliffe-Brown offers this conclusion:

> I would hold, as a reasonable hypothesis, that we have here the primary basis of all ritual and therefore of religion and magic, however these may be distinguished. The primary basis of ritual, so the formulation would run, is the attribution of ritual value to objects and occasions which are either themselves objects of important common interests linking together persons of a community or are symbolically representative of such objects.[7]

Rituals clearly serve important psychological and social functions. Their enumeration would be almost limitless, but we can mention a few of the most basic. Rituals of initiation, such as the Jewish bar mitzvah, can legitimize the transition from one stage of life to another. In so doing they can, like liturgical rites, also serve an important identity function. Rituals can also routinize behavior and help reduce

A bar mitzvah, meaning "Son of the Commandment." It is the ritual
initiation of a 13-year-old Jewish boy into responsible membership in the
community. (*Source*: Courtesy of ZEFA Picture Library [UK] Ltd.)

the anxiety and uneasiness associated with the loss of clear boundaries
or the experience of dislocation. Similarly, rituals can help to resolve
social tensions due, perhaps, to the scarcity and arbitrary distribution
of life's material goods or the seeming injustice in the apportioning
of social positions. Raymond Firth speaks of this ritual function in
his study of the natives of the small island of Tikopia:

> One can assume that every individual has emotional dispositions and
> tensions arising from his relation to the external world, including
> members of his own society. . . . What ritual has done is to provide
> routinization and canalization for such tensions. These are not left
> for random expression, but are assigned their time and place for
> explicit mention and acting out.[8]

Rites that allot social duties or offices, such as the investiture of a
bishop or tribal chief, or rites that allow for and channel the expression of pent-up emotion at certain times in socially accepted ways,
such as Mardi Gras, would be examples.

Rituals also serve to dramatize and therefore to articulate a community's archetypal patterns of belief and behavior and, in so doing, to
legitimize those beliefs and actions. In ritual, these patterns are per-

ceived as established by the gods or as having a sacred or divine sanction. Related to this is the fact that the ritual is performative; that is, it accomplishes something or reinforces the belief or behavior by the very fact of its periodic repetition. The philosopher Feuerbach said, "man is what he eats" or, to put it another way, we become what we habitually do.

These and other functions of ritual will be more obvious when we describe a number of specific rituals. Suffice it to say, the functionalists have greatly increased our appreciation of the place, indeed the indispensability, of ritual in human social life. However, it would be wrong to reduce religious ritual solely to functional analysis if that meant viewing it as simply or primarily serving some *other*—secular, psychological, or social—purpose. In other words, the danger of functionalism is in its reduction of a *religious* phenomenon, such as ritual, to a purely psychic or social reality. Such a reduction is an impoverishment, for it fails to do full justice to the *religious* dimension of the ritual itself. Needless to say, while all action has a function or purpose, there are social scientists who have shown far greater interest in and sensitivity to the specifically religious meaning of ritual action. The work of the anthropologist Victor Turner, discussed later, is a case in point.

A nice counterbalance to an extreme functionalist interpretation is the observation that rituals, like some other types of human activity, do not always serve a practical purpose. A good deal of human behavior is not instrumental, that is, is not a means to some other end but is, rather, an end in itself. Games and play are good examples. Another way, then, that ritual has been investigated recently is exploring the analogies between it and human play. The foremost work in this field is Johan Huizinga's influential *Homo Ludens: A Study of the Play Element in Culture*. Huizinga summarizes the formal characteristics of play as follows:

> We might call it a free activity standing quite consciously outside 'ordinary' life as being 'not serious,' but at the same time absorbing the player intensely and utterly. It is an activity connected with no material interest, and no profit can be gained from it. It proceeds within its own proper boundaries of time and space according to fixed rules and an orderly manner. It promotes the formation of social groupings which tend to surround themselves with secrecy and to stress their difference from the common world by disguise or other means.[9]

Huizinga points out how primitive and archaic religious ritual is closely related to play, and in this he is supported by the ethnographers who have demonstrated the sacred origin of many games. We observe that ancient religious ritual often is marked by play-acting and "make believe" in which the distinction between empirical reality and imagination actually breaks down. In ritual or play, fantasy and imagination are not sharply distinguished from the empirically real. In tribal rituals, for example, men carve monstrous masks, which stand for ghosts, and scare both themselves and the women of the tribe. Yet both the men and the women know that behind the masks are their own relatives. Both play and religious ritual have this dramatic and imaginary quality about them; both are "different from ordinary life." This perhaps explains the interest people take in the ritualized pageantry associated with the British monarchy. The colorful costumes from another era, the pomp, and the solemnity, are all touched with an aspect of fantasy and festivity. Ritual, like play, introduces us to the imaginative possibilities of "another world."

From what we know about our human capacity for self-transcendence, it makes a good deal of sense to see ourselves as *homo ludens*, as the player or the ritualist. Essential to our nature is the expressive need to act, to imagine new possibilities, and to engage spontaneously in festivity and celebration—the goal of which is in the activity itself. Without pressing the connection perhaps as closely as Huizinga has done, we can nevertheless appreciate the family resemblance that does exist between human play and religious ritual and how both reflect an indispensable dimension of human life.

Types of Sacred Ritual

We have looked at some of the ways in which ritual has been studied and interpreted. We now can examine the principal forms of religious ritual and illustrate these types with specific examples from a variety of traditions, both archaic and modern. There is no agreed-on typology of religious ritual, one reason being that rituals often overlap, both in form and in meaning. Nevertheless, there are some helpful distinctions that can be made. Rituals sometimes are differentiated by whether they are corporate, domestic, or personal. Another possible contrast is between rituals based on the cycle of nature and the seasons—for example, agricultural festivals or celebrations of the New Year—and those rituals that commemorate or recreate a historical or mythological event—for example, the birth of Christ or the Jewish Passover.

Another type of ritual consists of nonperiodic rites connected with the human life cycle, or rites of passage, as they have come to be called. These include rituals associated with such events as birth, initiation into adulthood, marriage, and death. Some scholars have distinguished these noncyclical rites of initiation and passage from other occasional rituals associated with the "life crisis" of an individual or community. Examples would be healing rites or rainmaking rites. In this chapter, we will analyze all these various types in terms of two paramount forms: (1) nonperiodic life-cycle and life-crisis rites and (2) periodic festivals based on calendar-fixed seasonal or historical events.

Life-Cycle Rites

The significance of rituals connected with critical events in the life of individuals was brought to the attention of scholars by Arnold van Gennep in *The Rites of Passage.* Van Gennep noted that there were numerous rituals that accompanied life's stages and crises.

> The life of an individual in any society is a series of passages . . . so that a man's life comes to be made up of a succession of stages with similar ends and beginnings: birth, social puberty, marriage, fatherhood, advancement to a higher class, occupational specializa-tion, and death. For every one of these events there are ceremonies whose essential purpose is to enable the individual to pass from one defined position to another.[10]

What life-crisis rituals do, according to van Gennep, is help individuals through the difficulties of such critical transitions, as well as assist society in accepting significnat changes in the status or the loss of their members. Victor Turner and Mircea Eliade would, however, give greater attention than does van Gennep to the sacred symbolism of these rites, which reveal the most profound values of a community. For example, it is through puberty rites, Eliade contends, that the individual passes "beyond the natural mode—the mode of the child— and gains access to the cultural mode; that is, he is introduced to spiritual values."[11]

Van Gennep called attention to the striking fact that rites of passage often reveal a common pattern, consisting of three distinct elements: separation, transition, and reincorporation. The first stage removes individuals from their old status. This is often shown by actual physical separation from other members of the society or by a simulation of death itself. The transition stage is frequently marked by some form of social isolation and a condition of statuslessness, a kind of limbo. During this time, the initiate—whether an adolescent girl or an elder, grieving son—is prepared for her or his new station. The third stage of reincorporation signals the passage to a new status or to normal social life, often symbolized by the wearing of new attire, a ring, or other forms of insignia.

Victor Turner has developed van Gennep's insight into the three stages of life-cycle rites by giving special attention to the transitional, or *liminal* (*limen,* signifying "threshold" in Latin), stage and its social and religious significance. Turner sees societal life as a process involving successive periods of structured differentiation, forms of hierarchy, and times of what he calls *communitas,* or the spontaneous bond of communion between members of a society. Life-cycle rites exhibit this alternating process in the life of both individuals and groups.

The liminal, or threshold, stage is a transitional one, and thus, according to Turner, it represents antistructure. It is likened to being in the wilderness, to darkness, and to death. In the liminal stage, the initiate is stripped of status, symbolized by uniform dress, loss of rank, and submissiveness. A rite of the African Ndembu tribe, undertaken for the installation of their chief, is a good example of Turner's understanding of the role of liminality. The Ndembu chief is, in fact, a condensed symbol for the tribe itself because he represents its territory, its community, and its fecundity. But before the chief-elect can be installed, he must be stripped of his status and reduced to that of the commonest tribesman. The Ndembu liminal rite begins with the construction of a hut known as the *kafu,* which means "to die," and it is here "that the chief-elect dies from his commoner state."[12]

The chief-to-be is clad in nothing but a ragged waistcloth and is led, with a ritual wife, to the *kafu,* as if they were infirm. In the hut, they sit crouched in a posture of shame and submissiveness and undergo a tirade of rebuke and humiliation by fellow tribesmen:

> Be silent! You are a mean and selfish fool, one who is bad-tempered. You do not love your fellows. . . . Meanness and theft is all you have! Yet here we have called you and we say you must succeed to the Chieftanship. Put away your meanness, put aside anger, give up adulterous intercourse, give them up immediately.[13]

Anyone in the tribe wronged by the chief-elect is entitled to revile him during this liminal period. The chief, by being ritually stripped of his status, is being prepared to facilitate the achievement of *communitas,* the sense of sharing a common humanity, a profound fellow feeling required of a chief. Turner points out that the elevation to a new status must be preceded by such a status reversal. In a real sense, the first must be last before becoming first. By so doing, human communion and fellow feeling are achieved.

The attainment of *communitas* is considered holy or sacred because it "breaks through the interstices of structure" and "transgresses or dissolves the norms that govern institutionalized relationships."[14] But rites of passage do not conclude in the liminal stage; they also include the rites of incorporation back into a structured society, revitalized by the experience of *communitas.* Turner argues that it is only the achievement of a sacred communion that makes ongoing social life possible.

The profound attraction of many of the world's great religious leaders lies, perhaps, in the fact that their lives can be viewed as condensed symbols of this ritual process. Buddha, Jesus, and Gandhi come to mind. During Holy Week the Pope often visits an Italian prison where he washes the feet of some of society's outcasts, thus showing his bond with all of suffering humanity.

Life-cycle rites can be observed in every religion because of their importance not only to the individual but also to the larger community. However, the number of rites and the importance of specific types of rites of passage vary greatly among the religions. In some cultures, marriage rites play a critical role whereas in others—for example, the Zuni Indians—it is absent or nearly so. Buddha once recommended 40 rites connected with life's stages. Today, devout Hindu Brahmans observe 16 *samskaras,* or sacraments. These are rites accompanying such events as conception, name-giving, **tonsure,** and the beginning of formal study, as well as those associated with birth, marriage, and death. It is striking that four of the seven authorized sacraments of the Roman Catholic Church are rites of passage: baptism; matrimony; extreme unction or anointing of the sick; and holy orders. Here we confine our examples of life-cycle rites essentially to

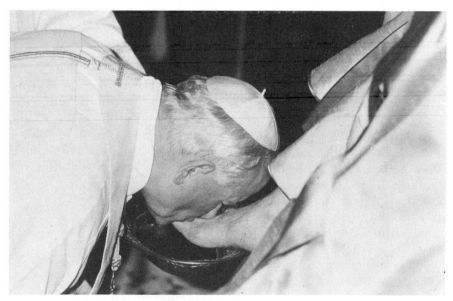

The Pope's washing of an Italian prisoner's feet, often undertaken during Holy Week, is an example of what the anthropologist Victor Turner calls the ritual achievement of *communitas.* (*Source*: Courtesy of AP/Wide World Photos, Inc.)

three: birth, social puberty, and rites of initiation into special societies or vocations.

BIRTH RITES In many primitive and archaic societies, birth rites begin long before the actual physical birth of the child and have to do with insuring the health and well-being of both the mother and the unborn. This is the case in Hinduism, where *samskaras* are performed at conception; at the quickening of the unborn (before the fetus moves in the womb); and at the hairparting of the pregnant mother, a rite that occurs around the fifth month when, it is believed, the mind of the child is developing and needs the mother's special care so as not to be shocked.

The actual birth ceremony is called *jātakarma* and is normally to be performed before the severing of the navel cord, although some latitude is allowed in this regard. The rite itself is preceded by preliminary ceremonies and precautions a day or two before the birth. The *jātakarma* proper commences with the *medhajanana* rite, or the production of intelligence. The father, using an instrument of gold, gives to the child honey and ghee (a purified butter] or ghee alone. It is believed that the ghee, the honey, and the gold are favorable to the child's mental development.

This is followed by the *ayusya*, or the rite of ensuring the long life of the child. Near the navel or the right ear of the child, the father murmurs:

> Agni is long-lived; through the trees he is long-lived. By that long life I make thee long-lived. . . . Sama is long-lived; through the herbs, etc. The Brahman is long-lived, through observances, etc. Sacrifice is long-lived; through sacrificial fire, etc.[15]

All the possible instances of long life are cited before the child, in the expectation that thereby the life of the infant will be enhanced. Also, five Brahman priests are brought in to breathe on the child because their sacred breath is obviously seen as productive of life. The father next performs a rite to insure the hardy and pure life of the child, imploring the babe: "Be a stone, be an axe, be an imperishable gold. Thou indeed are the self called son; thus live a hundred autumns."[16]

Following these ceremonies, the mother is then praised for bearing a son, the husband reciting: "Thou art Idā, the daughter of Mitra and Varuna; thou strong woman hast borne a strong son. Be thou blessed with strong children, thou who has blest us with a strong son."[17] The navel cord is then cut, and the child is bathed and given to the mother. A pot of water is put near the head of the mother to ward off demons, and a sacrificial fire is kept burning near the

An adult baptized by immersion in a pool that represents the waters of the Jordan. Baptisms universally represent ritual purification as well as incorporation into the religious community. (*Source*: Courtesy of Camera Press Ltd.)

maternity room door until the mother leaves her child-bed. When the ceremonies are over, presents are offered to the Brahman priests. Broadly similar patterns can be found in other primitive and archaic religions, although in some the elaborate ceremonials focus on the father rather than on the mother or child. In these prenatal and birth rites, with their symbolic gestures and **incantations**, a magical or sacramental purpose is apparent while the three-fold structure emphasized by van Gennep and Turner is not discernible, as it is in puberty rites and other forms of initiation.

SOCIAL PUBERTY—INITIATION INTO ADULTHOOD   Initiation rites are among the most important religious rituals and include not only initiation into adult status in society but also entrance into secret societies and admission to a special vocation, such as the enthronement of a king or the ordination and consecration of a nun, priest, or bishop.

In primitive and archaic societies, transition to adult status often coincides with physical puberty or sexual maturity. However, initiation into adulthood does not always take place at the time of physical puberty, especially in the case of boys. Nevertheless, social puberty rites have to do with the transition from the asexual world of childhood to an adult society that is differentiated by sexual roles. Rites marking the transition to adulthood reveal a rather common pattern in which the initiates are socially isolated and their behavior restricted, undergo certain ordeals to test their ability to take on their new responsibilities, are instructed in the secret knowledge of the community and shown the sacred objects, and finally are given the insignia of their new status and formally recognized as having made the transition. It is worth noting that this pattern can be recognized in contemporary college fraternity initiations as well.

Isolation and restricted behavior are common to the initiation rites of both girls and boys. Ordeals are a somewhat more-typical feature of rituals for boys, although girls often do undergo such ordeals as fasting, sitting motionless, and even whipping. Boys frequently are required to prove their physical prowess and their hunting feats. Another feature of puberty rites is the physical mutilation of the body, which marks the separation from childhood and incorporation into adult life. In the case of boys, this often involves circumcision or subincision, a slitting of the underside of the penis. In some societies, a similar act, called clitoridectomy, is performed on girls. Other means of signaling incorporation include removing a front tooth, filing teeth to points, piercing ear lobes and the septum for the insertion of ornaments, tattooing and scarifying the body, ornamenting the body with special clothing and bracelets, and haircutting and dressing.

Another important component of puberty rites is the instruction of the adolescents in the tribal law and in the sacred knowledge of the community.

> In this religious perspective, initiation is equivalent to introducing the novice to the mythical history of the tribe; in other words, the initiand learns the deeds of the Supernatural Beings, who, in the

dream times, established the present human condition, and all the religious, social, and cultural institutions of the tribe. All in all, to know this traditional lore means to know the adventures of the Ancestors and other Superhuman Beings when they lived on earth.[18]

The ordeals and instruction of the young are frequently accompanied by a dramatic ceremonial and dance, including the use of frightening masked figures and bull-roarers, which emit a roaring sound when whirled through the air—all intended to impress on the adolescents a sense of the *tremendum*, the sacredness of the occasion, which they are never to forget.

VOCATIONAL INITIATION RITES   In many societies, there are, in addition to the usual social puberty rites, initiation ceremonies for special groups or fraternities that consist of an elite class of persons who have demonstrated that they possess a special capacity to understand the sacred mysteries or are gifted with unique spiritual powers. Membership in a sacred society often cuts across tribal or social boundaries, and entrance can involve a series of rites extending over several years. However, the pattern of initiation is similar in, for example, North America, Oceania, and Africa. In the following passage, van Gennep describes initiation into membership in a secret society among the Congo tribes in Africa:

> They include all sorts of negative rites (taboos) and positive rites. The order of rites is as follows: the novice is separated from his previous environment, in relation to which he is dead, in order to be incorporated into his new one. He is taken into the forest, where he is subjected to seclusion, lustration, flagellation, and intoxication with palm wine, resulting in anesthesia. Then come the transition rites, including bodily mutilations . . . and painting of the body; since the novices are considered dead during their trial period, they go about naked and may neither leave their retreat nor show themselves to men; the *nganga* (a priest-magician) instructs them; they speak a special language and eat special food (dietary taboos).
> The trial period is followed by rites of reintegration into the previous environment. . . . The initiates pretend not to know how to walk or eat and, in general, act as if they were newly born (resurrected) and must relearn all the gestures of ordinary life. Before they enter the relearning process, which takes several months, the initiates bathe in a stream, and the sacred hut is burned.[19]

Initiation into a special religious vocation—be it that of a monk, nun, or priest—follows a similar pattern of separation, transition, and reincorporation. In Chinese Buddhism, this can be observed in the ritual known as tonsure, in which a monk shaves the head of a layman, often a youth, who thereby enters the *sangha*, or congregation of Buddhist monks or nuns. The ceremony in the shrine hall is simple but replete with symbolic meaning. A sermon is read by the master to the kneeling candidate, relating how Sakyamuni, the Buddha, stole out of his palace, cut off his hair, and renounced lay life. The candidate waves to his parents, symbolizing "leaving the home" and accepting an older monk as his new master. The young candidate then faces the altar and makes nine prostrations to the Three Jewels: the Buddha, the Dharma (the doctrine or teaching), and the Sangha. At that point, the master sprinkles the candidate's head with holy water and then receives a razor from the candidate, who beseeches: "I, your disciple . . . today beg Your reverence to be the Teacher who shaves my hair. . . . I wish to renounce lay life as your dependent."[20]

The master shaves all but the top tuft of hair, reminding the youth that it is not too late to withdraw from his vows. The candidate then answers: "I have made up my mind to renounce lay life and I will never regret or withdraw." Three times the question is put to the youth, and three times he replies. The master then cuts off the remaining hair, cutting off the candidate from all previous ties. The youth then dons a monk's gown, prostrates himself before the Buddha image, and joins the other monks in a chant. The ceremony ends with the novice returning to his family and the other spectators to receive their congratulations. From that day forward, he will begin to live like a monk and train for ordination, although he may not actually be ordained for several years at the age of 20.

MARRIAGE AND FUNERAL RITES   The classic features of life-cycle rites that we have observed so far are also evident in marriage ceremonies and in funeral or mortuary rites. As a "holy estate," marriage is hedged around by numerous taboos and customs, such as the throwing of rice or grain at the bride to insure her fertility, the seclusion of the bride and groom for a period, the changing of clothing before the marriage, and the tying of knots and the exchanging of rings to strengthen the marriage bond.

Funeral rites also reflect the three-fold pattern of separation, transition, and reincorporation. For most religions, death is viewed as a threshold leading from one mode of existence to another, a liminal period before rebirth to a new status. Similarly, mourning rites represent a time of separation and transition for the deceased's family and friends. The greater the role played by the deceased in the community—a ruler, for example—the more elaborate and extended are the funeral and mourning rites. The variety of rituals surrounding death are legion, and their features depend to a considerable degree on the society's attitude toward the role of the deceased in the afterlife state. Fear of the dead often means elaborate rites of purification or efforts to appease and to placate the spirit of the dead. The body may be removed from the house by special means to ensure that it will not return, or a stake may be driven through the corpse for the same purpose. In China, elaborate mortuary rites ensure both a safe and speedy journey of the deceased spirit to Heaven and its well-being in Paradise. The extraordinary number and the duration of these rites impresses the living kinsmen of the importance of the ancestors for the ongoing cohesion, health, and happiness of the family. The sage Hsün Tzu points to the unique importance of rites connected with both birth and death:

> Rites are strictest in their ordering of birth and death. Birth is the beginning of man, death his end. When both beginning and end are good, man's way is complete. Therefore the gentleman is reverent in his treatment of the beginning and careful in his treatment of the end, regarding both with the same gravity.[21]

Life-Crisis Rites: A Healing Ritual

Another prevalent type of nonperiodic ritual is the kind undertaken to meet a specific crisis in the life of an individual or a community, such as illness, miscarriage, failure in the hunt, or drought. Understandably, the concern for health is of particular urgency, and all religions—especially those in nonliterate societies—have rituals that invoke or ward off supernatural powers as a means of curing disease.

In primitive societies, it is generally believed not only that health is supernaturally given but also that disease is often supernaturally caused. Thus the crucial dealing with illness, the loss of soul, or evil possession are left to the work of religious professionals: diviners, medicine men, shamans, **exorcists**, and priests. Shamans, witch doctors, or medicine men play a particularly crucial role in technologically simple societies since it often is believed that they possess special ecstatic powers for dealing with the supernatural, including witchcraft and demons.

The shaman is uniquely able to undergo altered states of consciousness and to leave his body and travel to the other world of the spirits, and thereby to serve as intercessor and healer. The word *shaman* is Siberian, and it is in the northern regions that shamanism can be observed in its classic form. It is, however, found throughout the world and is a common feature of Native American Indian religious life. Mircea Eliade remarks that shamans "are predominantly the antidemonic champions; they combat not only demons and disease, but also the black magicians."[22]

The illustration of a life-crisis healing rite that we have selected here focuses on the prominent role of the shaman. It is taken from the anthropologist Derek Freeman's study of the Iban or Sea Dayaks,

a people of western Borneo, now a part of Malaysia. The Iban shaman
is called a *manang*, and his principal concern is caring for the psychic
welfare of his Iban clients. The Iban believe that every person has a
separable soul that can leave the body and wander about in the world
of the spirits and therefore become ensnared by an evil spirit. Sickness
is most often diagnosed as some misfortune that has befallen the soul
and, it is believed, the shaman can heal the soul by freeing it from
a malevolent spirit or by slaying the evil spirit.

The infant mortality rate among the Iban is very high, and most
women in the community have suffered the loss of a child. Child loss
is widely attributed to the work of an *antu buyu*—an incubus, or evil
demon, who descends on persons in their sleep, especially to seek
carnal intercourse with women. In their dreams, the incubus appears
to Iban women as a handsome and alluring male whose advances
they are unable to resist. However, the incubus is really a guise for
an animal, such as the monkey, that is metamorphasized to assume
an attractive human shape.

The intercourse with the evil spirit leads, of course, to fatal consequences for the women's offspring, as well as for the family. High
infant mortality is a powerful threat to the entire community. Slaying
the incubus and restoring a woman to health is one of the Iban
shaman's most important and formidable tasks. While most shamans
can perform rituals to ward off an incubus, only the exceptional shaman can actually ritually slay an *antu buyu*. Here we relate Freeman's
account of such an extraordinary feat by Manang Bungai, which took
place on New Year's Day, 1951.[23]

The seven-month-old daughter of an Iban couple died, and the
mother, named Rabai, was driven to hysteria and had to be restrained.
Several days later, she confessed that she had had a dream and that
she now realized she had been visited by an incubus who had assumed
the appearance of her husband. A rite was quickly performed to
protect the couple's home from the incubus that, it was believed, was
still haunting Rabai. Soon, however, the couple sought out Manang
Bungai in order that he might slay the incubus responsible for the
death of Rabai's infant daughter. On his arrival, Manang Bungai performed a divinatory rite with a quartz crystal, moving it rhythmically
in circles over the heads of several women who were assembled. By
this means, he was able to divine that Rabai, of all the women present,
was beyond all doubt being molested by some spirit.

Rabai's husband then prepared a spear for the shaman's deadly
struggle. However, it was decided that Manang Bungai should begin
his work in the nearby apartment of Sating, whose wife, Menun, had
lost two of her three children. Using the same divinatory rite, he
announced that Menun, too, had been molested by an incubus that was,
almost certainly, a monkey. He then continued with his preparations:

An opening in the rear wall of the apartment through which the incubus would enter was unshuttered, the sleeping mats were rolled up and removed, and a bait consisting of boiled rice and eggs was laid out on a winnowing tray. Bungai then took up his blinder, a magical substance indispensable to a shaman in that it is believed to have qualities which make him and his soul invisible to all evil spirits. . . . A small piece of this he rubbed on each of his shoulders and on his chest; he then set it smoldering and as its fumes drifted about the room he addressed these imprecatory words to all incubi and other malevolent spirits:

> There, you the troublesome ones, you the perverse ones,
> Be cursed, be enfeebled,
> Be abused, be bereaved,
> Trip and fall headlong;
> Be weak of bone, be weak of limb,
> Be weak of leg, be weak of hand,
> Be stupid, be senseless,
> So you may expire outright, perish utterly,
> We pray thus
> Because you so constantly plague us,
> That we freely die, till all be gone.[24]

Spear in hand and clad only in a loin cloth, Bungai then entered the apartment. A piece of fabric over the doorway concealed him from the crowd outside. After a few minutes, Bungai could be heard calling to the incubus as if he were a woman longing for her lover. Soon one of Bungai's associates whispered to the watching Iban that the incubus had arrived and had begun to eat the food. Bungai could now be heard singing to the incubus in soothing words. He now moved carefully, like a hunter stalking a wary prey, while chanting his magical words and thereby lulling the incubus into a sense of security. Suddenly there was the noise of a scuffle, accompanied by the agonized yelps of a monkey.

A few moments later, Bungai emerged, signaling to the spectators to enter the apartment. A trail of spattered blood led across the floor to the opening in the rear wall. Bungai stood in the center of the room, panting, holding his spear, which was smeared with blood and some hair. The shaman then told the excited assembly that he had speared the incubus deeply in the back and in the side as it was fleeing and invited those present to inspect his spear. The Iban were greatly impressed by Manang Bungai's feat and certain that the incubus had, indeed, been killed.

After a pause of about 30 minutes, Bungai summoned Menun and performed another divinatory rite. This time the quartz crystal showed that Menun's soul was healthy, and Bungai announced that the molesting incubus lived no more. Before completing his work, the shaman warned Menun and her family that this victory would be lost if certain ritual prohibitions (taboos) were not obeyed. He told them that, if the prohibitions were broken, another incubus could become attached to Menun. Bungai then performed a shamanistic rite, enclosing the apartment of Menun and Sating with magically protective walls. With this, the shaman's work of healing was ended.

Similar healing rituals are found in most tribal societies. Eskimo shamans, for example, go on spirit flights for the purpose of curing illness and retrieving lost souls. The belief in the intrusion of disease-causing objects is especially widespread among American Indians. The Sia Pueblo Indians have special medicine societies whose job it is to carry out elaborate rituals for the purpose of extracting foreign, disease-producing objects—thorns, sticks, or pebbles—from the bodies of the Sia who are in need of cures.

Calendar or Seasonal Rituals

All over the world, from time immemorial, societies have marked the seasons and important events in the cycle of the year with public rituals. These seasonal and calendar rites are closely associated with the rhythmic changes of nature; with the cycles of the sun and moon; with winter, spring, summer, and autumn; as well as with seed time and harvest. In agricultural societies, rites connected with planting, the first fruits, and the harvest are universal. On the other hand, in historical religions such as Judaism and Christianity, fixed calendar rites serve to commemorate and to represent archetypal historical events. Even some of these rites—Christmas and the Jewish Passover, for example—trace their roots to the annual cycle of the seasons.

Seasonal ritual is always directed to securing the well-being of both the community and the individual. They tend to follow a common ritual structure in which the evil, pollution, and eclipse of life's vitality, connected with the old year, are purged away. The pattern is marked by mortification and lenten austerities and rites of emptying (*kenosis*), followed by rites of revitalization, or the giving of new life, fertility, and prosperity. Theodore Gaster rightly observes that, for the primitive community, "life is not so much a progression from cradle to grave as it is a series of leases annually or periodically renewed."[25]

These "leases on life" follow a more or less uniform structure that Gaster describes in terms of four principal movements:

> First come rites of MORTIFICATION, symbolizing the state of suspended animation which ensues at the end of the year, when one lease of life has drawn to a close and the next is not yet assured.

> Second comes rites of PURGATION, whereby the community seeks to rid itself of all noxiousness and contagion, both physical and moral, and of all evil influences which might impair the prosperity of the coming year and thereby threaten the desired renewal and vitality.
>
> Third comes rites of INVIGORATION, whereby the community attempts by its own concerned and regimented effort, to galvanize its moribund condition and to procure that new lease of life. . . .
>
> Last comes rites of JUBILATION, which bespeak men's sense of relief when the new year has indeed begun and the continuance of their own lives . . . is thereby assured.[26]

Gaster has amassed a wealth of evidence from primitive and ancient religion to support this general pattern. For purposes of illustration, we will focus on one classic example, the New Year (Akitu) Festival of the ancient Babylonians. We will see, however, that the pattern is also discernible in a historical–calendric rite such as the modern Roman Catholic mass.

The Akitu was celebrated at the beginning of each year at the vernal equinox, during the first 12 days of the month of Nisan (March–April). The rites centered around the temple of the god Marduk (called Esagila) in Babylon and the ritual dramatization of the creation story, the *Enuma elish,** and Marduk's victory over Tiamat and the forces of chaos. The Akitu Festival is a threshold rite marking the transition from one status to another. You will note that the themes discussed by van Gennep and Turner are prominent. However, the ritual is an exemplary model of the seasonal pattern so common among agricultural societies. The seasonal theme is nonetheless tied closely to the political concern of ensuring the life and prosperity of the social order.

The first four days of Nisan are somber and melancholy, expressing a sense of the desolation of the winter season, the defilement of the people, and the impotence of the king. These are days of lenten *mortifications* and prayer. On the second day of the rite, the priests entreat Marduk

> [Have pity] upon the city, Babylon
> Turn thy face towards Esagila thy temple;
> Give freedom to them that dwell in Babylon, thy wards.[27]

Marduk is thought to be "bound" and the king is deposed or symbolically slain. On the evening of the fourth day, the entire *Enuma elish* is recited, marking the beginning of the passage from winter to spring, from chaos to cosmic renewal.

* For a discussion of the Babylonian creation myth, the *Enuma elish*, see Chapter 8.

The fifth day of Nisan ushers in the rites of *purgation* on the Day
of Atonement. The temple is purified, sprinkled with water, and fumi-
gated with incense. Incantations are recited by an exorcist, and a
sheep is beheaded and its body rubbed against the temple walls to
absorb all the pollution of the previous year. The head and body of
the sheep, or scapegoat, are then thrown in the river, and both the
officiating priest and the executioner are sent into quarantine in the
desert for the remainder of the festival. This purging is followed by
a ritual abdication of the king. The king's crown, ring, and scepter
are removed, and the priest strikes the king across the face. The
sovereign is forced to kneel and make an act of penitence and expiation in the presence of Marduk, offering a "negative" confession
declaring his innocence:

> I have not sinned, O Lord of the lands . . .
> I have not neglected the temple of Esagila . . .
> I have not rained blows on the cheek of a subordinate . . .
> I have cared for Babylon; I have not broken its walls.[28]

The king is then reinvested and resumes his regal status. During
the king's divestiture in the temple, there is a carnival atmosphere in
the streets of the city, accompanied by ritual combats symbolizing the
ascendency of chaos. The social order is overturned, slaves become
masters and masters become slaves, and a criminal is enthroned as
carnival king. However, once the king is restored and Marduk is
ritually released by his son Nabu, the rite moves into its third phase
with ceremonies of *invigoration*.

From the sixth to the eighth day of Nisan, the ritual liberation of
Marduk, his victory over Tiamat, the assembly of the gods, and Marduk's enthronement are all enacted. On the ninth day of Nisan there
occurs a triumphant procession of Marduk and the king from Esagila
to the House of the New Year's Feast, or Bit Akitu, accompanied by
a joyful populace. New life is assured. On the next day, a sumptuous
banquet is held for the king, the gods, the priests, and their atten-
dants. That night, Marduk and the king return to Esagila where a
sacred marriage is consummated between the king and a sacred female
temple slave. This signals the return to fertility, the impregnation of
Mother Nature, and the restoration of life. The rite ends with the
couple emerging from "the chamber of the bed" to partake of a final
elaborate feast of *jubilation* for the new life won:

> Around the shoulders of his beloved bride he has
>   laid his arms . . .
> The king, like unto the sun, sits beside her,
> A sumptuous meal is placed before her . . .

> The palace is in fest[ive mood], the king is glad,
> The people are passing the day in abundance.[29]

Seasonally, the Akitu festival marks the fertility of the new year but, politically, it also ensures divine approval of the king and the assurance of his vitality and authority — the return to cosmic order.

Vestiges of the four-fold seasonal pattern can be noted in some of the calendric rituals of the later historical religions. It can be seen, for example, in the Roman Catholic Mass, particularly in the pre–Vatican II (1965) liturgy. The liturgy begins with prayers of entreaty, confession, and acts of mortification. The priest and the people say the *confiteor*, a public confession of sin, which includes the following:

> I have sinned exceedingly in thought, word, and deed / (striking the breast three times as a sign of contrition), through my fault, / through my fault, / through my most grievous fault.[30]

At the conclusion of the first movement of the Mass, the priest leads the people in the *Kyrie*, a triple supplication: "Lord have mercy on us, / Christ have mercy on us, / Lord have mercy on us."

The second movement, that of *purgation*, begins, as does the Akitu ritual, with a reading from sacred scripture (the Bible, like the *Enuma elish*, is the archetypal Word), a homily or sermon on the readings from the Bible, and the recitation of the Creed. The central rite of the purgation, and the holiest point in the Catholic Mass, is the offering of the sacrifice at the altar, where the priest represents both the sacrificial offering of the people and Christ's eternal sacrifice on the cross at Golgotha. The priest offers the bread (signifying Christ's body), saying:

> Accept, O holy Father, / almighty and eternal God, / this host for the all-holy sacrifice, / which I, Thy unworthy servant, offer unto Thee, / my living and true God, / to atone for my numberless sins of wilfulness and neglect; / on behalf of all here present, / and likewise for all faithful Christians, living and dead, / that it may profit me and them / as a means of salvation unto life everlasting. Amen.[31]

Similar words are said at the offering of the chalice (wine) signifying Christ's blood.

Following the priest's consecration of the elements of the bread and the wine and the eucharistic sacrifice itself, the people join in the sacred meal, which introduces a series of rites of *invigoration*. This is indicated by a number of prayers, including the following offered by the priest:

> Most humbly we implore Thee, Almighty God . . . that those of us
> who, from this sharing in the heavenly sacrifice, shall receive the
> most sacred Body and Blood of Thy Son, may be filled with every
> grace and heavenly blessing . . . [32]

The Mass concludes with rites of *jubilation*: prayers of thankgiving,
sung Psalms and hymns, and benedictions. Grace has been conferred,
the mystical union with God effected, and eternal life assured.

Ritual and Sacrifice

A random study of seasonal and calendric rituals reveals a striking
feature that these religious rites share: so many of them include ritual
acts of sacrifice. This feature has long been noted by scholars, and
a number of interesting and influential ideas about the origin and
the purpose of ritual sacrifice have been suggested.

What is the religious intention or purpose of presenting offerings
and sacrifices? Obviously, innumerable human emotions can be expressed in these actions, including fear, guilt, adoration, gratitude,
and homage. Three dominant purposes have been highlighted by
scholars. Early commentators focused on what is called the rule of
do-ut-des—"I give that thou mayest give." In other words, offerings
signify a simple bargain or exchange, expressed succinctly in a Hindu
ritual: "Here is the butter; where are thy gifts?"

E. B. Tylor (1832–1917) believed that sacrifice evolved through
three stages: gift giving; homage; and abnegation, or renunciation.[33]
Gift giving clearly can express the *do-ut-des*—the giver obligating the
receiver (the god) to act in kind. Tylor saw the same rule at work
in homage. The person paying tribute seeks to gain the king's or the
god's good will and protection. Renunciation, however, expresses only
self-denial and, Tylor believed, is free of crudely practical motives.
He therefore considered such acts of renunciation as expressing higher
forms of sacrifice. Common to the *do-ut-des*, or Tylor's first function
of sacrifice, is *propitiation*. To propitiate means to cause to become
favorably inclined, to appease or conciliate another. From the dawn
of human life, offerings have been made to propitiate the spirits or
gods, to achieve their favor, and to minimize their hostility.

Robertson Smith (1846-1894) focused on a second important purpose of sacrifice: the securing of a social bond. Smith perceived that
ancient Semitic sacrificial rites often were accompanied by a sacred
feast or meal. The meal served to establish a covenant, or a mystical
union, between the god—symbolized by the sacrificial elements consumed—and those participating in the meal. The ritual also
strengthens the bond between the members of the community itself.

According to Smith, it is the establishing of community and not barter or propitiation that is the central purpose of sacrifice.

A third, and most important, function of sacrifice is expressed by the term *expiation* — the making amends or **atonement** — for defilement or transgression. According to this view, sacrificial rites of expiation assume some offense against the sacred or divine. In their most primitive form, rites of expiation are directed at the removal of pollution, release from which, it is believed, can free the community and the individual from deadly contagion. What is of critical importance to expiatory rites, however, is the belief that life can be restored not simply by ethical good works but only by costly self-sacrifice. Life must be offered in order that life may be preserved. Moreover, the focus of attention is not on the individual but rather on the transgression that affects the entire society. The community is defiled, and reconciliation needs to be effected. The defiled and sinful life therefore must be offered, sacrificed, and destroyed so that new life might be given.

The way in which corporate purgation and atonement is usually achieved is through the community's representative, or scapegoat. The word *scapegoat* has, in recent times, come to refer to someone who is blamed for someone else's errors and who bears the burden of blame, but this is a distortion of its original intention. Both primitive society and the ancient world shared a more-profound sense of society's corporate nature than we do today. It is sometimes called the sense of "corporate personality" — the belief that one person, perhaps the king or a totem animal, can *represent* the entire tribe or nation and can thereby be its sin bearer. Theodore Gaster points to the real function of the scapegoat as representative:

> The essential point about the scapegoat is that it removes from the community the taint and impurity of sins *which have first to be openly confessed*. There is no question of transferring to it either blame or responsibility; the sole issue is how to get rid of the miasma of transgression which one freely acknowledges. [Yet] there can be no assurance that every single person will indeed undergo that process; latent impurity may therefore remain. . . . There is thus only one method of securing clearance, namely, to pronounce a *comprehensive*, blanket confession of sins and to saddle the *comprehensive* taint upon some person, animal or object which will be forcibly expelled and thereby take it away.[34]

The representative is the sin remover, and expiation usually involves the offering — the sacrifice and death — of the victim, which removes or covers the pollution and sin. The Hebrew word for such rites of purgation or covering is *kippurim*, and the holiest day of the Jewish year is Yom Kippur, or the Day of Atonement. Originally, the rites of Yom Kippur focused exclusively on the removal of pollution, but in the later Temple and synagogue rites, it became more closely associated with the atonement of sins, understood in terms of the Jewish community's moral obligations under the Covenant with their God.

The earliest account of Yom Kippur is in Chapter 16 of the Book of Leviticus, where it is said to be instituted by Moses in connection with the tabernacle. The ritual is performed by the high priest called Aaron. Its purpose is to purify the priests, the sanctuary, and the people once a year. It consisted of numerous rites of fumigation; ablutions, or washings; and burnt offerings and sacrifices, culminating in a rite that sends into the desert a scapegoat bearing the collective sins of the people.

> And when he has made an end of atoning for the holy place and the tent of meeting and the altar, he shall present the live goat; and Aaron shall lay both his hands upon the head of the live goat, and confess over him all the iniquities of the people of Israel, and all their transgressions, all their sins; and he shall put them upon the head of the goat, and send him away into the wilderness by the hand of a man who is in readiness.
>
> The goat shall bear all their iniquities upon him to a solitary land; and he shall let the goat go in the wilderness.
>
> *(Leviticus 16:20–22)*

Aaron then removes his garments and bathes in a holy place before again dressing. Thereafter, he offers burnt offerings to make atonement for himself and for the people. The text concludes with the following "everlasting statute":

> And it shall be a statute to you forever that in the seventh month, of the tenth day of the month, you shall afflict yourselves . . . for on this day shall atonement be made for you, to cleanse you; from all your sins you shall be clean before the Lord.
>
> *(Leviticus 16:29–30)*

Rites of expiation follow another three-fold structure that can be observed on Yom Kippur. The rite begins with a ceremonial *offering*. Here something costly is selected, and a spiritual union is effected between the offerer and the offering. The offering is a genuine representative. This initial rite is followed by the actual *sacrifice*. The representative dies, which symbolizes the offerer's sacrifice of self and death. Life must be given if life is to be received and renewed. The third movement of the rite is the *receiving of new life*, resurrection and regeneration. This is often symbolized by the participation in a common meal or feast, or by the putting on of new raiment or other insignia. It is well known that the Christian liturgy of Holy Communion, or the sacrifice of the Mass, is rooted in the ancient Israelite atonement rites. In the liturgy of the Mass, Christ is the people's representative before the throne of God, paradoxically both the offering and the offerer.

More recently, a striking theory of sacrifice has been suggested, based on the thesis of Konrad Lorenz's *On Aggression*: Violence is deeply rooted in human behavior and serves an essential function in human society. The classicist Walter Burkert has built on Lorenz's idea that group demonstration of aggression toward outsiders creates a sense of close personal community. Burkert suggests that human solidarity was, in the primitive and ancient world, achieved through a sacred crime—that is, bloody, violent killing—which required amendment for the wrong. The **Paleolithic** Age was, after all, the age of the hunter with its indelible effects on all of humankind.

> Man can virtually be defined as 'the hunting ape.' ... The age of the hunter, the Palaeolithic, comprises by far the largest part of human history. No matter that estimates range between 95 and 99 percent: it is clear that man's biological evolution was accomplished during this time. By comparison, the period since the invention of agriculture—10,000 years, at most—is a drop in the bucket. From this perspective, then, we can understand man's terrifying violence as deriving from the behavior of the predatory animal, whose characteristics he came to acquire in the course of becoming man.[35]

According to Burkert, humanity's explosive aggression was transferred and released "in the dangerous and bloody hunt"; that is, in the hunting ritual, aggression between humans was redirected toward animal quarry, assuring order and peace within the community. However, this primordial human violence provoked feelings of fear and guilt that called for amendment; hence the emergence of the ritual of sacrifice. "Sacrificial killing," Burkert concludes, "is the basic experience of the 'sacred.'" *Homo religiosus* acts and attains self-awareness as *homo necans* [from the Latin *necare*, "to kill"].[36]

Burkert's theory has much in common with one proposed by René Girard in his important study *Violence and the Sacred*. Girard also sees violence as the matrix of *all* ritual, and hence religion:

> In a universe where the slightest dispute can lead to a disaster—just as a slight cut can prove fatal to a hemophiliac—the rites of sacrifice serve to polarize the community's aggressive impulses and redirect them toward victims that may be actual or figurative, animate or inanimate, but that are always incapable of propagating further vengeance. The sacrificial process furnishes an outlet for those violent impulses that cannot be mastered by self-restraint. ... The sacrificial process prevents the spread of violence by keeping violence in check.[37]

Girard has developed an elaborate theory concerning the relationship between the original human victim and the ritual surrogate or substitute victim, the scapegoat. Ritual victims are ambivalent figures, both belonging and yet not belonging to the community. Hence, the surrogate victim often is a slave or livestock. The fundamental point, however, is that the scapegoat keeps violence *outside* the community. It keeps the sacred at bay because, according to Girard, the sacred is not a beneficent power but the *tremendum,* a force of peculiar dread. It represents all those powers—tempests, forest fires, and plagues— that are outside our mastery. Chief among these is the chaotic threat of human violence—a power, according to Girard, that is "seen as something exterior to man and henceforth as a part of all other outside forces that threaten mankind. Violence is the heart and secret soul of the sacred."[38]

Girard makes the extraordinary claim that *all* religious ritual has its origin in the representative sacrificial victim and that all our great human institutions are founded on religious ritual. The sacrificial victim is, then,

> . . . the ideal educator of humanity, in the etymological sense of *e-ducatio,* a leading out. The rite gradually leads men away from the sacred [as malevolent power]; it permits them to escape their own violence, removes them from violence, and bestows on them all the institutions and beliefs that define our humanity.[39]

There appears to be no agreement on the origin or meaning of sacrifice, and it is likely that none of the theories we have surveyed fully explains this primordial and universal human phenomenon. It is a reasonable conjecture that there are multiple sources of ritual sacrifice and that its practice in any particular context may include several overlapping meanings. In any case, acts of renunciation, the covering or purging of impurity or sin, the strengthening of the bonds of community, and the warding off of violence are deeply human and are not to be dismissed as merely the aberrant actions of ancient peoples.

Rituals as Sacraments

It will be helpful to conclude this analysis of sacred ritual with a brief consideration of ritual as *sacrament.* By so doing, we can summarize some of the most salient characteristics of sacred rite. Broadly speaking, all *religious* ritual is sacramental in that it concerns the presence of the sacred or holy. Sacraments make use of temporal things—words, gestures, and objects—for a spiritual purpose, to make manifest the sacred or the supernatural. A classic definition of a sacrament, found in the catechism of the Anglican *Book of Common Prayer*, states that it is "an outward and visible sign of an inward and spiritual grace." An important addition would be that sacraments do not, like symbols, simply signify or represent the sacred; they also *work*. Effective action is essential to sacraments. Evelyn Underhill underlines this point:

> The water cleanses, the bread and wine feed, the oil anoints, the imposition of consecrating hands conveys new character, the marriage act unites; and all this in the interior and spiritual as well as in the exterior and natural sense. . . . *A valid sacrament, therefore, always leaves the situation different from what is was before.* (Italics added.)[40]

Sacraments, like initiation ceremonies, are *performative* in the sense that they actually accomplish something; they change the status or condition of the participants. In many sacramental religions, such as Roman Catholicism, the efficacy of sacramental rites is not fundamentally dependent on the individual's subjective condition or feelings. The sacrament functions, according to Catholic doctrine, *ex opere operato* ("by the work worked"); that is, the rite itself has a causal power or efficacy beyond its subjective or psychological effects. Mary Douglas registers this performative character of sacraments in her comments on the Roman Catholic **Eucharist**. "Symbolizing," she writes

> does not exhaust the meaning of the Eucharist. Its full meaning involves . . . sacramental efficacy. . . . The crux of the doctrine is that a real, invisible transformation has taken place at the priest's saying of the sacred words and that the eating of the consecrated host has saving efficacy for those who take it and for others.[41]

Sacraments do, of course, have profound psychological and sociological effects, as do all rituals. The function of *catharsis*, or the clarification and purification of the emotions in ritual action, should not be underestimated. Nor should the wider sociological effects of sacraments be minimized in the least. Sacraments, like all rituals, bring attitudes and beliefs to a heightened state of consciousness, thereby strengthening these convictions and, in turn, fortifying the community. As the Chinese Confucianist would say: "Men become truly human as their raw impulse is shaped by *li* [ritual]." However, since social scientists have given such elaborate attention to the emotional and social functions of ritual, it is worth emphasizing their purely sacramental or spiritual efficacy.

Sacramental rites are *performative*, but related to this is their *repetitive character*. Sacramental action must be undertaken periodically at certain specified times of the season, the life cycle, or the liturgical calendar. The habitual, recurrent, and rhythmical character of sacramental ritual

is crucial to its effect. Sacraments simply cannot be random and unfamiliar because they are based not only on what is believed to be a
venerable tradition but—more important—on an exemplary model,
on an authorized, sacred, archetypal pattern of behavior.

Another characteristic of sacraments is the *meticulous accuracy of their
performance*, which is often considered essential to their efficacy. Therefore, the form of a sacramental ritual becomes fixed and conventional.
Departure from the traditional "way" can cause anxiety as to whether
the rite is actually achieving its effect. For this reason, sacramental
rites are the most conservative aspect of a community's religious life
and can be a source of weakness if the rituals become too conventional
and routinized and lose their vitality and relevance. This is the cause
of periodic antiritual protests by religious prophets and puritans
against the dead monotony of formal liturgical routine, of "going
through the traces."

Such forms of antiritualism are probably a sign that a certain dead-
ness has, indeed, set in. But authentic ritual is neither lifeless nor
unfeeling; quite the contrary, we have seen that it engages both individuals and communities at the deepest levels of their being. We can
conclude, then, by calling to mind Mary Douglas's claim and warning
that "ritual structure makes possible a wordless channel of communication."[42] Put another way, ritual can represent or create a structure
of meaning that is capable of binding us together; of reviving our
sense of participation in a larger human, even cosmic, drama; and
of restoring us to genuine *communitas*.

Notes

1. Hsün Tzu, "A Discussion of Rites," in *Basic Writings of Mo Tzu, Hsün
   Tzu and Han Fei Tzu*, trans. by Burton Watson. (New York, 1967),
   p. 94.
2. Among Harrison's important works are: *Prolegomena to the Study of Greek
   Religion* (Cambridge, 1903); *Themis: A Study of the Social Origins of Greek
   Religion* (Cambridge, 1912); *Ancient Art and Ritual* (Cambridge, 1913).
3. Jane Harrison, *Ancient Art and Ritual* (Cambridge, 1913), p. 49.
4. Clyde Kluckhohn, "Myths and Rituals: A General Theory," in W. A.
   Lessa and E. Z. Vogt, eds., *Reader in Comparative Religion*, 4th ed. (New
   York, 1979), pp. 69–70.
5. A. R. Radcliffe-Brown, *Taboo*, as cited in Lessa and Vogt, eds., *Reader
   in Comparative Religion*, 4th ed. (New York, 1979), p. 52.
6. _____ , *Taboo*, p. 56.
7. _____ , *Taboo*, p. 56.
8. Raymond Firth, *The Work of the Gods in Tikopia* (New York, 1967),
   p. 25, 23.
9. Johan Huizinga, *Homo Ludens* (Boston, 1950), p. 13.

10. Arnold van Gennep, *The Rites of Passage* (Chicago, 1960), pp. 2–3.
11. Mircea Eliade, *Rites and Symbols of Initiation* (New York, 1958).
12. Victor Turner, *The Ritual Process* (Chicago, 1969).
13. Turner, *Ritual Process*, p. 101.
14. Turner, *Ritual Process*, p. 128.
15. Raj Bali Pandey, *Hindu Samskaras* (Delhi, 1969), p. 75.
16. Pandey, *Samskaras*, p. 76.
17. Pandey, *Samskaras*, p. 76.
18. Mircea Eliade, *Rites and Symbols of Initiation* (New York, 1958), p. 39.
19. van Gennep, *Rites*, p. 81.
20. Holmes Welch, *The Practice of Chinese Buddhism* (Cambridge, Mass., 1967), p. 274.
21. Hsün Tzu, "A Discussion of Rites," p. 96.
22. Mircea Eliade, *Shamanism* (New York, 1964), p. 508.
23. The following is taken from Derek Freeman's account, entitled "Shaman and Incubus," in Warner Muensterberger and Sidney Alexrod, *The Psychoanalytical Study of Society* IV (New York, 1967), pp. 315–43.
24. Freeman, "Shaman," p. 326.
25. Theodore Gaster, *Thespis; Ritual, Myth, and Drama in the Ancient Near East* (New York, 1961), p. 23.
26. Gaster, *Thespis*, p. 26.
27. Henri Frankfort, *Kingship and the Gods* (Chicago, 1948), p. 319.
28. Frankfort, *Kingship*, p. 319.
29. Frankfort, *Kingship*, p. 296.
30. The Rev. Richard E. Power, *Our Mass: A Manual for the Dialogue Mass* (St. John's Abbey, Collegeville, Minn., 1956), p. 5.
31. Power, *Our Mass*, pp. 26–27.
32. Power, *Our Mass*, pp. 44–45.
33. E. B. Tylor, *Primitive Culture* II (New York, 1958), pp. 461–62.
34. Theodore Gaster, *Festivals of the Jewish Year* (New York, 1974), pp. 142–43.
35. Walter Burkert, *Homo Necans: The Anthropology of Ancient Greek Sacrificial Ritual and Myth* (Berkeley, 1983), p. 20.
36. Burkert, *Homo Necans*, p. 3.
37. René Girard, *Violence and the Sacred* (Baltimore, 1977), p. 113.
38. Girard, *Violence*, p. 31.
39. Girard, *Violence*, p. 306.
40. Evelyn Underhill, *Worship* (New York, 1957), p. 43.
41. Mary Douglas, *Natural Symbols* (New York, 1970), pp. 47–48.
42. Douglas, *Natural Symbols*, p. 33.

Review Questions

1. Define a religious ritual. What characteristics of rituals make them so common and important?
2. According to scholars who employ functional analysis, rituals have certain *values* for persons and for communities that may

not be apparent to the participants. Can you think of social values (including some unconscious ones) that some specific rituals may serve in our society?
3. What are the similarities between religious ritual and human play?
4. Describe the three-fold pattern of life-cycle rites as developed by Arnold van Gennep and Victor Turner. According to Turner, what is the significance of what he calls the "liminal" period?
5. In our often-secular Western society, life-cycle rites are not as prevalent or as important as they are in some cultures. However, ritual baptisms, bar mitzvahs, weddings, and funerals are still common events. Indicate the symbolic meanings of some features of one or more of these rites that you have observed.
6. Desribe the four-fold ritual structure of seasonal rituals as described by Theodore Gaster. Indicate how this structure is illustrated in the movements of the Babylonian Akitu Festival.
7. Describe what is involved in the religious ritual of expiation, or atonement, including the several movements of the rite.
8. Define a sacrament and indicate the several characteristics of sacramental rites.

Suggestions for Further Reading

DOUGLAS, MARY, *Natural Symbols* (New York: Pantheon Books, 1970).

DURKHEIM, EMILE, *The Elementary Forms of the Religious Life* (New York: The Free Press, 1969).

ELIADE, MIRCEA, *Rites and Symbols of Initiation* (New York: Harper and Row, 1958).

GASTER, THEODORE H., *Thespis: Ritual, Myth, and Drama in the Ancient Near East* (New York: Doubleday, 1961).

GIRARD, RENÉ, *Violence and the Sacred* (Baltimore: Johns Hopkins Press, 1977).

GLUCKMAN, MAX (ed.), *Essays on the Ritual of Social Relations* (Manchester: Manchester University Press, 1962).

GRIMES, RONALD L., *Beginnings in Ritual Studies* (Lanham, Md.: University Press of America, 1982).

————, *Research in Ritual Studies* (Metuchen, N.J., and London: Scarecrow Press, 1985).

HEILER, FRIEDRICH, *Prayer* (Oxford: Oxford University Press, 1937).

HUIZENGA, JOHAN, *Homo Ludens: A Study of the Play Element in Culture* (Boston: Beacon Press, 1950).

KRISTENSEN, W. BREDE, "Cultus," *The Meaning of Religion* (The Hague: Martinus Nijhoff, 1971).

LESSA, WILLIAM A., and EVON Z. VOGT, *Reader in Comparative Religion: An Anthropological Approach*, 4th ed. (New York: Harper and Row, 1979).

TURNER, VICTOR, *The Ritual Process* (Chicago: Aldine Publishing Co., 1969.)

UNDERHILL, EVELYN, *Worship* (New York: Harper Torchbook, 1957).

VAN DER LEEUW, GERARDUS, "Outward Action," *Religion in Essence and Manifestation* II (New York: Harper Torchbooks, 1963).

VAN GENNEP, ARNOLD, *Rites of Passage* (Chicago: University of Chicago Press, 1960).

CHAPTER 6

Society and the Sacred: Social and Ethical Dimensions of Religion

OVERVIEW

We human beings are not isolated individual units or islands. To be a human being means, fundamentally, to be a social being. The wild boy of Aveyron, raised with animals and isolated from human community, was not considered fully human. In this chapter, we look at some—but by no means all—social dimensions of religion and some of the important ways in which religion and society relate, often in a reciprocal or symbiotic way. We shall begin with the debate over whether religion is essentially a reflection of more-fundamental social realities or whether religion is a powerful independent creator of profound social values, institutions, and behavior.

The focus of this chapter, however, is an analysis of a variety of types of religious societies and the social and religious dynamics of their development, change, and dissolution. One basic type of religious society is the natural community, that is, one based on kinship ties, race, nationality, or geography. A second type is the voluntary religious group whose membership is based on common beliefs, special functions, or sacred powers that extend beyond the natural ties of kinship or geography. These include secret societies that often maintain close affiliation with the kinship group while, at the same time, remaining autonomous.

Another type of voluntary group is the "founded" religion. It is established by a charismatic seer or prophet who brings a new revelation or spiritual message and whose authority commands disciples.

The "founded" religious community faces unique problems on the death of the founder, and the means employed by the community to sustain itself and to grow are discussed.

The church-type voluntary religious community is another example. It also experiences special strains and challenges often not encountered by natural religious communities. We shall explore the ways in which the church-type religion manages protest and reform, both from within—for example, the church-within-the-church and monasticism— and by secession. This shall lead us to an extended analysis of the sect-type religious group, a form of voluntary religious community that is found throughout the world. The ideal features of the sect-type are discussed, as are the distinctive features of several different groups that share sect characteristics, such as the evangelical or conversionist sect, the revolutionist sect, and the introversionist sect. Each of the several sect-type communities reflects a peculiar response to the wider society and to the world. The chapter appropriately concludes with several illustrations of how a religious community's understanding of ethical obligation determines whether its attitudes toward society and the world are world-accepting, world-denying, or world-transforming.

The Reciprocal Relationship Between Religion and Society

There is little doubt that social systems influence the form and even the substance of religion. It also is obvious that religious beliefs and values have served as critical forces in social and cultural change. The question, of course, has to do with the relative importance that is given to social and material conditions and, conversely, to the role of ideals and human agents as causal factors in human history.

An example of the perspective of Emile Durkheim and his followers can be seen in *The Birth of the Gods* by sociologist Guy Swanson. Swanson claims to have discovered definite correlations between certain social structures—primarily political sovereignty—and specific types of religious belief—monotheism, polytheism, reincarnation, and so on. He begins his study by asserting that "we assume that insofar as a group has sovereignty, it is likely to provide the conditions from which a concept of spirit originates."[1] He insists that people experience supernatural qualities because specific types of social relationships "inherently possess the characteristics we identify as supernatural," that is, certain "constitutional arrangements" that are often unconsciously taken for granted.[2] "Constitutional structures, and especially those of sovereign groups . . . are what men often conceptualize as personified and supernatural beings."[3]

Swanson is, of course, correct that religious ideas and structures often are drawn from and mirror social relations. We need only consider the use of filial imagery in many religious traditions, for example, the metaphor of Father in Christian language about God ("Our Father who art in Heaven") and its use of Father and Son in describing the relationship between God and Jesus Christ. It is also evident that the structure of the Roman Catholic Church reflects the organization of the old Roman Empire into parish, diocese, and province. Sexual relations and roles are another instance. In a religion such as Islam, the sexual patterns of Arabic society — in this case, a strongly patriarchal social structure — are mirrored by the limited role of women in the religion itself. Having recognized the obviously formative role of society on religion, it would nevertheless be wrong to assume a one-way social determinism.

Religious beliefs and practice also play a critical role in the change and evolution of societies. This was one of Max Weber's most important contributions to the study of religion. For Weber, religion is a powerful causal factor influencing social action and social structures. In this, he countered Marx's influential idea that religion is merely an epiphenomenon, that is, a mere reflection of more-fundamental realities. As we recall from Chapter 2, in his book *The Protestant Ethic and the Spirit of Protestantism*, Weber argues that the ethic of Protestantism preceded the emergence of *modern* capitalism and was a crucial factor in its development. In his study of the religions of China, India, and ancient Israel, he further demonstrated that varying religious conceptions of salvation shape economic behavior and other practical choices and decisions—and hence the fundamental value structure or ethos of these societies. An example is the influence of the Hindu belief in reincarnation on the practice of caste duty in India.

Weber did not, however, propose that religion is a wholly independent causality—as if it were free of, or only marginally influenced by, material conditions and social structures. For Weber, religious ideals and values and socioeconomic structures are interactive; the relationship is complex and dependent on many variables. Ideas are rooted in and shaped by material and social conditions, yet these beliefs are not static; they are embodied in persons and persons are not passive, inert things. As the carriers of ideas and values, persons participate in the process of social change. Religious prophets, sages, and saints often introduce quite unexpected new disclosures of truth and reality. While remaining at one level continuous with their social world, they introduce something radically new. One thinks of the great eighth and ninth century (B.C.E.) prophets of Israel, of Jesus within Judaism in the first century C.E., and of Gautama Buddha in 6th century (B.C.E.) India.

The dynamic, interdependent relationship between society and religion means that religion can often functionally serve society in a number of positive ways, some of which we have mentioned in our discussion of sacred ritual. Conversely, religion can be a disintegrating factor for a society, serving as engine of radical social change, even revolution. The same religious belief or activity can be viewed as functional or dysfunctional. For example, religion can provide a society with a world view or interpretation of human nature. However, it can also socialize ideas that can stand as obstacles to the development of knowledge or progress.

Types of Religious Communities

It is evident that, at both the ideational (ideas and values) and the institutional levels, religions are shaped by their material and social environments in significant ways. Since all religions involve some form of community or fellowship, It is worth exploring the relationship between social structures and types of religious groups, as well as the dynamics of change in these communities.

Natural Religious Communities

There are important differences to be observed between "natural" and "founded," or voluntary, religious groups. In natural religious communities, there is little differentiation between the religious and the sociocultural life of the community: family life, polity, the economy, warfare, medicine, and so forth. Religion is interwoven Into all these activities. Furthermore, natural religious groups are joined by biological–blood relations, kinship (clan and tribe), geography (region and nation), or culture. The individual is born into or marries into the group. On the other hand, "founded" religions are dependent on the unique authority of a charismatic leader, on the teachings or ideology that he or she professes, and on personal conversion to that teaching or doctrine. It is therefore voluntary rather than based on natural ties of blood or kinship.

The distinction is not quite this neat, however, since natural religious groups do contain special subgroups that are based on the possession of certain gifts, powers, or functions. Conversely, voluntary religions often divide into smaller subcommunities that, while based on commonly shared beliefs, nevertheless become so identified with blood and family ties that they are indistinguishable from natural religious communities. This has often been the case in Christian history, for example, in some ethnic groups within Eastern Orthodoxy and Roman Catholicism and, more strikingly, in communities such as the Amish and Hutterite Brethren. These groups make no effort to evangelize those outside and seek to perpetuate the community through procreation and nurture. In time, little distinction is made between cultural ethos and religion.

Because natural religions are maintained through blood, kinship, race, or nation, great attention is devoted to rites of passage and especially to the religious significance of fertility and procreation, puberty, marriage, death, and ancestor veneration or worship. All these rites represent vital links in maintaining the family bond over the generations. In voluntary religions, the members are bound by doctrines and ethical ties that do not require the same attention to rites ensuring the perpetuation of the extended family. Hence, in contemporary Western religion, birth and puberty rites often are marginal, if not wholly absent, and marriage and death rites are frequently quite private affairs, certainly no longer communal rites of immense importance. Such is not the case in natural religious groups, either primitive or modern. The imperative of marriage remains marrying within the clan, tribe, or racial group. For example, Abraham, father of the 12 tribes of Israel, expressed deep concern that his son Isaac not marry a daughter of the Canaanites (Genesis 24:2ff). Again, in the religious reforms carried out under the Israelite king Josiah in the seventh century B.C.E. (Deuteronomy 7:3–5) and during the restoration of Judea by Ezra and Nehemiah two centuries later, the matter of marriage is a central motif:

> In those days also I saw the Jews who had married women of Ashdod, Ammon, and Moab; and half of their children spoke the language of Ashdod, and they could not speak the language of Judah, but the language of each people. And I contended with them and cursed them and beat some of them . . . and made them take oath in the name of God, saying, 'You shall not give your daughters to their sons, or take their daughters for your sons or for yourselves.'
> *(Nehemiah 13:23–25)*

Another way natural religious communities join the family, clan, or nation in kinship is through ancestor veneration. Here, the deceased are bound together with the living in a seamless web of generations. This is a crucial aspect of caste Hinduism, Japanese Shinto, and Chinese Confucianism. It is also the central motif in the life of the Dahomey tribal nation of West Africa. It is believed that the ongoing life and well-being of each Dahomey sibling group or extended family is dependent on the appropriate care and veneration of the dead ancestors through the carrying out of costly, elaborate, and lengthy funeral ceremonies for all dead adults, as well as through rites in which the descendants are properly "established," or deified. This is because it is believed that the ancestors, though departed, continue to exert an influence on the sibling community, as do the living on their descendants. During the ceremonial funeral dance of the siblings, they are reminded:

> Your fathers and your kinsmen
> Shall never wear torn clothes because of the neglect of their
>   children who remain in life;
> And when fine clothes are worn,
> Your ancestors shall appear in *lubik pa*.[4]

Every sibling family is called on to build a special house in which the worship of the ancestors is held, including the conduct of sacrifices to provide for their care. If the deification ritual is not fulfilled, members of the family begin to die, the head of the community being the first. It is critical, therefore, that the ceremony of "establishing" the ancestors be completed by each of the Dahomey sibling groups.

Melville Herskovits summarizes this fundamental role of the ancestral cult:

> All persons eventually become deified as familial gods. . . . Whether of royal blood or commoner, however, the importance of the ancestral cult is paramount. In the life of every Dahomean, his ancestors stand between him and the gods who personify the forces of the universe that periodically threaten him with destruction. As an integral part of social organization, on the one hand, and of religious expression, on the other, the respect and worship of the ancestors may then be thought of as one of the great unifying forces that, for the Dahomean, give meaning and logic to life.[5]

The largest natural religious community is the race nation or nationality. The nation—or folk, as it is sometimes called—is not technically based on race. Nevertheless, the people believe that they share a common ancestry, history, and tradition. Here, the symbiotic relation between society and religion is especially striking because religion finds in the national–cultural institutions powerful means for its expression. Society, in turn, sees in religion the sacred legitimation of its order, its values, and its destiny.

National religions often trace the nation and its people back to a sacred origin, even as descendants of the gods, and view the king or emperor as representative or incarnation of deity itself. Here, there is a perfect symmetry between the divine cosmic order and the political order, between the macrocosm and the microcosm. This type of national religion was dominant in the ancient Near East, for example in Egypt, Babylonia, and Assyria. In each instance, the king served as the god's representative. This type was also present in ancient

Rome, where the emperor not only took on the high priestly role of Pontifex Maximus but also, finally, was deified as a god incarnate.

Examples of national religion are not, however, a thing of the archaic past. Japanese State Shinto is a vivid illustration of its presence in the twentieth century. According to Japanese mythology, the Japanese islands were created by the sexual union of two gods, the primal male and primal female (see Chapter 8), and the first human emperor, Jimmu Tenno, is portrayed as descended from the sun-goddess, Amaterasu. According to tradition, Jimmu Tenno established his capital on the island of Honshu in 660 B.C.E. Here, then, are the ingredients of a national religion: a divinely created land, people, and emperor—and a divine destiny.

Japanese Shinto was not, however, highly nationalistic until quite recently. For centuries, it represented a form of preanimism, that is, the worship of mana-like power, present in certain gods, persons, and objects associated with the rulers. Shinto's latent nationalism was revived, however, through its political restoration by the Emperor Meiji in 1868. State Shinto, as it is called, was purified of foreign—that is, Confucian and Buddhist—elements and, by constitutional and educational means, the focus of public attention was placed on reverence for and obedience to the emperor and on Japan's unique national destiny.

The Meiji Constitution (1889) asserted that "the Emperor is sacred and inviolable," and in a commentary on the constitution Prince Itō wrote that "the Sacred Throne was established at the time when the heavens and the earth became separated. The Emperor is Heaven descended, divine and sacred: He is preeminent above all his subjects . . . the law has no power to hold him accountable to it."[6]

An imperial decree on education (1890) joined obedience to the emperor with unswerving loyalty to the Japanese state and empire: "Always respect the Constitution and observe the laws: should emergency arise, offer yourselves courageously for the State; and thus guard and maintain the prosperity of Our Imperial Throne coeval with heaven and earth."[7] Shinto thus emerged from the Meiji period as a cult of nationalistic patriotism. It contributed, in the years before World War II, to a growing Japanese militancy and war fever. Schools taught young Japanese that Japan stood high above the other nations of the world, and that her people excelled other peoples. Here, religion was serving the national political interests of an expansive military power.

The uses of religion for political ends is not, of course, unique to natural religious communities; the history of Christianity and Islam make this point indelibly plain. We see in natural religious groups, however, a most powerful weaving of the natural, the societal, and the religious into an often-seamless fabric.

Voluntary Religious Communities

The relation between religion and the natural and social environment is never without some tension, even in the most stable and homogeneous of natural religious groups. There are unpredictable spiritual strains and demands. Closer communion with sacred power may be called for, which requires special talents or spiritual gifts, for example, an elite fraternity of priests or shamans. In an extreme case, certain social institutions may come to be seen as impediments to a genuine access to the sacred or the transcendent. Some religious fraternities may therefore separate or even break away from the larger natural group. It may even reach the point where the new group regards the larger society and its cultural values as of little import or, indeed, as actually evil.

A growing consciousness of "inwardness," of a new and distinct spiritual life, which challenges the customary bonds of society, is an important factor leading to voluntary religious groups even within the natural community. The new spiritual association is set off from other members of the same sex, kin, or race.

The voluntary religious group has certain distinct features. First, there is at least a partial break with the natural ties. The new spiritual unity often is based on religious function—for example, priesthood—but also, and more often, on a new spiritual insight or experience of the sacred or of spiritual power. This may entail a feeling of regeneration or conversion, deepening a sense of intimacy with the new fellowship but also loosening the ties with the natural kin who do not share in this sacred experience. The old natural ties of blood and kinship may now even count for naught.

Where the break with natural bonds becomes relatively complete, as in the universal voluntary religions such as Islam, Buddhism, or Christianity, those social relations that were essential to the natural religious community may also lose their hold. Marriage within the group, for example, may no longer be important. What is important is union with another person who is committed to the same spiritual doctrine or experience; or chastity and vows of celibacy may be considered the highest spiritual ideal—that of priest, monk, or nun—as in the case of Roman Catholicism and Theravada Buddhism. The religion no longer is sustained merely by procreation but, rather, by evangelization, proselytization, and conversion.

In voluntary religions, rites centering on the veneration of the ancestors also play little or no role. In fact, the Buddhist monk ritually severs ties with his natural family. Jesus turned to the multitudes following him and asserted, "If any one comes to me and does not hate his own father and mother and wife and children and brothers and sisters, yes, and even his own life, he cannot be my disciple"

(Luke 14:26). It is often remarked how Islam's radical monotheism transcends ethnic, racial, and national boundaries.

THE SECRET SOCIETY   Perhaps in only the universal "founded" religions are natural folk ties weakened; but natural bonds and folk beliefs continually assert themselves in the universal religions as well. This can be observed, for example, in the nationalism of the early Japanese Nichiren sect and in the growth of South Asian Buddhist nationalism today, and, of course, in the history of the various ethnic churches and denominations within Christianity. A more-common form of voluntary religious community is the secret society *within* the larger natural community. They are found in almost every natural religious group, and their membership is distinguished by the fact of selection or election. Their rites and teachings are secret, and they are the exclusive possession of the society. Admission follows a period of thorough instruction and severe testing to ensure the fitness of those enlisted.

The secret society often arises out of dissatisfaction with the traditional natural religion. This was true of the famous "mystery religions" of ancient Greece and Rome, such as the Eleusinian, Orphic, and Dionysian cults. The public and imperial cults lacked direct contact with the divine, and they offered no hope of immortality, which was promised by participation in the "mysteries."

Secret fraternities are especially common among the North American Indians, in West African tribal communities, and in Melanesia and Polynesia. The anthropologist Paul Radin has described the rich variety of subreligious groups among the North American Winnebago Indians, including special clans and professional associations, for example, of warriors. But the Winnebago also have many secret societies whose membership is dependent on receiving the blessings of the same spirit or on participation in the same "medicine" group.

One of these is the society of those especially blessed by the grizzly bear. The center of the society's cult is the ritual grizzly bear dance. Women are not allowed to participate in the rite. In the lodge constructed for the dance, there is a mound of earth representing the bear's cave. The dancing takes place around the lodge and around the earth mound, the movements representing those of the grizzly bear. The dancers vie with one another in exhibiting the powers with which they have been especially blessed, the purpose of the dance being to thank the grizzly bears for their favors. Radin describes the remarkable dance of Little Priest, a Winnebago who was seriously wounded and near death. The story tells of the special powers possessed by a member of this "medicine" group. It was decided that the grizzly bear dance would be performed for Little Priest since he had been blessed by the bears as a child.

The dance was to be given at the lodge of an Indian named Good Soldier. They carried Little Priest to the lodge in a blanket, so that they could sing for him and permit him to show the powers he possessed. He was unable to move on account of the wounds and the bruises he had gotten. The man who sang for him at the time was South-Wind. Little Priest told South-Wind that he was a grizzly bear and that he could heal himself.

As soon as the songs and dancing commenced Little Priest began to move his little fingers. Soon he was able to move his arm as far as his forearm, and gradually he regained the power of moving the entire arm. Finally he sat up and began to keep time on the drum. Then he tried to stand on his feet, but owing to his weakness it was only with the greatest difficulty that he could straighten out his body. Finally he stood erect. Then he started to walk around the lodge very slowly. The second circuit he made more easily, and by the time he had made the fourth circuit he was dancing just as the other dancers were with all his strength restored. Then he walked to the [mound], took some earth, rubbed it on his wounds, and they were healed immediately [8]

FOUNDED RELIGIONS[9]   Among the voluntary type of religious community is the "founded" religion with its own distinctive characteristics. As the name implies, the community is established through the unique role of a religious leader. This person is variously called a prophet, reformer, teacher, or master. He or she is, first, a *witness* to a new revelation or a new spiritual wisdom. The witness then speaks of this new spiritual truth as a prophet or enlightened master. But no founder produces a new religion *de novo*; he or she is usually a powerful reformer, building on the foundation of an existing religion. Zoroaster, Buddha, Jesus, and Muhammad were all reformers in this sense. But they were also more than reformers; what they established was also something new. What is distinctive about the founder is a decisive religious experience followed by the enlisting of disciples. The founder possesses a unique and compelling authority, usually both in his or her person and teaching. Max Weber spoke of this distinct power as *charisma*, "a certain quality of an individual personality by virtue of which he is set apart from ordinary men and treated as endowed with supernatural, superhuman, or at least specifically exceptional powers or qualities."[10]

It is this special charisma possessed by the prophet or seer that captivates disciples and sparks the new religious movement. The disciples are drawn together by their shared religious insight, which is interpreted to them by the founder. Their commitment to the founder and to the fellowship may demand a sharp break with the natural community, with the ties of family and kinship, and with the civil authority. It is this severing of kinship bonds, the claim of doctrine over blood, that Max Weber considers the achievement of the great universal, "ethical" religions.

The companions of the founder—who are also apostles spreading the new teaching—face a horrendous crisis at the death of their master. What is to be done when the personal charismatic authority of the leader is no longer present? How is the spiritual authority to be preserved and passed on? How are questions to be answered? Who or what is to guide and to inspire? Many voluntary religious groups never survive their leader's death. Two recent examples are the Father Divine Peace Mission in New York and the Peoples Temple in Jonestown, Guyana; these communities collapsed with the death of Father Divine (1965) and the Reverend James Jones (1978).

On the death of the founder, the future of the spiritual fellowship rests on its message and its organization, rather than on the leader's personal charisma. The community has reached a turning point. If it is to survive and be spared divisive conflicts among the followers, a number of things, characteristically, are to be done. First, the oral teachings and the practices of the founder must be collected, systematized, and established as an official canon of sacred writings. To simplify teaching and to establish conditions of membership, a standardized rule of faith or creed is often produced. The community frequently must defend its ongoing life in the wider society; hence, the necessity of creating apologetical writings. Worship and discipline must also be standardized, based on the teachings and practices of the founder. Most important, the *ecclesia*, or fellowship, must organize itself more formally, establishing a constitution, clear functions, and lines of authority. For example, in the primitive Christian *ecclesia*, there soon emerged deacons, presbyters, and the episcopate. As the authority of spiritually (charismatically) gifted persons declined, or became problematic for the community, a clearer distinction was made between "clergy" and "laity." All of this process is what Weber calls "the routinization of charisma"—the standardizing of doctrine, discipline, cult, and organization.

The English word *church* (*ecclesia*, meaning "people called by God") has a definite Christian origin. Not all large-scale voluntary religious communities have evolved organizational structures similar to that of the Christian Church. The Buddhist Sangha ("assembly"), or monastic order, does not include laymen and therefore is, in some respects, more like a Catholic monastic order. The Muslim *ummah* (the entire community of those "surrendered" to Allah) has more in common, perhaps, with the Christian *ecclesia*. What they all share, however, when compared to the Hindu caste or Confucian family, is a break with natural religious ties and, at least ideally, commitment to a spiritual message and life *universal* in its outreach. As they developed, Islam, Mahayana Buddhism, and Christianity all were required to develop organizational structures different from those of the early spiritual brotherhood, the inner circle of disciples. These larger structures, concerned with maintaining doctrine, discipline, and cult, can properly be called church-type organizations.

Protest and Change in Voluntary Religious Communities

All human organizations experience the stresses and strains brought on by discord among their members concerning beliefs and practice. Even the most closely knit kinship group will find within it both the highly zealous and the relatively indifferent, the orthodox conformist and the questioner. Furthermore, different persons have different needs and goals. This explains, in part, the emergence of special subgroups and secret societies in almost all natural religious communities.

Discord, protest, and calls for reform and change are, however, especially prevalent in voluntary religious groups, that is, in church-type communities. From the beginning, there is the tension between the "true believers" and those prone to lapse in their discipleship. There are the inevitable disagreements over the interpretation of scripture or doctrine, over cultic practice, and over authority. All these tensions make the church-type community more vulnerable to protest, conflict, and even secession.

Protest, reform, and renewal can be either individual or collective and can either take place within the community or result in withdrawal from it. If the reformer is to be socially effective, he or she must gain followers and can do so only by exhibiting the requisite authority. A list of reformers whose protest and renewal involved either a "purifying" of an original revelation or a more-radical "restatement" of the original faith would include St. Philip Neri, Martin Luther, John Calvin, John Wesley, Joseph Smith, and Mary Baker Eddy within Christianity; Nichiren and Shinran in Japanese Buddhism; and Muhammad ibn' Abd al Wahhab and Mizra Ghulam Ahmad in Islam. Here, we will describe successful reforms that were achieved *within* the larger voluntary church-type community and then those that were accomplished only through secession from the original church.

Reform From Within the Church

Calls for reform or more-radical change may be handled *within* the community in a number of ways. The dissidents may be shown the error of their ways and be brought back into conformity with the majority. In the Roman Catholic Church, many priests and bishops who in the 1860s vigorously opposed the majority's wish for an official declaration by the Church on the infallibility of the pope, were reconciled to this development when it was in fact declared a dogma in 1870. Often, a compromise is struck by which the protesters are somehow accommodated within the larger community.

THE *ECCLESIOLA IN ECCLESIA*   It often happens that a small group within the church becomes concerned about the community's "laxity" or carelessness with regard to doctrine, discipline, or worship. Yet the protesters do not wish to secede. This was true of Philipp Jacob Spener (1635–1705), the father of the movement within German Lutheranism called Pietism, and of John Wesley (1703–1791), the founder of Methodism, who organized Methodist societies *within* the established Church of England in order to renew the spiritual life of the people. What both men wished to do was to establish a spiritual "leaven" within the larger church community — a little church (*ecclesiola*) within the larger church (*ecclesia*). These men were not finally successful since their followers withdrew from the mother churches and organized the separate Moravian and Methodist church-type communities that exist today.

Spener introduced into Lutheranism small meetings for the purpose of prayer, devotions, and Bible study. He called for less emphasis on the difference between clergy and laity. He was not interested in the finer points of Lutheran theology but, rather, in the deepening of personal piety, sanctity, and devotion. Spener called these small meetings "colleges of piety" (*collegia pietatis*). Similar "churches within the Church" were found in early Puritanism and the early Society of Friends (Quakers) and also in such pious and mystical movements as Hasidism within orthodox Judaism and Sufism in Islam. Joachim Wach describes the common features of all these *collegia pietatis*:

> [It] is a loosely organized group, limited in numbers and united in a common enthusiasm, peculiar convictions, intense devotion, and rigid discipline, which is striving to attain a higher spiritual and moral perfection than can be realized under prevailing conditions.[11]

What is also common to the *ecclesiola in ecclesia* is, of course, an explicit protest against the larger church that, if too pronounced and too prolonged, may lead to division.

MONASTICISM   Another classic form of protest and reform from within is the institution of monasticism. In the Roman Catholic Church, this has been perhaps the best-known form of resolving conflict and of accommodating always-new eruptions of spiritual zeal and

calls for a stricter discipline. As early as the third century C.E., ancho-
rites—or desert hermits—joined in Christian communities to develop
a strict rule of spiritual life and work. In Western Christianity, the
rules of the monastic community were classically formulated by St.
Benedict in the sixth century C.E. Monasticism, however, is a common
feature of many of the great religious traditions. In early Buddhism,
it *was* the church (the Sangha).

Unlike the *ecclesiola in ecclesia*, which includes families engaged in
worldly activities, the monastic community calls for a more-fundamental rejection of worldly compromise; indeed, it calls for a denial of,
or near denial of, the world and its ways—and thus a more-radical
spiritual ideal. Some monastic orders, like the Cistercian Trappists
(men) and the Strict Observance Carmelites (women), require a relatively severe ascetical discipline, but most Catholic orders follow the
moderate rule established by St. Benedict.

While restrained in its discipline, the Benedictine rule nevertheless
does require a more demanding spirituality than would be possible
for the average layman. The monks' day is divided among worship,
work, and study. They share everything; dress cheaply and simply;

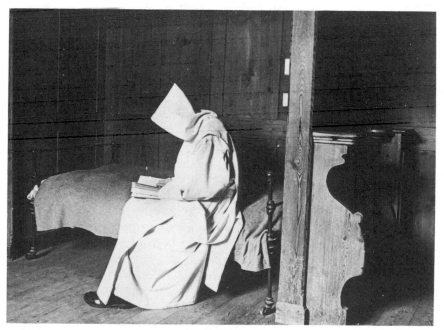

A Carthusian monk sits reading and in contemplation in his cell at St.
Hugh's Charterhouse monastery in Sussex, England. The monk passes
most of his life praying, studying, eating, and working in solitude.
(*Source*: Courtesy of Religious News Service.)

and eat twice a day on a diet of bread, vegetables, and fruit. Silence
is enjoined at all times. Poverty, chastity, and obedience are required.
The simplicity and rigor of the rule is evident in Benedict's 72 precepts, among which are the following:

> Not to be fond of pleasures.
> To become a stranger to the ways of the world.
> Not to be fond of much talking.
> Often to devote oneself to prayer.
> Not to give way to the desires of the flesh; and to hate one's
> own will.
> In all things to obey the abbot's commands, even though he
> himself should act otherwise.[12]

Later ventings of spiritual zeal and devotion in the Catholic Church
were legitimized through the establishment of new religious orders,
each one meant to direct certain spiritual gifts into official channels:
the Franciscans (providing humanitarian service, especially to the poor),
the Dominicans (preaching the faith), the Jesuits (defending the faith
against heresy and performing missionary work), and the Trappists
(encouraging liturgical worship, study, and silent contemplation).

The enthusiasm or the integrity of a movement within the church-
type community may become so powerful and the resistance so strong
as to propel the reformers beyond the pale of the church into dissent
and secession. Such a move may be long coming and undertaken
regretfully. Other forms of withdrawal may come, however, as a joyful
liberation from "Babel," from a sense that the older community has
lost its integrity and hence its capacity to save genuinely.

Secession From the Church-Type Community

When the new community breaks irrevocably with the original church,
it is because it has (1) discovered in the original teachings norms of
belief and practice once delivered to the saints, but that are now
overlooked or denied, or (2) it claims a new, independent revelation
or teaching that stands as a challenge to both the church and the
larger society and culture. In either case, the new teaching becomes
the standard of the new-founded community. The voluntary and universal nature of the church-type religious community invites such
movements of "renewal," as well as further "revelations" that often,
in turn, claim to be the definitive teaching forbidding new developments.

Examples of the first kind of secession would be the establishment
of independent Lutheran, Reformed, Anabaptist, and Anglican
churches *within* Christianity at the time of the Protestant Reformation

in Europe in the sixteenth century; the division *within* Judaism between Orthodoxy and the modern movements of Conservatism and Reform Judaism; or the emergence *within* Islam and Buddhism of several subsects or movements—each of which claims a new spiritual insight, teaching, or norm of authority. Examples of the second and more-radical type of protest would be the early Christian community's break with Judaism, involving the former's claim to be the New Israel; Buddhism's emergence out of and yet rejection of some of the fundamental doctrines of Hinduism; or the claims of Mormonism and Christian Science to have new revelations and new authoritative scriptures (the *Book of Mormon* and *Science and Health*) other than the Christian Bible. In all of these latter instances, as well as in some of the former, the reformer (Jesus, Buddha, Joseph Smith, and Mary Baker Eddy) caused his or her followers to secede from the mother community and to establish an independent, separatist group or sect.

The Sect

The word *sect* has long carried a disparaging connotation, implying something strange and deviant, perhaps even contemptible. It was, indeed, originally used by churches to describe heretical and schismatic groups. However, the word is used today by scholars simply to distinguish sociologically certain types of voluntary religious communities from others with different sociological features, for example, from the *ecclesia* or established churches; from the *ecclesiola in ecclesia*; and from a more-recent ecclesiastical institution, the **denomination**.

In *The Protestant Ethic and the Spirit of Capitalism*, Max Weber first noted the distinction between church and sect and discussed the factors involved in their development. These differences were explored more extensively by Weber's pupil, Ernst Troeltsch, in his study *The Social Teachings of the Christian Churches*. Since these two epochal studies, sociologists have worked on refining a **typology** of religious groups and, more important, on determining the social as well as the religious factors involved in the development and change of specific types of religious communities, especially the sect-type.

Sects differ from churches and denominations in a number of ways. While no sect perfectly exemplifies the ideal type, scholars are agreed that the sect is distinct in joining the following characteristics:

1. The sect tends to be exclusive.
2. The sect claims to have a monopoly on the religious truth.
3. The sect tends to be lay-organized and to reject or downplay a religious division of labor. Religious obligations are equal and shared by all in the group.

4. The sect is strongly marked by voluntarism; that is, each member usually is required to show some knowledge or change of life in order to be accepted.
5. The sect demands the total allegiance of the member in all areas of life; hence, membership in the sect is the individual's most important means of personal identification.
6. The sect exercises sanctions against the wayward to the point of expulsion of the deviant from the sect.
7. The sect is a protest group, not only against the church but also against the wider culture and the state.[13]

No actual sect conforms perfectly to all these features. Sects do tend, however, to be small, rigorous, and selective rather than broad and inclusive, as are established churches. Unlike churches, sects often are not deeply involved in the wider society; sects not infrequently are alienated from the surrounding culture. The rigor and alienation of sects also may express themselves in nonconformist dress or in a deviant style of living.

Following the work of Weber and Troeltsch, the American scholar H. R. Niebuhr sharply distinguished the sect-type religious community from the church-type. Most important, Niebuhr theorized that genuine sects are short lived and become denominations in the course of one generation. He claimed that if a sect, as a radical protest group, does not wither away, the upward social and economic mobility of its members and the change from voluntary membership to second-generation membership through birth will cause the sect to move to the status of a denomination. If it survives, the sect must focus on the nurture and education of its young, on organization, and on the acquisition and management of property. Moreover, the second generation rarely holds the convictions with the zeal of their parents; secular commitments and the desire for social respectability intrude. The sect thus becomes "denominationalized"; it becomes a form of church-type community that is limited by boundaries of social class, race, and ethnicity or region, and that displays more liberal and tolerant attitudes toward other religious groups, greater accommodation to the "secular" world, and rather more formality in worship and leadership.[14] The denomination, as Niebuhr observed, is a dominantly American type of religious association, although it has become common in other parts of the English-speaking world. This points to a weakness in Niebuhr's sect analysis. It is generally conceded today that Niebuhr mistook the sequence of development of a certain type of American "conversionist" sect for a universal and inevitable social process of sect growth and change.

More recently, sociologists have demonstrated that the sect typologies worked out by Weber, Troeltsch, and Niebuhr reflect too-narrow preoccupations with Western Christian forms of religious community. All three fail to do justice to the sect-type groups that are found in other religious cultures and in Western culture since the decline in the special status of the older European established churches. Bryan Wilson is prominent among those sociologists who have suggested a new typology of sect-type communities.[15] Wilson believes that the sect is a universal form of religious community, far more pervasive than the dominantly Western church or denomination. Furthermore, there are a number of distinctive types of sects or religious movements, some prone to "denominalization" while others are apparently immune to the alternatives of denominational development or dissolution.

Wilson proposes a typology of seven types of sects, each one expressive of a distinctive "response to the world." The *conversionist* sect is characteristic of fundamentalist and pentecostal groups within Protestant Christianity. These groups have little or no interest in programs of social reform. What is called for is a highly emotional, personal spiritual conversion experience. The evil of the world is transcended by this radically new, subjective experience of salvation here and now.

The *revolutionist* sect believes that salvation will come soon, but only with the destruction of the present natural and social order. This process of destruction will be supernaturally wrought, although the believers may participate in the process. What is looked for, however, is a new dispensation, a new order that is seen as historically imminent. Salvation will come only by divine action. An American example of this type of sect is the Jehovah's Witnesses. Wilson sees the revolutionist sect as one of the most distinctive sect movements in contemporary less-developed countries. The Jamaican Ras Tafarians typify the supernatural utopianism of this kind of religious group.

The *introversionist* sect neither attempts to convert individuals in the world nor expects the imminent destruction of the world and the coming of a new order. Rather, this group perceives the world as irredeemably evil and salvation as possible only through renunciation and withdrawal from the wider society and the establishment of a separate holy community. This type of sect is indifferent to general social reform or social revolution, or to the conversion of the worldly. It focuses on deepening the holiness of the community itself, which is the source of salvation. Various "holiness" and "pietist" movements would typify this form of sect. In America, the Old Order Amish and the Mennonites in Pennsylvania and Ohio or, perhaps, the Children of God would be examples.

A very different kind of religious movement is what Wilson calls the *gnostic*, or *manipulationist*, sect. What is distinctive about this kind of group, sometimes called a cult, is the fact that it fully *accepts* and pursues what others would see as worldly goals. What it seeks is not withdrawal from or an indifference toward the world but, rather,

The spiritual guru of the cult of the Divine Light Mission, Maharaj Ji,
speaks to his disciples in 1971 as he launched his mission in America.
(*Source*: Courtesy of Daily Camera.)

appropriation of the right spiritual means or techniques by which to
cope with or to achieve worldly goals. Salvation essentially means
health, happiness, success, status, wealth, or long life. Salvation is a
present, immediate possibility. Group fellowship in some of these
movements is minimal. Examples are Scientology and Transcendental
Meditation.

A somewhat similar type of group is the *thaumaturgical* sect; it, too,
is concerned with the curing of rather specific, personal, mundane
ills. These would include the healing of disease, avoidance of an imminent calamity, restoration after a loss, contact with a deceased loved
one, and so on. However, this kind of spiritualist group differs from
the manipulationist type in its direct appeal to supernatural powers
and interventions in obtaining cures, in receiving messages from
spirits, and in performing miracles. This group does not join together
to worship but, rather, to receive personal supernatural benefits or
to watch others obtain them. Miracles, magic, and oracles, rather than
esoteric knowledge or technique, are the means of salvation in this
type of spiritualist group, which flourishes today in less-developed
societies.

The last two sect types identified by Wilson are world-affirming but
are very different from the two previously described highly individualistic types. These latter two groups are not primarily concerned

with personal enrichment and compensation; their interest is focused on wider social and cultural goals. The *reformist* sect often begins as a revolutionist and introversionist movement but, while maintaining its structure, over time modifies its response to the outside world. This sect type accepts its place in the world and works cooperatively with secular groups; nevertheless, it seeks to remain untainted by worldly standards. It sees itself as the spiritual conscience of the secular world, ever open to supernatural guidance and inspiration. Its reformist agenda often differs little from that of secular idealists with whom it cooperates. Its hope for the amelioration of evil is not revolutionary but gradualist, and it is open, inevitably, to some accommodation to the larger society. The Society of Friends (Quakers) exemplifies this type of group. The Quakers are an interesting case study of the transformation of a sect that remains traditional in important respects and, at the same time, modifies its response to the world.

Wilson's last sect type is the *utopian*, a very complex type. Unlike the revolutionist, it does not look to the violent overturn of the present world; rather, it looks to the human reconstruction of the world on a communitarian basis and according to a divinely given plan. It is more radical than the reformist groups in that it calls not only for social improvement and reform but also for a total social reorganization in which evil is eliminated. The Oneida Community in nineteenth-century western New York, the Brüderhof communities, and the Peoples Temple in Guyana are examples of this type of religious society.

The varied characteristics of these sect types—in terms of ideology, organization, and response to the world—make some more vulnerable than others to change, development, and dissolution. Some can remain relatively stable over time while others, such as the conversionist type, are vulnerable to external influences that often bring rather rapid modifications in belief and organization. For example, the conversionist sect's emphasis on evangelism involves exposure to the secular world and hence to the acceptance of members with perhaps inadequate socialization into the beliefs and values of the sect. All this disturbs a strong sense of the community's values and strict social boundaries. Furthermore—while the conversionist sect initially disdains the cultural values accepted by the wider society and is hostile to clerical learning—as it grows, it also finds it difficult to avoid the move toward differentiation and specialization of religious roles and the training of clergy, which is typical of more-complex churches. Due to these and other sociological factors, the conversionist sect is especially vulnerable to dissolution as a sect and to transformation into a denomination.

It is obvious that a religious community's doctrines, for example, its attitude toward the secular world, will affect its stability and its development. But a sect's transformation is also clearly dependent on social factors that may not be readily apparent to the group itself. Max Weber made much of the effect of changing social class and economic status on the transformation of sects into churches or denominations. The upper classes usually have more investment in the economic and cultural life of the wider society and so are less prone to outbursts of religious enthusiasm and political radicalism. Education and growth in size are also potent social factors in the transformation of religious groups.

The Sacred and Social Ethics

All religious communities maintain and transmit a moral tradition, that is, a set of social values that are codified into normative ritualistic, legal, and ethical standards of obligation and action. In many of the great religions, there is no sharp demarcation between ritual, legal, and ethical–religious requirements. The Jewish *halakhah*, the Muslim *shari'ah*, and the Hindu *dharma* (see Chapter 11) involve a totality of ritual commandments, religious behaviors, and civil obligations and punishments. What distinguishes religious social ethics from secular morality is that the former accepts a complex of attitudes and practices based dominantly, if not solely, on the *acceptance of a sacred authority*. That authority may be located in the commands of a sacred book—the Hebrew Scriptures, the New Testament, or the *Quran*; in cosmic law— *rta* or *dharma* (Hinduism), or the *tao* (Confucianism); in the teachings and example of a charismatic leader—Jesus or Buddha; or, more often, in a combination of these.

The religious person's sense of obligation and right action is shaped by and conforms to a normative sacred authority. Conformity may be largely personal and demand an essentially interior or dispositional response—as, for example, in certain classical passages in the Hindu Bhagavad-Gita and in the writings of the Protestant reformer, Martin Luther. Other ethical obligations may be more focused on the community and be largely consequential, that is, measured by certain social results. The sacred ethical obligation may also involve degrees of possibility, success, and failure. The transgression of or failure to fulfill the sacred obligation may result in a variety of problems for the individual and for the community that require amelioration (see Chapter 9). Transgression and failure may bring a sense of defilement, shame, or guilt, all of which require purification, amendment of life, or liberation (see Chapters 10 and 12). What is important here, however, is that the nature of the sacred obligation and the character of the individual and communal response will reflect different responses to the wider secular world.

The ethical character of some religions naturally tends to a *world-indifference* or a *world-acceptance* that is reflected in the community's apathy toward and disinterest in social change. It often entails, by default, the legitimation of the social order. The ethical ethos of other religions may be *world-denying* and call for a "flight from the world." Here, the normative ethical obligation demands a separation from the world that is perceived as evil. The world is allowed "to go to the devil," so to speak. Other moral orientations demand that the religious community "be *in* but not *of* the world." In this case, the ethical obligation may be *world-transforming*, involving a very different and more-dynamic relationship between the religious community and the wider society.

Here, we will examine briefly how these different ethical–religious orientations reflect opposing responses to the world, each one involving profound social consequences. We refer to a number of other ethical issues and to other expressions of sacred ethical obligation elsewhere (see especially Chapters 5 and 9–12).

The World-Accepting Response

The central concept of ethical obligation in orthodox Hinduism is called **dharma**, which sets forth the ethical duties of individuals in each level of the social class (caste) and at each stage of life. Every social class has its own *dharma* to perform, a duty that reflects the very principle of social order as that order is portrayed in the cosmic myth of origin in the sacred text, the *Rig Veda*. Each individual is obligated to perform those ritual and ethical laws set by the caste or station in life into which he or she is born.

> Agriculture, cattle-tending, and commerce
>   Are the natural-born actions of artisans;
> Action that consists of service
>   Is likewise natural-born to a self.
> Taking delight in his own special kind of action,
>   A man attains perfection . . .
> Better one's own duty (even) imperfect,
>   Than another's duty well performed.
> Action pertaining to his own estate
>   Performing, he incurs no guilt.[16]

What is decisive for the Hindu caste system is its connection with the law of **karma**, or action, and the transmigration of souls (see Chapter 9). According to these doctrines, an individual's actions in this life have indelible consequences both for this life and for future lives. A person's chances of improvement in future earthly reincarnations depend on having fulfilled the obligations of his or her caste.

The effect of this ethical system is to induce a conservative acceptance of the social order, especially among the lower classes, who have the most to gain by a favorable transmigration.

A rather different illustration of a "world-accepting" religious–ethical response, but with not dissimilar conservative or politically quietistic consequences, can be found in the writings of Martin Luther on the relations of the church and temporal authority. He calls them "the two kingdoms." The foundation of Luther's political thought is rooted in his radical belief in the absolute sovereignty of God over the church and the civil order, using both to accomplish his purposes. Life consists of these two realms, over which God rules supreme and which serve His will, though in different ways. The church, or spiritual government, has no temporal authority; it is ruled solely by God's Word or Gospel. However, because Christians are few and the world is evil, God has established a second government—worldly authority—that rules by the sword. Without temporal authority humans would, in Luther's estimation, "devour one another." The temporal government is a blessed servant of God since it confers such necessary benefits as security, peace, and order. Christians therefore are called to support unequivocally the temporal authorities and those civic orders established by God to insure social stability.

In Luther's view, Christian principles cannot be expected to govern evil, worldly affairs. It would be like putting sheep together with wolves and lions. In other words, the Kingdom of God is not of this world. The two kingdoms must be kept separate as God's right and left hands. To resist worldly authority or to attempt to change it is to confuse and to conjoin the two kingdoms mistakenly.

The social consequence of Luther's ethical response to the world is to establish a radical distinction between a person's private and public morality. It thereby gives religious legitimation and support to the secular ordinances and governments that are perceived as "everywhere ordained of God" (Romans 13). In Luther's own day and in the later history of Lutheranism in Germany, this ethic resulted in the odd claim that Christians do not mix in secular political matters and yet that they must obey, support, and pray for the state, as if these were not political acts.

The World-Denying Response

A second type of ethical response to the world emphasizes that loyalty to the object of sacred obligation entails a rejection of society and its standards and values. Believers must be saved from the world, which usually means that the believers must withdraw from society into separated communities, or communes, where the pure or spiritual life can be practiced. The position is expressed, for example, in this New

Testament injunction: "Do not love the world or the things in the world. If any one loves the world, love for the Father is not in Him" (I John 2:15). The world is a realm under the dominion of evil, a realm of darkness to be shunned by the children of light. It is a society concerned with material and passing values, with "the lust of the flesh, the lust of the eyes and the pride of life."

In the early years of Christianity, when the end of "the world" seemed near, this response was a popular one. It is expressed not only in some New Testament writings but also in such popular works as *The Shepherd of Hermas* and *The Epistle of Barnabas*. Historically, this type of renunciation of the world has taken two rather distinct forms. The first is expressed in adherence to an extremely rigorous, puritanical morality of obedience to the sacred law. The second, and quite different, response is called antinomianism, or the belief that true believers have been spiritually freed from *any* moral obligation, not only from worldly ethical norms but even from the sacred commandments themselves. The rules that bind ordinary believers are not meant to pertain to, indeed are intended to be subverted by, the elect saints or spiritual elite. This second form of world-denying response has shown itself from time to time within Christianity, but it has never gained a foothold and has always been viewed as a heresy. For Christians, radical "renunciation of the world" has normally taken the form of strict obedience to the commands of the Gospel and fear of, rather than contempt for, the world's contamination.

Tertullian (145–220 C.E.), the father of Latin theology, is a classic representative of Christian puritanical world-denial. He counseled believers to withdraw from civic meetings, from certain occupations, and from politics:

> As those in whom all ardor in the pursuit of honor and glory is dead, we have no pressing inducement to take part in your public meetings: nor is there aught more entirely foreign to us than affairs of state.[17]

Tertullian also taught that military service and the swearing of an oath to Caesar were contrary to the Gospel. He demanded of Christians the uncompromising morality of nonresistance to evil, loving of enemies, and prohibitions against anger and lustful thoughts. In modern times, the Mennonites and Amish perhaps best represent this ascetic or puritanical response of ethical world-denial.

The antinomian response was particularly virulent in Christianity in the late Middle Ages, a time of great social upheaval and change. One expression of it was the heresy of the Free Spirit in the thirteenth and fourteenth centuries. Foremost among this lawless type was a Parisian mystical group called the Amaurians. They denied the reality

Members of the Old Order Amish in Washington to seek exemption from government programs. (*Source*: Courtesy of Wide World Photos, Inc.)

of sin and even thought of themselves as divine and above promiscuous behavior. For the Amaurians and similar groups, spiritual liberty from the world meant freedom from all laws and morality, which was a sign of their divinity and salvation.

During the Hellenistic period—the centuries just before and after the coming of Christianity—a number of religious movements taught their adherents that this evil world was a prison house of the immortal soul and that the world and all the things in it were to be despised. All laws and virtues were ridiculed and held in contempt. To these Gnostics—meaning secret knowledge—(see Chapter 10) salvation required a bypassing or overleaping of all earthly concerns that were seen as mere obstacles and distracting temptations on the path to an other-worldly salvation. This resulted in a radical worldly pessimism and a moral nihilism, a disregard of all moral restraints. Indeed, for some Gnostics, the rejection of morality became a positive obligation.

The Church Father Irenaeus (135–202 C.E.) contrasts the Gnostics with Christian teaching and speaks of their doctrine:

> To us [the Christians], they [the Gnostics] maintain, a moral life is necessary for salvation. They themselves, however, according to their teaching, would be saved absolutely and under all circumstances, not through works but through the mere fact of their being by nature

'spiritual.' For, as it is impossible for the earthly element to partake of salvation ... so it is impossible for the spiritual element to suffer corruption, whatever actions they may have indulged in. . . . Therefore 'the most perfect' among them do unabashed all the forbidden things of which Scripture assures us 'that they which do such things shall not inherit the kingdom of God.'[18]

A similar antinomian response to the world is found in the school of magical Buddhism called Left-handed Tantra, which is found in Tibet. Like Gnosticism, Tantra makes a sharp distinction between the truly initiated and the uninitiated and therefore between a common and an esoteric, elite doctrine. Left-handed Tantric Buddhism appears to teach the very opposite of the ascetic ideals of the Theravadin Buddhist monk. The initiate into the Tantric mysteries and exercises no longer is subject to the ethical obligations regarding food and sexuality that are, for example, so central to the classical Buddhist Eightfold Path to Enlightenment (see Chapter 11). In fact, to the horror of the Theravadin monk, Tantra cultivates the passions and sensual pleasures as vehicles of enlightenment. This view is expressed in a Tantric poem, *Disquisition on the Purification of the Intellect*, which includes the following verses:

> The mystics, pure of mind,
>   Dally with lovely girls,
> Infatuated with the poisonous flame of passion,
>   That they may be set free from desire . . .
> As a washerman uses dirt
>   To wash clean a garment,
> So, with impurity,
>   The wise man makes himself pure.[19]

The antinomian's detachment from the world devalues it to the point where religion and morality are seen as totally distinct. Morality is perceived as a mere stock of social taboos. To fear the world and its ways and to take ascetic flight show that one has not yet gained genuine "freedom of the spirit." Antinomianism represents the paradoxical denial of the vain world by embracing its very evil and foolish passion.

The World-Transforming Response

It is true to say that most religions teach their adherents that they should "be *in* but not *of* the world." The radical other-worldly, antinomian response is exceptional in this regard. Generally, even the world-accepting religions embrace the world only "indifferently," provisionally, or penultimately. The Kingdom of God, Nirvana, and Paradise are not *of* this world. Nevertheless, many of the world's great religions see the concentration of human effort leading to salvation *as requiring* participation *in* the world, indeed, on the conversion and transformation of a "fallen" or degenerate but sacred social and political order.

This form of response can be seen, for example, in Confucianism, where all efforts are bent (see Chapter 9) on recreating Chinese society and the state according to the true principles of cosmic order or the Mandate of Heaven. This demands cooperation with the state in order to transform it. Here, the faithful neither are separated from the world nor do they merely endure the world in the hope of a transhistorical salvation; rather, they are called to serve Heaven in and through their worldly activity. Human culture may be corrupt, but it is part of God's or Heaven's good creation. It requires conversion, not replacement; it calls for activity *within* the institutions of society but in order to transform them so that they might be in accord with cosmic order or God's Word or Law.

This world-transforming response often requires of the converted or the elect of God what Max Weber calls an "inner-worldly asceticism." It is a discipline that prepares the disciple to undertake the obligation of transforming society in accordance with the sacred commands of God. However, such an inner-worldly discipline may prepare the believer, whether consciously or not, to become a social reformer, perhaps even a revolutionary bent on establishing a **theocratic** society modeled on the divine plan.

In such a case, every individual must come under the influence of those sacred ordinances that are to inform the civil as well as the religious life of the community. In the West, this transforming impulse, whose logic often leads to a theocratic ideal of a church-dominated state and society, is best seen in sixteenth- and seventeenth-century Calvinism. It is present in John Calvin's effort to establish a theocracy in Geneva and in a similar effort by the New England Puritans. In both instances, God's will for the whole of civil life is claimed to be known through God's infallible Word as it is interpreted by the elect "saints."

Not all Puritans were theocrats. They did believe, however, that God had called them, through their several vocations, to labor in the affairs of the practical life in order to transform society into a holy commonwealth. "God," wrote a Puritan divine, "doth call every man and woman . . . to serve him in some particular employment in this world, both for their own and the common good."[20] Numerous Puritan treatises were composed to expound the responsibilities of Christians in their several civil and vocational callings, such as *Navigation Spiritualized, The Religious Weaver*, and *Husbandry Spiritualized*. The Christian's duty was to Christianize the world of business as well as the social order.

The world-transforming response, even in its radically theocratic
form, remains an important force in the major world religions today.
It is apparent in certain expressions of Evangelical Christianity in
America but, perhaps most dramatically, in Shi'ite Islam in Iran under
the leadership of the Ayatollah Rudollah Khomeini.

Traditionally, Islam never has separated what is Caesar's from what
is God's. In Arabic, there is no dichotomy between the spiritual and
the temporal. The spread of Islam has always been perceived by the
faithful as a sign of God's providence and favor. And for the Muslim,
the *Quran* and the traditions of the Prophet Muhammad contain the

The Ayatollah Khomeini, returning from exile in 1979, is greeted by the
supporters of his Islamic revolution and the newly approved Islamic
Republic. (*Source*: Courtesy of Camera Press.)

complete blueprint for humanity. In contemporary Iran, this plan is applied by the *mujtahid*—the experts in religious science and Islamic law—to every aspect of human life, thereby transforming Iranian society into a holy commonwealth. This is powerfully set forth in Imam Khomeini's authoritative treatise on *Islamic Government*:

> The nature and character of Islamic law and the divine ordinances of the *shari'a* [divine law] furnish additional proof of the necessity for establishing government, for they indicate that the laws were laid down for the purpose of creating a state and administering the political, economic, and cultural affairs of society.
>
> First, the laws of the *shari'a* embrace a diverse body of laws and regulations, which amounts to a complete social system. In this system of laws, all the needs of man have been met; his dealings with his neighbors, fellow citizens, and clan, as well as his children and relatives; the concerns of private and marital life; regulations concerning war and peace and intercourse with other nations; penal and commercial law; and regulations pertaining to trade and agriculture. . . . It is obvious, then, how much care Islam devotes to government and the political and economic relations of society, with the goal of creating conditions conducive to the production of morally upright and virtuous human beings.[21]

This survey has provided some indication of how a religious community's understanding of its sacred ethical obligations profoundly reflects a response to the world and how it, in turn, shapes the community's understanding of the wider society and the social responsibilities of the faithful. A complete discussion of religion and society would include a number of other significant themes—for example, the relation of religion to gender, economic, and racial status, that is, to social stratification. The important subject of social and religious pluralism, its effect on modern secularization and the future of religion is another topic that, fittingly, is discussed in the Postscript. It is time now, however, to turn from the analysis of some of the universal forms of religious experience given in Chapters 3–6 to a consideration of some classic expressions of belief about deity, cosmogony, and human condition, and the paths of salvation and enlightenment.

Notes

1. Guy E. Swanson, *The Birth of the Gods* (Ann Arbor, 1960), p. 21.
2. Swanson, *Birth of the Gods*, p. 22.
3. Swanson, *Birth of the Gods*, pp. 26–27.
4. Melville J. Herskovits, *Dahomey: An Ancient West African Kingdom* I (Evanston, 1967), p. 202.
5. Herskovits, *Dahomey*, p. 238.

6. F. H. Ross, *Shinto: The Way of Japan* (Boston, 1965), p. 139.

7. Ross, *Shinto*, p. 140.

8. Paul Radin, "The Winnebago Tribe," *Thirty-Seventh Annual Report of the Bureau of Ethnology* (Washington, D.C., 1923), pp. 348–49.

9. This discussion of founded religions is dependent on Joachim Wach, *Sociology of Religion* (Chicago, 1944).

10. Max Weber, *The Theory of Social and Economic Organization* (New York, 1947), pp. 358–59.

11. J. Wach, *Sociology of Religion*, p. 175.

12. *The Rule of Saint Benedict*, trans. by Cardinal Gasquet (London, 1925), pp. 17–22.

13. For this ideal-type characterization I am dependent on Bryan Wilson, *Religion in Sociological Perspective* (Oxford, 1982), pp. 91–92.

14. H. Richard Niebuhr, *The Social Sources of Denominationalism* (New York, 1929).

15. Bryan Wilson, *Religious Sects* (London, 1970); *Magic and Millennium* (London, 1973), pp. 18–31; and "The Sociology of Sects," *Religion in Sociological Perspective* (Oxford, 1982).

16. The *Bhagavad Gita*, trans. by Franklin Edgerton (New York, 1964), pp. 87–88.

17. Tertullian, *Apology*, xxxviii, in *Anti-Nicene Fathers*, vol. III.

18. Irenaeus, *Against Heresies* I 6.2–3. Cited in Hans Jonas, *The Gnostic Religion* (Boston, 1963), pp. 270–71.

19. W. Theodore DeBary, ed., *The Buddhist Tradition* (New York, 1969), pp. 119–20.

20. Richard Steele, *The Tradesman's Calling*, etc. (1684), p. 1.

21. "Islamic Government," *Islam and Revolution: Writings and Declarations of Imam Khomeini*. ed. and trans. by Hamid Algar (Berkeley, 1981).

Review Questions

1. Many scholars, following Durkheim's lead, have focused on the influence of material and social conditions in the development of religious belief and practice. Give some specific examples of the way in which religion mirrors social beliefs and practice. Give some examples of societies whose religious beliefs have been especially instrumental in changing social beliefs and behavior.

2. Describe some of the characteristics of a natural religious community and the voluntary religious community.

3. What are the special features of the "founded" religion? What special problems does it face on the death of the founder and how does it deal with these problems?

4. Describe, with examples, the form that religious protest and reform often take within the church-type religious community. Give some examples of protest and reform that led to secession from the original church-type community.

5. Describe the chief characteristics of the ideal sect-type religious

group. Describe the distinctive features of some of the sect-types distinguished by Bryan Wilson.
6. Compare and contrast the positions of the world-accepting, world-denying, and world-transforming religious communities.

Suggestions for Further Reading

BERGER, PETER, *The Sacred Canopy* (New York: Doubleday, 1967).

DURKHEIM, EMILE, *The Elementary Forms of the Religious Life* (Glencoe, Ill.: The Free Press, 1954).

HILL, MICHAEL, *A Sociology of Religion* (New York: Basic Books, 1973).

NIEBUHR, H. RICHARD, *The Social Sources of Denominationalism* (New York: Henry Holt, 1929).

O'DEA, THOMAS, *The Sociology of Religion* (Englewood Cliffs, N.J.: Prentice Hall, 1966).

ROBERTSON, ROLAND, *The Sociological Interpretation of Religion* (New York: Schocken Books, 1970).

———— , (ed.), *Sociology of Religion* (New York: Penguin Books, 1981). A collection of classic essays.

TROELTSCH, ERNST, *The Social Teachings of the Christian Churches* (New York: Macmillan, 1931).

WACH, JOACHIM, *Sociology of Religion* (Chicago: University of Chicago Press, 1944).

WEBER, MAX, *Ancient Judaism* (Glencoe, Ill.: The Free Press, 1952).

———— , *The Protestant Ethic and the Spirit of Capitalism* (New York: Scribners, 1930).

———— , *The Religion of China* (Glencoe, Ill.: The Free Press, 1951).

———— , *The Religion of India* (Glencoe, Ill.: The Free Press, 1958).

———— , *The Sociology of Religion* (Boston: Beacon Press, 1964).

WILSON, BRYAN, *Magic and Millennium* (New York: Harper and Row, 1973).

———— , *Religion in Sociological Perspective* (Oxford: Oxford University Press, 1982).

———— , *Religious Sects* (New York: McGraw-Hill, 1971).

YINGER, MILTON, *The Scientific Study of Religion* (New York: Macmillan, 1970).

WORKS ON COMPARATIVE SOCIAL ETHICS

CHIDESTER, DAVID, *Patterns of Action: Religion and Ethics in a Contemporary Perspective* (Belmont, Calif.: Wadsworth, 1987).

GREEN, RONALD, *Religious Reason: The Rational and Moral Basis of Religious Belief* (New York: Oxford University Press, 1978). For the advanced student.

LITTLE, DAVID, and SUMNER B. TWISS, *Comparative Religious Ethics* (San Francisco: Harper & Row, 1978). For the advanced student.

PART III

Classic Forms of Religious Belief and Practice

CHAPTER 7

Deity

OVERVIEW

In this chapter, we shall describe a variety of ways in which deity or sacred power has been experienced and conceived in the history of religion. We shall organize our exploration along a continuum through various forms of polytheism, **pantheism**, dualism, monotheism, and **monism**. A scheme such as this can be useful as long as it is not taken as representing a series of mutually exclusive types. Many religions reflect a curious mix of animistic, pantheist, and theistic beliefs or tendencies. Neither must the scheme be thought to represent an evolutionary or progressive development from, say, primitive mana to sophisticated philosophical conceptions of monism or monotheism. We know that high gods are present among the most primitive of societies and that animistic spirits, totems, and other deities are not uncommon in the religious life of the higher civilizations.

As we shall see, when the human imagination begins to reflect on deity, tensions and paradoxes arise between, for example, the immanence and the transcendence of the sacred, or between the rich plurality of sacred power and the quest for a primordial sacred unity or oneness.

The way in which deity is humanly experienced raises questions of momentous importance because it points to the deepest sources of human security, social order, and moral action. The perception of deity deeply affects a society's understanding of nature, of the human condition, and of what constitutes human salvation or liberation.

We have learned that sacred power is the ultimate object of religion. We also know that sacred power can be present in any object, person, or spiritual being when it is approached in awe and fear, or when it is perceived as the source of both purity and danger. Our primitive

163

ancestors are one with us in our common awareness of a distinction between what is ordinary and profane and what is "other," sacred, and set apart as holy. Primitive man, however, was not as prone as we are to draw sharp distinctions between the "natural" and the "supernatural." Any object or event that elicits unique feelings of awe and aversion possesses sacred power. It is set apart as having special import, although it is present in such a seemingly earthy object as a bear's skull or a stone weapon. For the primitive, sacred power is always particular, immediate, and tangible.

Polytheism and the Worship of Nature

Until relatively recently (2000 B.C.E.), the religious life of most prehistoric and primitive societies was *polytheistic*. These deities often were associated with certain realms and forces of nature—the sun, the sky, the earth, and the waters—as well as with totem plants and animals, all of which represented sacred power, the giver, sustainer, and destroyer of life.

We know little of the religion of prehistoric man—our Neanderthal and Cro-Magnon hominid ancestors—but some things appear evident. The early Neanderthal hunters, who inhabited the lands skirting the Alps, treated the fearsome cave bear—which they stalked and killed— with great reverence. We know that they deposited the undamaged head of the bear, with the brain intact, in an altar-like stone chest in the dark recesses of the caves that they inhabited. These hidden chambers, with their bear skull niches, are the earliest human sanctuaries and shrines.[1] The reverence shown the bear points, of course, to its deity, to its sacredness as the dispenser of hunting fortune and providence. The bear cult is practiced even today by tribes in the sub-Arctic regions of northern Asia.

For the hunters of the late Paleolithic period, as for primitive societies today, the hunter and the hunted joined in a mysterious and magical relationship. The animal is providence, the source of life, but it is also humankind's feared adversary. The later Paleolithic hunters adorned their caves and weapons with pictures of their game animals. In the presence of these images, they performed magical rituals and sacrifices meant to ensure the success of the hunt. These pictures— such as the one of the "great sorcerer" in the Trois Frères cave at Ariège, France—are evidence of the belief in spirits that personified sacred, magical power.

The religious practice of the **Neolithic** Age (7000–3000 B.C.E.) reflects the different life of the farmer and the tiller of the land. The traces of religion that exist from this period are symbols and images

Paleolithic mural from a cave in France depicting an
owl-masked shaman arrayed in reindeer antlers and
animal skins. He is probably leading a magical hunting
ceremony, the animal features representing the objects
of the hunt that the shaman seeks to subject to his power.
(*Source*: Courtesy of the Department of Library Services,
American Museum of Natural History.)

associated, in the main, with the polytheistic worship of nature—the
sun, the sky, and the earth—the fundamental realities for the farmer.
Sky and earth, representing the primal pair of male and female, are
common in the nature cults of the Neolithic Age. The sky is the
supreme deity in some cults; in others, worship centers on the Great
Goddess of earth and vegetation. Together, however, the two deities
represent cosmic fertility. The theme is expressed in the hymns of
the Pleiades of Dodona:

> The Earth is our mother, the Sky is our father. The Sky fertilizes
> the Earth with rain, the Earth produces grains and grasses.

Polytheistic cults are generally characteristic of primitive and Neolithic religion. Each cult reflects the practical needs and concerns of these early societies. The French scholar Georges Dumezil has shown, for example, that the earliest Indo-European communities were divided into three classes — priests, warriors, and animal breeders or farmers — and that each class possessed a distinctive religious cult; for example, one was devoted to the gods of martial power and another to the gods representing nature's fecundity. There were sky gods of creation and order; gods of the storm and of might and force; and maternal gods of the earth.

Sky Gods

More needs to be said about the distinctive role of the sky gods of cosmic order and sovereignty, as well as about the female goddesses of earth and fertility. The school of ethnology associated with Wilhelm Schmidt discovered sky or high gods among primitive societies to be so universal as to argue for the existence of a primitive monotheism. While serious objections can be raised about calling belief in high gods monotheism, Schmidt and his disciples are quite right in claiming an almost-universal belief in a creator god who dwells in the sky and who fertilizes the earth with his vivifying rain. This supreme god — for instance, among many African tribes — is often regarded with indifference because he has withdrawn into the sky, his work of creation already accomplished. In some instances, it is evident that the sky god is the personification of an abstract concept, the first cause, for example, to explain the origin of the cosmos. The African cults tend to center around the lower gods whose sacred powers impinge on the tribe's daily activities. Here, we see a characteristic phenomenon of all religions: the move away from the otherness or absolute transcendence of the sacred and toward more immanent, dynamic, and accessible forms of sacred power, especially in rites and sacraments.

However, when sacred power becomes too localized, as in the belief in mana or in animism, the pendulum often moves in the opposite direction, toward more-transcendent, less-localized expressions of deity. Ascendance and dominion are quite naturally associated with the sky, and so it is intelligible why the sky became the abode of the all-knowing supreme Creator.

When we move from primitive religion to the great polytheistic religions of the historical civilizations of Greece, Egypt, and Mesopotamia, we observe that the sky god is connected not only with creation but also with sovereignty — a rather new conception of sacred power that guarantees cosmic order. The Indo-European peoples worshiped a sky god under various names derived from the same root word that meant both sky and "to shine." In Latin, the word is *deus*; in Sanskrit, *deva*; and in Iranian, *div*. In the Indian Vedic hymns, he is the god Varuna, who is "visible everywhere" and who sees all. Varuna, it is said, "even counts how often men wink their eyes." It is he "who knows all, spies out all secrets, all deeds and intentions" (*Rig Veda* VIII, 41, 3; 1, 25). Varuna rules as king since it is the common characteristic of these later sky gods that they see all and know all, and are keepers of the law.

Perhaps the best known of the sky gods of antiquity is Zeus, head of the Greek **pantheon**. Homer, in the *Iliad*, says that "the portion of Zeus is the broad heaven, in brightness and in cloud alike" (XV, 192). Zeus not only dwells in the sky but also is spoken of as the sky itself. It is Zeus who sends the rain and hurls the lightening and the thunderbolts. He is ruler and father, although his sovereignty is achieved after considerable struggle. This is recounted in Hesiod's *Theogony*, which chronicles Zeus' rise to supremacy among the Greek gods. According to Hesiod, Earth (Gaea) and Heaven (Uranus) were the original divine pair. From them were born the Uranides, the six Titans (including Kronos) and the six Titanides (including Rhea). Hesiod records that Uranus hated his children and hid them in Gaea's body. This infuriated Gaea, who called on her children "to punish the criminal outrage of a father." When Uranus approached Gaea "drunken to penetrate the body of Earth," Kronos castrated his own father with his sickle. Kronos became his father's successor and married his sister, Rhea. The two had five children: Hestia, Demeter, Hera, Hades, and Poseidon, each one given rule over a realm of nature.

Knowing, however, that he would also one day feel "the blows of his own son," Kronos swallowed his children. On the day that Rhea was to give birth to Zeus, she went to Crete and hid the infant from Kronos in a cave. When Zeus grew up he, in turn, forced his father to disgorge his brothers and sisters and freed his father's brothers, whom Uranus had chained. In gratitude, the brothers offered Zeus the thunder and the lightening, with which Zeus henceforth commanded "both mortals and immortals." With the help of three 100-armed Giants, Zeus defeated Kronos and the Titans and was thereby able to bring new order to the cosmos. Finally, Zeus defeated the great monster, Typhon, and cast him down into Tartarus. Zeus then divided the cosmic dominions between himself (the sky), Poseidon (the ocean), and Hades (the subterranean world). The earth and Olympus belonged to the three in common. However, through a series of marriages and liaisons with Hera, Demeter, and Leto, among others, Zeus both absorbed and replaced these popular goddesses in both power and popular veneration.

The Greek high god Zeus enthroned with raised hand, as if holding a royal scepter. (*Source*: From the Henry L. Pierce Fund, 98.678, courtesy of the Museum of Fine Arts, Boston.)

Here, then, begins the unification of divine power in one god, Zeus, which leads to what can be called *monarchical polytheism*, a form of polytheism, as seen in Homer, featuring one triumphant and superior god—"the father of gods and men" (*Iliad* I, 544).

The sovereign Zeus is invoked in a variety of aspects: as Zeus Chthonios (god of agriculture), as Zeus Herkeios (god of the hearth and household), as Zeus Polieus (god of the city-state), as Zeus Katharsios (god of purification), and so on. Zeus' mastery and omnipotence are illustrated in the *Iliad* in his challenge to the other Olympian deities:

> Then you will see how far I am strongest of all the immortals. Come, you gods, make this endeavor, that you may learn this. Let down out of the sky a cord of gold; lay hold of it all you who are goddesses, yet not even so can you drag down Zeus from the sky to the ground, not Zeus the high lord of counsel, though you try until you grow weary.[2]

Mother Goddesses

If the sky is our father, the earth is our mother. If sky gods can be traced back to the earliest societies, so also do we find a primeval worship of female earth deities. This is attested to in the discovery of prehistoric female figurines with exaggerated breasts, thighs, and abdomen—for example, the Paleolithic image of the Venus of Laussel discovered in a rock shelter in the Dordogne, France. Though universal, the worship of the "Great Mother" Earth is especially pronounced in the ancient Mediterranean and Near Eastern religions. So conspicuous is her cult that we can see traces of it still in the simple worship of the Virgin Mary in some Roman Catholic and Orthodox communities in southern Europe and the East. A vivid illustration from Cyprus is cited by D. G. Hogarth:

> In honour of the Maid of Bethlehem the peasants of Kuklia in Cyprus anointed lately, and probably still anoint each year, the great corner stones of the ruined temple of the Paphian Goddess. As Aphrodite was supplicated once with cryptic rites, so is Mary entreated still by Moslems as well as Christians, with incantations and passings through perforated stones, to remove the curse of barrenness from Cypriote women, or increase the manhood of Cypriote men.[3]

The Paleolithic "Venus" of Laussel, with exaggerated breasts and hips, symbolizes fertility, the central feature of prehistoric mother-goddess cults. (*Source*: Courtesy of the Department of Library Services, American Museum of Natural History.)

The Neolithic discovery of agriculture radically changed the nature of religious life from that of the previous era of Paleolithic hunters. A new relationship was divined between the human community and vegetation, centering on the mysteries of birth, death, and rebirth. The fertility of the earth and the harvest were perceived as bound up with feminine sexual fecundity. Women are associated with the earliest practice of agriculture and, of course, it is natural that women should be connected with birth and creation. However, it was also understood that the birth of vegetation requires the "death" of the seed before a new birth is ensured. Human life was thereby assimilated into the cyclical drama of the agricultural year.

The slow transformation of the feminine Mother Earth into the Great Goddess of life and rebirth can be observed in the influential religions of the ancient Near East: in the history of the Mesopotamian goddess Ishtar; the Syrian Astarte (meaning "womb"); the Egyptian Isis; and the Greek Demeter. Isis was the most important of the Egyptian goddesses. She was adored in her role both as wife and as mother and was called the "divine mother." She personified the feminine creativity of the earth and was represented nursing the infant god Horus, who was sitting on her lap.

In Egyptian mythology, Isis is depicted as the daughter of Geb and Nut, the primal earth and heaven, and as the wife of her brother Osiris. According to the myth, Osiris is murdered by his evil brother, Set, but his dismembered body is recovered by Isis. She embraces her husband, who then revives briefly and impregnates her with the god Horus. Horus, in turn, defeats Set and rules as lord of the upper world. Horus is able to bring his father back to life. However, Isis is perceived as responsible, if indirectly, for the revival of the divine king Osiris, the most popular of the Egyptian deities.

The cult of Isis–Osiris, associated as it was with the themes of death and rebirth, had deep human appeal and spread far beyond Egypt. Isis became assimilated to and identified with a number of Semitic, Greek, and Roman goddesses. She became the object of the most fervent adoration, especially during the Roman period, and, despite the Christian prohibition against the feast of Isis in 394, the mysteries of Isis continued to be celebrated until as late as the sixth century of the Christian era.

Ishtar played a role in Mesopotamia similar to that of Isis in Egypt and Rome. Ishtar is the mother and lover of the young god Tammuz, who represents the spring vitality whose vigor fades with the autumnal vegetation. In the Akkadian myth *The Descent of Ishtar to the Nether World*, the theme of the "dying and rising" god is vividly enacted. The young god Tammuz dies and goes to the land of the dead, where he is rescued by Ishtar. In reviving Tammuz, Ishtar also gives new birth to nature and to humankind.

The Egyptian goddess Isis, here nursing her son Horus,
is the exemplar of motherhood, the patroness of
childbearing, the protector of children, and the symbol
of immortality. (*Source*: Courtesy of the Fitzwilliam
Museum, Cambridge University.)

Before the resurrection of Tammuz, the *Descent of Ishtar* portrays the disastrous results for nature from Ishtar's detention in the nether world:

> The countenance of Popsukkal, the vizier of the great gods
> Was fallen, his face was clouded.
> He was clad in mourning, long hair he wore ...
> His tears flowing before Ea, the king:
> Ishtar has gone down to the nether world, she has not
>   come up.
> Since Ishtar has gone down to the Land of No Return,
> The bull springs not upon the cow, the ass impregnates not
>   the jenny,
> In the streets the man impregnated not the maiden.
> The man lay down in his own chamber
> The maiden lay down on her side.

Through the intervention and ransom of the gods, Ishtar returns to the upper world, along with Tammuz:

> As for Tammuz, the lover of her youth,
> Wash him with pure water, anoint him with sweet oil;
> Clothe him with a red garment, let him play on the flute
>   of lapes.

The myth ends with these words of Ishtar:

> On the day when Tammuz *welcomes* me
> When with him the lapes flute (and) the carnelian ring wel-
>   comes me,
> When with him the wailing men and wailing women welcome
>   me,
> May the dead rise and smell the incense.[4]

The myth of Tammuz–Ishtar personifies the ceaseless movement of the seasons, life coming to fruition, its decline in the summer heat, its death, and its restoration again in the springtime. Ishtar was but one of the many goddesses representing the fecundity and life-giving powers of Mother Earth.

The ancient association of the earth goddess with life-giving fertility remains alive in folk religion to the present day. It would be quite wrong, however, to think that female deities simply represent the fecundity and nurturing of Mother Earth, as a manifestation of early matriarchal forms of human social organization. Today, scholars largely reject the idea of the priority of matriarchal society. Nor is it possible to predict the type or role of female deities in a particular historical context from an analysis of that community's social structure. For example, there is no necessary correlation between the presence of exalted female goddesses and the high social status of women—or the reverse. There are too many historical, environmental, and socioeconomic variables to be confident with such simple correlations. Therefore, it is important to recognize the multiple and often ambivalent characteristics of mother goddesses. They are pregnant with life but also virginal; they are chaste and yet promiscuous; they are matrons of suffering but demanders of blood sacrifice; they create but also destroy; and they protect and unify yet also fiercely divide by conflict. This ambivalence can be perceived in the goddesses of the ancient Near East and Mediterranean world but, perhaps even more graphically, in the popular myth and devotion of India.

Among the most popular of Indian religious cults are those known collectively as *sakti* (meaning "energy"). They are distinct in conceiving sacred power as manifest and paramount in the wife of the god or in the female consort. The *sakti* cults render devotion to all that is associated with the eternal female, which often is perceived as *the* active principle of the universe. Some Hindu sects stress the maternal nature of deity, the Mother Goddess, such as Umā, the wife of the god Śiva. Others focus on *sakti* as the personification of the tender and devoted wife, for example, the beautiful Pārvati, another consort of Śiva. *Sakti* also symbolizes female voluptuousness, sexual desire, and sexual joy. The sexual union of female energy with the male is a common theme of *sakti* imagery and devotion. The eternal virgin is a popular theme as well, represented by a girl in her middle teens. Finally, there is *sakti* in the form of terror, cruelty, destruction, and death. Here, *sakti* is best personified by the goddess Kali, or Durga. But Kali also reflects the multiple and ambivalent character of the Hindu goddesses. She is represented as the power of creation, protection, and destruction, as well as the power in which all things rest after their dissolution, the power beyond life and death, the One, the Supreme.

As goddess of terror and destruction, Kali brings bloodshed, pestilence, and death. She is black and pictured wearing a necklace of human skulls. In two of her multiple hands, she carries a sword and dagger; in another is the head of a demon dripping with blood. Blood also trickles down her chin and neck. In the past, human sacrifices were offered to Kali; today, in Bengal she is pacified with the blood of goats. As a young man, Sri Ramakrishna, one of the great leaders of the modern Hindu renaissance, became attached as chief priest to the Dakshineswar Kali temple near Calcutta. His devotion to Kali, as divine Mother and representative of cosmic power, was the source of his own intoxicated mystical visions and his profound spiritual insight. A leader of the Ramakrishna Mission describes the image of Kali in the Dakshineswar temple—Kali in all her terror, yet reflecting as well the complex qualities that she represents to her devotees:

The fearsome Kali stands on the body of the god Śiva,
her lord. (*Source*: Courtesy of Jack Van Horn.)

> Within the main temple is a basalt figure of the goddess Kali, dressed
> in gorgeous apparel of gold brocade and decked lavishly with
> precious ornaments. She stands on the white breast of Śiva, who is
> lying stock-still on a thousand-petalled lotus. A garland of skulls
> hangs loosely from her neck, and a girdle of human arms runs
> round her waist. She has two pairs of arms, one on each side. With
> the lower left hand she holds a severed human head ... while with
> one of the right hands she offers boons and with the remaining
> one she allays fears. Seeing her holy consort Śiva beneath her feet,
> she blushes and expresses her delicate sentiment, like an Indian
> lady, by biting her protruded tongue. Her three eyes strike dismay
> into the hearts of the wicked, and yet pour out affection for the
> devotees. Thus stands in her benignly cruel majesty, Kali, the divine
> Mother.[5]

A few words by way of conclusion are necessary before we turn to
other forms of sacred power. The religious life of mankind, until
approximately 2000 B.C.E., was largely animistic and polytheistic. A
belief in high or sky gods and mother goddesses was common even

in the earliest societies. However, between the Neolithic Age and the emergence of our historical period, a move toward greater organiza- tion and even abstraction in the conception of sacred power can be observed in a number of cultures. In place of the myriad spirits— dwelling in every tree, rock, or river—one god often is given dominion over a particular aspect of nature or department of life; Poseidon is god of the seas, Aphrodite is goddess of love, and Ares is god of war. The great sky gods and representatives of Mother Earth often assimilate the roles of local deities and replace their cult. Zeus and Isis are good examples of this process.

Roughly at the time (800–600 B.C.E.) when the Hebrew prophets were reproving the Israelites for their worship of idols and false gods, speculative minds in Greece were challenging the all-too-anthropomor- phic depiction of the gods of the Homeric pantheon. "Is the ultimate, is sacred power," they asked, "to be identified with the mental limita- tions and the moral crudities of animals or of humans writ large?" Men, wrote the Greek Xenophanes, erroneously portray the gods in their own likeness:

> Homer and Hesiod have ascribed to the gods all things that among men are a shame and a reproach—theft and adultery and deceiving one another.
>   Mortals think that the gods are begotten, and wear clothes like their own, and have a voice and a form.
>   If oxen or horses or lions had hands or could draw with them and make works of art as men do, horses would draw the shapes of gods like horses, oxen like oxen; each kind would represent their bodies just like their own forms.
>   The Ethiopians say their gods are black and flat-nosed; the Thra- cians that theirs are blue-eyed and red-haired.[6]

Xenophanes was confident that deity was "one god greatest among gods and men, not like mortals in form, not yet in mind. He sees all over, thinks all over, and hears all over."[7] In both Greece and India, the protest against forms of polytheism often moved toward pantheistic and monistic conceptions of deity. However, before com- menting on these, we must look at a rather different idea of sacred power, namely, forms of cosmic dualism.

Dualism

Dualism perceives the world as constituted by or as living under the ordering of two coequal, and often coeternal, sacred powers. Some forms of dualism, as in certain ancient Chinese texts, conceive the world as *balanced* between dual polar forces that are neither antithetical nor hostile to one another. In other forms of dualism—for example, in late expressions of Iranian Zoroastrianism—the two coequal powers are locked in an eternal conflict.

Chinese *Yin-Yang*

The *yin-yang* dualism of China is very ancient and reflects a benign, complementary conception of two primordial sacred cosmic forces or principles. The origin of *yin-yang* is traced to ancient occult or magical teachings, but it later was taken up by Confucianist and Taoist writers. It is reflected, for example, in the Confucianist appendix to the *I-Ching*, or *Book of Changes*, written during the Ch'in and Han periods (221 B.C.E.–9 C.E.) by Hsi Tz'u. The original *I-Ching* was produced between 900–700 B.C.E. It was made up of eight trigrams, each consisting of broken and unbroken lines:

Originally the trigrams, in their multiple combinations, were but symbols of actual changes in nature. Later, the trigrams were invested with real *power* by which, it was thought, changes actually did occur. The trigrams became the basis of Chinese cosmogony, science, and even social ethics. The unbroken line stands for the power of *yang*, the broken line for *yin*. Together, they represent the bipolar forces of nature, rather like positive and negative electrical charges. According to this bipolarity, nature, including human nature, requires and operates through the interplay of such forces as light and darkness, heat and cold, and male and female.

In Hsi Tz'u's "Great Appendix," the trigrams *Ch'ien* (= Heaven) and *K'un* ( ) = Earth)—made up entirely of undivided and divided lines, respectively—are the representations par excellence of the *yang* and *yin*. It is believed that the other six trigrams were produced through the intercourse of *Ch'ien* (father) and *K'un* (mother). The process of universal change is described as follows in the "Great Appendix" to the *Book of Changes*:

> Heaven is high, earth is low; thus the *ch'ien* and the *k'un* are fixed. As high and low are thus ordered, honorable and humble have their places. Movement and rest have their constancy; according to these strong and weak are differentiated. Ways coincide according to their species and things fall into classes. Hence good fortune and bad fortune come about. In the heavens phenomena appear; on earth shapes occur. Through these, change and transformation becomes manifest. Therefore the strong and the weak [lines in the trigrams]

interplay, and the eight trigrams act and react upon each other. Things are roused by thunder and lightning; they are fertilized by wind and rain. Sun and moon revolve on their courses with a season of cold and then a season of heat. The way of the *ch'ien* constitutes the male, the way of the *k'un* constitutes the female. The *ch'ien* knows the great beginning; the *k'un* gives things their completion.[8]

Chinese thinkers perceived a perpetual interplay between the negative, passive, dark, feminine, destructive *yin* and the positive, light, masculine, creative *yang*. These bipolar powers are mutually related phases in the ceaseless transformation of nature. They interact harmoniously, each one necessary to the proper functioning of the other. The Chinese sages even saw the *yang* and *yin* as embodying the two schools of Confucianism (representing the active, like *yang*) and Taoism (representing the passive, like *yin*), symbolizing the complementary principles of the Chinese tradition. In an imaginary dialogue, the Taoist philosopher Chuang Tzu (365–290 B.C.E.) tells Confucius of his having voyaged to the world's beginning and relates what he saw:

> I saw Yin, the Female Energy, in its motionless grandeur; I saw Yang, the Male Energy, rampant in its fiery vigour. The motionless grandeur came out of the earth; the fiery vigour burst out from heaven. The two penetrated one another, were inextricably blended and from their union the things of the world were born.[9]

Dualism of Cosmic Struggle

There is a quite different form of cosmic dualism that reflects an enduring conflict, rather than a harmony, between two primordial sacred powers. It can be seen in the religions of Egypt, Mesopotamia, and India, as well as in ancient Judaism and Christianity. They all reflect dualistic tendencies, but they rarely, if ever, adopt a thoroughgoing dualism. In Egypt, for example, Re, the sun-god, representing life and truth, is pitted against Apophia, the serpent of darkness. In Babylon, the god Marduk struggles against Tiamat, the monster of chaos (see Chapter 8) while, in the Bible, the final victory of God over the powers of darkness is portrayed in his victory over the sea monster Leviathan. In each case, the satanic power of darkness and chaos is overcome by the God of light and life who, in victory, establishes his kingdom or rule.

In Zoroastrianism, the ancient religion of Persia (Iran), we have a good example of the development of a more-radical cosmic dualism of conflict. The founder of the religion was the prophet Zoroaster (or, more properly, Zarathustra; the former is a Greek corruption of this Iranian name) who, according to Persian tradition, was born in the seventh century B.C.E. Some scholars contend that, if not legen-

dary, Zarathustra may have lived as early as 1000 B.C.E. In any case,
tradition relates how he was brought before the celestial assembly and
was instructed by Ahura Mazda (later Ohrmazd), the supreme deity
and Wise Lord of Light, in the true religion. The result of this
encounter was Zarathustra's reform of ancient Persian polytheism,
transforming it into a tempered form of monotheism centered on the
worship of Ahura Mazda.

What is significant about Zarathustra's prophetic revolution, however, is his dramatic portrayal of a cosmic struggle between the dual
forces of good and evil, climaxing in a titanic **apocalypse** at the end
of time. According to Zarathustra, Ahura Mazda's supremacy and his
Good or Holy Spirit (Spenta Mainyu) are constantly challenged by
Angra Mainyu, the Bad Spirit, and his satanic *daevas*, or evil spirits.

The hymns written by Zarathustra, called the *Gathas*, portray the
entire world as divided between good and evil powers and between
moral right and wrong. According to the *Gathas*, this cosmic moral
division occurred in the beginning when Ahura Mazda created the
world and gave his creatures, including the two Spirits, freedom of
choice:

> Now the two primal Spirits, who revealed themselves in visions as
> Twins, are the Better and the Bad in thought and word and action.
> And between these two the wise one chose aright, the foolish not
> so. And when these twin Spirits came together in the beginning,
> they established Life and Not-Life, and that at the last the Worst
> Existence (Hell) shall be the followers of the Lie, but the Best
> Thought (Paradise) to him that follows Right. Of these twain Spirits
> he that followed the Lie *chose* doing the worst things; the holiest
> Spirit chose Right.[10]

Zarathustra did not himself teach a thoroughgoing dualism, for he
had no doubt about the ultimate issue in the struggle between the
two powers. In the fullness of time, Ahura Mazda would triumph
over evil. Centuries later, however, Zoroastrianism resorted once again
to older polytheistic gods and from this there evolved a more-radical
dualism between the Good Spirit, now called Ohrmazd, and Ahriman,
the Evil One. According to the *Bundahism*, a text from the ninth
century C.E., in the beginning light and darkness existed together with
no link between the two powers:

> Ohrmazd [Spenta Mainya] was on high in omniscience and goodness:
> for Indefinite Time he was ever in the light. That light is the Space
> and place of Ohrmazd: some call it the Endless Light . . .
>   Ahriman [Angra Mainyu] slow in knowledge, whose will is to smite,
> was deep down in the darkness: he was and is, yet will not be. The
> will to smite is his all, the darkness is his place: some call it the
> endless Darkness.[11]

In the *Vendidad*, a priestly text also of the ninth century C.E., Ohrmazd is portrayed as creator of all that is good, while Angra Mainyu is seen as creator of all that is evil and noxious—the two creators being coequal. Angra Mainyu, unlike satan or the devil in the Christian and Moslem traditions, creates his own *daevas* and all other harmful creatures: snakes, wolves, locusts, as well as evil men and their vices and lusts.

The power of Ahriman (Angra Mainyu) and his army of evil spirits is portrayed as finally regnant over this world. Water, earth, and plants are all defiled. Even Righteous Man, who held Ahriman at bay for 3,000 years is, finally, unable to withstand the Evil One. Ahriman is pictured exulting in his power and the ruin he has wrought:

> Perfect is my victory: for I have rent the sky, I have befouled it with murk and darkness, I have made it my stronghold. I have befouled the waters, pierced open the earth and defiled it with darkness. I have dried up the plants, and have brought death to the Bull, sickness to Gayomart. Against the stars have I set up the planets, frought with darkness. I have seized the kingdom. On the side of Ohrmazd none remains to do battle except only man; and man, isolated and alone, what can he do?[12]

This late Zoroastrian dualism profoundly affected the other religions of the ancient Near East with its worldly pessimism and sense of engagement in an intractable struggle against formidable powers of evil. None of the great monotheistic faiths of the West that came in contact with Persian religion—Judaism, Christianity, and Islam—succumbed fully to its radical dualism and pessimism. We know, however, that in the centuries just prior to the beginning of the Christian era, dualistic tendencies and historical pessimism found their way into Judaism. Philo, a Jewish philosopher of this time, speaks, although briefly, of God creating the world by means of two divine powers, one the creator of good and the other the creator of evil. According to the Rule of Qumran—one of the important, recently discovered scrolls from Dead Sea caves—two spirits were created by God, the Prince of Darkness and the Prince of Light, and together they rule this world.

Radical dualism came closest to capturing Christianity in the first two centuries of its life. The challenge came primarily from Gnosticism (from the Greek *gnosis*, meaning secret knowledge), a religio-philosophical movement of the Greco–Roman world, comprising many sects within paganism, Judaism, and Christianity. Gnosticism, like late Zoroastrianism, was thoroughly dualistic. It taught that this world was created by a Demiurge who was inferior to the Supreme Being. The human soul, a spark of the divine, had fallen from its heavenly home and was imprisoned in a mortal, material body. The soul could be saved from its horrible state only by acquiring true knowledge (*gnosis*), which would free it to return to its heavenly home. The Gnostic Christians rejected the Genesis account of Creation and taught that the true God of light had nothing to do with this vile and evil material world. According to the Gnostic Christians, this world was created and is now ruled by inferior powers, including the Old Testament God, Yahweh. Gnostic doctrine was widespread within Christianity by the second century, but it was then condemned by the Church at Rome in the middle of that century. Thereafter, its influence waned.

Manicheanism is a third historically influential form of radical dualism in the West. For a century, it was Christianity's chief rival. Manicheanism was founded in the third century C.E. by a Mesopotamian teacher named Mani. An eclectic thinker, Mani wanted to combine Gnostic Christianity with elements of Zoroastrianism and Greek philosophy. The world, according to Mani, is ruled by two independent, eternally opposing powers; Light, which he associates with the soul, and Darkness, or matter. Mani relates how Darkness attacked Light, causing the two to be mixed and the soul to be befouled. Mani further tells how the soul can be freed from the Darkness, its material prison. Some historians believe that the writings of St. Augustine (354–430 C.E.), which are so infused with strong, dualistic contrasts were deeply, if unconsciously, influenced by Manichean doctrine. St. Augustine had been a Manichee for 9 years before his conversion to Christianity.

Hellenistic–Gnostic and Persian ideas are unquestionably present in early Christian writers—St. Paul and St. John, for example—and most obviously in the apocalyptic world view that dominated Christianity in the first and second centuries. However, like Judaism and Islam, Christianity also came to view dualism as a mortal threat to both its doctrines of God and creation and repudiated it as a heresy. However, in Chapter 10 we shall see that as a **theodicy**, or explanation for the reality of evil, dualism has had great appeal.

Pantheism and Monism

Earlier, it was pointed out that the protest against animism and polytheism often took the form of pantheism and even monism. Pantheism (from the Greek words for "all" and "God") is the belief that all existing things are in some sense divine. Pantheism and monism (from the Greek word for "single") are often indistinguishable if, for example, it is believed that there is only one divine Being or Reality and that all finite things are simply modes or appearances of that One.

The Greek Stoic philosophers were pantheists. They attacked popular polytheism and taught that there is but one sacred Being, which

they called the **Logos**, or Reason. They identified this divine Logos
with a rarified element, the ether, or with the basic element, fire.
They further taught that each person is a spark of this divine Logos
and participates in the Logos through the exercise of reason (see
Chapter 9). Perhaps to satisfy more-popular religious sentiments, some
Stoics did personify the Logos, calling it Zeus and offering it hymns
and prayers.

A more-significant religious move from polytheism to pantheism and
monism can be observed in the historical development of Hinduism,
the religion of India. It is most evident in the contrast between the
ancient Vedic hymns and the later speculations found in the writings
called the *Upanishads*. The religion of early Hinduism is that of the
ancient Aryans and is reflected in three collections of hymns: the
Rig-Veda; the *Sama-Veda*; and the *Yajur-Veda*, used by different groups
of priests. This Vedic religion was polytheistic, and its pantheon included many gods, the most prominent being Indra, Varuna, Agni,
Soma, Rudra (later Śiva), and Vishnu. Indra, the most popular and
often invoked, is the warrior-king and god of the storm. Varuna is
the guardian of *rta*, the law or cosmic order, while Agni and Soma
are clearly associated with the sacred Vedic ritual sacrifice. Both Śiva
and Vishnu emerge as the great Supreme Beings of later Hinduism.

As was the case in Greece, the earthy, life-affirming but simple
polytheism of the ancient Vedic period was, in time, found wanting.
R. C. Zaehner speaks of the change:

> Toward the end of the Rig-Vedic period, it becomes clear that a
> plurality of gods becoming ever less distinguishable from each other
> was beginning to be an embarrassment, for these later Vedic seers
> were becoming increasingly interested in what constituted the unitary
> and unifying principle of the universe, and in this quest the multi-
> plicity of gods was a scandal.... So according to the new way of
> thinking the personalities of the various gods shrank and became
> little more than mere names marking a single reality. This 'they
> called Indra, Mitra, Varuna, Agni.... What is but one the wise call
> by manifold names' (Rig-Veda 1.164–46). Here Vedic polytheism is
> already slipping into classical Hindu pantheism.[13]

By the end of the Vedic period, the many gods are perceived "as
but marking a single reality." The thrust of this reflection is carried
further along in the *Upanishads* (meaning "sitting near a teacher"),
the great Hindu speculative treatises, often in the form of dialogues
written between 700 and 300 B.C.E. The *Upanishads* include a mixture
of theistic and pantheistic tendencies, but the latter is characteristic
of many texts. In reflecting on the origin and explanation of the
phenomenal world, the Indians first posited fire as the primal element,
then space, and then the more-abstract notions of being and nonbeing.

But the conception that finally gained ascendancy in the *Upanishads* is called Brahman.

In the *Rig-Veda*, *brahma* is interpreted as meaning "hymn," "prayer," or "sacred knowledge." However, it also came to signify the sacred *power* inherent in the hymn or in knowledge; it was then associated with the world-ground, with the power that pervades and upholds the cosmos, in which all things live and have their being. In the *Brihad-Āranyaka Upanishad*, it is written: "As a spider might come out with his thread, as small sparks come forth from the fire, even so from this Soul [Brahman] came forth all vital energies, all worlds, all gods, all beings."[14]

All things, including the human soul, are actual only through their participation in Brahman. The *Chāndogya Upanishad* declares: "Verily this whole world is Brahma. Tranquil, let one worship It as that from which he came forth, as that into which he will be dissolved, as that in which he breathes."[15] Here, we encounter the first explicit statement of Indian pantheism, but it is latent in much earlier speculation.

According to the *Chāndogya Upanishad*, the human soul, all that is subjective, is merely a mode or phase of Brahman, the One. The term that came to be used for the soul or inner self, in contrast to the body, is Ātman. "Yajnavalkya," asks an inquirer, "explain to me him who is the Brahman present and not beyond our ken, him who is the soul of all things." The answer is that Brahman "is your soul":

> He who dwelling in the earth ... in the waters ... in the fire ... in the atmosphere ... the wind ... the sky ... the sun. ... He who dwelling in all things, yet other than all things, whom all things do not know, whose body all things are, who controls all things from within—He is your Soul, the Inner Controller, the Immortal.[16]

The soul is spoken of here as Brahman, but this form of Hindu pantheism is not fully monistic. As the *Brihad-Āranyaka Upanishad* makes plain, finite entities are the body of Brahman who is "yet other than all things." The world, including the soul, is divine since Brahman is immanent in all things. However, there is not a perfect unity or monism but rather a plurality in unity. This is evident in the well-known parable of the bees and the honey, which is found in the *Chāndogya Upanishad*.

> As the bees, my dear, prepare honey by collecting the essences of different trees and reducing the essence to a unity, as they are not able to discriminate 'I am the essence of this tree,' 'I am the essence of that tree'—even so, indeed, my dear, all creatures here, though they reach Being, know not 'We have reached Being.' ...
> That which is the finest essence—this whole world has *that* as its soul. That is Reality. That is Ātman (Soul). That art thou, Svetaketu.[17]

While Ātman and Brahman are one, because the individual soul loses its individuality in Brahman, distinctions do remain. Nevertheless, a tremendous change has taken place. The goal of religion now is knowledge of the pantheistic unity of the soul and world in Ātman–Brahman. The diligent performance of ritual sacrifice to the many Vedic gods is perceived as crude and a fraud: "So whoever worships another divinity [than his Self], thinking 'He is one and I another,' he knows not."[18]

Classical Hinduism did not remain entirely satisfied with the ambiguous relationship between the One and the world of plural beings that characterized Indian pantheism. In the relatively late *Māndūkya Upanishad*, the move to a thoroughgoing monism is evident. It is a state beyond waking, beyond dreaming, or even beyond dreamless sleep. It is spoken of as a fourth state, that

> . . . has cognizance neither of what is inside nor what is outside, nor of both together; it is not a mass of wisdom, it is not wise nor yet unwise. It is unseen, there can be no commerce with it; it is impalpable, has no characteristics, is unthinkable; it cannot be designated. Its essence is its firm conviction of the oneness of itself; it causes the phenomenal world to cease; it is tranquil and mild, devoid of duality. . . . [19]

This extreme form of monism, or absolute nonduality, was developed in the *Vedanta Sūtra* (*Vedanta* meaning "the end of Vedas") in the first century before the Christian era. The Indian philosophy of nonduality thus came to be called the *Vedanta*. However, the greatest systematizer of radical Hindu *Advaita* (nondualism) *Vedanta* was a later thinker named Śankara (788–820 C.E.). Śankara begins his teaching with the assertion of the *Māndūkya Upanishad* that the Ultimate or Real is "unthinkable" and "cannot be designated"; that is, it has no attributes. According to Śankara, it follows that the phenomenal world of subjects and objects, the world of plurality, "ceases" or, rather, is an illusion or appearance. Śankara introduces the concept of *māyā* to signify the illusory phenomenal world, which gives us only an "apparent" and not a real knowledge of the relationship of the One and the many. According to Śankara, belief that the objects of our sense experience are real is the work of ignorance. In one of his favorite similes, he says that *māyā* is like perceiving a rope as a snake in the twilight. The 'snake' is simply imposed on the rope through our ignorance. Likewise, it is the work of ignorance to believe in the independent and contingent reality of the individual self or soul. True knowledge is achieved only when we realize that the self, Ātman, and Brahman are not distinct, that the soul is identical with Brahman, which alone exists, timeless and eternal. Such knowledge is liberating, but it cannot be described because it transcends the limits of space and time. The Hindus call it *sat chit ānanda*, "being-awareness-bliss."

A type of pantheism, with liberating effects not unlike those described by exponents of Vedanta, is observable in certain forms of "natural mystical experience." Numerous examples are cited in William James's *The Varieties of Religious Experience*. The recollection of the English poet, Tennyson, is typical:

> I have never had revelations through anaesthetics, but a kind of waking trance—this for lack of a better word—I have frequently had, quite up from boyhood, when I have been all alone. This has come upon me through repeating my own name to myself silently, till all at once, as it were out of the intensity of the consciousness of individuality, individuality itself seemed to dissolve and fade away into a boundless being, and this not a confused state but the clearest, the surest of the sure, utterly beyond words—where death was an almost laughable impossibility—the loss of personality (if so it were) seeming no extinction, but the only true life. I am ashamed of my feeble description. Have I not said the state is utterly beyond words?[20]

Tennyson's experience of the dissolving of individuality and the sense of death being "an almost laughable impossibility" is not unlike the Vedantist's efforts to describe the ineffable bliss of "the One without a second."

If we review our comparison of forms of deity, we see that pantheism and monism are located at one extremity of the spectrum and mana or animism at the other. The two, however, join in the conviction that sacred power is immanent in and through all things. Polytheism appears to conceive of sacred power as more fully personalized, as in the youth and beauty of the god Apollo, although some forms of polytheism appear to be indistinguishable from animism. The polytheistic religions of the ancient Mediterranean world and the Near East also tend to move toward hierarchical patterns, exhibiting a division of labor within the pantheon of gods, with one god becoming preeminent in power and authority. On occasion, the various gods are simply the names for one supreme deity.

While the problem in the East was how to reconcile the fact of a world of plurality with the intuition of a single world-soul or ground, the problem for the Western historical religions was how to reconcile the presence of sacred power *in* the world with its wholly otherness or *transcendence of* the world. The crisis that faced Greco–Roman religion, and the Semitic religions as well, came at the point when their pantheon of gods began to appear all too earthly and human. The gods' moral weaknessess and errors exposed their lack of genuine transcendence. In the East, the move against polytheism often—but by no means always—took the form of pantheism and monism. In the West, the protest against and reform of polytheism usually took the form of *monotheism*, or the worship of one god.

Monotheism

Monotheism is not the same as belief in a high god or even a creator god in the sky. In primitive religion, the high god often is considered superior, but his remoteness frequently results in the god's eclipse by more-popular gods of the local polytheistic cult. Marduk was "a great king above all gods" in Babylon, but, even in ancient Mesopotamia, the other gods of the pantheon also had their dominions and functions. Monotheism, as we know it today, is a rather late development in the history of religions and is most appropriately associated with the emerging faith of ancient Israel. However, monotheistic tendencies are present in a number of movements that sought to reform polytheism, for example, by Zoroaster in ancient Iran and, perhaps most notably, in Egypt for a brief time under the Pharoah Amenhotep IV about 1375 B.C.E.

Amenhotep was a devotee of the sun-god, Aton, and when he ascended the throne he suppressed all polytheistic cults and had the names of all gods erased from the monuments. He set up a new priesthood and changed his own name to Ikhnaton (meaning "profitable to Aton"). He declared Aton to be "the sole god whose powers no other possesseth," the Creator and Sustainer, ruling the entire cosmos. No cult image was allowed, other than the simple sun disc with its emanating rays. The singing of hymns and the giving of offerings were the principal acts of worship. The simplicity of Ikhnaton's monotheism is reflected in an inscription in one of the tombs at El-Amarna:

> Beautiful in thine appearing in the horizon of heaven,
>   thou living sun, the first who lived!
> Thou riseth in the eastern horizon and
> Thou fillest every land with thy bounty.
> Thou art beautiful and great and glisteneth, and art
>   high above every land.
> Thy rays, they compass the lands, so far as all that
>   thou hast created.
> Thou art Re, and thou reachest unto their end and
>   subduest them for thy dear Son.
> Though thou art far away, yet are thy rays upon earth;
>   Thou art before their face — thy going.[21]

King Ikhnaton and Queen Nefertiti
presenting offerings to the Egyptian
sun god, Aton, the one Creator and
Sustainer. Aton is transcendent, yet
his rays encompass the entire earth.
(*Source*: Courtesy
of The Metropolitan Museum of Art.)

Ikhnaton's religious reform was short lived, however, and after his death in 1350, the Egyptians returned to their earlier polytheistic ways. It is therefore correct to say that monotheism, as we understand the term, has its origin in the great Semitic religions of the West: principally in Israel, and later in Judaism, Christianity, and Islam, all of which began as protests against polytheism.

The religion of the early Israelite tribes was not monotheistic. Before the ninth century B.C.E., the patriarchs and the kings of Israel did not worship a universal Creator god but, rather, a tribal god who was nevertheless conceived as unique in power and moral authority. **Henotheism**, a term coined by Max Müller, perhaps best describes the religion of Israel in both the Patriarchal and the Mosaic periods. Henotheism refers to those religions that, while recognizing the reality of many gods, worship and believe in the efficacy of only one god. The early Israelites lived in a polytheistic environment, but from the time of Moses they considered their God Yahweh as unique in power and authority.

The ancient Israelites did not arrive at a knowledge of Yahweh by examining the order of nature or by rational speculation, as did the

Greeks. Rather, Yahweh was revealed to Israel through her historical experience and, most notably, through the Exodus from Egypt, the Covenant sealed at Mount Sinai, and the exile in Babylonia. According to the account in the Book of Exodus, Moses was tending the flock of his father-in-law, Jethro, in the desert when an angel of the Lord appeared to him in a flaming bush that was not consumed:

> God called to [Moses] out of the bush, 'Moses, Moses!' And he said, 'Here am I.' Then he said, 'Do not come near; put off your shoes from your feet, for the place on which you are standing is holy ground.' And he said, 'I am the God of your father, the God of Abraham, the God of Isaac, and the God of Jacob.' And Moses hid his face, for he was afraid to look at God.
>
> Then the Lord said, 'I have seen the affliction of my people who are in Egypt, and have heard their cry because of their taskmasters; I know their sufferings, and I have come down to deliver them out of the hand of the Egyptians, and to bring them out of that land to a good and broad land, a land flowing with milk and honey. . . . Come, I will send you to Pharaoh that you may bring forth my people, the sons of Israel, out of Egypt. . . . Then Moses said to God, 'If I come to the people of Israel and say to them, 'The God of your fathers has sent me to you,' and they ask me, 'What is his name? what shall I say to them?'

The answer Moses received is a most significant event in the history of religions. God said to Moses, "I am who I am." And he said, "Say I am [YHWH*] has sent me to you" (Exodus 3:4–14).

Whether the divine name Yahweh predates Moses is a matter of dispute, but it is generally agreed that Moses' interpretation of the **theophany** both in the desert and later on Mount Sinai gave birth to a new conception of deity. It is not a fully conceived monotheism but a henotheism that, for all intents and purposes, can be called "practical monotheism." Yahweh is a transcendent, holy God who nevertheless enters into a solemn covenant with the people Israel, promising them, for their strict loyalty, peace and prosperity. Yahweh also is "a jealous God" (Ex. 20:5; 24:14), a conviction associated with the first commandment of the Decalogue or Ten Commandments: namely, that Israel will have "no other gods before me" (Ex. 20:3). Yahweh demands exclusive worship and no idols or images are to be made of him. However, the period of Israel's history from the entrance into Canaan (the thirteenth century B.C.E.) — rife with polytheistic cults — to the religious reforms of King Josiah (621 B.C.E.), testifies to Israel's violent struggle against pagan idolatry (see Judges 2:11–13; II Kings 16:3–4).

---

* The divine name YHWH is here connected with the verb *hayah*, to be. In ancient Hebrew texts only consonants and not vowels were written to reproduce the name.

The great Prophets of the ninth to the sixth centuries B.C.E. enlarged Israel's understanding of the meaning of Yahweh's "jealousy" to include his sovereignty and providential care over the entire creation. In the eighth century, for example, the prophet Amos triumphantly affirmed Yahweh's control over the affairs of *all* nations (Amos 1:1–2:3). Likewise, the prophet Isaiah heaped scorn on the gods of the nations as worthless idols and warned Israel of the wrath of God. He saw Yahweh as no tribal god but as the Lord of all the nations that are subject to his decrees. Yahweh even uses the enemy nations to chasten unrighteous Israel:

Oh, Assyria, the rod of my anger, the staff of my fury!
Against a godless nation I send him and against the people
  of my wrath I command him.

(Isaiah 10:5–6)

A century later, Jeremiah denounced the gods as simply "no gods" (2:11; 5:11) and worthless:

They are both stupid and foolish; the instruction of idols is
  but wood! . . .
But the Lord is the true god;
he is the living God and the everlasting King.
At his wrath the earth quakes,
and the nations cannot endure his indignation.

(Jer. 10:8, 10)

During the Exile in Babylon, Israel's God speaks through the prophet known as Second Isaiah, in terms that are unquestionably monotheistic.

I am the Lord and there is no other,
  beside me there is no God;
I gird you, though you do not know me,
that men may know, from the rising of the sun
and from the west, that there is none beside me;
I am the Lord, and there is no other.
I form the light and create darkness.
I make weal and create woe,
I am the Lord, who does all these things.

(Isaiah 45:5–7)

A genuine monotheism can thus be observed evolving in Israel in the period from the Exodus from Egypt (1250 B.C.E.) to the Exile in Babylon (sixth century B.C.E.). Israel's understanding of God developed out of the nation's experience of Yahweh's loving care, providential intervention, and wider sovereignty over all the nations. Yet underlying this experience of God's providence were certain convictions about God's other attributes or character. Yahweh was, first, a *personal* God, not a remote sky-god, but a God who intervenes in human affairs—a *personal providence*. Furthermore, there was neither a time when Yahweh was not nor a time when he will not be. He is from everlasting to everlasting, *eternal*. All things come from his hand as *Creator*. Yahweh is also wise and benevolent, and his councils will not, finally, be thwarted—that is, he is what the theologians later will call **omniscient** and **omnipotent**. These rather abstract concepts were, of course, only tacit in Israel's faith in God, but they were later fully defined by the theologians in all three of the great monotheistic traditions. The distinctiveness of Western theism, as well as some of its unique problems, is connected, as we shall see, with this rather elaborate philosophical development of biblical monotheism. Classical Western monotheism is, in fact, the result of the joining of biblical theism and Greek philosophical speculation, especially in the centuries between the Jewish thinker Philo (20 B.C.E.–54 C.E.) and the great Catholic theologian Thomas Aquinas (1225–1274 C.E.).

Before describing in detail God's attributes as defined by theologians in the West, we can get a sense of their conceptual dexterity and of the complexity of philosophical monotheism by listening to one of them. Our example is the orthodox Islamic theologian and mystic, al-Ghazālī (1058–1111 C.E.), a contemporary of the equally brilliant Christian theologian, St. Anselm. Al-Ghazālī's statement joins all the elements of classic monotheism:

> 81. Praise be to God, the Creator . . . He is one in essence, unequalled, unique, sole, incomparable, alone without opponent or rival. He exists from the beginning, without predecessor, from all eternity, beginningless; he endures, none follows him, he is everlasting without end. . . . He is no substance and there are no substances in him; he is not an accident and there are no accidents in him. . . . He is high above heaven and earth, and yet is 'closer to man than his own arteries' . . . for his presence is not like that of a body . . . he is not in things nor are things in him. . . . He is exalted above change and alteration; for him there are no happenings, no misfortune can befall him, but rather he possesses everlastingly the properties of his majesty, beyond the reach of decay, and for the attributes of his perfection he needs no growth or process of perfection.

> 82. He knows all things knowable. . . . He knows the inward motives and impulses and the most secret thoughts, with an external knowledge which he has had before all time. . . . He wills all that exists, and determines events. . . . What he wills takes place and what he does not will, does not take place. . . . From eternity he willed the existence of things in the times appointed for them, and they

come into being at those times and no others, precisely in accordance with his knowledge and will.

> 83. He brought forth the creation to reveal his power . . . not as though there were for him any necessity or need for the creation. . . . It is proof of his generosity, and not a necessity, that he showers mercy and good things upon his servants, a pure gift on his part, for he could have punished his servants with every possible affliction, suffering, and illness.[22]

Viewed in isolation, each of the divine attributes described by al-Ghazālī appears abstract, the product of intellectual analysis; however, each one is the result of reflection on the religious experience of believers who, in the first instance, personally felt the reality of standing in the presence of an unseen and awesomely majestic God. The classical attributes of God derive, then, from a more primal experience of God's overwhelming *holiness*. As the *Qur'an* says: "He is *the* God, other than whom there is none; He is the knower of the seen and unseen . . . the Sovereign, the Holy" (59:22).

God's holiness is traditionally symbolized by the spatial imagery of height. Height stands for God's transcendence, for the fact that God is above and distinct, although not remote, from the world. Unlike pantheism, monotheism insists that the world is not a part of God; God and the world remain distinct. Furthermore, God's holiness reflects his self-sufficiency. God does not need the world. Why God created the world, except as an act of love, remains a mystery. One fundamental aspect of God's holiness and transcendence is the fact that "his ways are not our ways." The holy God remains, finally, mysterious and not fully knowable.

A primary tenet of *mono*theism is that God is *one* — the belief in the unity of God. It became a critical doctrine for both Judaism and Christianity in their encounters with Greco–Roman polytheism between roughly 300 B.C.E. and 300 C.E., and later, of course, for Islam. Defenders of these religions argued that God is, by definition, the object of absolute devotion, but that a god who *shares* his being and powers with other gods cannot be such an object. Thomas Aquinas later insisted on the self-evidence of God's oneness, simplicity, or unity on the grounds of his perfection:

> For God, as we have seen, embraces in himself the whole perfection of existence. Now many Gods, if they existed, would have to differ. Something belonging to one would not belong to the other. And if this were a lack the one God would not be altogether perfect, whilst if it were a perfection the other God would lack it. So there cannot be more than one God. And this is why philosophers in ancient

times, bowing, so to speak, to the truth, held that if the source of things was unlimited it could not be many.[23]

Implied in God's perfection is the further belief that he is not limited as are all finite creatures. God is *infinite*—that is, nonfinite. This emphasis can be observed in efforts at all costs, especially in Islam and Judaism, to avoid **anthropomorphism**, or the tendency to view God in too-human terms. This can be seen in the writings of the Mu'tazilites, Islamic thinkers of the ninth century C.E., who sought to speak of God in only negative terms:

> The Mu'tazila agree that God is one; there is no thing like him . . . he is not a body, not a form, not flesh and blood, not an individual, not substance nor attribute . . . no movement, rest, or division . . . no place comprehends him, no time passes over him . . . he is not comparable with men and does not resemble creatures in any respect . . . he is unlike whatever occurs to the mind or is pictured in the imagination.[24]

Since monotheists deny that God suffers all those limitations common to finite, created beings, it is understandable that negative predicates often must be used in speaking of God, for example, that he is *immutable*. However, the term most used by Medieval theologians to refer to God's infinity is his *aseity* (from the Latin *a se esse*, meaning "being from oneself"), self-existence or necessity. God is not dependent on any other reality for his being or his character. God is not created, nor is there anything that can limit or destroy him. According to Aristotle, the essence of finite *homo sapiens* is not existence since we all one day will die. Humans are essentially rational, though finite, beings. But God's unique essence is, indeed, to exist—he alone possesses *aseity*, necessary existence. It follows from God's infinity and aseity that he is *eternal*. God is without beginning or end; if God had a beginning, there obviously would have to be another being or prior cause that brought him into existence. This would deny God's infinity, independence, and perfection. However, God's eternity is not to be confused with everlastingness, as in a temporal series. God is outside the temporal series; God is timeless.

Three additional divine attributes follow from God's infinity and aseity. First, monotheism must conceive of God as the Creator of all that exists. The biblical doctrine of creation is discussed at length in Chapter 8, and so we need refer to it only briefly here. For monotheism, creation means creation *ex nihilo*—creation out of nothing—since there can be nothing that is prior to God or that God is required to create. God does not form a pre-existent material into an ordered cosmos. God and his creation, the world, are distinct, the latter being wholly dependent on the former. Creatures are dependent on God not only for their being but also for their continued existence. God's creative activity is continuous.

In this latter respect, classical monotheism differs from **deism**, which teaches that God created the world but no longer has any commerce with it; rather, that God simply allows the world to continue according to the laws which he originally established. This conception of deity was popular in the eighteenth century, both in Europe and in America, among free thinkers who were offended by miracles and the orthodox claim that God intervened directly in worldly events on special occasions. According to the Deists, as they were called, belief in God is a rational necessity because it is required to explain the existence of a world of contingent or non-self-existent beings. The Deists argued that without a first cause or first mover, the world remains inexplicable; out of nothing comes nothing (*ex nihilo nihil fit*). This deistical conception of God is analogous to that proposed by Aristotle (384–322 B.C.E.) in his proof of the necessity of an unmoved mover:

> 18. . . . all things that are in motion must be moved by something.
> Now this may come about in either of two ways. Either the movent is not responsible for the motion, which is to be referred to something else which moves the movent, or the movent is itself responsible for the motion. Further, in the latter case, either the movent immediately precedes the last thing in the series, or there may be one or more immediate links, e.g., the stick moves the stone and is moved by the hand, which again is moved by the man . . .
> If then everything that is in motion must be moved by something, and the movent must either itself be moved by something else or not, and in the former case there must be some first movent that is not itself moved by anything else . . . (for it is impossible that there should be an infinite series of movents, each of which is itself moved by something else, since in an infinite series there is no first term) — if then everything that is in motion is moved by something, and the first movent is moved but not by anything else, it must be moved by itself . . .
>
> 22. . . . the following considerations will make it clear that there must necessarily be some such thing, which, while it has the capacity of moving something else, is itself unmoved and exempt from all change.[25]

Aristotle is arguing that the fact of a world process, without beginning or ending, requires either that the process itself be necessary (but the finite and contingent cannot be necessary) or that such a process implies an agent whose existence is itself necessary and eternal.

The Aristotelian argument became the foundation of Western natural theology and what is called the **cosmological proof** of the existence of God.

In Aristotle's work, classic monotheism found an intellectual resource of incomparable value. However, monotheism could not accept the idea of an "absentee" God, one who sets the world in motion but has since left it to run on its own. Monotheism asserts that God's *creativity is continuous*. Thomas Aquinas, for example, argues that every being remains in existence through the immediate and continuous creativity of God alone:

> Since the infinite must be everywhere and in all things, we have now to consider whether this applies to God. God is in all things, indeed, as part of their essence, or as a quality, but in the manner that an efficient cause is present to that on which it acts. An efficient cause must be in touch with the product of its action immediately, and this by its own power. Now since God's very essence is his existence, created existence is his proper effect. This effect God causes, not only when things first begin to be, but so long as they continue to be. While a thing endures, therefore, God must be present to it according to its mode of being. Existence is most intimate to each and deepest in all reality since it is the heart of all perfection. Hence, God is in all things, and intimately.[26]

Two additional divine attributes are implied by God's creativity, as well as by his infinity and aseity. One such perfection is *omniscience*, or the belief that God is all-knowing. We finite humans develop our knowledge piecemeal through experience. We are fallible. According to monotheism, God knows all things perfectly. There is nothing that falls outside his preknowledge or is not dependent on his will. Events that come to be in future time are already known to God but, according to Aquinas, without his imposing on them the necessity of existing. God is omniscient, but the creation is also given a relative freedom or autonomy.

Finally, God's infinity and creativity imply his *omnipotence*, the belief that God is able to do all things within his nature. The last three words are important, since omnipotence does not mean that God can act contrary to the very laws he himself has created. Monotheists, therefore, insist that it is only reasonable to believe that God's power of action is always within his own, so to speak, self-imposed limits — limits imposed, for example, by creating this world rather than some other and by creating human beings with genuine freedom.

The attributes of omniscience and omnipotence are, however, problematic for monotheism when they are joined with God's infinite *goodness and love* — qualities essential to monotheistic belief. This question naturally arises: If God is both omnipotent and infinitely good and loving, then why does he permit evil? We will not pursue the question here since we will do so at length when we consider the various responses to the problem of evil and suffering in Chapter 11, on types of theodicy.

In this chapter, we have observed the many ways in which human beings have experienced the reality of sacred power—from animism and polytheism through highly philosophical conceptions of monotheism and monism. As we have seen, any object, person, or event—from a stone or a bear's skull to the world itself, or the power that infinitely transcends this created world—can be and have been the object of religious awe and worship. Another universal religious concern has been the origin and order of the natural and human world. Cosmogony, or accounts of the origin and order of the world, is our next subject of study.

Notes

1. For this account, I am dependent on J. Maringer's *The Gods of Prehistoric Man* (New York, 1960).
2. *The Iliad of Homer*. Trans. Richmond Lattimore (Chicago, 1951).
3. D. S. Hogarth, *A Wandering Scholar in the Levant* (London, 1896), pp. 179–80. See, for example, "An Italian Religious Feast" in James J. Preston, ed., *Mother Worship* (Chapel Hill, 1982), pp. 95–122.
4. *Ancient Near Eastern Texts*. Ed. James B. Pritchard (Princeton, 1950), pp. 108–9.
5. Swami Nirvedananda, "Sri Ramakrisna and Spiritual Renaissance," in H. Bhattacharyya, ed., *The Cultural Heritage of India*, IV (Calcutta, 1956), p. 661.
6. *Greek Religious Thought from Homer to the Age of Alexander*. Ed. F. M. Cornford (London, 1923), p. 85.
7. Cornford, *Greek Religious Thought*, p. 87.
8. *I-Ching*, Hsi Tz'u, 1. As cited in W. T. deBary, ed., *Sources of the Chinese Tradition* (New York, 1960), pp. 211–12.
9. Arthur Waley, *Three Ways of Thought in Ancient China* (New York, 1956), p. 16.
10. James Hope Moulton, *Early Zoroastrianism* (London, 1913), p. 349.
11. *Greater Bundahishn* 2:12–36. Cited in R. C. Zaehner, *The Dawn and Twilight of Zoroastrianism* (London, 1961), p. 248.
12. R. C. Zaehner, *Zoroastrianism*, p. 264.
13. R. C. Zaehner, *Hinduism* (London, 1966), p. 39.
14. *The Thirteen Principal Upanishads*. Trans. Robert E. Hume (London, 1921), p. 95.
15. Hume, *Upanishads*, p. 209.
16. Hume, *Upanishads*, p. 110–11.
17. Hume, *Upanishads*, p. 246.

18. Hume, *Upanishads*, p. 84.
19. *Māndūkya Upanishad* 7. Trans. and cited in R. C. Zaehner, *Hinduism*, p. 56.
20. William James, *The Varieties of Religious Experience* (London, 1902), p. 384. See R. B. Martin, *Tennyson: The Unquiet Heart* (Oxford, 1980), p. 28–9.
21. Davies, *Rock-Tombs of El-Amarna* (London, 1903–8). Cited in E. O. James, *The Concept of Deity* (London, 1950), pp. 94–5.
22. AL-Ghazālī, *Resuscitation of the Sciences of Religion*. Trans. and cited in C. Hartshorne and William L. Reese, *Philosophers Speak of God* (Chicago, 1953), p. 107.
23. Thomas Aquinas, *Summa Theologica*, Blackfriars ed. (London, 1964), 1a, 11, 3.
24. Montgomery Watt, *The Formative Period of Islamic Thought* (Edinburgh, 1973), pp. 246–7.
25. *The Works of Aristotle*. Trans. under editorship of J. A. Smith and W. D. Ross (Oxford, 1912), pp. 256a, 2–20; 258a, 14–23.
26. *Summa Theologica* 1a, 8, 1. *Philosophical Texts*, ed. Thomas Gilby (Oxford, 1951), p. 234.

Review Questions

1. Describe what takes place in the movement from animism or diffuse forms of polytheism to what is called monarchical polytheism.
2. Contrast the dualism of Chinese *yin-yang* with the Western forms of dualism found in late Zoroastrianism, or in Gnosticism and Manicheanism. Can you detect any dualistic tendencies in contemporary Western religion, for example, in some expressions of Christianity or Islam?
3. Characterize pantheistic forms of deity or sacred power. How does monism differ from pantheism? Scholars have remarked that mystic union or at-one-ment with nature is frequently experienced in early youth, as described here by Tennyson. Have you ever had such a "natural mystical experience"? If so, describe it.
4. Describe the several attributes of deity as developed in classical monotheism. How does monotheism differ from deism?

Suggestions for Further Reading

PRIMITIVE AND ANCIENT CONCEPTIONS OF DEITY

ELIADE, MIRCEA, *From Primitives to Zen* (New York: Harper & Row, 1977).
———, *Patterns in Comparative Religion* (New York: Sheed and Ward, 1958).
GUTHRIE, W. K., *The Greeks and Their Gods* (London: Methuen, 1950).

JAMES, E. O., *The Ancient Gods* (London: Weidenfeld and Nicholson, 1960).
_____ , *The Concept of Deity* (London: Hutchinson, 1950).
MARINGER, JOHANNES, *The Gods of Prehistoric Man* (New York: Alfred A. Knopf, 1960).

MOTHER GODDESSES

HAWLEY, JOHN S. and DONNA WULFF (eds.), *The Divine Consort: Rādhā and the Goddesses of India* (Berkeley: University of California Press, 1983).
JAMES, E. O., *The Cult of the Mother Goddess* (New York: Praeger Publishers, 1959).
NEUMANN, ERICH, *The Great Mother: An Analysis of the Archetype* (Princeton: Princeton University Press, 1955).
OLSON, CARL (ed.), *The Book of the Goddess: Past and Present* (New York: Crossroad, 1986).
PRESTON, JAMES J. (ed.), *Mother Worship* (Chapel Hill: University of North Carolina Press, 1982). The essays in this volume call in question the generalizations of James, Neumann, and others.

NON-WESTERN FORMS OF DUALISM, POLYTHEISM, THEISM, AND MONISM

BHATTACHARJI, S., *The Indian Theogony* (Cambridge: Cambridge University Press, 1970).
DANIELOU, ALAIN, *Hindu Polytheism* (New York: Pantheon Books, 1964).
DAS GUPTA, S. N., *A History of Indian Philosophy*, 5 vols. (Cambridge: Cambridge University Press). This and the Radhakrishnan work, cited below, are a mine of information on Indian Vedantic monism.
NEEDHAM, JOSEPH, *Science and Civilization in China* II (Cambridge: Cambridge University Press, 1956). An account of Chinese *yin-yang* dualism.
O'FLAHERTY, W. D., *Hindu Myths* (Baltimore: Penguin Books, 1975).
RADHAKRISHNAN, S., *Indian Philosophy*, 2 vols. (New York: Macmillan, 1923).
SMART, NINIAN, *Doctrine and Argument in Indian Philosophy* (London: Allen and Unwin, 1964).
ZAEHNER, R. H., *The Dawn and Twilight of Zoroastrianism* (New York: Putnam, 1961). On classic Iranian dualism.

STUDIES OF WESTERN THEISM

EICHRODT, WALTHER, *Theology of the Old Testament*, 2 vols. (Philadelphia: Westminster Press, 1961). The beginnings and development of Hebrew monotheism.
HARTSHORNE, CHARLES, and WILLIAM L. REESE, *Philosophers Speak of God* (Chicago: University of Chicago Press, 1953). An excellent anthology of texts representing classical forms of theism, pantheism, and panentheism.
HICK, JOHN, *The Existence of God* (New York: Macmillan, 1964). An excellent collection of classic texts on the ontological, cosmological, teleological, and moral arguments for theistic belief and contemporary theistic problems.

OWEN, H. P., *Concepts of Deity* (London: Macmillan, 1971). A study of Western theism, pantheism, process theology, and the view of contemporary theologians.

TWO CLASSIC WESTERN TEXTS

AQUINAS, ST. THOMAS, *Summa Theologica* I, Questions 1-26. *Basic Writings of Saint Thomas Aquinas*, ed. Anton C. Pegis (New York: Random House, 1945).

CALVIN, JOHN, *Institutes of the Christian Religion*, Book I. (Philadelphia: The Westminster Press, 1936).

CHAPTER 8

Cosmogony

OVERVIEW

Among humanity's most persistent questions are the following: "How did our world come to be and to achieve its natural and social order?" and "Where are we and the world going?" This chapter explores a variety of religious responses to the first question. A cosmogony is an account of the generation or creation of world order (from the Greek *kosmos*, meaning world, and the root of *gignesthai*, meaning to be born). As we shall see, interest in beginnings is not the result of idle speculation; it is intimately tied to basic concerns about the natural and social order, the status of the gods and humankind, and human action.

We shall begin by underlining this practical basis of cosmogony and then present a typology of cosmogonic myths, those primarily found in primitive and archaic societies. We shall conclude, however, by reflecting on the mythic elements in modern, "scientific" *cosmology* or characterizations of the cosmos — for example, in the Marxian and Freudian world view — and on the mistake involved in attempting to justify religious cosmogony by means of scientific explanation.

Our typology includes accounts of generation or procreation from a primal substance(s), the sexual union of a primal male and female, generation from a cosmic egg, and the ordering of a primal chaos through the conflict of divine forces. Sometimes, as in Chinese Taoism, the world is viewed as an ongoing, infinite process of becoming, with no conception of a fixed or final sacred order. A pervasive cosmogonic theme is that of divine craftsmanship; the ordering of the world of pre-existent matter through the agency of a god or, as in the philosopher Plato's speculation, through the creative work of an intelligent and purposeful Mind, or *Nous*.

The crucial differences between the Greek and ancient Hebrew (Genesis) accounts of creation are discussed, including the very differ-

198

ent implications of each conception for such important matters as the
nature of God and the problem of evil. These very problems have,
however, convinced some religions—for example, Jainism in India and
certain schools of Buddhism—to insist on the futility of cosmogonic
speculation and to focus their attention on the practical matter of
achieving liberation from evil and suffering.

The chapter concludes with an examination of **cosmology** in a scientific age and with a critical analysis of the effort, by Creation Science, to claim a *scientific* basic for a particular religious cosmogony.

The Practical Basis of Cosmogony

The creation of a world, in the sense of an original beginning, is an
idea that many Westerners take for granted. A number of our unwit-
ting assumptions about cosmology—that is, about the nature of the
world and our place in it—are derived from the Bible. Also, we may
not be conscious of the fact that the idea of *a beginning* of the world
is a relatively sophisticated idea, involving some sense of detachment
from our environment and the capacity to imagine a state of affairs
radically different from what we experience daily. It would be quite
natural to think of our environment as always the way it is observed
now to be. Primal man did, nevertheless, speculate about the origin
and ordering of the world. The rudiments of such imaginative thinking can be found in efforts to answer questions about the origin of
some regularly observed feature of nature or social life, such as the
tribe.

Until the emergence of Greek and Indian philosophic speculation
in the first millennium B.C.E., cosmogony was cloaked in the vivid,
concrete imagery of myth. For the purpose of our discussion here,
we can refer again to Eliade's comment that "myth narrates a sacred
history; it relates an event that took place in primordial Time, the
fabled time of the 'beginnings.'"[1] Of special interest is Eliade's claim
that myth is related to a creation, to how something came into existence. Furthermore, Eliade insists that myths of origin are not primarily concerned with conveying scientific knowledge of a first cause;
rather, they are interested in putting us in touch with those sacred
orders or those exemplary patterns that are presupposed before any
meaningful activity can be undertaken.

Cosmogonic myth often represents the exemplary model for every
future creative act, and therefore many **etiological** (meaning the description of the cause or reason of a thing) myths begin with a rehearsal of the original cosmogony. Only after such a rehearsal does the
mythic narrative go on to relate, for example, the genealogy of the
royal family, the history of the tribe, or the origin of one of its

institutions. Eliade illustrates the point by a custom of the Osage Indians:

> When a child is born among the Osages, 'a man who had talked with the gods' is summoned. When he reaches the new mother's house he recites the history of the creation of the Universe and the terrestrial animals to the newborn infant. Not until this has been done is the baby given the breast. Later, when it wants to drink water, the same man—or sometimes another—is called in again. Once again he recites the Creation, ending with the origin of Water. When the child is old enough to take solid food, the man 'who had talked with the gods' comes once more and again recites the Creation, this time also relating the origin of grains and other foods.[2]

We see that the interest here is not at all speculative. It is quite necessary to re-establish contact with the sacred time of the original "beginning" in order to ensure the renewal of nature, ongoing human life, or social institutions.

While it is true that existential anxiety about the maintenance and renewal of the natural world and the social order is the essential interest underlying archaic cosmogonic mythology, an intellectual element is not wholly absent and, as previously stated, this requires a certain detachment from the environment. The origins of cosmogonic speculation are uncertain, but some conditions would appear to have been critical and formative.[3] The archaeological evidence of the Paleolithic (or Old Stone) Age, especially of the female figurines with exaggerated maternal features, points to the phenomenon of birth as perhaps supplying the initial conception of a "beginning." But Paleolithic art does not reveal any interest in the larger natural environment. However, the subsequent Neolithic revolution (c. 4500 B.C.E.) changed man from a food gatherer and hunter to a cultivator and agriculturalist. Humans became acquainted with the generative powers of Nature and its fecundity.

The Neolithic Age also saw the invention of the craft of potterymaking, and we later see the image of the fashioning of a lump of clay as a recurring one in depictions of world beginnings. But whatever the sources of such speculation, cosmogonic myths were little developed before the third millennium B.C.E., when the earliest known creation texts appear. The imagery found in these texts varies considerably. Surprisingly, many of them reflect, if crudely, modern theories of catastrophic and continuous creation. The dominant themes, however, are those of sexual fecundity and union, fertilization, procreation, and generation. Conflict, conquest, and the ordering of chaos are other common subjects, as is craftsmanship. It is worth noting, however, that some of these ancient myths also depict creation as resulting from a divine thought or will—an idea we often erroneously associate exclusively with the emancipation of thought from nature mythology in the great historical religions. The typology of cosmogonic myths here employed is necessarily selective; nevertheless, it gives some sense of the variety of imaginative conceptions of creation and order that we find in the history of the world's religions.

Emergence or Procreation From a Primal Substance or Being

The ancient Egyptians, like so many archaic and primitive cultures, accepted many accounts of the creation and felt no need to reject one for another. Among the earliest Pyramid Texts (c. 2400 B.C.E.) are various accounts of life emerging from the primordial watery abyss (Nun). The sun and creator-god, Re-Atum, according to one text, appears on the "primeval hillock" produced by the silt of the flooding Nile River. Re-Atum is self-created: "I am Atum when I was alone in Nun; I am Re in his (first) appearances, when he began to rule that which he had made. . . . 'I am the great god who came into being by himself.'"[4]

Re-Atum proceeds to engender the first male and female pair of gods, Shu and Tefnut, by several means. In one text, the creation of air (Shu) and his consort, moisture (Tefnut), is accomplished by a violent sneeze:

> O Atum-Kheprer, thou wast on high on the (primeval) hill; thou didst arise as the *ben*-bird of the *ben*-stone in the *Ben*-House in Heliopolis; thou did spit out what was Shu, thou did sputter out what was Tefnut. Thou didst put thy arms about them as the arms of a *ka* [the vital force of Atum].[5]

In a second text, Re-Atum appears in the aspect of Khepera ("he who comes into existence") and—in **androgynous** or bisexual fashion—fertilizes himself through masturbation, pouring his seed into his mouth and producing Shu and Tefnut:

> I am he who came into being in the form of Khepera, I was the creator of what came into being ... after my coming into being many [were] the things which came into being coming forth from my mouth. . . . I, even I, had union with my clenched hand, I joined myself in an embrace with my shadow, I poured seed into my mouth my own, I sent forth issue in the form of Shu, I sent forth moisture in the form of Tefnut.[6]

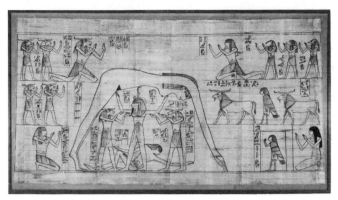

The Egyptian sky god, Nut, held apart from the earth,
Geb, by the god of air, Shu. (*Source*: From the William
Sturgis Bigelow Collection, courtesy of the Museum of
Fine Arts, Boston.)

Here, we observe that generation of the elements of the cosmos is
accomplished by the god alone without union with a female principle.
The myth goes on to describe the creation of man and woman from
the tears of Khepera. This is followed by the appearance of other
living things—the earth god, Geb, and the sky god, Nut—who, in
turn, produce the gods Isis and Osiris.

A common theme in archaic cosmogonies is this form of emanation
of the primal elements or beings from a watery chaos or nonbeing,
or from a primeval being—a god or being itself. As we have seen,
in the Egyptian Pyramid texts Atum appears out of the watery abyss
and creates through his own fecundity. In the Greek Orphic religion
(600 B.C.E.), the first god, Protagonos, is also androgynous and bears
within himself the seeds of all the future gods and men. A more-
sophisticated version of this theme is found in the *Chandogya Upanishad*, the Hindu philosophical text written about 700 B.C.E. The
Upanishads are consumed with the question of the relation of being
to nonbeing. In the following passage, emergence from the abyssmal
waters of nonbeing is rejected, for how could something come from
nothing? Being is everexistent and the manifold world is the result
of Being's own procreation:

> In the beginning, my dear, this world was just Being, only one,
> without a second. To be sure, some people say: 'In the beginning
> this world was just Non-being, one only, without a second; that from
> Non-being Being was produced.'
>
> But verily, my dear, whence could this be?, said he. How from
> Non-being could Being be produced? On the contrary, my dear, in
> the beginning this world was just Being, one only, without a second.

It bethought itself: 'Would that I were many! Let me procreate myself!' It emitted heat. The heat bethought itself: 'Would that I were many! Let me procreate myself!' It emitted water. Therefore whenever a person grieves or perspires from the heat, then water . . . is produced.

That water bethought itself: 'Would that I were many! Let me procreate myself!' It emitted food. Therefore whenever it rains, then there is abundant food. So food for eating is produced just from water.[7]

The Sexual Union of a Primal Male and Female

In many religions, the appearance of the elements, the seasons, and the myriad beings that make up the natural environment are the result of the sexual union of a primeval male and female. It represents the coming together of the primal opposites—often the earth and the sky. This can be seen in the interaction of *yin* (the earth, female) and *yang* (the sky, male) in Chinese mythology, as well as in the primal role of Uranos, the sky-Father, and Gaea, the earth-Mother, in Greek myth—for example, in Hesiod's *Theogony*.

A similar theme is found in the Luiseño Indian (California) cosmogony. According to the Luiseño, in the beginning nobody was there, only space (Kyuvish) and emptiness (Atahuish). The myth then tells of the creation of the primal pair, Tukomit—the sky (male)—and Tamayowut—the earth (female):

> She lay with her feet to the north; he sat by her right side; and she spoke: I am stretched, I am extended, I shake, I resound. . . . Then he answered: 'I am night, I am inverted (the arch of the heavens). I cover. I rise, I ascend . . . I seize, I send away (the souls of men).' . . .
>
> Then as the brother took hold of her and questioned, she named each part of her body, until they were united. He assisted with the births with the sacred stick, and the following came forth singly or in pairs; ceremonial objects, religious acts, and avenging animals.[8]

The myth tells how Sky and Earth then gave birth to the mountains and rocks; to grasses, trees, and birds; to the badger, the buzzard, the eagle; and finally to Towish, the spirit of man that survives the body, and to Wiyot, from whom spring all the human generations. Here we see the practical concern to explain and legitimate not only the natural order but also ceremonial and religious activity.

One of the most elaborate expressions of creation by sexual union is found in the Japanese *Kojiki* ("Records of Ancient Matters," 712 C.E.) and *Nihongi* ("Chronicles of Japan," 720 C.E.). These texts include most of the themes we have surveyed so far. In the beginning there is chaos, but gods spontaneously appear, including the primeval male and female. The interest in the gods and the origin of the cosmos is, however, only preliminary to the central interest of this Japanese chronicle: the divine creation and destiny of the Japanese islands. The *Kojiki* speaks of an original chaos from which numerous deities appear, either spontaneously or from a reed shoot in the mud. However, the *Nihongi* begins—as does the Chinese myth of the creator god, P'an Ku—with the feminine and masculine principles not yet divided but forming a great cosmic egg:

> Of old, Heaven and Earth were not yet separated, and the In [feminine] and Yo [masculine] not yet divided. They formed a chaotic mass like an egg, which was of obscurely defined limits, and contained germs. The purer and clearer part was thinly diffused and formed Heaven, while the heavier and grosser element settled down and became earth. . . . Heaven was therefore formed first, and Earth was established subsequently. Thereafter Divine Beings were produced between them.[9]

The eighth generation of the gods produced Izanagi (the male-who-invites) and Izanami (the-female-who-invites), who create the Japanese islands:

> Izanagi and Izanami stood on the floating bridge of Heaven, and held counsel together, saying:
> 'Is there not a country beneath?' Thereupon they thrust down the jewel-spear of Heaven, and groping about therewith found the ocean. The brine which dripped from the point of the spear coagulated and became an island which received the name of Ono-goro-jima— the pillar of the world.[10]

The *Nihongi* further relates the birth of the eight Japanese islands. It is then that Izanagi and Izanami join in creating the rivers, the mountains, and the wind that blows away the mists covering the world. Izanami's last child is the god of fire, who accidentally but fatally scorches his mother, who descends to Yomi (Hades). In his grief, Izanagi searches for Izanami. After he finds her, she forbids him to look on her decaying body. But Izanagi refuses and, in her fury, Izanami pursues the terror-stricken husband, who endeavors to escape to the light of day. Izanagi then undertakes elaborate bathings in the river to wash away the pollution and decay of death. From this purifying bath, many things are born. From his left eye is born Ama-terasu, the sun goddess, giver of life, from whom the Japanese emperors are

The Japanese god Izanagi about to thrust his spear into the ocean; the Japanese islands were created from the drippings off his spear. (*Source*: From the Henry L. Pierce Fund, courtesy of the Museum of Fine Arts, Boston.)

descended. Here is the divine source of imperial authority and the divine destiny of the Japanese islands. From Izanagi's right eye springs the moon god, Tsuki-go-mi, Guardian of the Night, and from his nostrils comes the fearsome storm god, Susa-no-wo. To these three illustrious deities, Izanagi invests the government of the cosmos—and especially the contest for supremacy between Ama-terasu, the life-giving sun, and Susa-no-wo, the god of death and destruction.

The Cosmic Egg

We noted that the *Nihongi* assumes in its cosmogony the presence of a primeval cosmic egg. This theme is widespread and is found in the myths of India, Polynesia, Greece, China, Finland, and South America. Like water, the egg is naturally associated with birth, life, and fecundity. The egg is the incubator of life. It is obvious, then, why the egg is often used in rituals and celebrations of the New Year and the giving of new life. Colored eggs are given as New Year's gifts in Persia, while Easter eggs serve as gifts in Christian Europe and North America. The image of the egg is, as Eliade points out, not so much to remind us of ordinary birth as it is "the *repeating of the archetypal birth* of the cosmos, the imitation of the cosmogony."[11]

Some commentators believe the cosmic egg symbolism, with its bisexual characteristics, represents a stage beyond that of the earth-Mother and sky-Father—an attempt to overcome the sexual dualism and primal chaos associated with the earlier theme. The power of creativity is present from the beginning. This can be observed in many Hindu texts, including the *Laws of Manu* and the *Upanishads*. In the former, we read the following:

> 8. He (the Self-existent) desiring to produce beings of many kinds from his own body, first with a thought created the waters and placed his seed in them. 9. That (seed) became a golden egg, in brilliancy equal to the sun; in the (egg) he himself was born as Brahman, the progenitor of the whole world.[12]

The account of creation in the *Chandogya Upanishad* is similar:

> In the beginning this [universe] was non-existent. It became existent. It grew. It turned into an egg. The egg lay for the period of a year. Then it broke open. Of the two halves of the eggshell, one half was of silver, the other of gold. That which was of silver became the earth; that which was of gold, heaven. What was the thick membrane [of the white] became the mountains; the thin membrane [of the yolk], the mist and the clouds. The veins became the rivers; the fluid in the bladder, the ocean. And what was born of it was yonder Aditya, the sun. When it was born shouts of 'Hurrah' arose, together with all beings and all objects of desire.[13]

In the Tahitian creation story, the supreme being Ta'aora exists within an egg "which revolved in space in continuous darkness." There was then no sun or moon, no land, no man or beast, and no sea or water—no living thing.

> But at last Ta'aora was filliping his shell, as he sat in close confinement, and it cracked and broke open. Then he slipped out and stood upon the shell and cried out, 'Who is above there? Who is below there?' No voice answered. Vexed, Ta'aora 'overturned his shell and raised it up to form a dome for the sky and called it

Rumia.' Still angry at no response, 'he took his spine for a mountain range ... his vitals for broad floating clouds, his flare and his flesh for fatness of the earth ... his feathers for trees and shrubs, and creepers to clothe the earth ... and the blood of Ta'aora got heated and drifted away for redness for the sky and for rainbows.'[14]

Creation by Conflict and the Ordering of Chaos

In the Japanese cosmogony, we observed that sexual union is a dominant theme. However, unlike some other myths to which we have referred, the union is not basically quiescent and harmonious; on the contrary, it is turbulent and ends in conflict and violence. The Japanese myth reveals the practical concern with the struggle between the powers of chaos, darkness, and death and those of life and order. This is a most important cosmogonic motif because in this type of myth the cosmos is created or, rather, *ordered* through a battle with the terrible powers or monsters—the Dragon, the Serpent, or the Leviathan—that symbolize chaos and disorder, or even repressive order.*

We observed earlier that in the Egyptian myth creation emerges from the primal, boundless, deep waters (Nun), but that the waters appear motionless and entirely benevolent. However, even here, according to some texts, cosmic order is threatened by Apophis, the dragon or water monster symbolizing hostile darkness. The sun's rising each day on the eastern horizon heralds the victory of Amon-Re and the pharaoh (the image of Amon-Re) over chaotic darkness (Apophis). As we might expect, each day in the Temple of Amon-Re the Egyptians ritually recited the myth "The Repulsing of the Dragon" as a spell against Apophis. The recitation included the following triumphant declaration:

> He Is One Fallen To The Flame, Apophis with a knife on his head. He cannot see, and his name is no more in this land. I have commanded that a *curse* be cast upon him. . . . He is fallen and overthrown. . . . [15]

---

* Not all myths depicting the struggle with chaos represent the latter in purely negative terms, for example, meaningless nonbeing or complete disorder. Recent studies of both ancient Near Eastern and Chinese creation mythology have made it clear that chaos can be the source of creativity itself. See, for example, the brief discussion of the Taoist *hun-tun* (Chaos) at the conclusion of this section.

The theme of a primal chaos, represented by the warfare between the forces of nature and overcome and ordered by a high god, is a common one in Greek mythology. As we saw in Chapter 7, Hesiod's *Theogony* relates not only the story of the birth of the gods but also, more basically, the establishment of the Olympian order and the final triumph and authority of Zeus. Hesiod describes in vivid and violent language the struggles, lustings, and treachery of the gods; all, however, for the purpose of ensuring cosmic order and justice through the reign of Zeus. When Zeus conquered the Titans, his work was not done; he was yet faced with the conflict with the monster Typhon. Only after that was relative order achieved. And so

> When the Olympian gods had brought their struggle to a successful end and had forcibly vindicated their rights against the Titans, Mother Earth advised them to invite Zeus ... to be king and lord of all the gods. Zeus in return distributed rights and privileges among them.[16]

The Babylonian creation epic, *Enuma elish* ("When on high"), is a classic example of a cosmogony involving this kind of conflict and the bringing of order out of chaos. The epic comes from the middle of the second millennium B.C.E. It was introduced briefly in Chapter 5 in the discussion of the Babylonian Akitu or New Year's Festival and temple ritual. The creation myth itself deserves attention here. The text primarily honors Marduk, the Babylonian high-god, ruler of the lesser gods and creator of heaven and earth. But the conflict of the elements and the ordering of the cosmos serves as the background and justifies Marduk's rise to sovereignty.

The myth begins with watery chaos, consisting of three elements: Apsu, representing the sweet water; Ti'amat, the sea; and Mumma, their son, the mist. As yet, there is neither sky nor firm ground, although in time the union of Apsu and Ti'amat brings forth Lahmu and Lahamu, representing the silt formed by the waters. From a later pair, Anu, the sky-god, is born; Anu, in turn, engenders Nudimmut— also known as Enke—and Ea—the wise god of the subterranean sweet waters, but also here representing the earth itself. The practical import of the myth is not difficult to discern at this point. Mesopotamia is a land produced by the soil of the flooding Tigris and Euphrates rivers, which is deposited at the meeting of the sea on the Persian Gulf. The silt is formed where the fresh water meets the salt water.

The myth proceeds to tell the manner in which the primal elements are ordered and how a cosmic government is established and assured. This is accomplished through a prolonged conflict between two principles: the older gods representing primordial inactivity and the younger gods symbolizing movement, energy, and activity. Restlessly surging back and forth, the young gods disturb Ti'amat and Apsu, who responds:

> Their ways are verily loathsome unto me.
> By day I find no relief, nor repose by night.
> I will destroy, I will wreck their ways,
> That quiet may be restored. Let us have rest.[17]

The young gods dash about in panic and only Ea proves equal to the challenge. He casts a sacred spell on Apsu, who falls into a profound sleep. Ea then removes Apsu's royal crown—and in so doing possesses his might and splendor—and kills him, imprisoning his son, Mummu. On Apsu, Ea established a spacious dwelling and here Marduk is born, endowed with awe-inspiring majesty.

The older gods chide Ti'amat for failing to come to the aid of Apsu, urging her to avenge her spouse's death. Ti'amat finally yields, chooses the wicked Kingu to be her spouse, and entrusts him with command of the army and authority over "the tablets of destinies." A formidable demonic and chaotic power now threatens the young gods. Ea this time is no match for Ti'amat—even his powerful spell fails him. Anu, the sky-god, then proceeds against Ti'amat with the combined approval and authority of the gods, but he also fails. Authority alone cannot defeat the mighty Ti'amat. In desperation, the gods ask Ea to seek out his son, Marduk, "whose strength is mighty." Marduk is prepared to do battle, but he demands a high price:

> If I indeed, as your avenger
> Am to vanquish Ti'amat and save your lives
> Set up the Assembly, proclaim supreme my destiny
> When in Bushukinna jointly you sit down rejoicing,
> Let my words, instead of you, determine the fates.
> Unalterable shall be what I may bring into being;
> Neither recalled nor changed shall be the
>   command of my lips. . . . [18]

The gods agree to Marduk's terms—"Of Marduk, of their champion, they decreed the destiny"—and confer on him kingship: political authority joined with the power of physical force. The gods plea, "Go and cut off the life of Ti'amat." Arrayed in his dazzling and terrifying might, Marduk is challenged to battle by the fearsome and angry Ti'amat. Marduk, however, shoots an arrow through Ti'amat's jaws, piercing her heart and killing her. The enemy gods attempt to flee Marduk but are imprisoned. Marduk takes from Kingu the "tablet of destinies" and fastens it on his own breast. Finally, Marduk cuts the

Marduk in battle with Ti'amat. The winged Marduk
attacks Ti'amat with double tridents. Wings outstretched,
the fierce Ti'amat retreats. (*Source*: Wall panel in the
palace of Ashur-nasiripal II, 885–860 B.C.E. Reproduced
by Courtesy of the Trustees of the British Museum.)

body of Ti'amat in two, lifting up one half to form the sky and
fashioning the earth with the other half. Marduk then establishes
Anu, Enlil, and Ea in their appropriate dominions. The conflict between Marduk and Ti'amat again explains a realistic feature of life
in Mesopotamia. The battle has to do with the spring flooding of the
Mesopotamian plain and the contest between the waters and the wind.
In spring, the land reverts to a watery chaos until the winds can fight
back the waters and bring back dry land.

The creation myth concludes with Marduk assigning all the gods
their stations and their duties, organizing the calendar, and creating
and organizing the heavenly bodies. On plea from the gods, the new
king agrees to relieve them of all toilsome and menial tasks. He
addresses Ea:

> Blood I will mass and cause bones to be,
> I will establish a savage, 'man' shall be his name.
> Verily, the savage-man I will create.
> He shall be charged with the service of the gods,
> That they might be at ease.[19]

Ea has another plan. He suggests that the gods in assembly determine
which of the prisoners was guilty of contriving to make Ti'amat rebel.
The gods declare that the guilty one is Kingu. He is executed, and
from his blood mankind is created under Ea's supervision.

> They imposed upon (Kingu) his guilt and severed
>   his blood (vessels).
> Out of his blood they fashioned mankind.[20]

Mankind, it is important to note, is created for the purposes of serving the gods and relieving them of burdensome work. The epic poem ends with an account of the gods—toiling for the last time—building their king the city of Babylon and a temple in his honor. The focus of the *Enuma elish* is not primarily on the origin of the physical cosmos but, rather, on the more-pressing issue of establishing a natural and a social order.

We noted earlier that not all cosmogonic myths conceive of chaos as unambiguously evil or as representing the powers of death and destruction. Ancient Chinese Taoist cosmogony is a case in point. The early Taoist sages taught that the reality of Tao or "the Way," as it is often translated, is an "uncarved Block." By this they meant that it was not to be thought of as an already determinate order but, rather, a becoming, a process capable of infinite possibility. The Tao, they said, is both "nameless" and "nameable"; that is, the Tao as creative process is a joining of "nonbeing" and "being." The *Tao Te Ching* says: "Being and non-being produce each other"—in other words, they are the polar aspects, the *yin* and the *yang*, of Tao. "This is but to say that only becoming (coming into being which illustrates some mixture of being and non-being) is; not-becoming (either being or non-being abstracted from its polar relation with its opposite) is not."[21]

The Taoist sages intuited that there is no simple, final, and permanent order; there is no privileged rational order among lesser orders or disorder. As one commentator has written, the Taoist "does not feel obliged to single out any specific order as the true one. His vision of nature is as if it were an uncarved block, a matrix of actualizable orders, passive to infinite patterning. The primary fact about the Taoist universe is that it is the sum of all orders.... There are as many actualizable worlds as there are events in the process of becoming."[22]

In the Taoist cosmogony, chaos (nonbeing) is a polar element with cosmos (order, being) in Becoming itself (*Tao*), the harmonious *yin-yang* of the creative process of nature. In some Near Eastern myths, the monster representing chaos is similarly a source, not only of disorder but also of ongoing creativity and the battle with the monster chaos is a necessary and perennial aspect of life itself.

Creation by Divine Sacrifice

It is interesting to note that, in the figure of Kingu, the *Enuma elish* included an account of creation by divine sacrifice—although in this case the creation of man, not of the cosmos. However, some fragments preserved of a work written by a priest of the temple at Babylon in the third century B.C.E. indicate that the creation of man as a rational animal was made possible by Marduk's own self-sacrifice. There are, however, many cosmogonic myths that trace the beginning of the world itself to a divine sacrifice or the sacrifice of a primal man.

The latter type is found in Chinese narratives about the god P'an Ku, stories that were especially popular in Southern China from the third to the sixth centuries C.E. P'an Ku is an immensely fecund deity and in one variant he is pictured as the divine embryo within the cosmic egg. Yet in another version, P'an Ku creates the world by his own death:

> The world was never finished until P'an Ku died. Only his death could perfect the universe: from his skull was shaped the dome of the sky, and from his flesh was formed the soil of the fields; from his bones came the rocks, from his blood the rivers and seas; from his hair came all vegetation. His breath was the wind; his voice made thunder; his right eye became the moon, his left eye, the sun. From his saliva or sweat came rain. And from the vermin which covered his body came forth mankind.[23]

Long before the appearance of the rather philosophical speculations about creation—that is, about being and nonbeing—in the Hindu *Upanishads*, many types of creation myths were present in the ancient Vedic hymns. One of the most popular is the account of creation resulting from the sacrificial dismemberment of the primeval man, Purusa. According to this hymn, the sacrifice of Purusa produces not only the physical elements of the cosmos, the animals, and the seasons, but also the sacred Vedic chants and formulas.

Most important, however, the myth tells of the origin of the four orders, or classes (*varnas*), of ancient Indian society that became the basis of the Hindu caste system: "His mouth was the *brahman* [priestly class], his arms were made into nobles [or warriors, *ksatriyas*], his two thighs were the populace [*vaisyas*] and from his feet servants [*sūdras*] were born."[24]

The creation of the world and the social order from a divine being is a perfectly understandable idea because they both are seen as rooted in a primordial sacrality.

Creation by a Divine Craftsman

To this point, we have used the words *cosmogony* and *creation* interchangeably. However, an important distinction needs to be made. The cosmogonic accounts we have surveyed are not, strictly speaking, mythic expressions of *creation*; rather, they are imaginative narratives of *generation* or *procreation* from some primal substances(s) or being—the abyssmal waters, the divine body, the embryonic egg, and so on. Technically, creation means *creatio ex nihilo*, or creation out of nothing. Such an idea was unthinkable in many primitive and archaic cultures. It was even inconceivable to the Greeks. *Creatio ex nihilo* finds its most distinctive expression in the theologies of the three Western mono-theistic faiths—Judaism, Christianity, and Islam—and is derived from their interpretations of the Creation story in the book of Genesis.

Greek cosmogony employed, among others, the image of the *creative artisan* or *craftsman*—which is often, although erroneously, associated with the idea of creation. It will be instructive to look first at myths of the divine craftsman before we turn to accounts of *creatio ex nihilo*. Examples of the former are common in Egyptian and in North American Indian texts, but the following illustrations are taken from the Greeks.

It is common to hear it said that the Greeks were responsible for the transition from mythological cosmogony to philosophical and scientific cosmology. The problem with such a claim is not only that it leaves out of account the important philosophic and scientific developments in other ancient civilizations, but also that it distorts the history of Greek thought itself. It is wrong to speak of a movement "from myth to reason" in Greek thought if it implies that the later Greeks wholly supplanted mythic thinking with scientific explanation.

The earliest Greek philosophers—the Ionians, Thales, Anaximander, and Anaximenes (sixth century B.C.E.)—attempted to establish that the world evolved from a single material substance, without reference to the elaborate cosmogonic and theogonic myths of Homer and Hesiod. Nevertheless, neither these pre-Socratic philosophers nor Plato could avoid the use of mythic imagery in their cosmological speculations. They conceived the world animistically as a living, divine organism and they spoke of the origin and evolution of the cosmos in images of piloting and craftsmanship that implied intelligent direction and design.

Thales held that water is the primary stuff from which all things evolve. Aristotle conjectured that Thales formed the idea from the fact that the seeds of all things are moist and from the fact that evaporation and freezing may, after all, turn water into air and perhaps even earth. Anaximenes thought the prime element was air, or breath, while for Heraclitus the essence of all things was fire, which symbolized the strife and tension immanent in all existence. What these Ionian philosophers discovered was the fact that, despite all change and becoming, there must be something permanent, which may undergo change but itself exists eternally. What they did *not* explain was motion, or the *cause* of cosmic evolution. They assumed that the primal substance possessed its own inherent power. Empedocles (fifth century B.C.E.) and Anaxagoras (fifth century B.C.E.) went further and tried to explain the *power* responsible for the order and evolution of the cosmic process. In mythic fashion, Empedocles posited the forces of Love and Hate, or Harmony and Strife. Love, he said, brings the four primal elements of earth, air, fire, and water into a cosmic harmony. Hate and Strife separate the elements, causing discord and the cessation of individual existences. The world process moves, then, in periodic cycles of unity and dissolution—an idea common to Hindu and Buddhist cosmology as well.

Anaxagoras introduced a radically new principle—*Nous*, or Mind—to explain motion and cosmic evolution. *Nous* does not create matter, for that is eternal; rather, *Nous* sets matter in motion. *Nous* is a kind of *Deus ex machina* (literally "a god from a machine," that is, a thing introduced to solve a difficulty), says Aristotle, brought in to explain change and the origin of all particular things. Anaxagoras spoke of *Nous* as infinite and alone. Yet *Nous* is also present in all living things. Anaxagoras is obviously seeking to distinguish an intelligible principle, that is, mind—the source not only of movement but also of intelligent design—from brute matter, an effort that reaches its highest development in Greek cosmology in Plato's (428/7–348/7) *Timaeus*.

Plato wrote *Timaeus* in part to show that the cosmos is the work of intelligence, "that Mind orders all things." Plato did not, however, think it possible to give an exact scientific account of cosmic origins. He presented his own mythic vision as, in his own words, a most "likely account." Plato believed that the material world of becoming requires some eternal cause that he called the divine Demiurge or Craftsman. This god is good, and "he desired that all things should come as near as possible to being like himself."

> Desiring, then, that all things should be good and, so far as might be, nothing imperfect, the god took over all that is visible—not at rest, but in discordant and unordered motion—and brought it from disorder into order, since he judged that order was in every way the better. . . . Taking thought, therefore, he found that, among things that are by nature visible, no work that is without intelligence will ever be better than one that has intelligence. . . . In virtue of this reasoning, when he framed the universe, he fashioned reason within soul and soul within body, to the end that the work he accomplished might be by nature excellent and perfect as possible.[25]

This important passage requires several comments. First, we should note that Plato's Demiurge is divine, creative Reason, but it *is not a Creator God*. According to Plato, the Demiurge "took over" pre-existing material and fashioned it as perfectly *as possible* "so far as might be." The Demiurge is not to be confused with an omnipotent Creator but must instead be seen as a persuasive power working on disordered, intractable material. Later in the dialogue, Plato speaks of the generation of the cosmos as "a mixed result of the combination of Necessity and Reason." Necessity is also called the Errant Cause, and it represents the purposelessness or the chance element in existence that is not informed by Reason. The cosmos is fashioned "by the victory of reasonable persuasion over Necessity."

For Plato, the Demiurge's creative work is limited by two additional eternal realities. One is "the Receptacle—as it were, the nurse—of all Becoming." The Receptacle is not matter but the Space in which all the material elements of the world of becoming appear. The Demiurge thus takes over the Receptacle (Space) and the material elements and fashions the cosmos after the model of the Forms, the other coeternal reality. Plato writes that the Demiurge "took thought to make, as it were, a moving likeness of eternity (the Forms)." Here we see Plato portraying an eternal Craftsman persuading and shaping a somewhat recalcitrant, purposeless Necessity into a cosmos, according to pre-existent, eternal Forms or Ideas. One result of Plato's mythic cosmogony is that he escapes the difficult problem of attributing imperfection and even natural evil in the world to God, a problem faced by the believer in an omnipotent Creator. The Western monotheist insists, of course, that God is perfect but also that the Creator is omnipotent and cannot be limited, like the Demiurge, by any other *coeternal* matter or form.

Creation From Nothing

When we turn to the idea of creation from nothing, it is important to mention that many creation accounts, quite independent of Genesis, conceive of the deity as creating by divine *fiat*, that is, simply by word or by will. The Quiche Maya, a great tribe of the southern branch of the Mayan civilization, spoke of the two powers—Tepeu and Gucumatz, or sun-fire—as existing in the beginning in the dark waters. The cosmos is then perceived as emerging from their deliberation and word.

> There was only immobility and silence in the darkness, in the night. Only the Creator, the Maker, Tepeu, Gucumatz, the Forefathers, were in the water surrounded with light.... By nature they were great sages and great thinkers. In this manner the sky existed and also the Heart of Heaven, which is the name of God and thus He is called.
>   Then came the word. Tepeu and Gucumatz came together in the darkness, in the night, and Tepeu and Gucumatz talked together.

They talked then, discussing and deliberating; they agreed, they united their words and their thoughts.

Then while they meditated, it became clear to them that when dawn would break man must appear. Then they planned the creation. . . .

Thus let it be done! Let the emptiness be filled! Let the water recede and make a void, let the earth appear and become solid; let it be done. Thus they spoke. Let there be light . . . Earth! they said, and instantly it was made. . . . So it was that they made perfect the work, when they did it after thinking and meditating upon it.[26]

In this Mayan creation story, the cosmogony is a deliberative and willed action and is not conceived solely in terms of procreation or involuntary emergence. The Zuni myth of the genesis of the world is similar:

Before the beginning of the new-making, Awonawilone (the Maker and Container of All, the All-father Father) solely had being. There was nothing else whatsoever throughout the great space of the ages save everywhere black darkness in it, and everywhere void desolation.

In the beginning of the new-made Awonawilone conceived within himself and thought outward in space, whereby mists of increase, steams potent of growth, were evolved and uplifted. Thus, by means of his innate knowledge, the All-contained made himself in person and form of the Sun whom we hold to be our father and who thus came to exist and appear. With his appearance came the brightening of the spaces with light . . . [27]

In each of these myths, the role of divine forethought and will is at least analogous to the Creation narrative in the book of Genesis, the text that remains the classic example of *creatio ex nihilo*.

Scholars agree that there are two distinct accounts of the Creation in Genesis. One is found in Chapters 1–2:4a and is the work of a rather late hand, a Priestly [P] writer of the middle of the fifth century B.C.E. The second account, in Chapters 2:4b–25, is the work of two sources, the Jahwist (J) and Elohist (E), representing the southern kingdom of Judah and the northern kingdom of Israel. The J and E sources are woven together in Genesis into one continuous narrative. They can, nevertheless, be distinguished on various grounds, including their different viewpoints, but also by the fact that the two writers use different names for God: Jahweh and Elohim. The interests of the later Priestly and the earlier J and E writers are markedly different, and this is reflected in the central focus and the order of their respective Creation narratives. These differences can be seen most easily by setting them out in parallel columns.[28]

P
(Gen. 1–2:4a)

The original state of the earth is a watery chaos.

The work of creation is divided into six separate operations, each assigned to one day.

The order of creation is:

(a) Light.
(b) The firmament-heaven.
(c) The dry land-earth.
    Separation of earth and heaven.
(d) Vegetation—three kinds.
(e) The heavenly bodies, sun, moon, and stars.
(f) Birds and fishes.
(g) Animals and man; male and female together.

J–E
(Gen. 2:4b–25)

The original state of the earth is a waterless waste, without vegetation.

No note of time is introduced into the account.

The order of creation is:

(a) Man, made out of dust.
(b) The Garden, to the east, in Eden.
(c) Trees of every kind, including the Tree of Life, and the Tree of the knowledge of Good and Evil.
(d) Animals, beasts, and birds (no mention of fish).
(e) Woman, created out of man.

It is evident that the J–E tradition focuses on the creation of man, his dependence on and obedience to God, the tree of the knowledge of good and evil, the temptation, the fall, and paradise lost. We will discuss this narrative in detail in Chapter 9, where we compare accounts of the human problem. Here we concentrate on only the distinctive cosmogonic features of the Priestly narrative. First, we note that the geographical background of the Priestly account is not an uninhabitable waste, without rain and vegetation (the Palestine of J–E), but is, rather, an original watery chaos, representing the point of view of the Mesopotamian myths, especially the Babylonian creation epic. Scholars point out that the Hebrew word for the chaos of waters, *tehom*, is a corruption of the name Ti'mat, the chaos-monster slain by Marduk. The rending of sky and earth from one another also resembles the splitting of Ti'mat's body in two. There also is a general resemblance to the Babylonian order of creation in the Priestly narrative of the six days. The Babylonian background is clearly present, and yet, as we will see, the Priestly writer transforms this material in significant ways.

At first glance, the opening chapter of Genesis does not appear to support the idea of *creatio ex nihilo*. We read: "In the beginning God created the heavens and the earth. The earth was without form and void, darkness was upon the face of the deep and the Spirit of God was moving over the face of the waters" (1:1–2). Reference to "the deep" and to "the waters" would indicate the presence of a coeternal,

Michelangelo's portrayal of the Creation of Man "in the image and
likeness of God," from The Sistine Chapel, Vatican City, Rome. (*Source*:
Courtesy of Alinari/Art Resource, NY.)

uncreated substance. However, in the total context of the Priestly
story, scholars agree that God is perceived as the sole agent in creation
and is a being who exists entirely transcendent, free and independent,
of his creation. This is affirmed both in the first verse—"In the
beginning God created the heavens and the earth"—and by the impo-
sition of the divine fiat again and again in the successive acts of
creation. For instance, the statement that "God made the firmament
and separated the waters . . . " (1:7) is preceded by "God said, let
there be a firmament . . . and let it separate the waters" (1:6). The
same pattern is followed throughout the successive creative acts. Thus,
while the inclusion of the second verse appears to express an idea
not entirely consistent with *creatio ex nihilo*, the fact is that "the deep"
(*tehom*) plays no role in the account of the creation. There is no
shaping of pre-existent matter, no theogony, no conflict of divine
forces. Creation is achieved by divine command.

To summarize the discussion so far, *creatio ex nihilo* is an account
of cosmic origin and order that denies the existence of any other
reality as coeternal with God. It also denies that the world is of the

same substance or identical with God, that is, divine. This creationist model implies that God alone is self-existent, creates solely by divine reason and will, and is related to a world that is entirely contingent and dependent on the deity's own creative and providential activity. This biblical view of creation was a new and radical idea. The Latin poet Lucretius insisted that "from nothing, nothing comes"; the ancients conceived of creation in terms of generation, procreation or, most sublimely, as the work of an intelligent craftsman. Yet the artist uses materials that are ready at hand.

It was pointed out in Chapter 7 that monotheism responds to questions left unresolved in other forms of theistic belief, for example, in polytheism, monism, or deism. However, *creatio ex nihilo* poses a number of other questions with which monotheists must contend. What, for example, is the transcendent and self-existent God's relation to the finite creation? Why did a God possessing aseity, or self-existence, and perfection create a mutable world in the first place? Is the Creator-God's omnipotence and wisdom consonant with the suffering and evil evident in the creation?

The Rejection of Cosmogonic Speculation

Before we leave the subject of cosmogony, a few additional points need to be discussed briefly. The first has to do with the fact that not all religions possess cosmogonic myths, or, if they do, they play a rather insignificant role in the religion's thought and life. The highly imaginative and speculative character of cosmogony is reason enough why some practically minded religions have remained indifferent to or highly skeptical of accounts of world beginnings, particularly toward the idea of *creatio ex nihilo*. Jainism, a religion that began in ancient India as a protest against Hindu ritualism, is an example. The goal of Jainism is to free the soul from its imprisonment in karmic matter and the cycle of rebirth, which is a result of its attachment to the material world. The Jain path leading to release regards cosmogonic speculation not only as full of contradictions but also as irrelevant to salvation and therefore to be avoided:

> Some foolish men declare the Creator made the world.
> The doctrine that the world was created is ill-advised,
> and should be rejected . . .
>
> How could God have made the world without any
> raw material?
> If you say he made this first, and then the world,
> you are faced with an endless regression.

If you declare that this raw material arose naturally
you fall into another fallacy, For the whole universe
might thus have been its own creator, and have
arisen equally naturally . . .

If he is ever perfect and complete, how could the will
to create have arisen in him? . . .
If, on the other hand, he is not perfect, he could no more
create the world than a potter could . . .

If out of love for living things and need of them he
made the world,
Why did he not make creation wholly blissful,
free from misfortune? . . .

Good men should combat the believer in divine creation,
maddened by an evil doctrine.

Know that the world is uncreated, as time itself is,
without beginning and end . . .

Uncreated and indestructible, it endures under the
compulsion of its own nature.[29]

In the sixth century B.C.E., Gautama, the Buddha (meaning the "Enlightened One"), also voiced his disapproval of cosmogonic theorizing. His antimythological and antimetaphysical temperament has since characterized Theravada Buddhism in Southern Asia. Gautama's religious teaching (see Chapters 9, 11, and 12) is essentially a spiritual therapy directed at freeing persons from the suffering caused by ignorant, egoistic desire or craving. The story is told of Malunkyaputta, a monk and disciple of Gautama, who was addicted to speculation. One day, as he sat in meditation, he began to fret about whether or not the world was eternal and how, if not, it had begun. He went to the Buddha to seek answers to these puzzlements. Gautama replied:

Well, Malunkyaputta, anyone who demands the elucidation of such futile questions which do not in any way tend to real spiritual progress and edification is like one who has been shot by an arrow and refuses to let the doctor pull it out and attend to the wound. If the wounded man were to say, 'So long as I do not know who the man is who shot me . . . until then I will not allow the arrow to be pulled out or the wound to be attended to'—that man, Malunkyaputta, will die without ever knowing all these details.[30]

Buddha was advising his disciple that the wise man will seek to be treated immediately and in a practical way by a physician and will not demand answers to secondary and futile questions that cannot contribute to his present need.

"A holy life, Malunkyaputta," the Buddha continues,

> does not depend on the dogma that the world is eternal or not eternal and so forth. Whether or not these things obtain, there still remain the problems of birth, old age, death, sorrow ... all the grim facts of life—and for their extinction in the present life I am prescribing this Dhamma [Doctrine]. Accordingly, bear it in mind that these questions which I have not elucidated ... I have not elucidated purposely because these profit not, nor have they anything to do with the fundamentals of holy life nor do they tend toward Supreme Wisdom, the Bliss of Nibbana [Nirvana].[31]

Buddha's advice to his disciple sounds very modern in its indifference to **metaphysical** questions about cosmic beginnings or endings, questions that appear irresolvable. But below the surface of Buddha's brilliant analysis of the human plight in the world lie, of course, fundamental assumptions about the essential nature of things and the implications for human action. Humankind's perennial resort to cosmogonic speculation—to myth and metaphysics—is, many will insist, inherently human. For cosmogony, as we have seen, has to do with judgments about what is real, the fundamental order of the world, the status and duties of humans, and the purposes of the gods.

Cosmogony Today

There is one final question. The cosmogonies surveyed in this chapter are, in every case, imaginative and intuitive efforts to answer etiological questions about the origin of the primal elements, the cosmos itself, its natural and political order, or human institutions and duties. Whether or not they were originally understood literally, in our modern sense, is not the critical point. Clearly, they were taken as "true stories" because each cosmogony offered a structure of meaning and value that adequately accounted for the perennial features of life as observed—for example, the annual victory over the spring floods, the intelligible order and design of nature or the social order, the institution of kingship, or humankind's lowly status or dominion over the earth.

Today, we are living in a scientific age in which few educated persons still think of cosmology in such mythic terms. Or do we? Certainly, the scientist setting forth the nebular hypothesis, the "big bang" theory, or the theory of "continuous creation," attempts to avoid poetic and anthropomorphic language. However, the scientist is not always successful; human language is intractably anthropomorphic. Charles Darwin, despite his materialist doctrine of natural selection and evolution, could not always avoid using human language of purpose and intelligent design in discussing natural evolution in *The Origin of Species*. Scholars perceive in Marxist dialectical materialism profound cosmogonic assumptions that inform the Marxist theory of history and ethical action, for example, the role of labor, the processes of production, and the proletarian revolution.

Most revealing, perhaps, are the cosmogonic suppositions to be found in that most modern of scientific theorists, Sigmund Freud. We know that Freud was a severe critic of all religious cosmogonies. He believed they revealed an unhealthy wish to find the world congenial to and supportive of our human values, desires, and hopes. Freud asserts, quite beyond doubt, that the *world* has no meaning. That does not, however, prevent him from producing his own quite remarkable and imaginative vision—in *Civilization and Its Discontents*—of those primal forces at work in the world that, it turns out, are to guide our behavior.

As Freud sees it, everything is ruled by two cosmic forces: what he calls Eros, or the life-instinct, and Thanatos, or death-instinct. The latter is the drive to aggressive destructiveness. Freud describes our condition dramatically:

> And now, I think, the meaning of evolution of civilization is no longer obscure to us. It must present the struggle between Eros and Death, between the instinct of life and the instinct of destruction, as it works itself out in the human species. This struggle is what all life essentially consists of, and the evolution of civilization may therefore be simply described as the struggle for life of the human species. And it is this battle of the giants that our nursemaids try to appease with their lullaby about Heaven.[32]

Freud realizes, of course, that civilization is imperilled by the aggressive death-instinct. As he sees it, the only means that civilization can employ to inhibit socially destructive Thanatos is to turn aggression toward others into aggression against the self:

> His aggressiveness is introjected, internalized; it is, in point of fact, sent back to where it came from—that is, it is directed towards his own ego. There it is taken over by a portion of the ego, which sets itself over against the rest of the ego as **super-ego**, and which now, in the form of 'conscience,' is ready to put into action against the ego the same harsh aggressiveness that the ego would have liked to satisfy upon other, extraneous individuals. The tension between the

harsh super-ego and the ego that is subjected to it, is called by us
the sense of guilt. . . . Civilization, therefore, obtains mastery over
the individual's dangerous desire for aggression by weakening and
disarming it . . . [33]

In Freud's vision, civilization is purchased at the heavy price of
individual neurotic illness, that is, aggression toward one's own self.
In this somber view, human ethical activity is fundamentally
pathological.

Our brief discussion of Freud can serve to alert us to the fact that
mythic visions of nature's order or our human plight are not foreign
to our present scientific culture. They can be found lurking, often
unconsciously, in the background of what purport to be scientific
claims, or at least claims free of religious or metaphysical assumptions.

Traditional religious cosmogonies do, quite naturally, fail to meet
our scientific explanations. There are those, however, who do claim
to find in ancient cosmogonic myth conjectures surprisingly, though
quite coincidentally, similar to modern geological and cosmological
theories. Both the Egyptians and the Incas believed, for example, that
the earth was a creation of the sun. Anaxagoras spoke of the heavenly
bodies "breaking off" from a revolving mass of hot matter. The ancient Mesopotamian cosmogony spoke, as do modern evolutionists, of
life beginning in the abyssmal ocean.

Yet it is dangerous to press these similarities too far. There may
be some analogies between ancient cosmogony and modern scientific
cosmology, but the effort to harmonize the two literally is really a
fruitless task and too often has shown itself to be an intellectually
dishonest enterprise. The attempt has, sadly, discredited religion in
the minds of many moderns during the past century and a half.

The conflict between science and religion unfortunately has recently
been rekindled through the attempt, by those who espouse Creation
Science, to legally require the teaching of the biblical account of Creation *as science* in science courses in the public schools. On examination, the creation scientists' argument appears strangely negative.
Rather than offering compelling reasons as to how a scientist might
establish a comprehensive *scientific* explanation of cosmology based on
the Genesis account of a *divine, miraculous Creation*, the creationists
simply attempt to show that the received scientific view of evolution
(for example, Darwinism) faces a number of serious problems. These
are especially associated with the mechanism of Darwinian natural
selection and with the gaps in the fossil record, which raises questions
about the gradual development of new forms of life. The argument
seems to be this: If the scientists cannot agree on the details of evolution, then divine Creation must be a preferable *scientific* theory.

The scientific community has, perhaps, contributed to popular questioning of evolution by long conveying the impression that evolution is a proven, infallible "fact." As one historian of science has commented:

> Clearly evolution is not a "fact" in the sense that the man in the street understands the word. . . . A scientific theory is not a fact; it is a working hypothesis of great explanatory power employed because it continues to guide research along fruitful lines. . . . If ordinary people can be persuaded to adopt this more sophisticated view of scientific activity, they will realize that evolutionists cannot be expected to answer all the questions put to them. They will also realize that a decision to abandon evolutionism in favor of creationism could be justified if creationism shows that it can be elaborated into a comprehensive explanatory system that can serve as a better guide to research.[34]

As it turns out, Creation Science is not a science but a religious belief of a very specific kind. Members of the Creation Research Council acknowledge subscribing to a statement of faith committing them to belief in special, miraculous creation; to a worldwide Noahic Flood; and to opposition to evolution as being contrary to the teaching of the Bible. It is difficult to see how these creation scientists can describe their methodology as scientific if they start with several extra-scientific conclusions and refuse to change them, regardless of any possible evidence to the contrary. Furthermore, since it is clear that biblical Creation is a particular religious belief, there is no reason why it, rather than the Japanese or the Babylonian account of creation, should be singled out to be taught in U.S. public schools—in view of the constitutional separation of church and state.

After reading this chapter, we should be wary of any claim that there is only one or, at most, two possible "models" of cosmogony. Scientific evolution can teach us much but so, in different ways, can those mythopoeic accounts that we have explored in this chapter. They can provide us with profound insights into the human moral and spiritual world. They are not scientific; they are poetry and myth but, as such, are uniquely able to illuminate dimensions of our existence.

The simple fact is that the ancient writers of Genesis were not interested in a scientific description of nature but, rather, were attempting to say some extremely important things about God, man, and nature in the light of Israel's experience of having entered into a covenant relationship with its God, Yahweh. The point is that human beings not only are interested in giving scientific explanations but also have engaged and continue to engage in value judgments about the meaning and significance of the natural and social world and the cosmic process itself.

Notes

1. M. Eliade, *Myth and Reality* (London, 1964), pp. 5–6.
2. M. Eliade, *Myth and Reality*, p. 33.
3. The following discussion is dependent on S. G. F. Brandon's essay, "The Dawning Concept of Creativity," in *Creation Legends of the Ancient Near East* (London, 1963).
4. James B. Pritchard, ed., *Ancient Near Eastern Texts Relating to the Old Testament* (Princeton, 1955), pp. 3–4.
5. J. B. Pritchard, *Ancient Near Eastern Texts*, p. 3.
6. E. A. Wallace Budge, *The Gods of the Egyptians*, I (New York, 1969), pp. 308–13.
7. Robert E. Hume, ed. and trans., *The Thirteen Principal Upanishads* (London, 1971), pp. 214–15, 241.
8. A. L. Kroeber, *Handbook of the Indians of California* (Washington, D.C., 1925), pp. 677–78.
9. *Nihongi*, I., W. G. Aston, trans. (Yokahama, 1896), p. 1ff.
10. *Nihongi*, p. 1ff.
11. M. Eliade, *Patterns in Comparative Religion* (New York, 1967), p. 414.
12. George Buhler, trans., *The Laws of Manu*, in *Sacred Books of the East*, XXV (Oxford, 1886), p. 5. Cited in C. Long, *Alpha: Myths of Creation* (New York, 1963), p. 129.
13. Swami Nikhilananda, trans., *The Upanishads*, IV (New York, 1959), pp. 218–19. Cited in C. Long, *Alpha*, p. 138.
14. Teuira Henry, *Ancient Tahiti*, Bernice P. Bishop Museum, *Bulletin* 48 (Honolulu, 1928), pp. 339–40. Cited in C. Long, *Alpha*, pp. 145–46.
15. J. B. Pritchard, *Ancient Near Eastern Texts*, p. 7.
16. Hesiod, *Theogony*, trans. Norman O. Brown (New York, 1953), p. 78.
17. J. B. Pritchard, *Ancient Near Eastern Texts*, p. 61.
18. J. B. Pritchard, *Ancient Near Eastern Texts*, p. 65.
19. J. B. Pritchard, *Ancient Near Eastern Texts*, p. 68.
20. J. B. Pritchard, *Ancient Near Eastern Texts*, p. 68.
21. David L. Hall, "Process and Anarchy—A Taoist Vision of Creativity," *Philosophy East and West* 28 (1978), p. 276.
22. D. L. Hall, "Process and Anarchy," p. 278.
23. Barbara C. Sproul, *Primal Myths: Creating the World* (London, 1980), p. 202.
24. Wendy D. O'Flaherty, *Hindu Myths* (New York, 1976), pp. 27–28.
25. F. M. Cornford, *Plato's Cosmology: The "Timaeus" of Plato translated with a Running Commentary* (London, 1937), p. 33.
26. *The Popal Vuh*, trans. Adrian Recinos. Cited in B. C. Sproul, *Primal Myths* (London, 1980), pp. 289–90.
27. Cited in C. Long, *Alpha*, p. 191.
28. The parallelism is taken from S. H. Hooke, *In the Beginning* (Oxford, 1947), p. 21.
29. *Mahapurana*. Cited in W. Theodore de Bary, ed., *Sources of Indian Tradition* I (New York, 1966), pp. 76–78.

30. *Majjhima Nikaya* I, 166. Cited in Kenneth Morgan, ed., *The Path of the Buddha* (New York, 1956), p. 18.
31. G. Morgan, *The Path of the Buddha*, p. 19.
32. Sigmund Freud, *Civilization and Its Discontents* (New York, 1961), p. 77.
33. S. Freud, *Civilization*, p. 78.
34. Peter Bowler, *Evolution: The History of an Idea* (Berkeley, 1984), pp. 341–42.

Review Questions

1. Scholars point out that religious cosmogonies are not interested in a scientific explanation of the world but are etiological in a practical sense. Can you give examples, from the several myths discussed in this chapter, of this practical interest or purpose?
2. The Babylonian creation myth and the Chinese Taoist cosmogony both have to do with the relations of chaos and order. How do these two cosmogonies essentially differ?
3. Compare or contrast the main features of the cosmogonies that feature creation by divine conflict, creation by a divine craftsman, and *creatio ex nihilo*. What theological issues are raised by *creatio ex nihilo* that are not faced by the other two cosmogonies? What significant features of the natural world, human life, and God are reflected in the Genesis account of creation?
4. Some practical religions, like Confucianism and certain schools of Buddhism, either minimize or avoid cosmogonic speculation. Is is possible *not* to hold certain notions or beliefs about the nature of—that is, the meaning and order of—the natural and social world? Do you agree that it is unwise to attempt to harmonize religious cosmogony with modern scientific evidence, as do some in the Creation Science movement today? Or is it important to attempt such a unification of religious cosmogony with scientific explanation? Give reasons for the position you take on this question.

Suggestions for Further Reading

ANDERSON, BERNHARD W., *Creation versus Chaos: The Reinterpretation of the Mythical Symbolism in the Bible* (New York: Association Press, 1967).

BRANDON, S. C. F., *Creation Myths of the Ancient Near East* (London: Hodder and Stoughton, 1963).

BROWN, NORMAN O., "Introduction," *Hesiod's Theogony* (New York: The Liberal Arts Press, 1953).

DE BARY, W. THEODORE (ed.), *Sources of Indian Tradition; Sources of Chinese Tradition; Sources of Japanese Tradition* (New York: Columbia University Press, 1958–1960).

DUNDES, ALAN (ed.), *Sacred Narrative* (Berkeley: University of California Press, 1984).

ELIADE, MIRCEA, *Gods, Goddesses, and Myths of Creation* (New York: Harper & Row, 1974).

FRANKFORT, H., and H. A. FRANKFORT, et al., *Before Philosophy: The Intellectual Adventure of Ancient Man* (Harmondsworth, Middlesex: Penguin Books, 1951).

GIRARDOT, N. J., *Myth and Meaning in Early Taoism: The Theme of Chaos* (Berkeley: University of California Press, 1983).

GUTHRIE, W. K. C., *In the Beginning: Some Greek Views of the Origin of Life and the Early State of Man* (Ithaca, N.Y.: Cornell University Press, 1957).

KRAMER, SAMUEL N. (ed.), *Mythologies of the Ancient World* (Garden City, N.Y.: Doubleday, 1955).

KUNTZ, PAUL (ed.), *The Concept of Order* (Seattle: University of Washington Press, 1968).

LONG, CHARLES, *Alpha: Myths of Creation* (New York: Collier Books, 1963; Scholars Press, 1983).

LOVIN, ROBIN W,, and FRANK E. REYNOLDS (eds)., *Cosmogony and Ethical Order* (Chicago: Chicago University Press, 1985).

PRITCHARD, JAMES B. (ed.), *Ancient Near Eastern Texts Relating to the Old Testament* (Princeton: Princeton University Press, 1950).

SPROUL, BARBARA C., *Primal Myths: Creating the World* (London: Rider, 1980).

CHAPTER **9**

The Human Problem

OVERVIEW

In this chapter, we shall explore the ways in which religious traditions understand the root of the human problem. While we may seriously disagree on the cause of human ignorance, distress, and strife, most human beings agree that life is not what it should be. We are often overwhelmed by a sense of our own weakness and inadequacy, by feelings of hostility and estrangement, or by a profound disquiet provoked by moral guilt and failure. We seek enlightenment, reconciliation, forgiveness, and peace.

We begin by looking briefly at some modern, secular theories and asking whether they have probed the human problem at its deepest level. We then turn to four classic diagnoses of the human problem—the Stoic, the Christian, the Buddhist, and the Confucianist—and discuss each one in some detail. While they are strikingly different, each one insists that the cause of the human problem and its cure can be understood only in terms of the human self's relation to a primordial or ultimate sacred order.

As you think about these alternative accounts of the human problem, keep in mind certain questions about what is at stake. What are the assumptions concerning the self, human nature, and human freedom—for example, about the human capacity to know the truth or the good and to do it? Are different conceptions of nature and of deity or the ultimate reflected in these contrasting views of the human problem and the true goal of human existence, that is, in their accounts of salvation or enlightenment? Conceptions of the human problem usually are inextricably related to beliefs about cosmogony and about deity or the ultimate.

228

Modern Views of Our Human Plight

In 1961, Richard Alpert was a young, up-and-coming professor of psychology at Harvard University. He was, by any measure, a success. Suddenly, his life, despite its outward glitter, turned empty and meaningless. This is how he described his situation:

> I had an apartment in Cambridge that was filled with antiques and I gave charming dinner parties. I had a Mercedes-Benz sedan and a Triumph and a Cessna 172 airplane and an MG sportscar. But I felt that something was wrong with my world and that all the stuff I was teaching was just like little molecular bits of stuff, but they didn't add up to a feeling of wisdom.[1]

Alpert tried LSD, but he said it was like coming into the kingdom of heaven and then being cast out again and again. He began to feel depressed. He gave up drugs, went to India to study under a guru, and found deep spiritual insight. He changed his name to Ram Dass and became "a new man." Now, we might say that Richard Alpert was simply one of those overdriven, discontented intellectuals, but the fact is that other examples come easily to mind—middle-aged corporate executives, for instance, whose lives suddenly turn empty and who begin to question the mad scramble for wealth and power. Why are we humans so driven to seek pleasure, status, and knowledge and yet so frequently disappointed and anxious? The answer has to do with the fact that we are self-transcendent and therefore are insatiable in our desires and never fully satisfied with those temporal aspirations that prove precarious, transient, and ultimately negligible. Because we are spiritual as well as biological creatures, we are a problem to ourselves.

A number of modern secular theorists have probed the human problem and have tried to discover the reasons for our persistent anxiety and alienation. Karl Marx argued that man is alienated and unhappy because, in an industrial, capitalist society, his work and the objects he produces are alien to him. Humans are estranged and miserable, according to Marx, because they find no satisfaction in their productive work. This may be true, as far as it goes, but we have to wonder whether Marx touches the human problem at its deepest level.

As we have seen, Sigmund Freud saw human unhappiness and neuroses as inherent in the conflict within the individual between the erotic and self-preserving "life" instinct (Eros) and the sadistic, aggressive "death" instinct (Thanatos). He saw it as well in the discontent brought about by the conflict between the individual's drive to express his or her libidinal, erotic energies and the frustrating demands of

society and civilization that thwart those essential drives. Freud's rather
antisocial characterization of human nature is similar, in this respect,
to Konrad Lorenz's theory of innate human aggression, as proposed
in his book *On Aggression*. Both Freud and Lorenz hold out guarded
hope for the future of humanity, based on our ability to exercise
those rational capacities that just might redirect our aggressive antisocial behavior along more socially constructive lines. However, the
question whether reason is the cause or the cure of our seemingly
intractable problem has been questioned by some of the great religions,
as we shall see.

Whatever the cause of our unease and strife, few thoughtful persons
would deny that we humans have, over the millennia, sensed a tragic
flaw, a falling short of our potential, a missing the mark of life as
it was meant to be or should be. Something, we feel, is "out of joint."
We recognize that we are ignorant, estranged, anxious, or morally
guilty and are in need of enlightenment, reconciliation, salvation, or
atonement. And so we ask, "What is it about human consciousness
and behavior that causes us such unrest and suffering? What is it
that can free us from this tragic plight?" To provide answers to these
questions is a primary function of the world's religions. The differing
views of human nature that these religions propose naturally result
in different conclusions about the character of the problem and the
variety of prescriptions for its cure.

The classical Greek philosophers saw humankind's problem as essentially ignorance. According to Plato, virtue—and, therefore, happiness—is a matter of the exercise of intellect and is to be found in a
knowledge of what is perfect and unchanging, rather than in mere
appearances or opinion. The individual, therefore, must be brought
out of the shadowy cave of ignorance and into the light of knowledge
and truth. In *The Republic*, Plato offers his blueprint for a perfect
state. Since only the highly educated have attained true knowledge
and can discern truth from opinion, it is they who must rule if social
harmony is to be secured. "There will be no end to the troubles of
states, or of humanity itself," writes Plato, "till philosophers become
kings in this world, or till those we now call kings and rulers really
and truly become philosophers" (*Republic*, 473).

Plato's prescription of humankind's ills is called *rationalism* because
he assumes that the solving of our problem lies in overcoming ignorance and in acquiring knowledge *and* virtue through the employment
of reason. He further assumes that human nature is capable of dis-
cerning the unchanging Truth from what is relative and perhaps
self-serving, and that humans are able to act virtuously once the nature
of true virtue is understood. For Plato and all rationalists, reason is
redemptive.

While offering very different solutions, both classical Chinese Confucianism and contemporary Marxism would say that the human problem lies in unnatural, corrupt, or alienated social relationships. We are essentially what we eat; that is, we are products of our habits and our social relations. While we are basically human-hearted and social, we are nevertheless corrupted by false habits and relations. By a return to the way of the ancients or, in the case of Marxism, to truly productive relationships—that is, by a reorganization of society as we now know it—envy, acquisitiveness, strife, and suffering will be largely rectified, if not eliminated.

Judaism and, more particularly, Christianity see the genesis of the human problem neither in ignorance nor in unnatural social relations as such, for these are more fundamentally traceable to a hardened heart and a sinful will. The problem is rooted in our rebellion against and disobedience of God's will. Our redemption and reconciliation can come only through confession of our moral guilt and through repentence and conversion, or the turning of the will from self to God.

Buddhism's answer to the human problem is perhaps the most radical of all because it sees the self as, in fact, illusory and this deception as the source of human suffering and social unrest. According to Buddhism, our illusion about a permanent self is the root of our craving and egoistic desire, and hence of our unease and pain. Only by the rigorous adoption of a spiritual discipline can we hope to achieve that enlightenment by which egoistic craving is overcome, desire stilled, and peace achieved.

Every religion, of course, holds some conviction about life and its predicament, even if only unconsciously and inarticulately. Here, we select four distinct and explicit theories of human nature and the source of the problem to illustrate the range of possibilities. Our examples are taken from Stoicism, Christianity, Theravada Buddhism, and Confucianism.

Stoicism

Stoicism was founded by Zeno about the year 306 B.C.E. in Athens. The golden age of Greece and of Athens was past by then. The noble order of independent Greek city-states had fallen before the military empire of Alexander and his generals. The old moral guides and confidence were now gone. There was need of a new philosophy and religion for the Hellenistic age, one that could stand firm against the rising chaos. Until the coming and triumph of Christianity, Stoicism filled that role.

The burning question for Greco–Roman society remained the ethical one: how persons should live, because to many it appeared that human hopes and plans were at the mercy of impersonal, unpredictable forces. Chance, the great god Tyche, seemed to rule the world. And Tyche was a capricious deity, lifting people to the heights on one day and dashing their hopes on the next. Men and women saw themselves as playthings of fate, of powers outside their control. This world may be our only home, but it appeared to many to be an alien, even a hostile, place. For the educated Greek, Stoicism offered a noble response to this sense of fatedness, a means of spiritual liberation in a time of historical uncertainty and change.

According to Stoicism, this world is not a meaningless chaos, as we might surmise; on the contrary, the world is an ordered whole, governed and permeated by a Divine Reason, Law, or God. The evolutionary process is not chaotic, the Stoics argued, but is under the rule of a Divine Purpose by which all things—from the smallest worm to the intellect of man—are governed. The Stoics called this law of growth *Phusis*, or Nature. *Phusis* is what shapes living things into their perfect form, and each thing is a germ or spark of this Divine Logos or Reason. The Stoics viewed the world pantheistically as a divine organism, each thing a microcosm of the animating, germinating Divine Reason. To live according to nature is to live according to this Divine Nature or God.

Since we are a part or a spark of the Divine, the nature of the ethical life is clear. Goodness is living in accordance with Nature or fitting our aims and conduct so they may be in accord with Divine Reason. The Stoics insisted that happiness cannot be found in the pursuit of pleasure because pleasure often means the rule of passion over reason. Personal happiness can come only when we adjust our hopes and actions to the laws of Nature. To do otherwise is to resist the inevitable—and to be miserable. If evil befalls a person, it is after all only temporary; indeed, seen in the long run, it is not even evil because all events are but parts of a larger Whole.

The Stoic was thereby able to accept dispassionately both pain and pleasure, poverty and fortune, and health and sickness. The human soul, being a spark of the divine, has the same freedom as God. Therefore, it can act either with or against Nature, or God. However, to act against Nature is to court disaster, for true freedom is to live according to Nature. Freedom is not the rejection of all restraints; that is simply license. On the contrary, true freedom is the voluntary acceptance of the natural law, Reason or Fate, that must be obeyed whether we will to or not. "The Fates," writes Seneca, "lead him who is willing; they constrain him who is unwilling." The Stoics teach that a person must accept the apparent vicissitudes of life and fortune— such as bereavement, pain, poverty, and death—because every person, although a slave or poor, can be spiritually free. Death is, of course, inevitable and therefore must be accepted calmly as Nature's law. So writes the great Stoic philosopher, Epictetus:

> We act very much as if we were on a voyage. What can I do? I
> can choose out the helmsman, the sailors, the day, the moment.
> Then a storm arises. What do I care? I have fulfilled my task:
> another has now to act, the helmsman. Suppose even the ship goes
> down. What have I to do then? I do only what lies within my power,
> drowning if drown I must, without fear, not crying out or accusing
> heaven, for I know that what is born must needs also perish. For
> I am not immortal, but a man, a part of the universe as an hour
> is part of the day. Like the hour I must be here and like an hour
> pass away. What matters it then to me how I pass . . . for by some
> such means I must needs pass away.[2]

According to the Stoics, true goodness, and thus happiness, is to
know that we must live according to Nature or, to put it another
way, to recognize the difference between what lies within our nature
or power and what lies beyond it. Things that lie outside our nature
must be of no concern. Such "externals" are to be regarded with
indifference, with *apatheia*, since we cannot control them. Now, such
things as our physical appearance, our mental gifts, our nationality,
and, of course, death itself lie outside our control, and thus it is folly
to fret and fuss about them.

The wise person, therefore, sees the vanity of much worldly, human
striving since so much that happens lies outside our capacity to change
or is merely temporary and passing. The great Stoic emperor Marcus
Aurelius counseled the following:

> Think often on the swiftness with which things that exist and are
> coming into existence are swept past us and carried out of sight . . .
> all is as a river in ceaseless flow. . . . Is he not senseless who in such
> an environment puffs himself up, or is distracted or frets as over
> a trouble lasting and far reaching.[3]

On brief reflection, it would appear that the counsel of *apatheia*
conflicts with the Stoic appeal to civic duty. How can we work dili-
gently for the welfare of humanity if so much of our effort is, in
the long run, vain striving? Why work to increase our wealth and
prosperity if worldly goods are in themselves worthless and to be
regarded with indifference? The Stoic reply is forthright: Every
created thing, from the acorn to the cobbler to the king, is created
for a function, a purpose. Nature shapes everything to achieve its
form or end—for example, the end of the acorn is to be an oak
tree. Gilbert Murray describes the Stoic's view:

> A good bootmaker is one who makes good boots; a good shepherd
> is one who keeps his sheep well; and even though good boots are,
> in the Day of Judgment sense, entirely worthless . . . yet the good

bootmaker or good shepherd must do his work well or he will cease
to be good. To be good he must perform his function; and in performing that function there are certain things that he must 'prefer'
to others, even though they are not really good. He must prefer a
healthy sheep or a well-made boot to their opposites. It is thus that
Nature, or Phusis, herself works when she shapes the seed into the
tree, or the blind puppy into the good hound. The perfection of the
tree or hound is in itself indifferent, a thing of no ultimate value.
Yet the goodness of Nature lies in working for that perfection.[4]

Epictetus taught that life is like a drama or a game. The role of
the actor or the athlete is to play the part well, no matter whether
the play is insignificant or the game is lost:

> Remember that you are an actor in a play, and the Playwright
> chooses the manner of it: if he wants it short, it is short; if long,
> it is long. If he wants you to act a poor man you must act the part
> with all your powers; and so if your part be a cripple or a magistrate
> or a plain man. For your business is to act the character that is
> given you and act it well; the choice of the cast is Another's.[5]

The person capable of cultivating *apatheia* is free and thus happy;
no "externals" can assail him or her, neither poverty nor riches,
neither health nor sickness. It is, finally, the way we take things that
make them good or evil.

What disturbs our minds, according to Epictetus, is not events but
the view we take of events. For instance, death is nothing dreadful,
or else Socrates would have thought it so. The only dreadful thing
about death is our judgment that it is dreadful. The person who
achieves this knowledge, who cultivates indifference to externals, is a
wise man or woman and is freed of anxiety, fear, envy, and desire.

Stoicism sees the human problem as rooted in ignorance. The cure
it proposes is essentially naturalistic and psychological because the
healing of human distress is achieved by knowledge, by self-education,
and by the attainment of wisdom. The Stoic expects no change in
external conditions; liberation involves a change of mental and emotional viewpoint, not a change of the world. There will not be any
reward for Stoic self-sacrifice and its contempt for pleasure by a promise of recompense in another life or in another world—which, the
Stoic would say, is only to postpone the pleasure for a time. To follow
Nature or God suffices for the Stoic. "Shall not the fact," writes
Epictetus, "that we have God as maker and father and kinsman relieve
us from pains and fears?"

The Stoics' noble and selfless creed was admired by many of the
early Christian Fathers, including St. John Chrysostom and St. Augustine. Epictetus' *Enchiridion* was adapted for monastic life in the Middle

Ages. But, as we will see, the Christian diagnosis of the human condition, its problem, and its solution is strikingly different.

Christianity

The Christian view of human nature and the human predicament is rooted in the biblical portrayal of man and woman, especially as it is found in the early chapters of the book of Genesis. To be human, according to Christianity, is to be in a sense both angel and devil. Pascal called man "a monster, a chimera, the glory and the shame of the universe." This paradoxical vision of what it is to be human may be clarified by a brief analysis of the story of the Creation and human Fall in Genesis.

The first thing that is evident in Genesis 1–2 is the fact that man (the Hebrew *ha'adam* means man in the generic sense of humankind or human being) is a finite creature. Being human does not entail any notion that we are naturally divine or immortal. "The Lord God formed man of dust from the ground, and breathed into his nostrils the breath of life, and man became a living being" (Gen. 2:7). Human life is *created* and therefore is derivative and dependent. Human beings do not choose life, and they cannot prevent its end in death. God has the power over human breath—life and death are, according to the Bible, "in God's hands." To be human, then, is to be a part of nature, created from the dust of the earth to which we will return. Human life does not have an existence in and of itself; life is a gift of God.

While human life entails radical finitude and dependence, it is not for that reason worthless or evil. For, according to Genesis, God "saw everything that he had made, and behold, it was very good" (Gen. 1:31). There is nothing essentially evil about human creatureliness and finitude. The ancient Hebrews did not consider the body as distinct from or inferior to the soul or spirit, or evil as such. For the ancient Hebrew, there is no sharp dualism between the body and the soul, as we find in certain Hellenistic religions, for example, Gnosticism. To be human is to be "a living being," a psychosomatic (*psyche* means soul and *soma* means body) unity. Finite human life is declared good.

Not only is human existence good but also, according to Genesis, humankind is given a unique place in God's creation. Humanity is the crown and the glory of God's work. This is indicated by the fact that "God created man in his own image, in the image of God he created him; male and female he created them" (Gen. 1:27). To be created "in the image and likeness of God" is to be given a unique status, one in which all creation is placed under human dominion:

> And God blessed them, and God said to them, 'Be fruitful and multiply, and fill the earth and subdue it; and have dominion over the fish of the sea and over the birds of the air and over every living thing that moves upon the earth.
>
> *(Gen. 1:28)*

Human dominion—or, better, vice-regency over creation—is further underlined by the fact that we are called on to name all the animals, which in ancient Israel implied a power and authority over what is named.

Human life is given a unique status in the biblical cosmogony. Man and woman are *like* God—but they are *not* God. It is just this "likeness" that is humanity's glory; but it is also the root of the human problem. The human "image and likeness" is the source of the temptation to play God, and thus to rebel against God. From the early years of Christianity until the time of the Protestant Reformation, theologians saw the image of God (the *imago Dei*) as essentially present in the human exercise of *reason*. Roman Catholic theology has traditionally distinguished between two conceptions of the human "likeness" to God. One has to do with those special supernatural endowments that are associated with sanctifying grace and that were lost as a result of the Fall. However, there is also the natural gift of reason, essential to what it means to be *homo sapien* (like wisdom). Reason is intrinsic to our being human, and it is *not* lost in the Fall. This two-fold nature of the *imago Dei* is described by a contemporary Roman Catholic philosopher in a summary of the teaching of the Medieval theologian, Thomas Aquinas:

> The quality of being the image of God is co-essential to man because it is one with the rationality of his nature. To be a mind is to be *naturally capable of knowing and loving God*. To be able to do this is one with the very nature of thinking. It is as natural for man to be the image of God as to be a rational animal, that is, as to be man. [But there is also a special supernatural endowment.] *The first effect of grace is, therefore, to perfect this resemblance of man to God* by divinizing his soul, his mind and consequently his whole nature. From the moment he has grace, man can love God with a love worthy of God since his love is divine in its origin. (Italics added.)[6]

According to Roman Catholic teaching, our nature is "wounded" as a consequence of the Fall and thus susceptible to sin and evil; however, it is not so deep a wound as to destroy our natural human power of reason and free will.

Classical Protestant theology—for example, in the thought of Martin Luther (1483–1546) and John Calvin (1509–1564)—has rejected the Roman Catholic distinction between the two forms of the divine like-

ness and has claimed that the Fall did, indeed, involve the loss of
something essential to human existence. According to Luther, the divine image that was lost in the Fall is *the freedom of the human will.*
You can see how these opposing views of the image of God and the
effects of sin would have important implications regarding the way
to salvation (see Chapter 11).

In non–Roman Catholic Christianity, the *imago Dei* has been identified with unique human characteristics other than reason—for example, with human creativity, such as in the mastery of nature and in
artistic genius, or in man's unique addressability or moral response
and responsibility. One of the most compelling modern views of the
imago Dei is the idea of human *self-transcendence.* It is most fully developed in the writings of the Protestant theologian Reinhold Niebuhr
(1892–1971). According to Niebuhr, humans are unique in their capacity to stand clear of their actions, even their world, and to judge
them from beyond the self. For example, humans alone write histories
and conceive of systems of ultimate and universal value. The self is
capable of transcending the processes of nature and even its own
rationality:

> The human spirit has the special capacity of standing continually
> outside itself in terms of indefinite regression. . . . The rational capac-
> ity of surveying the world, of forming general concepts and analyzing
> the order of the world is thus but one aspect of what Christianity
> knows as 'spirit.' The self knows the world . . . because it stands
> outside both itself and the world, which means that it cannot under-
> stand itself except as it is understood from beyond itself and the
> world.[7]

Human self-transcendence involves self-determination or freedom,
which is the key to genuine selfhood. Nevertheless, self-transcendence
or self-determination is the source not only of human creativity but
also of human destructiveness. This is why, Niebuhr would argue, it
is not possible to identify virtue with reason per se. Self-transcendence
can make humans both saints and devils. Humans can be more deadly
than the brute animals just because they can transmute the brute's
instinctive will to survive into an egocentric will to power; that is,
freedom allows humans, encompassed by natural limits, to attempt to
defy those limits with infinite ambitions and pretensions. It is just this
ambiguous situation that makes humans conscious of their vulnerability
and insecurity and that leads to anxiety, the root and precondition
of what Christianity calls sin or destructive self-assertion.

According to Christianity, sin is the human propensity to put our
own egoistic interests at the center of things. This can be seen in the
variety of ways Christianity has attempted to describe sin. In the Old

Testament, sin is seen largely as a turning away from God, disobedience or distrust; a hardening of the human heart. The prophets thus
saw sin as a straying from God, a faithlessness and a breaking of the
Covenant that had been sealed at Mount Sinai. The medieval theologians tended to see sin as less a turning away from God than a turning
in, a self-absorption. They called sin *concupiscence*, or lust. It was often
associated with sexual or fleshly lust, but it should be seen as having
a wider application. Concupiscence is also a lusting of the mind (for
example, in the figure of Faust) or the spirit. It is a never-satisfied
egoistic striving.

Christian theologians have seen all these forms of egoistic sin—disobedience, the hardening of the heart, concupiscence, and sensuality—
as derived from and best described in terms of human *pride*. St.
Augustine so defined sin:

> For 'pride is the beginning of all sin.' And what is pride but an
> appetite for inordinate exaltation. Now, exaltation is inordinate when
> the soul cuts itself off from the very Source to which it should keep
> close and somehow makes itself and becomes an end to itself. This
> takes place when the soul becomes inordinately pleased with itself
> ... and falls away from the unchangeable Good which ought to
> please the soul far more than the soul can please itself.[8]

Subsequently, St. Augustine's view of sin dominated Western orthodox Christianity, and we find Luther and Calvin also describing
sin in Augustinian terms as a self-love and a false confidence. Calvin
writes of human sin:

> They worship not him, but a figment of their own brains in his
> stead. This depravity Paul expressly remarks: 'Professing themselves
> to be wise, they become fools.' He had before said 'they become
> vain in their imaginations.' But lest any should exculpate them, he
> adds that they were deservedly blinded, because not content with
> the bounds of sobriety, but arrogating to themselves more than was
> right, they willfully darkened and even infatuated themselves with
> pride, vanity and perverseness. Whence it follows, that their folly is
> inexcusable, which originates not only in a vain curiosity, but in
> false confidence, and in immoderate desire to exceed the limits of
> human knowledge.[9]

Christianity views sin as not primarily connected with the body or
finitude but with the spirit—that is, associated with human freedom
or, rather, with a perverted exercise of the human will or desire. So
pervasive and inevitable (though not necessary) is sin that St. Augustine spoke of it as *original*. St. Augustine found explicit biblical warrant
for viewing sin as an inevitable human defect in St. Paul's association

of sin with Adam, the first man: "Therefore as sin came into the world through one man and death through sin, and so death spread to all men because all men sinned" (Romans 5:12). While sin is a certainty, in that no person can claim to be free of its taint, it is not necessary because, if it were, it would deny human responsibility. Augustine thus follows St. Paul in affirming sin's original or universal character while insisting on human responsibility: "So they are without excuse; for although they knew God they did not honor him as God or give thanks to him. . . . Claiming to be wise, they became fools" (Romans 1:21–22). St. Augustine joins these two convictions of sin's inevitability and human moral responsibility in the following passage:

> Man's nature, indeed, was created at first faultless and without any sin; but that nature of man in which every one is born from Adam, now wants the Physician, because it is not sound. All good qualities, which it still possesses . . . it has of the Most High God, its Creator and Maker. But the flaw, which darkens and weakens all those natural goods, it has not contracted from its blameless Creator but from that original sin, which it committed by free will.[10]

St. Augustine maintains that sin condemns humankind to ignorance and prideful lust, and that sin is not merely a psychological state but a condition of being. This is the stark reality of the human predicament. Before the Fall of Adam, humans possessed both the ability not to sin (*posse non peccare*) and the ability to sin (*posse peccare*). But since the Fall, humans are capable only of the latter and are justly condemned to damnation. Traditional Christianity has consistently maintained that the cause of humanity's unease and tragic plight is an evil, disordered will, a turning to self rather than to God—and that mankind can do nothing to save or deliver itself from this bondage to sin and the sting of death. Only God's grace, freely bestowed, can redeem and liberate the self from its sin. This is expressed by St. Augustine at the conclusion of the passage cited above:

> The grace, however, of Christ, without which neither infants nor adults can be saved, is not bestowed for any merits, but is given *freely*, on account of which it is also called, *grace*.[11]

Many modern Christian theologians have rejected the Augustinian implication that every human inherits biologically not only the propensity to sin but also Adam's guilt. However, they, too, affirm the belief contained in the Adamic myth of the Fall: that we humans are all born into a social matrix of sinful pride and egoism. The individual cannot escape this tendency to sin and should not search for scapegoats in evil social institutions or in other persons—for example,

Polish Roman Catholics at confession. Each person must confess his or her sins privately before the priest, who may prescribe certain penances before absolution of sin is given. (*Source*: Courtesy of Elliot Erwitt, Magnum Photos, Inc.)

Hitler. All Christian theologians would insist that, while there surely is an inequality of personal guilt for evil, the taint of egoism is universal and every human is to some extent personally responsible for evil. Thus, while rejecting literal interpretations of St. Augustine's doctrine of the Fall and original sin, modern Christian thinkers maintain a belief in the universal reality of sin and the necessity of God's prior action or grace in justifying and in freeing the individual of moral guilt. How Christianity, in both its Catholic and its Protestant forms, understands the ways to and the goal of redemption or salvation is discussed in Chapters 11 and 12.

Theravada Buddhism

Buddhism has given the world a radical and an influential body of teachings regarding the human problem. Siddhartha Gautama—the Buddha (563?–483? B.C.E.), or enlightened one—lived in north India, the son of a ruler of the kingdom of the Sakyas. He taught how we should live in order to avoid pain and achieve supreme happiness and bliss, but knowledge of the right path requires that we know what is the true nature of human life and the truth about the processes of nature itself.

At the heart of Buddha's teaching is the Indian doctrine of *karma* (or *kamma* in Pali). The word means "action," "doing," or, more accurately, "volitional action." According to Buddhism, every living being exists by virtue of an individual force or energy peculiar to that being—the *karma* of each living thing. *Karma* is the way each being manifests itself in its own unique way and thus creates a self or personality. Now, our volition or action may be relatively good or bad. Good *karma* produces good "fruits," or effects, and bad *karma* produces bad effects. In every moment of a being's life, that individual is fashioning the life that will follow. Each being, the Buddha taught, is the architect of his or her own destiny: "The self is Lord of the self, who else is the Lord?" asked the Buddha.

The law of *karma* should not, however, be confused with the theistic idea of "moral justice," which implies a Supreme Being who metes out divine rewards and punishments. The law of *karma* is simply the law of cause and effect, and good and bad karma will continue to manifest themselves in another life after the death of this individual existence.

We have said that each being is an individual, something that is. It is more accurate, however, to say that Buddhism teaches that each being is a *becoming*, an event, a process. The cause of this process is *karma*. Every cause is the effect of a previous cause, world without beginning or end. Thus, Buddha taught what is called the "dependent origination" of all things. However, beings are not only in a state of becoming or process but also in a state of *compoundedness* and *conditionedness*. Every becoming is simply a compounded process that can be analyzed into the several elements or conditions of which it is composed. These elements are called *dhammas*, meaning that which "bears" certain qualities. According to Buddhism, these elements, which are both corporeal and mental, are found in five aggregates called *khandhas*. G. P. Malalasekera describes the *khandhas* as follows:

> The five aggregates together constitute what is called the "I" or "personality" or the "individual." The aggregates are not parts or pieces of the individual but phases or forms of development, something like the shape, color, and smell of a flower. . . . There is no "stuff" or substratum as such but only manifestations, energies, activities, processes. . . . Every living being, since it is a process, is described as a flux, a flowing, a stretching forth, a continuity, or, more frequently, as a combustion, a flame. There is no "substance," no "self" or "soul," underlying the process, unifying it.[12]

Buddhism teaches that nothing in reality corresponds to what we in the West call "I" or "self." The self is simply an abstraction of what in fact is a compoundedness of energies and activities. There is no enduring, substantial self beyond or underlying this aggregate of energy processes. This implies the Buddhist doctrine of *an-atta* (*an-atman* in Sanskrit), or the not-self. Buddha taught that what we call the enduring self, soul, or ego is in reality only an aggregate of phenomenal processes.

The not-self doctrine leads naturally from an analysis of the self or, rather, of its unreality, to the discussion of the human problem. According to Buddhism, the belief in a self is the indispensable condition for the emergence of suffering, which is the root of all unhappiness and sorrow. Buddha addressed the reality of suffering, and its cause and cure, in his famous sermon given near Benares immediately after his enlightenment. Because this discourse contains the Four Noble Truths that are the foundation of Buddha's *Dharma*—Truth or teaching—it is important that we quote the first part of the sermon in full:

> Thus have I heard: at one time the Lord dwelt at Benares at Isipatana in the Deer Park. There the Lord addressed the five monks:
> 'These two extremes, monks, are not to be practised by one who has gone forth from the world. What are the two? That conjoined with passions and luxury, low, vulgar, common, ignoble, and useless, and that conjoined with self-torture, painful, ignoble, and useless. Avoiding these two extremes the Tathagata ["one who has found the Truth," that is, Buddha] has gained the enlightenment of the Middle Path, which produces insight and knowledge and tends to calm, to higher knowledge, enlightenment, Nirvana.
> And what, monks, is the Middle Path? ... This is the noble Eightfold Way, namely right view, right intention, right speech, right action, right livelihood, right effort, right mindfulness, right concentration. This, monks, is the Middle Path ...
> 1. Now this, monks, is the noble truth of pain: birth is painful, old age is painful, sickness is painful, death is painful, sorrow, lamentation, dejection and despair are painful. In short the five groups of grasping [*khandhas*] are painful.
> 2. Now this, monks, is the noble truth of the cause of pain: the craving, which tends to rebirth, combined with pleasure and lust, finding pleasure here and there, namely, the craving for passion, the craving for existence, the craving for non-existence.
> 3. Now this, monks, is the noble truth of the cessation of pain: the cessation without a remainder of craving, the abandonment, forsaking, release, non-attachment.
> 4. Now this, monks, is the noble truth of the way that leads to the cessation of pain: this is the Noble Eightfold Way.[13]

The First Noble Truth of the Buddha is the reality of *dukkha*, usually translated as pain or suffering. *Dukkha* should not, however,

Tibetan Buddhist *mandala* depicting the Wheel of Life, which symbolizes the causes of suffering. The black monster embracing the Wheel is Impermanence, which devours existence. (*Source*: Neg. #329316, courtesy of the Department of Library Services, American Museum of Natural History.)

be understood simply as ordinary pain, sorrow, and suffering; it includes the deeper sense that imperfection and impermanence are constitutive of life. According to Buddha, whatever is impermanent is *dukkha*, and, since nature itself is constituted by change and conditionedness, it is permeated by *dukkha*. Buddha insisted this includes the aggregates that make up the "individual": "The five aggregates of attachment are *dukkha*."

Dukkha includes, then, the sense of impermanence, imperfection, and incompleteness that life exhibits—the persistent conflict between our desires and hopes and our actual attainments. It involves a sense of unease, of anxiety, of what Thoreau described as our lives of "quiet desperation." Buddhism would contend that most of us try to minimize these unpleasant facts of life. Edward Conze refers to this tendency:

> Most of us are inclined by nature to live in a fool's paradise, to look on the brighter side of life, and to minimize its unpleasant sides. To dwell on suffering runs normally counter to our inclinations. Usually we cover up suffering with all kinds of 'emotional curtains.' . . . This is illustrated by the widespread use of 'euphemisms' which is nothing but the avoidance of words that call up disagreeable associations. . . . A man does not 'die,' but he 'passes away,' 'goes to sleep' . . . etc.[14]

Conze suggests that a special effort of meditation is needed to realize the great amount of concealed suffering in what we unwittingly consider pleasant. For example, we frequently experience pleasure at the expense of others. Wealth, for instance, often is achieved at the expense of poverty-stricken laborers. Furthermore, pleasure is tied to unconscious anxiety because we are concerned about losing it—for example, wealth or youthful beauty. This is called "suffering from reversal." It is what the poet Shelley meant by "that unrest which men miscall delight." Buddha speaks of six occasions when suffering is present: birth; sickness; old age; the phobia of death; association with what we dislike or abhor, such as a personal weakness; and separation from what we love—for example, a friend, child, or a beloved environment.

Buddhists insist that to focus on *dukkha* is not to be pessimistic but, rather, to be *realistic*, to see things as they truly are. Only by facing the reality of *dukkha* can a person understand its cause and achieve its cessation. A Buddhist, they point out, is not gloomy and melancholy but is like the Buddha himself—serene, contented, and happy. However, before *dukkha* can be overcome it is essential to understand its cause. This is the Second Noble Truth.

When asked how "individuality" arises, Buddha replied by pointing to the Second Noble Truth, the cause of *dukkha*: "It is that craving [*tanhā*]", he said, "which gives rise to ever fresh rebirth and bound up with pleasure and lust, now here, now there, finds ever fresh delight."[15] *Tanhā* is thirst, craving, unsatisfied longing, a will to live that gives rise to and upholds the continuity of the ego or "self." Buddhists often describe *tanhā* by using the image of heat or a flame, a burning desire. However, it is important to realize that *tanhā* is not only egoistic craving for sense pleasure, wealth, or power. It is also a thirst for and attachment to ideas and ideals, views, opinions, theories, conceptions, and beliefs. According to the Buddha's analysis, all the troubles and strife in the world, from little personal quarrels in families to great wars between nations and countries, arise out of this selfish 'thirst.' From this point of view, all economic, political and social problems are rooted in this selfish 'thirst.'[16]

The Third Noble Truth is that there is liberation from suffering through a cessation of craving. Where there is no craving, there is no suffering. The goal of enlightenment, Nirvana, is known by the term *Tanhākkhaya*, or the "Extinction of Thirst." The Fourth Noble Truth is the truth of the Way leading to the cessation of suffering, or the Eightfold Path that leads to enlightenment and Nirvana. The Buddhist Path and the goal of Nirvana are discussed in Chapters 11 and 12.

Before we consider a fourth tradition, note that both Christianity and Buddhism see the human problem as rooted in anxiety and egoistic desire, although they hold radically different notions of the true nature of the "self." Also, as we will see in Chapter 11, Christianity requires a profoundly metaphysical solution—redemption through God's grace—to the human problem, while Theravada Buddhism renounces such a solution altogether. A very different conception of human nature and the human problem is found in Confucianism in traditional China.

Confucianism

Confucianism's this-worldly, practical view of the human problem and its resolution has led some scholars to deny that Confucianism is in any proper sense a religion; rather, that it is merely a humanistic code of manners. But that view fails to appreciate the sacred dimension of China's ancient way. Confucius's fundamental doctrine of *li*—of social rite or ceremonial, the "rules of social propriety"—is perceived by Confucianists as a sacred Rite or Way. *Li* involves the acquiring of a human virtue and power *consistent with the Mandate or Approval of Heaven*. It is heaven brought down to earth.

Confucianism is known in China as the "way of the ancients," or the "way of the sages," a rule of behavior that the pre-Revolutionary Chinese assumed had existed from time immemorial. Confucius was not regarded as the founder of the "Way" but nevertheless was spoken of reverently as the First Teacher, foremost in rank among the ancient "sages." He saw himself, however, as only a "transmitter" of the "way of the ancients."

Confucius was born around 551 B.C.E. in the province of Lu (now

Shantung) and died in 479. He spent most of his life as a tutor to the sons of the ruling class and never achieved his ambition of holding a high government position, whereby he might have put his precepts into practice. What we know of Confucius is largely derived from the *Analects*, or "Selected Sayings," written by him and his disciples. During the Sung Dynasty (960–1279 C.E.) the *Analects* and the *Book of Mencius* (written by a later idealistic Confucianist) were added, among others, to the ancient, hallowed Six Classics.

What was the human problem that afflicted the China of Confucius's time, and what did he prescribe for its cure? The Master, as he was called, lived in a period of terrible social and political instability, resulting from the disintegration of the feudal society typical of the early Chou Dynasty (1027?–256 B.C.E.). China was divided by a number of independent, warring states, each pursuing its own interest. Confucius believed that the solution to the incessant strife was a return to the Golden Age, to the social rites and the values of the earlier Chou rulers who, Confucius taught, had won the Mandate of Heaven because of their virtuous and peaceable ways. Confucius believed that a society perseveres through the instilling of a correct pattern of behavior. The pattern is exemplified in the lives of those in authority and is thereby passed on to others as a "pattern of prestige." Confucius devoted himself to transmitting this ancient Grand Harmony. "I transmit," he wrote, "but do not create. I have been faithful to and love antiquity."[17]

The Confucian sage Hsün Tzu (298–238 B.C.E.) also traced the human problem to an unrestrained pursuit of personal desire and to the undoing of the ancient rules of social propriety:

> Whence do the rules of decorum arise? From the fact that men are born with desires, and when these desires are not satisfied, men are bound to pursue their satisfaction. When the pursuit is carried on unrestrained and unlimited, there is bound to be contention. With contention comes chaos; with chaos dissolution. The ancient kings disliked this chaos and set the necessary limits by codifying rules of decorum and righteousness.... It is through rites that Heaven and earth are harmonious.... He who holds to the rites is never confused in the midst of multifarious change; he who deviates therefrom is lost.[18]

It follows from the Confucian analysis of the human problem that its cure lies in education. Assimilation of the ancient rites is the following of antique ways not simply for nostalgia's sake but rather for the specific purpose of modifying social conduct. Every aspect of life— the school, the theater, entertainments, public ceremonies, the lessons of history, and manners in the home—must be pressed into the service of nurturing the traditional values and patterns of behavior. The

American social philosopher Walter Lippmann describes the social imperative of such a process and the dire consequences of its failure. Social life

> has to be transmitted from the old to the young, and the habits
> and the ideas must be maintained as a seamless web of memory
> among the bearers of the tradition, generation after generation. . . .
> When the continuity of the tradition of civility is ruptured, the
> community is threatened. Unless the rupture is repaired, the community will break down into factional . . . wars. For when the continuity
> is interrupted, the cultural heritage is not being transmitted. The
> new generation is faced with the task of rediscovering and reinventing and relearning by trial and error most of what [it] needs to
> know. . . . No generation can do that.[19]

According to Confucianism, learning is essentially the imitation of exemplary models, the teacher providing a direct, living model of virtuous behavior. Confucius therefore taught that "a gentleman who associates with those who possess the Way and is rectified by them, may be said to be fond of learning."[20] It is evident that Confucianism is optimistic about human nature because it contends that every person has an innate capacity to learn virtue and that education should be available to all.* Moreover, it believes that men of wisdom and virtue, from whom we can learn the way, are always to be found among us. "In the presence of a worthy man, think of equaling him. In the presence of a worthless man, turn your gaze within."[21]

It is critical, of course, that we associate with the wise and worthy and not with the unworthy person since our patterns of behavior are picked up, often unconsciously, from our environs. Therefore, it is important to live in the right locality. "It is humaneness which is the attraction of a neighborhood. If from choice a man does not dwell in the midst of humaneness, how can he attain to wisdom?"[22] Confucius would say that "man is what he does," that we are shaped by our actions and habits. For this reason, he saw ritual (*li*) as the foundation of the educative process.

The word *li*, usually translated "ritual," originally meant "to sacrifice" and had to do with ritual sacrifices in a religious context. Later, the word came to mean ceremonious activity on special secular occasions; finally, it came to be associated with the "social propriety" or decorum expected in all human relationships. The Confucian sages believe that social unrest and war are the result of a decline in social ritual and that its restoration will result in a harmonious social order.

---

* Confucius and Mencius held optimistic or Idealist views of human nature.
  However, Hsün Tze was a Realist and taught that "the nature of man is evil; his
  goodness is acquired training"—a product of moral learning.

The sage Confucius lecturing his pupils, passing on the "way of the
ancients" through precept as well as through his own example of virtuous
living. (*Source*: Courtesy of Howard Sochurek, *Life* Magazine, © 1955
Time-Life, Inc.)

Ritual, they teach, humanizes our relationships; therefore, it is the
essential means of governing a society. The ruler is the model from
whom others take their cue:

> Yen Hui asked about humaneness. The Master said: 'To subdue
> oneself and return to ritual is humane. If for one day a ruler could
> subdue himself and return to ritual, then all under Heaven would
> respond to the humaneness in him.'[23]

A statement attributed to Confucius in the *Record of Rites* underlines
the pre-eminent place he gave to ritual in the amelioration of human
strife:

> Of all things to which the people owe their lives the rites are the
> most important. If it were not for the rites, they would have no
> means of regulating the services paid to the spirits of Heaven and
> Earth; if it were not for the rites, they would have no means of
> distinguishing the positions of ruler and subject, high and low, old
> and young; if it were not for the rites, they would have no means
> of differentiating the relations between male and female, between
> father and son, and between elder and younger brother, and of
> linking far and near by the ceremony of marriage.[24]

Westerners often are skeptical of the formality of oriental "bowing and scraping." We consider it perfunctory and rather inauthentic. However, this is to fail to recognize the true depths of Confucian ritual behavior. Beneath the seemingly excessive outward formality is a genuine inward and spiritual grace, the interrelation of action and sentiment. Ritual action shapes behavior and therefore character, and, in turn, character reinforces action. "Manners," the adage rightly declares, "make the man."

Confucius suggests a number of means by which *li* and the social virtues associated with "propriety" are to be advanced. One is the *rectification of names*. What Confucius meant by this term is semantic clarity regarding the use of words—a clarity that issues in moral exactitude and order. Semantic confusion results when *li* is forsaken, because then we have "no means of differentiating the relations between male and female, between father and son," and so on. Confucius said that if names—for example, ruler, son, and elder brother—are not correct, then language cannot be in accord with the true nature of things. A father cannot be a true father or a son a true son. As long as our words are askew, our actions will be incorrect, and strife and unhappiness will prevail. In a stable social order, names must have clear meanings. It is necessary that we know what it means to be a father *and* that a father *be* a father. The Confucian gentleman is known to embody the supreme virtue of humaneness (*jen*), but Confucius says, "If a gentleman abandons humaneness, how can he fulfill the name?"[25]

Confucius considered the rectification of names to be the first order of government. When Duke Ching of Ch'i asked his advice about government, Confucius replied, "Let the prince be a prince, the minister a minister, the father a father, and the son a son."[26]

To govern means to rectify not only names but also the realities to which they correspond. Confucius believed that true government begins, literally, at home. The regulation of the home depends on the cultivation of personal life. In turn, the ordering of national life is accomplished only by the humanizing of home life. Thus, a second means of advancing *li* and social order is through the Five Great Relationships. They have to do with the rights and responsibilities of ruler and subject, father and son, husband and wife, elder brother and younger brother, and elder and younger friends. At the heart of these relationships are the rules governing the family—the foundation of Confucian society. The key to the family is the child's respect for his or her parents, or *filial piety*.

Confucianism demands the deference and respectful obedience of the young toward their elders, and especially toward their parents. The Chinese are surprised at the West's exaltation of youth and are horrified at our neglect of the aged. A Confucian son's obligations to his father are extraordinarily demanding, including a period of over 2 years of mourning and retirement from normal activities following the death of the father. In this regard, it is interesting to note that Confucianism did not reject ancestor worship, despite its this-worldly, practical approach to life. The ancestral shrine remained at the center of the Confucian home, a sign of family solidarity. Confucius regarded the moral discipline and example of filial piety as, once again, essential to government. When someone asked why he did not take part in government, Confucius replied,

> What does the *Book of History* say about filial piety? 'Only be dutiful towards your parents and friendly towards your brothers, and you will be contributing to government.'[27]

Confucius taught that the moral ideal is exemplified in the *chun-tzu*, the gentleman or superior man. It is he, and not the skillful administrative expert, who should hold the reins of government. The *chun-tzu*—poised, sincere, and adequate for every occasion—rules by *te*, the virtue and power of his moral character. Confucius taught that the good society is achieved neither by law nor by physical power, but through the example of moral virtue and character. Confucius said:

> If you lead the people by means of regulations and keep order among them by means of punishments, they will be without conscience in trying to avoid them. If you lead them by virtue [*te*] and keep order among them by ritual [*li*,] they will have a conscience and will reform themselves.[28]

The power of *te* is what we today might call *charisma* in the sense that it represents "the power of a specific person to accomplish his will directly and effortlessly through ritual, gesture, and incantation."[29] Confucius speaks of this in another aphorism in the *Analects*: "He who rules by means of virtue may be compared to the pole-star, which keeps its place while all the other stars pay homage to it."[30]

Compared to St. Augustine or Freud, Confucius was highly optimistic about human nature and the cure of social strife. He believed that there is an ancient Harmony and order in the world and that it is possible for human beings to understand it and to recover it by adopting a code of social behavior. Unlike St. Augustine or Luther, Confucius did not consider human nature "fallen" or the will in bondage and requiring divine grace. He taught that the "way of the ancients" is open to all since every person is born with the innate capacity to develop humaneness (*jen*), even to become a sage.

A number of striking differences have been noted in the Stoic, Christian, Buddhist, and Confucian understanding of the human problem. Despite these fundamental differences, all four contrast with their modern secular substitutes in the conviction that there is, beyond the appearances of this empirical world and the present time, a sacred order. That order—*Phusis*, the Kingdom of God, Nirvana, and the Grand Harmony—is the only true goal of human striving and, they insist, the only real hope for eradicating our pain and suffering, our illusions, and our anxious guilt.

Notes

1. Richard Alpert, *Be Here Now*. As cited in William G. McLaughlin, *Revivals, Awakenings, and Reform* (Chicago, 1978), p. 204.
2. Epictetus, *Discourses* II, 5, in Whitney J. Oates, *The Stoic and Epicurean Philosophers* (New York, 1940), pp. 288–89.
3. Marcus Aurelius, *Thoughts* (Oxford, 1948).
4. Gilbert Murray, "The Stoic Philosophy," in *Essays and Addresses* (London, 1921), p. 100.
5. Epictetus, *Enchiridion*, in Whitney J. Oates, *The Stoic and Epicurean Philosophers*, p. 472.
6. Etienne Gilson, *The Christian Philosophy of St. Thomas Aquinas* (London, 1957), pp. 345–46.
7. Reinhold Niebuhr, *The Nature and Destiny of Man*, I (New York, 1941), pp. 13–14.
8. St. Augustine, *The City of God*, Book XIV, Ch. 13. (New York, 1958), pp. 308–9.
9. John Calvin, *The Institutes of the Christian Religion*, Book I, Ch. 4 (Philadelphia, n.d.).
10. St. Augustine, "Treatise on Nature and Grace," Ch. 3. In *The Nicene and Post-Nicene Fathers* V, ed. by Philip Schaff (Grand Rapids, 1971), p. 122.
11. St. Augustine, "Treatise on Nature and Grace," p. 122.
12. G. P. Malalasekera, "The Status of the Individual in Theravada Buddhism," *Philosophy East and West*, 14 (July, 1964), p. 147. I am dependent on Malalasekera for much that follows.
13. *Samyutta-Nikaya*, V, 420. As cited in Bhikshu Sangharakshita, *A Survey of Buddhism* (Boulder, 1980), pp. 113–14.
14. Edward Conze, *Buddhism: Its Essence and Development* (New York, 1959), p. 44.
15. *Digha-Nikaya*, XXII. Cited in Sangharakshita, *A Survey of Buddhism*, p. 98.
16. Walpala Rahula, *What the Buddha Taught* (New York, 1962), p. 30.
17. Confucius, *Analects* (7.1). Cited in Raymond Dawson, *Confucius* (New York, 1981), p. 11.
18. Hsün Tzu, XIX, 3. *Sources of Chinese Tradition*, ed. William T. de Bary et. al. (New York, 1960), pp. 122–23.
19. Walter Lippmann, *The Public Philosophy* (Boston, 1955). As cited in Huston Smith, *The Religions of Man* (New York, 1959), p. 164. I am indebted to Smith for this striking passage. The reader may wish to

consult Smith's brilliant and sympathetic treatment of Confucianism in the above volume.

20. *Analects* (1.14). Dawson, *Confucius*, p. 10. Dawson's exposition of Confucius' teaching has been very helpful.
21. *Analects* (4.17). Dawson, *Confucius*, p. 16.
22. *Analects* (4.1.). Dawson, *Confucius*, p. 17.
23. *Analects* (12.1). Dawson, *Confucius*, p. 30.
24. Dawson, *Confucius*, p. 32.
25. *Analects* (4.5). Dawson, *Confucius*, p. 56.
26. *Analects* (12.11). Dawson, *Confucius*, p. 57.
27. *Analects* (2.21). Dawson, *Confucius*, p. 67.
28. *Analects* (2.3). Dawson, *Confucius*, p. 73.
29. Herbert Fingarette, *Confucius — The Secular as Sacred* (New York, 1972), p. 3.
30. *Analects* (2.1). Dawson, *Confucius*, p. 73.

Review Questions

1. Why are human beings uniquely a problem to themselves?
2. What is the source of the human problem according to Marx, Freud, and Plato? What do Plato's and Freud's views of the resolution of the human problem have in common?
3. Describe the Stoic view of the cause and cure of the human problem. What is distinctive about the Stoic view of freedom? How does the Stoic doctrine of *apatheia*, or indifference, square with the Stoic appeal to civil duty?
4. What is the root of the human problem according to Christianity? How do the Roman Catholic and Protestant views of the "image of God" and the Fall differ? What are some of the ways in which sin has been described in the Christian tradition? What is meant by sin being "original"?
5. Understanding the human problem in Buddhism requires a grasp of certain basic concepts, including *karma, khandhas*, and *an-atta*. Describe what is meant by these concepts. The cause and cure of the human problem is described by Buddha in the famous Deer Park sermon. Describe in full the first two Noble Truths of the sermon — *dukkha* and *tanhā* — which have to do with suffering and its cause.
6. Describe how the Confucianist concept of *li* (ritual) addresses the human problem. What is involved in the "rectification of names" and in the Five Great Relationships?
7. What do you see as the foremost differences in the Stoic, Christian, Buddhist, and Confucianist understanding of the human problem? Do you see any similarities in any of their views of human nature or the human plight?

Suggestions for Further Reading

For studies of several religious and secular views of human nature and the human problem, see the following:

RADHAKRISHNAN, S., and P. T. RAJU, *The Concept of Man: A Study in Comparative Philosophy* (London: George Allen and Unwin. 1966).

STEVENSON, LESLIE, *Seven Theories of Human Nature* (Oxford: Clarendon Press. 1974).

_____ , *The Study of Human Nature* (Oxford: O.U.P., 1986).

For a discussion of the religious views of the human condition treated in this chapter, see the following:

STOICISM

MURRAY, GILBERT, "The Stoic Philosophy," *Essays and Addresses* (London: Allen and Unwin, 1921).

COPLESTON, FREDERICK, *A History of Philosophy* I (London: Burns Oates, 1956).

CHRISTIANITY

AQUINAS, ST. THOMAS, *Basic Writings of St. Thomas Aquinas* (Questions 75–79 from the *Summa Theologica*) (New York: Random House, 1948).

AUGUSTINE, ST., *Basic Writings of St. Augustine* I ("Nature and Grace" and "On Original Sin") (New York: Random House, 1948).

CALVIN, JOHN, *Institutes of the Christian Religion* (Philadelphia: Presbyterian Board of Christian Education, n.d.).

NIEBUHR, REINHOLD, *The Nature and Destiny of Man*, vol. I (New York: Scribner's, 1964).

BUDDHISM

MALALASEKERA, G. P., "The Status of the Individual in Theravada Buddhism," *Philosophy East and West* 14 (Honolulu: University of Hawaii Press, 1964).

RAHULA, WALPALA, *What the Buddha Taught*, Chs. 2–4 and 6 (New York: Grove Press. 1962).

SANGHARAKSHITA, BHIKSHU, *A Survey of Buddhism* Chapter One, XII–XVI (Bangalore: Indian Institute of World Culture, 1966).

CONFUCIANISM

DAWSON, RAYMOND, *Confucius* (New York: Hill and Wang. 1981).

FINGARETTE, HERBERT, *Confucius — The Secular as Sacred* (New York: Harper & Row. 1972).

SMITH, HUSTON, "Confucianism," *The Religions of Man* (New York: New American Library. 1958).

CHAPTER 10

Theodicy

OVERVIEW

The word *theodicy* comes from the Greek words *theos* and *dike* ("God" and "justice") and means "justifying the ways of God" in the face of the chaos and evil in the world. The word was coined by the philosopher Leibniz in an influential work entitled *Essais de Théodicée* (1710). Since then, the term has been principally employed in Christian theology and refers to the attempts of theologians to justify the goodness and omnipotence of God in the face of the world's real evil.

More recently, social scientists have adopted the term theodicy to describe a wide range of religious and ideological explanations or legitimations of the anomic, that is, the chaotic and evil experiences faced by both individuals and societies. Here, the word *theodicy* will be used in this broader sense, and we shall include in our discussion religions that, while offering explanations for evil and suffering, do not hold monotheistic assumptions—for example, God's goodness or omnipotence. Our analysis shall follow rather closely a typology introduced by the sociologist Peter Berger.[1]

Theodicies derive from the fact that evil and chaos must not only be endured but also be explained if a sense of fatedness, meaninglessness, and despair are to be held at bay. The world's religions propose a variety of explanations or legitimations for the fact of evil, many of which have proven enormously compelling and have endured in very different times and places. The power of these theodicies lies in their capacity to provide convincing explanations for the awful reality of suffering and evil. Perhaps surprisingly, what humans seek most is not happiness but the assurance that, evil notwithstanding, life has meaning and purpose.

The first type of theodicy we examine is one in which persons lose all sense of individuality through complete identification with the larger community—the tribe, nation, or race—or through absorption

254

in some larger cosmic reality. The prototype is often found in primitive religion, where the life of the individual is subsumed within and indistinguishable from that of the ongoing life of the community. Personal suffering is minimized in face of the assurances of the continuing life and prosperity of the clan or tribe. In mysticism, the individual's mundane suffering becomes insignificant, even laughably unreal, through the rapturous loss of self in union with the One or God.

A very common type of theodicy is one in which compensation for present suffering is perceived as coming imminently in the future here on earth. Present sufferings can be endured because they are relativized in the expectation of a future change of fortune. This form of theodicy is common in the West—for example, in ancient Israel, in some of the radical sects of the Protestant Reformation, in Marxism, and even in the Shi'ite revolutionary movement in present-day Iran. However, it is a type that is also associated with what anthropologists call Cargo Cults that are found throughout the Third World.

Perhaps the most common religious theodicy is that which looks to the reversal of present suffering and evil in a future life beyond this earth in Heaven or Paradise. It is prominent in Western theism but also in certain schools of Mahayana Buddhism. Cosmic Dualism offers a rather different explanation for evil. As we saw in Chapter 7, dualism regards this world as created by and presently under the rule of satanic powers. Since the God of Light did not create this earth, he cannot be held accountable—as is often the case in monotheism—for present evil. Dualism looks to the end of this earthly suffering only in a distant cosmic victory of the God of Light over Darkness.

Max Weber regards the classical theodicy of India, of *karma* and *samsara*, as the most rational or plausible of all religious explanations of present evil. According to this theodicy, our present existence is simply the result of our past karmic actions. We reap, inexorably, those effects of our past actions while we sow those karmic seeds that will determine, unalterably, our future destiny on the wheel of rebirth or reincarnation. We have no one to blame but ourselves. We shall illustrate this theodicy with citations from both Hinduism and Theravada Buddhism.

Western monotheism faces unique problems in its justification of evil since it teaches that the God who created the world *ex nihilo* is also omnipotent, omniscient, and perfectly good or benevolent. Why, then, is there so much evil and pain? In the final segment of this chapter, we explore a number of theistic justifications or explanations of evil, using the Book of Job as our basic source. As we shall see, theologians have regarded suffering as a punishment for sin, as a test of faith, and as a necessary condition for "soul-making." More recently, they also have challenged traditional notions of God's omnipotence. Finally, though, theism calls for both agonizing protest *and* faith before the mystery of God's ways that pass human understanding.

The Persistent Demand for Theodicy

Suffering and evil have always tortured and oppressed the human body and the human spirit. In the sixth century B.C.E., a Greek by the name of Kallinos lamented, "There is no wit in man. Creatures of a day we live like cattle, knowing nothing of how the god will bring each one to his end. . . . Thus evil is with everything. Yea ten thousand dooms, woes and grief beyond speaking are the lot of mankind."[2]

Albert Camus estimated that 70 million human beings have been displaced, enslaved, and killed *in the twentieth century alone.* The figures have risen dramatically since Camus wrote. Drought and famine persist in Ethiopia and the Sudan. The holocaust of the innocent did not end with the Nazi horror in Eastern Europe; it continues with the Khmer Rouge in Cambodia and today in the Middle East, and elsewhere. Wars persist and grow more deadly, starvation recurs, and man's inhumanity to man and the injustices of life are ever-present to us on the evening television news. The sick horror that we all feel in the presence of evil, injustice, and suffering raises for us, as for countless millions in the past, the problem of theodicy.

Basically, what a theodicy does is to place our own life, which may be riven with tragic suffering and the threat of chaos, in a larger framework of meaning that bestows a sense of order, purpose, and even repose. Berger explains how rites of passage often involve an implicit theodicy:

> Social ritual transforms the individual event [the crises encountered at various stages of life] into a typical case, just as it transforms biography into an episode in the history of society. The individual is seen as being born, living and suffering, and eventually dying, as his ancestors have done before him and his children will do after him. As he accepts and inwardly appropriates this view of the matter he transcends his own individuality as well as the uniqueness, including the unique pain and the unique terrors, of his individual experience. . . . He is made capable of suffering "Correctly." . . . In consequence, the pain becomes more tolerable, the terror less overwhelming.[3]

The religious legitimation of suffering and evil often is unconscious. So, while theodicies may entail rather complex metaphysical doctrines, as in Buddhism and Christianity, they as often represent the unsophisticated convictions of ordinary people. When such a person explains a drought as a judgment of God, he or she is engaging in theodicy.

For example, take the simple and moving testimony on television of a young American soldier whose legs had been blown off by a land mine in Vietnam. He had been involved, to his own deep remorse, in the annihilation by flame throwers of an entire Vietnamese village, including the death of innocent women and children. Some time after that event, he suffered his own tragic, crippling injury. He saw it, however, as God's judgment on his own monstrous crime and a merciful release. His personal suffering strangely satisfied his sense of justice and he accepted his condition, not grudgingly or stoically, but with an apparent sense of relief, satisfaction, and peace. The young man was engaging, unawares, in theodicy.

Theodicy of "Mystic Participation"

A common way of justifying the "slings and arrows of outrageous fortune" is for individuals to see themselves as a "typical case." Berger described how this often takes place in rites of passage, but also through the loss of self in mystic participation or absorption in a larger social or spiritual reality. In such cases, what defines the self is not its unique individuality but, rather, its participation in and identification with a corporate group, clan, tribe, nation, or race. Thus, the Chinese Confucian father could die a "happy death" knowing he lived on in his sons and their sons. The soldier can sacrifice his life in battle with the assurance that, spiritually, he lives on in his tribe or nation.

This form of theodicy is especially common in primitive societies where a heightened sense of individuality is not developed. The sociologist Lucien Levy-Bruhl (1857–1939) called this identification, or merging of the self with others, the "law of participation." He maintained that individuals in primitive societies suffered less from personal anomie or misfortune because of their "mystical participation" in the ongoing life of the tribe and of nature itself. The individual may suffer personal loss, but the tribe lives on and nature is immortal:

> Every individual *is* both such and such a man or woman, alive at present, a certain ancestral individual, who may be human or semi-human . . . and at the same time he *is* his totem, that is, he partakes in mystic fashion of the essence of the animal or vegetable species whose name he bears. The verb "to be" . . . encompasses both the collective representation and the collective consciousness in a participation that is actually lived, in a kind of symbiosis effected by identity of essence.[4]

The continuity of individual–society–nature places the "individual's" birth, growth, and death within the larger life and rhythm of the tribe and of nature itself. The sting of our own misfortune and death is thus relativised by a form of "objective immortality" in the ongoing life of the family or clan. Such a sense of "corporate personality" was an essential feature of life among, for example, the ancient Semitic tribes, including Israel. In ancient Israelite psychology, the "soul" was considered to be more than the individual, conscious ego; it was everything that we associate with a name—renown, property, progeny, and so forth. The "soul" may thus live on even when the individual ego dies.

Theodicies of "participation" are present in all those forms of mysticism that emphasize the absorption or annihilation of the self in its union with the divine. In this form of mystic union, all sense of ego and individuality is lost in union with the All or the One. In the blissful passivity that accompanies such an "oceanic" experience, the individual's own sufferings and trials become as nothing, trivial and unreal. The symbolism of the ocean is prominent in this form of mysticism, as is evident in the reminiscence of the German mystic Malwida von Meysenbug, cited by William James:

> I was alone upon the seashore as all those thoughts flowed over me, liberating and reconciling. . . . I was impelled to kneel down . . . before the illimitable ocean, symbol of the Infinite. I felt that I prayed as I had never prayed before, and knew now what prayer really is: to return from the solitude of individuation into the consciousness of unity with all that is, to kneel down as one that passes away, and to rise up as one imperishable. Earth, heaven, and sea resounded as in one vast world-encircling harmony. It was as if the chorus of all the great who had ever lived were about me. I felt myself one with them, and it appeared as if I heard their greeting: 'Thou too belongest to the company of those who over came.'[5]

Such a "consciousness of unity," of escape from "the solitude of individuation," leaves the soul "imperishable," free of mundane anxieties and threats. They now are seen as inconsequential, even imaginary.

A Future, This-Worldly Theodicy

It is common to associate the religions of the biblical tradition—Judaism, Christianity, and Islam—with the belief that the evils and sufferings of this life will be compensated for and that justice will be meted out in a future life in heaven or, as the case may be, in hell. Indeed, it can be claimed that this form of theodicy has been the dominant one in at least two of these biblical faiths. We know, however, that in early Israel there was no belief in a future life; that Israel's hope lay in the promise that their God, Yahweh, would redeem Israel from the oppression and injustice of her enemies and, in the

Western consciousness has been deeply influenced by the biblical vision of a future peaceable Kingdom or new age on earth, where all will live in justice and harmony. (*Source*: Courtesy of Abby Aldrich Rockefeller Folk Art Center, Williamsburg, Virginia.)

future, would establish her in triumph and prosperity. Palestine was envisioned as a new Eden, a Paradise regained, which would be established through a "righteous remnant." Once holy Zion was secure, a world reign of justice and peace would ensue; the desert would bloom; the poor would be rewarded; and flocks, corn, and fruit would multiply. This hope of early Israel was sorely tested through the centuries. Out of Israel's travail, there emerged a radically different but essentially this-worldly eschatology. This shift in eschatology is discussed in Chapter 12.

In the centuries prior to the Christian era, Israel began to look to the intervention of a supernatural figure, called "the Son of Man," who would put down the ever-growing power of Satan and would establish a kingdom of his saints. This form of supernatural, yet this-worldly, hope persisted long after the vision weakened its hold on the Jewish imagination. Norman Cohn describes, as follows, the features of this eschatological theodicy:

> The world is dominated by an evil, tyrannous power of boundless destructiveness—a power moreover which is imagined not as simply

human but as demonic. The tyranny of that power will become more and more outrageous, the sufferings of its victims more and more intolerable—until suddenly the hour will strike when the Saints of God are able to rise up and overthrow it. Then the Saints themselves, the chosen, holy people who hitherto have groaned under the oppressor's heel, shall in their turn inherit dominion over the whole earth. This will be the culmination of history.[6]

What is distinctive about this **millenarian** form of theodicy is that compensation for the suffering of the present time is postponed into the future, but *a future realized on this earth* and not in some other-worldly heaven. Moreover, the coming justice is imminent; it will come soon and it will be total. That is, there will be a *revolutionary* transformation in which the just will be rewarded and the unjust will be put down. Supernatural intervention will be accompanied by human action. For the "saints," the present sufferings can be endured because they are relativized in relation to the expectation of an imminent, future change of fortune.*

Historical experience would appear to confirm that such a future, this-worldly theodicy is most likely to attract support during times of natural disaster and social upheaval, when a sense of present historical injustice and pessimism is widespread. The period between the eleventh and sixteenth centuries in Europe was just such a time. Europe witnessed a number of social convulsions associated with the breakup of feudal society and with the horror brought on by the Black Death, the Crusades, and the various peasant uprisings before and during the Protestant Reformation. Examples from the Czech and German peasant revolts are especially revealing of this type of future-oriented theodicy.

In the early fifteenth century, a socioreligious reform known as the Hussite movement burst forth in Bohemia. It soon joined zealous religious reform with social revolution. In the 1390s, the writings of the English reformer John Wycliffe (d. 1384) became known in Prague. They particularly influenced the Czech preacher John Huss

---

* This kind of realized millenarian theodicy can be observed in the Shi'ite movement that is distinctive of Iranian revolutionary Islam under the leadership of the Imām Khomeini. Traditional Shi'ite Islam is more other-worldly, as we will soon see. According to present Iranian Shi'ism, the coming of the Imām at the end of time to initiate a thousand years of peace and justice, and to redress the wrongs of individuals and the community, is believed to be occurring at the present time. Through its revolution, the Iranian people have taken on a kind of Imāmic function in bringing about the fulfillment of a golden age here on earth. The evil world of suffering is now being transformed, and justice and virtue will be rewarded in this life as well as the next. The hope for a future Paradise for the martyr and the righteous is present but is balanced by a more-earthly, revolutionary theodicy.

(1372–1415), who later was burned at the stake by the Roman Church for his heretical teachings. Huss's mantle was soon taken up by more-radical leaders. In 1419, a large gathering of disaffected Czech peasants met on a hilltop that they identified as the biblical Mount Tabor, the place of Christ's transfiguration and the renewal of the Church. The Taborites, as they came to be called, soon broke all ties with the feudal order and organized into a new society that stressed a sharing of all goods in common. They taught that a new age of the Holy Spirit was about to dawn: All feudal institutions and their lords and priests would be destroyed. So began a series of savage wars against the authorities. A member of the Taborite community, John of Pribram, who later opposed the movement, describes the incendiary teachings of the prophets of Tabor:

> And they said that the elect of God would rule in the world for a thousand years with Christ, visibly and tangibly. And they preached that the elect of God who fled to the mountains would themselves possess all the goods of the destroyed evil ones and rule freely over all their estates and villages. And they said, 'You will have such an abundance of everything that silver, gold, and money will only be a nuisance to you.' They also said and preached to the people, 'Now you will not pay rents to your lords any more, nor be subject to them, but will freely and undisturbedly possess their villages, fish-ponds, meadows, forests, and all their domains.'[7]

A century later, a similar vision gripped the German Protestant reformer Thomas Münzer. He began as a follower of Luther but soon renounced Luther and embraced a more-radical, apocalyptic vision. Münzer taught that the Last Days were at hand and that the powers of evil and the Antichrist ruled. The very excesses of tyranny were a sign to Münzer that the great consummation was at hand. Soon God would raise up his elect, the poor—who, empowered by force of arms, would annihilate the evil ones—at which point the millennium would begin. Münzer challenged the Saxon princes to come to the aid of the Elect to destroy Satan, that is, the evil lords and priests. If they would not assist, the Elect would do it themselves.

Münzer was soon convinced that the princes—those "godless rascals"—were unfit to play any role in bringing about the new Kingdom. Their tyrannous failure was a sign that the "last days" were at hand. The Elect peasants alone would serve as God's sword. First they must put down the princes:

> At them, at them, while the fire is hot! Don't let your sword get cold! ... One can't speak to you about God so long as they [the princes] are reigning over you. At them, at them, while you have daylight! God goes ahead of you, so follow, follow! ...[8]

Implicit in Münzer's apocalyptic message was the promise that despite the injustice and suffering of the present time, the Elect peasants would soon be vindicated and consoled and the unjust brought down and punished.

Similar millenarian, this-worldly theodicies are found within Islam. From time to time, Islamic peasant movements have nourished the belief that a time of justice and well-being on earth was imminent and would be ushered in by, for example, the return of the Mahdi or savior who would triumph over the Antichrist. As we have seen, it is a prevalent theme in the Shi'ite tradition of Islam today. A similar millenarian theodicy is found in movements that may have little relation to ancient biblical apocalypticism, for example, in the Taiping Rebellion in China and in numerous Cargo Cults.

The phenomenon of Cargo Cults is of great interest to anthropologists because they represent a curious, often bizarre response to conditions of rapid socioeconomic change and deprivation. In these cults, a prophet appears to announce the imminent end of the world that will result from a series of apocalyptical disasters. With the destruction of the old order, a savior figure arrives to bring all the goods that previously had been denied. During the interim, the people are called on to prepare for the Golden Age by building storehouses and depots to receive the goods, known as "cargo." In the period of waiting, the cult members' actions reflect a complete break with the old order; pigs and cattle are slaughtered, all savings are squandered, and work ceases. Often, an **antinomian** spirit prevails, with boisterous revelries and ecstatic dancing.

The John Frum Cargo Cult was just such a movement in the southern island of Tanna in the New Hebrides. The cult is described, with many others, by Peter Worsley in *The Trumpet Shall Sound*. The islands of the New Hebrides had long suffered from labor recruiters who had taken the natives from their islands, often by force, to work on plantations in Australia and elsewhere. In 1940, a native named John Frum began to prophesy. The natives came to regard him as the earthly manifestation of Karaperamun, the island's highest mountain. Here is Worsley's description of the movement:

> John Frum prophesied the occurrence of a cataclysm in which Tanna would become flat, the volcanic mountains would fall and fill the riverbeds to form fertile plains, and Tanna would be joined to the neighboring islands of Eramanga and Aneityum to form a new island. Then John Frum would reveal himself, bring in a reign of bliss, the natives would get back their youth, and there would be no sickness; there would be no need to care for gardens, trees or pigs. The Whites would go; John Frum would set up schools to replace the mission schools and would pay chiefs and teachers. . . .
> Natives now started a veritable orgy of spending in European

stores in order to get rid of the European's money, which was to be replaced by John Frum's with a cocoanut stamped on it. Some even hurled their long-hoarded savings into the sea, believing that 'when there would be no money left on the island the white traders would have to depart.' . . . [9]

John Frum was soon arrested by the authorities, but the movement continued and new leaders came along to proclaim themselves to be John Frum. Worsley reports that the activity of the cult varied in intensity during the following decade, depending on the changing social and economic conditions of the island.

One of the obvious weaknesses of a future, this-worldly theodicy is its possible empirical disconfirmation. Münzer prophesied total victory over the armies of the German princes, and his followers were slaughtered by the thousands. The Millerites—followers of the New England farmer William Miller—predicted that, according to the Bible, the end of the world would occur in 1843. The end did not come. New predictions were then forthcoming. Finally, the day was set for October 22, 1844. That day also passed, and there was no deliverance. This failure caused the collapse of the Millerite movement. However, not all millenarian movements died out as quickly. Various explanations—miscalculations, claims that the time is not yet ripe, or that God is testing the group's faith—can be advanced. The response to the failure of prophecy is examined by Leon Festinger in *When Prophecy Fails* (1956), an exploration of how people cope with such conditions of "cognitive dissonance." Festinger studied, first-hand, a group in Lake City, Minnesota, that claimed to have received a message—from a planet called "Clarion"—of a great Deluge that would destroy the world. The group's rationalizations and responses to disconfirming evidence were striking but not unexpected. The classic example of a this-worldly theodicy today is Marxism, which will be discussed at length in Chapter 12.

Other-Worldly Theodicy

The form of theodicy that would appear to be most common among the great religions—certainly the three missionary religions, Christianity, Islam, and certain schools of Mahayana Buddhism—is one that looks to a recompense for the evil and injustice of this life in a life after death in a blessed Heaven or Paradise. It is voiced, for example, in the famous hymn "Jerusalem the Golden":

1. Jerusalem the Golden, With milk and honey blest,
   Beneath thy contemplation Sink heart and voice oppressed;

> I know not, O I know not What joys await us there,
> What radiancy of glory, What bliss beyond compare. . . .
>
> 4. O sweet and blessèd country, The home of God's elect!
> O sweet and blessèd country, That eager hearts expect!
> Jesus, in mercy bring us, To that dear land of rest,
> Who art, with God the Father, And Spirit ever blest.

The vision of a Heaven or Paradise is prominent in much of the devotional and even the great poetical literature of the West. Dante's *Paradiso* is the supreme example. We need not illustrate the theme with numerous examples, but a particularly apt type is found in the traditional Shi'ite sect of Islam. It is especially appropriate because the conventional Shi'ite theodicy so strongly underlines the compensation for present suffering, and especially for martyrdom, in an other-worldly Paradise.

The Shi'ite movement arose over a dispute concerning the succession to the Prophet Mohammed. The causes of the sectarian division are complex but, essentially, the Shi'ite claim that only members of Mohammed's family should be considered his legitimate successors separates it from the larger Sunni tradition in Islam. Ali—the fourth caliph, or supreme ruler, and a cousin of Mohammed—is considered by Shi'ites to be the first legitimate successor. They regard the assassinations* of Ali and his two sons, Hasan and Husain, to be glorious and revered martyrdoms. The role of the sacrificial death of the innocent has since profoundly shaped the Shi'ite understanding of suffering and theodicy. The dramatic re-enactment of the historic martyrdoms—called passion plays—gives special prominence in Shi'ite Islam to a future reward for present suffering in an other-worldly Paradise. The theme is prominent in the play honoring Husain. As he faces death, Husain offers the following reflections:

> *Husain*: Trials, afflictions and pains, the thicker they fall on man, the better dear sister, do they prepare him for his journey heavenward. We rejoice in tribulations, seeing they are but temporary, and yet they work out an eternal and blissful end. Though it is predestined that I should suffer martyrdom in this shameful manner, yet the treasury of everlasting happiness shall be at my disposal as a consequent reward. Thou must think of that, and be no longer sorry. . . .

At the play's end, the angel Gabriel, through Mohammad, gives Husain the keys to Paradise, which he had desired. Gabriel speaks:

---

* While the historical evidence is lacking for the death by assassination of all the successors, such martyrdoms are held as an article of belief.

"Peace be unto thee, O Muhammad the elect, God hath sent thee a message saying, 'None has suffered the pain and afflictions which Husain has undergone. None has like him, been obedient in my service.'" Husain then replies: "O my friends, be ye relieved from grief, and come along with me to the mansions of the blest. Sorrow has passed away, and it is now time for joy and rest; trouble has gone by, it is the hour to be at ease and tranquility."[10]

The Shi'ite can face martyrdom joyful in the assurance that his or her suffering hastens the day when the Imām will come, but also in the promise of immediate heavenly bliss.

Dualism

Dualism is not a prevalent doctrine in the modern world religions, either East or West. However, as indicated earlier, its appeal was very great in the centuries just before and after the beginnings of Christianity, in Zoroastrianism, Mithraism, Manichianism, and Gnosticism. Its attraction in certain forms of contemporary popular Gnosticism is still clearly discernible. We have learned that, according to dualism, all evil and suffering are to be ascribed to powerful, satanic forces that created and now rule this world, including our bodily existence. The god of light and truth did _not_ create this material world and therefore cannot be held accountable for our earthly suffering. The earth, by its very nature, is a realm of darkness and disorder. The victory of order over chaos and the defeat of evil and suffering will take place, as in Zoroastrianism, in a distant cosmic victory of Light over Darkness or, as in Gnosticism, in a return to a world of Light wholly beyond this material world.

The Mandeans were one of the Gnostic sects of late antiquity, and a few thousand Mandeans live today in religious communities along the rivers of southern Iraq and Iran. In the Mandean _Ginza_, or "Treasure," the vivid contrast between the world of Light and Darkness is portrayed:

> 278. In the name of the great Life! I cry to you, I instruct you, and I say: (you) true and believing men (you) perceiving and separate ones: separate yourselves from the world of imperfection which is full of confusion and replete with error. First I gave you instruction about the King of Light, blessed be he in all eternity. And I told you about the blessed worlds of light in which there is nothing perishable. . . . Now I will speak to you about the worlds of darkness and what is in them, hideous and terrible whose form is faulty.
>
> Beyond the earth of light downwards and beyond the earth Tibil southwards is that earth of darkness. . . . Darkness exists through its own evil nature, (is) a howling darkness, a desolate gloom which knows not the First or the Last. But the King of Light knows and

perceives the First and the Last, that which is past and that which is to come. And he knew and perceived that evil was there, but he did not want to cause it harm, just as he said: 'Harm not the wicked and the evil, until it has done harm itself.' Its own evil nature exists from the beginning and to all eternity. The worlds of darkness are numerous and without end. He (the King of Light, or: One) said: 'Broad and deep is the abode of evil, whose peoples showed no fidelity to the place which is their endless habitation, whose kingdom came into being from themselves. Their earth is black water and their heights gloomy darkness.'[11]

Because this world is a realm of desolation, sin, and darkness, earthly existence is radically devalued—to the point that moral license and promiscuity are often encouraged as indifferent. Such a profound earthly pessimism, which considers evil as the natural condition of this earthly life, does not have enduring popular appeal. However, as a theodicy it does resolve the nagging question that confronts the monotheistic faiths: How can a good and omnipotent Creator God allow the presence of so much unspeakable suffering and sorrow? But before surveying forms of monotheistic theodicy, we need to examine what Max Weber calls the most rational of all the religious answers to the presence of evil: the *karma–samsara* doctrine found in Hinduism and later in Buddhism.

The Karma–Samsara *Theodicy*

The classical Indian theodicy is built on two related doctrines: *samsara* and *karma*. *Samsara* is the wheel of rebirth, or reincarnation, the doctrine that each soul passes through a sequence of bodies. The soul's human embodiment brings with it self-consciousness, freedom, and responsibility. Every human thought and action thus has its effect and—as the Bible also affirms—"as a man sows, so shall he reap." The law of *karma*, we have learned, is the law of cause and effect. Each person is the effect of the actions of a previous embodiment and, in turn, is the architect of their own habits and character, and hence of their destiny in a future rebirth. As the *Chandogya Upanishad* asserts:

> ... those who are of pleasant conduct here—the prospect is, indeed, that they will enter a pleasant womb, either the womb of a *Brahmim* [priest], or the womb of a *ksatriya* [warrior], or the womb of a *vaisya* [trader and agriculturist]. But those who are of stinking conduct here—the prospect is, indeed, that they will enter a stinking womb, either the womb of a dog, or the womb of a swine, or the womb of an outcast [*candala*].
>
> *(V.X.7)*

Most of us would prefer to deny such a doctrine and to claim that our present and future lives are not of our own making, but are rather the work of fate, or of "social conditions," or lie "in the hands of God." The Hindu* rejects all such "excuses" that would place the blame elsewhere. The Hindu would repudiate Job's protestations of innocence before God and would side with Job's friends, who tell him that his suffering is the result of his own unrighteousness. However, for the Hindu, Job's suffering may be the effect not of his present but also of his previous lives: The acts done in former births never leave any creature. Since all deeds are under the control of *karma*, we must always have in mind how we can restore the balance and rescue the self from evil consequences.

Hinduism teaches that rescuing oneself "from evil consequences" cannot be achieved by pretending that they are not real. It is thus essential to fulfill the obligations of our present state. Progress between stages of rebirth depends in large measure on fulfilling the **dharma** appropriate to our present condition or caste. The Hindu is assured that, if called on to carry out what appear to be evil actions associated with his or her caste duties, no evil *karma* will attach to such actions. The warrior thus need not fear that being a good soldier will result in the sowing of more evil effects in a future existence. *Dharma* is dutiful action without attachment to consequences.

The point is made dramatically in the *Bhagavadgita* (the *Gita*), the much-loved, popular Hindu scripture. Two related families, the Kauravas and the Pandavas, are about to engage in battle, and the warrior Arjuna recoils from fighting his own people. He turns to his charioteer, Krishna (the human incarnation of the god Vishnu), and tells him that it is not right for him to slay his kinsmen. Arjuna casts away "his bow and arrow, his spirit overwhelmed by sorrow." However, Krishna advises him that his real duty is to fulfill his *dharma*—so long as he does so with detachment:

> Further, having regard for thine own duty, thou shouldst not falter; there exists no greater good for a *ksatriya* [warrior] than a war enjoined by duty. . . . Therefore, arise, O Son of Kunti [Arjuna], resolve on battle. Treating alike pleasure and pain, gain and loss, victory and defeat, then get ready for battle. Thus thou shall not incur sin.[12]

The rationale of this Indian theodicy is plain to see since the individual has no one to praise or to blame for successes or for misfortune and suffering. The law of *karma* assures a completely intelligible explanation for both happiness and evil. However, it is also true that,

---

* We speak here of classical Hinduism. In the popular Hindu cults, *karma* has been essentially replaced by theism.

joined with the doctrine of *dharma*, this Indian theodicy constitutes an extraordinary justification of the socioeconomic status quo.

The most radical form of the *karma–samsara* theodicy is found in another, heterodox Indian religion, Theravada Buddhism, an offshoot of Hinduism. We have learned that the Buddha's teaching about the cause and cure of human suffering is the foundation of early Buddhism. Buddha's insight into human pain (*dukkha*) and his theodicy is briefly summarized in his famous Four Noble Truths. You will recall that when his disciple, Mālunkyaputta, asked him the answer to some puzzling metaphysical questions, Buddha dismissed them as a waste of time. For whatever views we hold on such questions, there remains "old age, decay, death, sorrow, pain, grief, distress."

Buddha connected his profound realism about suffering with the doctrines of *karma* and *samsara*. In the Wheel of Life, there is that inexorable chain of causation, the dependent origination of all things. And since nothing exists independently, all beings are the effect of previous causes. Every action produces its effect and the pleasant and painful consequences cannot be escaped:

> Even a flight in the air cannot free you from suffering. After the deed which is evil has been committed. Nor in the sky nor in the ocean's middle, nor if you were to hide in cracks in mountains, can there be found on this wide earth's corner where Karma does not catch up with the culprit. . . . The iron itself creates the rust, which slowly is bound to consume it. The evil-doer by his own deeds is lead to a life full of suffering.[13]

Karma ensures that everything that comes to us is the fruit of previous seeds. The Buddha thereby explained the apparent inequalities of life to a puzzled king:

> The King said: 'Revered Nagasena, what is the reason that men are not all the same, some being shortlived, some weakly, others healthy, some ugly, others comely, some of few wishes, others of many wishes, some poor, others rich, some belonging to low families, others to high families . . . ?'
>
> The Elder said: 'But why, sire, are trees not all the same, some being acid, some salt, some bitter, some sharp, some astringent, others sweet?'
>
> 'I think, revered sir, that it is because of a difference in seeds.'
>
> 'Even so, sire, it is because of a difference in *kammas* [*karmas*] that men are not all the same.'[14]

The doctrines of *karma* and *samsara* give us the clue to the profound sense of rightness that is so distinctive of the Buddhist theodicy. It is captured in the words of the Burmese Buddhist philosopher, Maha Thera U Thittila:

> We must never forget that *kamma* is always just—it neither loves or
> hates, it does not reward or punish, it is never angry, never pleased.
> It is simply the law of cause and effect.
>   *Kamma* knows nothing about us. It does not know us any more
> than fire knows us when it burns us. It is the nature of fire to
> burn, to give out heat; and if we use it properly it gives us light,
> cooks our food—but if we use it wrongly it burns us and our prop-
> erty. . . . It is foolish to grow angry and blame fire when it burns
> us because we made a mistake. In this respect *kamma* is like fire.[15]

Theravada Buddhism strips religion of all its usual elements—gods,
demons, saviors, cosmologies, heavens, and hells. What is left are a few
fundamental laws—*dukkha, karma,* and *samsara*—that explain why things
are the way they are. There can be no excuses, no appeal to blind
chance or to the prevenient action of an omniscient God. Buddhism
says, in effect, you have made your bed, now you must lie in it—unless
and until you find enlightenment and release. A modern apologist
for Buddhism sums up the matter:

> Only *Karma* can explain the mysterious problem of Good and Evil,
> and reconcile man to the terrible *apparent* injustice of life. For when
> one acquainted with the noble doctrine looks around him, and observes
> the inequalities of birth and fortune, of intellect and capacities; when
> one sees honour paid to fools and profligates, and their nearest neigh-
> bor, with all his intellect and noble virtues, perishing of want and for
> lack of sympathy . . . that blessed knowledge of Karma alone prevents
> him from cursing life and men, as well as their supposed Creator.[16]

Monotheistic Theodicies

Ethical monotheism presents a very different complex of beliefs and
issues. For Western monotheism, the problem of theodicy is sharply
put by the philosopher David Hume: "Is he [God] willing to prevent
evil, but not able? then he is impotent. Is he able, but not willing?
then he is malevolent. Is he both able and willing? whence then evil?"[17]
   The great theistic faiths of the west—Judaism, Christianity, and
Islam—all recognize the stark reality of both moral and natural evil
and innocent suffering. They also affirm the sovereignty, providence,
and benevolence of God. How can they hold all these beliefs at once?
Are they not required to deny either God's omnipotence, his benevolence, or the reality of evil? The response to this dilemma has been
varied, and there is no better source for their study than the biblical
Book of Job. At least four theodicies are suggested in Job; we will
explore three here and the fourth at the end of the chapter.

Suffering as Recompense for Sin

One justification of suffering is to see it as a punishment for sin. This was the traditional answer of the biblical Deuteronomic historians who completed a compilation of ancient Hebrew historical works after the exile in Babylon in 587 B.C.E. They interpreted the history of the kings and the people of Israel and Judah, especially in their relations with their foreign neighbors, strictly in terms of divine reward and punishment. The story of King Manasseh is a good example. In the sixth century B.C.E., the king allowed idolatrous practices to be performed in the Jerusalem temple. The historian of II Kings records the consequence:

> And the lord said by his servants the prophets, 'Because Manasseh, King of Judah, has committed these abominations . . . and has made Judah also to sin with his idols; therefore thus says the Lord, the God of Israel, Behold I am bringing upon Jerusalem and Judah such evil that the ears of every one who hears of it will tingle.'
>
> *(21:10–12)*

This is the view that is taken by Job's three friends, Eliphaz, Bildad, and Zophar, who maintain that Job's sufferings are the result of his

Job's three friends insist that his suffering is punishment
for his sins, but Job resists their explanation. (*Source*:
"The Just Upright Man is laughed to scorn" [Job xii.4],
by William Blake. From the Rosenwald Collection,
courtesy of the National Gallery of Art, Washington, D.C.)

sin. When Job challenges God to justify the enormity of the affliction that he has borne—miseries that "outweigh the sands of the seas"—the friends are horrified at his impiety. They find Job's questioning of God's justice intolerable. Bildad expresses their reaction:

> How long will you say these things and the words of your mouth be like a great wind? Does God pervert justice? Or does the Almighty pervert the right? If your children have sinned against him he has delivered them into the power of their transgression.
>
> If you will seek God and make supplication to the Almighty, if you are pure and upright, surely then he will rouse himself for you and reward you with a rightful habitation. And, though your beginning was small, your latter days will be very great.
>
> *(Job 8: 1–7)*

This traditional explanation of suffering is, as we will see, challenged by the whole movement of the poem of Job. Nevertheless, its perfect symmetry has always lent it a popular appeal—in Christianity and Islam as well as in Judaism.

Suffering as a Test and as a Necessary Condition of "Soul-Making"

The belief in a just balancing of righteousness and prosperity, of evil and suffering, although possibly attractive in the abstract, does not long stand up to the test of experience. Another possible explanation of evil is offered in Job: that suffering is a divine test or a trial of faith. In the prologue to the long poetic dialogue between Job and his friends, God is portrayed as allowing Satan to "entice" him to allow all manner of evil to be heaped on a God-fearing Job to test his faith:

> And the Lord said to Satan, 'Have you considered my servant Job, that there is none like him on the earth, a blameless and upright man, who fears God and turns away from evil?' Then Satan answered the Lord, 'Does Job fear God for nought? Hast thou not put a hedge about him and his house and all that he has on every side? Thou hast blessed the work of his hands, and his possessions have increased in the land. But put forth your hand now and touch all that he has, and he will curse thee to thy face.' And the Lord said to Satan, 'Behold, all that he has is in your power ... '
>
> *(Job 1:8–12)*

God's only request is that Satan spare Job's life. Satan proceeds to smite Job with the loss of all his possessions and his sons and his daughters, and finally afflicts him with running sores from head to foot. At this extremity, Job's wife calls on him to "curse God and die!" But Job answers, "You talk as any wicked fool of a woman might talk. If we accept good from God, shall we not accept evil?" Throughout the ordeal Job does not voice one sinful word. Seated among the ashes, he utters his final resignation, "Naked I came from my mother's womb, and naked shall I return; The Lord gave and the Lord has taken away; blessed be the name of the Lord" (Job 1:21).

The Job here depicted passes the divine trial of faith, but we may find it difficult to admire him fully. He does not strike us as a genuine flesh-and-blood human being. What is perhaps worse is the depiction of God! The Almighty allows Job to be stricken with the most harrowing and painful evil, and all *gratuitously*, that is, without just cause. God's motive appears hardly fitting for a loving father; it strikes us as more like the sadistic pleasures of a tyrant. The Job and the God who are portrayed in the long dialogue itself are very different.

Despite the grotesqueness of the prologue's test of Job's faith, the idea that the believer can be purged and refined in the crucible of suffering is a deep-felt and universal religious conviction. It plays an important role in Islamic piety. The *Qur'an* is quite explicit:

> Surely We [Allah] will try you with something of fear and hunger, and diminution of good / and lives and fruits, yet give thou good tidings / unto the patient / who, when they are visited by an affliction, / say, 'Surely we belong to God, and / to Him we return'.[18]

The *Qur'an* also points to the necessity for enduring an immediate pain to achieve a greater good. The eminent Muslim theologian al-Ghazālī gives us, as example, the ancient practice of blood-letting (cupping) of an infant:

> The mother feels tender concern for the little one and forbids cupping, but the father, who is intelligent, inflicts it forcibly on him. The ignoramus thinks that the mother, and not the father, is the compassionate one. But the reasonable person knows that the father's infliction of cupping on the child represents perfect compassion . . . and that the mother is (the child's) enemy in the guise of a friend.[19]

To see the trial of faith only as a cruel test imposed by a less-than-beneficent God is to fail to recognize the other elements that enter into any profound divine-human encounter. These would include the "medicinal" role of suffering and the place of suffering in shaping character and in teaching individuals such virtues as humility, patience, and fellow-feeling. Furthermore, there is in the presence of evil the attendant experience of the divine mystery, which places our suffering beyond our finite comprehension. Before we turn to this latter theme, we need to look more deeply into the relationship between suffering and the forming of character.

Those monotheistic theodicies that focus on God's limitless power and sovereignty tend to place the blame for moral evil on the fact of the Fall of Adam and the ever-present, intractable character of human sin. After all, a good deal of suffering—even pestilence and famine—can be traced to human sloth and hard-heartedness. When confronted with the inexplicable fact of natural evil, these same theodicies—for example, Islam and Calvinism—appeal to radical faith in the face of the divine mystery. However, there is another tradition in Western monotheism that takes a different tack. It sees God's purpose as including the creation of finite, imperfect creatures who, through their own freedom, can develop personal spiritual insights and moral character. According to this theodicy, human moral growth requires the kind of world that includes the reality of pain and loss. This position is found in the writings of a number of Christian theologians, including the early Church Father St. Irenaeus (120–202 C.E.) and the important liberal Protestant theologian Friedrich Schleiermacher (1768–1834). A contemporary formulation is developed by the philosopher John Hick.

Hick begins by acknowledging it is not possible to show that all human pain serves God's purpose. However, he does believe it is possible to show that the divine purpose could not be advanced in a world that was "designed as a permanent hedonistic paradise," that is, in an environment where the end was simply human pleasure and comfort. This, he argues, is exactly the assumption of the skeptic. Since this world does indeed include hardship, danger, and pain, the nonbeliever concludes that the world could not have been created by a perfectly benevolent and omnipotent God. Hick points out the crucial difference:

> An essential premise of this argument concerns the nature of the divine purpose in creating the world. The skeptic's assumption is that man is to be viewed as a complete creation and that God's purpose in making the world was to provide a suitable dwelling-place for the fully formed creature. Since God is good and loving, the environment which he has created for human life to inhabit is naturally as pleasant and comfortable as possible. . . .
>
> Christianity, however, has never supposed that God's purpose in the creation of the world was to construct a paradise whose inhabitants would experience a maximum of pleasure and a minimum of pain. The world is seen, instead, as a place of 'soul-making' in which free beings, grappling with the tasks and challenges of their existence in a common environment, may become 'children of God' and 'heirs of eternal life.'[20]

Having set out these alternative conceptions, Hick proceeds to make the case for his "negative theodicy." He asks us to suppose that the world is a hedonistic paradise, that is, free of all possibility of pain and suffering. What kind of world would it be? Hick argues that it would, to say the least, be quite extraordinary and, finally, not very appealing:

> For example, no one could injure anyone else: the murderer's knife would turn to paper or his bullets to thin air ... fraud, deceit, conspiracy, and treason would somehow always leave the fabric of society undamaged. Again, no one would ever be injured in an accident: the mountain climber, steeplejack, or playing child falling from a height would float unharmed to the ground....
>
> To make possible this continual series of individual adjustments, nature would have to work by 'special providences' instead of running according to general laws which men must learn to respect on penalty of pain or death. The laws of nature would have to be extremely flexible: sometimes gravity would operate, sometimes not ... there could be no sciences, for there would be no enduring world structure to investigate....
>
> Courage and fortitude would have no point in an environment in which there is, by definition, no danger or difficulty. Generosity, kindness, the *agape* aspect of love, prudence, unselfishness, and all other ethical notions which presuppose life in a stable environment, could not even be formed. Consequently, such a world, however well it might promote pleasure, would be very ill-adapted for the development of the moral qualities of human personality. In relation to this purpose it would be the worst of all possible worlds.[21]

If, indeed, it is within God's purpose to create human beings who, though imperfect, can develop free and uncoerced into more-perfect children of God, then this present world of danger and pain is a more plausible environment for such a purpose than is a hedonistic paradise. The great monotheistic faiths would agree that this is, in fact, God's purpose and that both moral and natural evil are, therefore, compatible with belief in a God who is both omnipotent and perfectly good.

If we keep our attention trained on individual "soul-making," much can be said for such a theodicy. But the innocent suffering that we have witnessed in the twentieth century—the Jewish Holocaust, Hiroshima, the blood bath in Cambodia, and the thousands of starving infants in Ethiopia—these forms of demonic evil strike us as somehow radically incompatible with any notion of "soul-making." Can God's purpose include such unspeakable, large-scale suffering? Or even the innocent suffering of a single infant?

Hick fully acknowledges that a theodicy of "soul-making" never can be *emotionally* satisfying in view of human genocide or the torture of a single child. He insists, nevertheless, that it remains *intellectually* compelling since we cannot expect God to revoke our freedom when its wrong exercise becomes intolerable to us. Finally, however, the theist must fall back on a radical trust that the mystery of present suffering will be lifted and God's action justified in the *eschaton*, the end time of resurrection and final judgment.

A Theodicy of Submission: The Mystery of God's Sovereignty

In the last analysis, John Hick appeals to faith in the face of God's mysterious ways that pass human understanding. This is, no doubt, the monotheist's ultimate refuge, whatever intellectual explanations may appear as plausible justifications of God and evil. The *locus classicus* is again the Book of Job.

After his three friends gave their brief for Job's suffering as his recompense for sin, Job presents the final defense of his own case. Once again, he portrays himself as a pious and righteous man, indeed as something of a paragon of virtue. He ends his plea:

> Let me call a witness in my defense!
> Let the Almighty state his case against me!
> If my accuser had written out his indictment,
> I would not keep silence and remain indoors.
> No! I would flaunt it on my shoulder and wear
> it like a crown on my head; I would plead the whole record
> of my life and present that in court as my defense.
> *(New English Bible, Job 31: 35–37)*

Job's persistent self-justification does not cause God to remove his rod of suffering. Neither does God feel called on to reply to Job's questions or to defend his own conduct; rather, the Almighty appears to Job in the whirlwind, brutally pressing him with questions and convicting him of his ignorance. What Job receives in reply is neither recompense nor comfort, but anger, sarcasm, and mockery:

> Who is this whose ignorant words cloud my design in darkness? Brace yourself and stand up like a man; I will ask questions, and you shall answer. Where were you when I laid the earth's foundations? Tell me if you know and understand. Who settled its dimensions? Surely you should know. Who stretched his measuring-line over it? On what do its supporting pillars rest? Who set its cornerstone in place, when the morning stars sang together and all the sons of God shouted aloud? ... Have you descended to the spring of the sea or walked in the unfathomable deep? Have the gates of

death been revealed to you? Have you ever seen the door-keepers of the place of darkness? Have you comprehended the vast expanse of the world? Come, tell me all this, if you know. . . . Brace yourself and stand up like a man; I will ask questions and you shall answer. Dare you deny that I am just or put me in the wrong that you may be right?

(New English Bible, Job 38: 2–7; 16–18; 40:7–8)

Job challenges the very government of the universe while at the same time he sits in self-absorption, riveted on the injustice of his own condition. God calls on Job to cast his view beyond his own parochial horizon. Job, after all, is not God's only concern—nor is man. Finally, then, in the presence of the wondrous mystery of the whole, vast creation, Job forgets his case; his focus is suddenly and profoundly widened and deepened:

Then Job answered the Lord: I know that thou canst do all things and that no purpose is beyond thee. But I have spoken of great things which I have not understood, things too wonderful for me to know. I knew of thee then only by report but now I see thee with my own eyes. Therefore I melt away, I repent in dust and ashes.

(New English Bible, Job 42:1–6)

Job does not repent of any sins that had brought affliction on him. He is vindicated before his three friends. Suffering as a recompense for sin can only be, at best, partially true. Job repents of his ignorant charges against God and of his lack of faith. No longer does he cry out to be delivered from innocent suffering. Job can only put his hand to his mouth and confess his error in speaking of things beyond his comprehension. Suffering is, in a sense, dissolved as a problem before God's sovereign majesty and mystery.

Job's experience is essentially the normative theodicy of the Western monotheistic faiths. In Islam, the problem of evil and suffering is always seen in the perspective of Allah's providential will. The Arabic word *aslama* means "to submit" to Allah, the Lord of the Universe. For the pious Muslim, the most certain thing in life is that all occurs within Allah's omnipotent but mysterious will. Any denial of complete predestination seems to imply a power other than God controlling the universe.

Al-Ghazālī points out that all explanations of evil are, finally, inadequate. We must accept the mystery of God's predestination:

Do not doubt in any way that God is the most compassionate of the compassionate . . . for beneath this is a mystery, disclosure of which the law forbids. Be content then with prayer, do not hanker after disclosure! You have been informed by hints and signs if you

are among his people. Reflect! . . . for I deem you one endowed
with insight into God's secret of predestination.[22]

Despite all appearances of evil to the contrary, submission to Allah
teaches the Muslim both patience and endurance. God, after all, is
in perfect control. All comes from God, whether it be good fortune
or seeming calamity. This kind of spiritual resignation can, of course,
translate into a divine determinism and fatalism, as it did in some
forms of Islamic theology. In orthodox Islamic thought, this extreme
determinism is, however, balanced with doctrines of human freedom
and divine compassion.

Preoccupation with the divine unity, omnipotence, and predetermi-
nation may appear to outsiders as strange, even inhumane. On the
contrary, such a faith has given millions of theists a deep sense of
cosmic order, of the moral *rightness* of things, and a profound spiritual
repose—in the midst of recurrent evil and innocent suffering. While
Job's theodicy of radical submission is present in the later theological
traditions of all three Western biblical religions, its association with
an extreme **predestinarian** theodicy is most clearly present in certain
forms of Calvinism within Christianity.

John Calvin is the father of the Reformed (Presbyterian) tradition
in Protestantism. While Islamic theodicy is primarily concerned to
protect the unity of God, Calvin's theodicy is framed by two formative
doctrines: the Providence of God and the sin and depravity of mankind. Calvin was deeply influenced by St. Augustine's (see Chapter 9)
teaching on the fall and original sin. According to Calvin, all humans
are infected with the hereditary corruption of Adam's fall. Thereby,
humankind has lost its original freedom and is enslaved to sin. However, Calvin makes a distinction:

> The will, therefore, is so bound by the slavery of sin, that it cannot
> exact itself, much less devote itself to any thing good. . . . We must
> . . . observe this grand point of distinction, that man, having been
> corrupted by his fall, sins voluntarily, not with reluctance or con-
> straint . . . but with the bias of his own passions and not with external
> compulsion: yet such is the depravity of his nature, that he cannot
> be exacted and biased to anything but what is evil.[23]

According to Calvin, humankind is under the inevitability of sinning
and yet the blame for sin and its suffering is placed on *voluntary*
action. It is this paradox that relates his ideas of the fall and sin to
God's providence. Calvin considers God's providential rule to mean
that God creates persons so that each will freely follow the path that
he, God, has predestined. Some are predestined to heaven and others
to hell:

> Predestination we call the eternal decree of God by which he has determined in himself, what he would have to become of every individual of mankind. For they are not all created with a similar destiny; but eternal life is foreordained for some, and eternal damnation for others.[24]

But why should God impute responsibility to humans for those things that are rendered necessary by divine predestination? Calvin gives the following reply:

> The reprobate wish to be thought excusable in sinning, because they cannot avoid a necessity of sinning, especially since this necessity is laid upon them by the ordination of God. But we deny this to be a just excuse; because the ordination of God ... is guided by equity, unknown indeed to us, but indubitably certain.... For though, by the eternal providence of God, man was created to that misery to which he is subject, yet the ground of it he has derived from himself, not from God.[25]

Like the *Qur'an*, Calvin appeals to the justice of God that passes human understanding but that is "indubitably certain." Since God's sovereign ways "pass finding out," who are we, Calvin asks, to question his will? The human response must be one of silence and reverent submission in the presence of so awesome a mystery.

> None, therefore, will attain just and profitable views of the providence of God, but he who considers that he has to do with his Maker and Creator of the world, and submits himself to fear and reverence with all becoming humility.... Those who have learned this modesty, will neither murmur against God on account of past adversities....[26]

In one passage in the *Institutes*, Calvin speaks of those who are predestined from the womb to death and perdition, that their "name may be glorified in their destruction" (III, XXIII, 6). Here, it would appear, is a rejoicing in the mysterious counsels of God *in extremis*.

To the observer, a theodicy of radical submission may appear irrational, a form of **masochism**. But that is a superficial perception. What underlies the experience of divine sovereignty and omnipotence is a profound religious sentiment. Job and al-Ghazālī and Calvin are telling us that, despite all appearances to the contrary, God cannot but have chosen the best. Not that evil and suffering are unreal; rather, that the pain and sorrow will somehow be used by God or, in the *eschaton*, be shown by God to be justified. Faith rests in that assurance.

The three types of monotheistic theodicy that we have explored so far hold in tension the reality of evil and the perfect goodness and omnipotence of God. Some critics would argue that Calvin, for example, so emphasized the sovereignty of God as possibly to call into question God's goodness and compassion. God's omnipotence is sustained but, seemingly, at the terrible price of denying any plausible meaning to the attribute of divine love. God's love and goodness have no analogy to what we know as human love and goodness. No monotheistic theodicy has, of course, explicitly denied God's goodness, and few (Christian Science may be a modern exception) deny the reality of evil. However, in the past two centuries, a number of Western philosophers and theologians have called for a thorough examination and revision of the idea of divine omnipotence. It is, they believe, the only way of making theism intelligible in a world of real suffering and evil.

Process Theodicy

The most impressive arguments for the incoherence of the classical view of divine omnipotence are offered by theologians who have appropriated the metaphysical doctrines of twentieth-century Process philosophy, particularly those of Alfred North Whitehead (1861–1947) and Charles Hartshorne (b. 1897). According to these Process philosophers, all reality is constituted by process and change, from the least to the greatest, God not excluded. Furthermore, this process is social, that is, the world consists of entities—again, from mere particles of matter to God—that freely respond to and are responded to by the free activity of other entities. Nothing whatever, not even God, *wholly* determines the being of something else. This metaphysical doctrine has important implications for the idea of "power," because power here is, by its very nature, social; that is, it presupposes free relationships between distinct individuals or agents, including the relationship between God and his creatures.

Process theology therefore argues that nothing, not even God, can *wholly* determine the being of others. A contemporary theologian puts it as follows:

> This means that even the greatest possible power over other things—even the omnipotent power than which no greater can be conceived—could not be all the power there is but only all the power that any one actual thing could be conceived to have, consistently with there being other actual things having lesser power over which its omnipotent power could alone be exercised. . . .
>
> The conclusion seems obvious, then, that the coherent meaning that 'all-powerful' or 'omnipotent' could have is not all the power there is—since nothing can have that . . . but only all the power that any one individual could conceivably have consistently with their

being other individuals who as such must themselves also have some
power, however minimal.[27]

Process theologians argue that such a conception of divine power
is more in keeping with the biblical picture of God's relations with
his creatures; moreover, that it certainly is more consistent with the
idea of divine love and omnibeneficence that, they insist, must presup-
pose the real freedom and responsibility of finite selves. Process theology can accept the real existence of evil as in no way incompatible
with belief in a God *whose power and goodness alike are the greatest
conceivable* "since such evil as exists may be attributed to decisions
other than God's own for which he cannot be reasonably held responsible."[28] God cannot eliminate evil; he can only minimize it while
maximizing the possibilities for good.

Many contemporary theists have found this to be an attractive solution to the problem of evil. Others, however, regard it as quite unsatis-
factory because God's action appears to be only a persuasive one. God
does not seem to be fully in control; his will and purposes can be
frustrated, or, indeed, defeated. A finite or limited God struggling to
maximize good may be admirable but, say the critics, he is no match
for the earthly powers of evil and thus not the proper object of our
ultimate trust and hope.

A Theodicy of Protest

Many sensitive theists will insist that philosophical arguments justifying
God in the face of evil are not only shallow but also downright diabol-
ical. Intellectual arguments, they contend, end up legitimating evil.
These believers are wary of all answers. While remaining believers,
they engage in a theodicy of protest, more properly, an *antitheodicy*.
They agree with Dostoevsky's Ivan Karamazov in refusing to approve
any theodicy that entails acceptance of the torturing to death of even
one terror-stricken, innocent child. Surely, much evil is the result of
human freedom and sin, but, they argue, God cannot so easily be
removed from responsibility. The cost in evil for human freedom is
too high. God allows far too much suffering and waste.

These protesters are also repelled by the notion of a "limited" God
who, so to speak, "holds his breath" while we humans foolishly act
out our carnage, a God who then tries to make the best out of a
bad job. Such a God, they claim, is not worth bothering about. God,
they insist, is the Lord of Creation. He cannot be exonerated because
of human freedom. God, too, is guilty; he, too, must bear a large
share of responsibility for evil. God must be put in the dock and
interrogated; he must be called to account.

To put God on trial may appear blasphemous—but, in fact, it may be paying God the highest compliment. To contest against God is at least to take his reality seriously. It would, in some ways, be much easier to deny that God exists and have done with it. The believing protester wants both to interrogate God and to resist nihilistic despair. The most powerful expression of this form of angry, faithful quarrel with God is found in the novels and essays of the Jewish writer Elie Wiesel, who experienced the Holocaust first-hand. His testimony and protest express a long tradition of Jewish faith going back to Job.

Wiesel learned from one of his teachers that the Jew alone realizes that "he may oppose God as long as he does so in defense of his [God's] creation."[29] In his play *The Trial of God*, Wiesel tells of the aftermath of a *pogrom*, the organized massacre of Jews, in Russia in 1649. God is put on trial for his crimes against humanity by Berish, one of only two Jewish survivors. Sam, a brilliant attorney, offers all the usual defenses of God: God has his reasons that are beyond our understanding, and so forth. But Berish will not hear of it and responds:

> I lived as a Jew and it is as a Jew that I shall die—and it is as a Jew that, with my last breath, I shall shout my protest to God. And because the end is near [another pogrom is imminent], I shall shout louder! Because the end is near, I'll tell Him that He's more guilty than ever![30]

This rejection of all attempts to "justify the ways of God to man" may not be satisfying to the philosophic mind, but Berish's "No!" to all forms of consolation can also strike one as refreshing and real. But the "No!" is only penultimate. There is the other side of the quarrel, voiced by Job: "Though he slays me, *yet will I trust in him*." (Job 13:15). This side is beautifully related in a tale told by Wiesel. It may sum up the ultimate stance of any profound theistic belief. A family of Jews is left in the desert without provision of food or drink.

> One evening they collapsed with fatigue. They were four to fall asleep; they were three to rise. The father dug a grave for his wife, and the children recited the **Kaddish**. And they took up their walk again.
>
> The next day they were three to lie down; only two woke up. The father dug a grave for his older son and recited the *Kaddish*. And with his remaining son he continued the march.
>
> Then one night the two stretched out. But at dawn only the father opened his eyes. He dug a grave in the sand and this is how he addressed God: 'Master of the Universe, I know what you want—I understand what you are doing. You want despair to overwhelm me. You want me to cease believing in You; to cease praying to You, to cease invoking Your name to glorify and sanctify it. Well, I tell you: No, no—a thousand times no! You shall not succeed! In spite of me and in spite of You, I shall shout the *Kaddish*, which

is a song of faith, for You and against You. This song you shall not still, God of Israel.[31]

Notes

1. The sociologist Max Weber was the first to use the term *theodicy* in this wider sense and the one who developed a useful typology of theodicies. More recently, the American sociologist Peter Berger has adapted and expanded upon Weber's work in his book, *The Sacred Canopy*. The account of theodicy in this chapter is heavily dependent on Weber and Berger, especially the latter's distinctive typology.
2. W. K. C. Guthrie, *The Greeks and Their Gods* (London, 1950), pp. 130–31.
3. Peter Berger, *The Sacred Canopy* (New York, 1967), pp. 54–55.
4. Lucien Levy-Bruhl, *How Natives Think*, trans. L. A. Clare (London, 1926), p. 91.
5. William James, *The Varieties of Religious Experience* (New York, 1902), p. 395.
6. Norman Cohn, *The Pursuit of the Millennium* (London, 1970), p. 21.
7. Howard Kaminsky, *A History of Hussite Revolution* (Berkeley, 1967), pp. 340–41.
8. N. Cohn, *Millenium*, p. 248.
9. Peter Worsley, *The Trumpet Shall Sound: A Study of 'Cargo' Cults in Melanesia* (London, 1957), pp. 154–55.
10. Lewis Pelly, *The Miracle Play of Hasan and Husain* II (London, 1879), p. 347f.
11. Werner Foerster, *Gnosis: A Selection of Gnostic Texts* II, trans. and ed. by R. McL. Wilson (Oxford, 1974), p. 159.
12. *Bhagavadgita* II, 31; 37–38. In S. Radhakrishnan and C. A. Moore, *A Source Book in Indian Philosophy* (Princeton, 1957), pp. 108–9.
13. *Dharmapada Karmavarga* IV, 4–5, 8, 19. Cited in John Bowker, *Problems of Suffering in Religions of the World* (Cambridge, 1970), p. 248.
14. *Milindapanha* 65. Cited in Bowker, *Problems of Suffering*, p. 249.
15. U. Thittila, "The Fundamental Principles of Theravada Buddhism," in Kenneth W. Morgan, ed., *The Path of the Buddha* (New York, 1956), pp. 86–87.
16. Christmas Humphreys, *Karma and Rebirth* (London, 1943), p. 54f.
17. Hume's *Dialogues Concerning Natural Religion*, ed. N. K. Smith (Oxford, 1935), p. 244.
18. Arthur J. Arberry, *The Koran Interpreted* II (London, 1955), p. 48.
19. Abu Hamid al Ghazālī, *al-Maqsad al-asnā* (Beirut, 1971), pp. 68–69. As cited in Eric L. Ormsby, *Theodicy in Islamic Thought* (Princeton, 1984), p. 253.
20. John Hick, *Philosophy of Religion* (Englewood Cliffs, 1964), p. 44.
21. J. Hick, *Philosophy of Religion*, p. 45.
22. Al-Ghazālī, in Ormsby, *Theodicy*, pp. 69–70.
23. *Institutes* II, iii, 5. *A Compend of the Institutes of the Christian Religion by John Calvin*, ed. Hugh T. Kerr (Philadelphia, 1964), p. 49.

24. *Institutes*, III, XXI, 5. H. T. Kerr, *A Compend*, pp. 128–29.
25. *Institutes* III, XXIII, 9. H. T. Kerr, *A Compend*, pp. 133–34.
26. *Institutes* I, XVII, 2–3. H. T. Kerr, *A Compend*, p. 36.
27. Schubert Ogden, "Evil and Belief in God: The Distinctive Relevance of a 'Process Theology,'" *The Perkins Journal* (Summer, 1978), pp. 32–33.
28. Ogden, "Evil and Belief in God," p. 33.
29. Elie Wiesel, *A Jew Today* (New York, 1978), p. 6.
30. Elie Wiesel, *The Trial of God* (New York, 1979), p. 157.
31. E. Wiesel, *A Jew Today*, pp. 135–36.

Review Questions

1. Describe the characteristics of a theodicy of mystic participation. Can you think of examples of such a theodicy in addition to those cited in the text?
2. What are the chief features of a millenarian, this-worldly theodicy, such as that of the Taborites or the John Frum Cargo Cult?
3. How does a radically dualistic theodicy differ from millenarian or monotheistic theodicies that may reflect, at least temporarily, dualistic features?
4. Explain the Hindu–Buddhist theodicy in terms of the *karma–samsara–dharma* complex of doctrines. Why is this theodicy called the most "rational"?
5. Despite the problematic depiction of God in monotheistic theodicies that portray suffering as a test, many theologians have defended suffering as a necessary condition of human "soul-making." Describe John Hick's defense of what he calls a "negative theodicy."
6. How does a process theodicy respond to the monotheist's insistence on God's omnipotence and love and the reality of evil?
7. Which, if any, of the theodicies outlined in this chapter do you find most meaningful or compelling? Why?

Suggestions for Further Reading

GENERAL DISCUSSION OF THEODICY IN THE WORLD'S RELIGIONS

BERGER, PETER, *The Sacred Canopy* (New York: Doubleday, 1967), Chapter 3.
BOWKER, JOHN W., *Problems of Suffering in Religions of the World* (Cambridge: Cambridge University Press, 1970).
HEBBLETHWAITE, BRIAN, *Evil, Suffering, and Religion* (London: Sheldon Press, 1976).
HERMAN, ARTHUR L., *The Problem of Evil in Indian Thought* (Delhi: Motilal, Banarsidass, 1976).

O'FLAHERTY, WENDY DONIGER, *The Origin of Evil in Hindu Mythology*
(Berkeley: University of California Press, 1980).

THE PROBLEM OF EVIL IN THE CONTEXT OF WESTERN MONOTHEISM

CAMUS, ALBERT, *The Rebel*, trans. Anthony Bower (New York: Vintage
Books, 1956).

DAVIS, STEPHEN (ed.), *Encountering Evil* (Atlanta: John Knox Press, 1981).
An interesting collection of essays and critiques by five philosophers.

DOSTOEVSKY, FYODOR, *The Brothers Karamazov*, trans. Constance Garnett
(New York: Modern Library, n.d.), Book V, Chapter 4.

FARRER, AUSTIN M., *Love Almighty and Ills Unlimited* (London: Collins,
1962).

HICK, JOHN H., *Evil and the Love of God* (London: Macmillan, 1966).

HUME, DAVID, *Dialogues Concerning Natural Religion*, Kemp Smith ed.
(Indianapolis: Bobbs Merrill, n.d.), Book XI.

GRIFFEN, DAVID, *God, Power, and Evil: A Process Theodicy* (Philadelphia:
Westminster, 1976).

ORMSBY, ERIC L., *Theodicy in Islamic Thought* (Princeton: Princeton
University Press, 1984).

PIKE, NELSON (ed.), *God and Evil* (Englewood Cliffs, N.J.: Prentice Hall,
1964). An excellent collection of philosophical essays.

RUBENSTEIN, RICHARD, *The Cunning of History* (New York: Harper &
Row, 1978). The meaning of evil and theodicy in the context of
the Holocaust and modern genocide.

WIESEL, ELIE, *Night* (New York: Avon Books, 1969). Wiesel's account of
his own experience in Birkenau, Auschwitz, Buna, and Buchenwald
concentration camps.

_____ , *The Trial of God* (New York: Random House, 1979). A dramatic
portrayal of the Jewish "quarrel with God," in the context of a
seventeenth-century pogrom in Russia.

CHAPTER 11

Ways to Liberation and Salvation

OVERVIEW

Human life is burdened by a tragic flaw. At least that is what the great religions teach. Viewed realistically and without illusion, they tell us that life is marked by estrangement and by a sense of failure, loss, moral regret, pain, and unease. Our empirical self, or ego, compares pitiably with our potentially real, spiritual self. Life, it is felt, is in need of liberation, healing, transformation. The conditions from which we humans need to be delivered range from the most basic physical threats—for example, an absence of food and bodily safety— to the spiritual need to sacrifice our finite, private self to that which is truly absolute and enduring.

The ways or means of achieving liberation or salvation have varied greatly in the history of religion and range from coercive magic, used to foil an enemy or to ensure a harvest; to acts of passionate entreaty and ecstatic devotion; to highly disciplined ethical patterns of behavior; to pure mystical flights of union with the divine. There are, however, three or four discernible "paths" or ways that can be observed in all the historical religions and are recognized as classical types. These are the way of *faith*, the way of *devotion*, the way of *disciplined action*, and the way of *meditation* and *insight*. While these patterns can be distinguished, they obviously often are combined. For example, the devout Muslim may reveal a highly patterned life of ethical and devotional behavior, but the Muslim discipline also reflects a life of radical faith and trust in Allah's providential care and goodness—and, perhaps, may be accompanied by occasional flights of mystical insight. The fact is that the great religions—Hinduism, Christianity, Buddhism, Judaism, and Islam—have at one time or another, in one or another

285

tradition or school, emphasized one of these traditional ways over the others as normative, as *the* way. However, these paths are not mutually exclusive, and in religious traditions such as Hinduism and Roman Catholicism all three or four ways may coincide.

Personal needs and temperaments differ greatly, and it is obvious that different persons are drawn to one or another way as religiously more suitable and effective. Some persons are attracted to highly emotional expressions of religion, as in certain forms of revivalistic Protestantism; other persons require a daily discipline of activities, of prayer and good works, carried out in a ritualistic manner that may appear merely routine to the emotionally charged temperament; and there are those rarer types who are neither very emotional nor practical but are essentially contemplative and meditative and who seek spiritual wisdom or insight largely in private.

It is true, however, that certain religions do appear to favor or to reflect one way of salvation as more characteristic of its normative life. Protestantism, for example, is characterized by the ways of faith and devotion, is less drawn to disciplined sacramental action, and gives almost no attention to the way of mystical insight. Both orthodox Judaism and Islam reflect a very practical religious life, one that is punctuated by a daily pattern of religious acts. Theravada Buddhism, on the other hand, is normatively meditative and reflects the way of knowledge or insight.

If we are attentive to the fact that the several ways of salvation are not discrete and exclusive paths but, rather, are overlapping and often combined, an analysis of these classic types can be instructive. Here, we shall describe four types and illustrate each with examples from a variety of traditions.

The Way of Grace Through Faith

It would appear obvious that any religion holding a belief in a transcendent sacred power, be it personal or impersonal, must assume an act of faith on the part of the believer. It may be that we live, move, and have our true being in and through Sacred Power, but such a reality is not necessarily transparent in the world of sensory experience. Believers must at least assent to the unseen reality of the Tao or Brahman, Nirvana or God, for it is not demonstrable in the same sense as a physical object. Faith, therefore, can mean the mental assent to the existence of such an unseen reality. In such a case, faith is synonymous with belief, the intellectual apprehension of a religious truth. However, the faith we are speaking of here is not intellectual assent (*assensus*) alone but, rather, the total response of a person—

heart, mind, and will. It is what the theologians call trust (*fiducia*), a total, confident reliance on divine grace, on unmerited love and favor.

Faith in this second sense implies that the believer feels incapable of taking any action that can lead to liberation from the condition binding him or her to sin, craving, or ignorance. The self has reached a condition of complete helplessness and abasement; the will is in bondage to evil or ignorance and is wholly dependent on the grace and love of the divine for its release. The way of faith is common in all three of the Western monotheistic traditions but is, perhaps, most often associated with orthodox Protestantism. Since its beginnings in the Reformation, Protestantism has accentuated the stubborn reality of human sin. It logically follows that the deeper the sense of sin, the greater is the need for help from beyond the self. Because the individual can do nothing to be saved—not the least good work—he or she must eradicate every vestige of self-assertion and humbly cast the self before the mercy-seat of God. The believer is liberated or saved by divine grace through faith alone. However, the way of faith is not exclusive to Western religion. It is present in both popular Hinduism and, as we will see, in some traditions of Mahayana Buddhism in China and Japan.

Martin Luther

The Protestant Reformer Martin Luther (1483–1546) represents the classic expression of the way of faith in the West. Before his break with Rome, Luther was a diligent Augustinian monk. His learning and holy striving brought him an appointment as professor of biblical theology at Wittenburg. But, despite his piety, Luther was plagued by the fact that he felt incapable of attaining the righteousness of God—that is, of standing morally satisfied before a righteous and demanding God. He could not know God as a merciful and forgiving God because of his own unrighteousness. "How," he asked, "can I find a gracious God?" The more this afflicted him, the more he tried to prove his righteousness and merit, by which he would be worthy of eternal life. He tried every possible spiritual and ascetic discipline: fasting, good works, pilgrimage, self-denial, and austerity. Nothing relieved his doubts. He could not acquire the monastic ideal of a proper balance between spiritual "dread" of God's righteous judgment and "security" in God's loving mercy. In desperation, he came to believe that Christianity was a cruel hoax. He felt he was eternally lost and fell into an abyss of despair.

Luther came to hate the word *righteousness*. He interpreted it as meaning God's demand of justice and his punishment of the sinner for his unrighteousness. However, as he studied the apostle Paul's Letter to the Romans, he came on this statement: "the righteous shall

live from faith to faith" (Romans 1:17). Here, righteousness was dis-
closed not as demanding justice by God but as a gift from God, as
disclosing the mercy of God. Luther later wrote of his new discovery:

> Now I felt exactly as if I had been born again and believed that I
> had entered Paradise through widely opened doors. As violently as
> I had formerly hated the expression "righteousness of God" so I
> was now as violently compelled to embrace the new conception of
> grace, and thus for me the expression of the Apostle really opened
> the Gates of Paradise.[1]

About the same time, Luther made a second discovery. The Latin
Vulgate (the official Roman) version of the Gospels read, "do penance,
for the Kingdom of God is at hand." However, the great scholar
Erasmus produced a new Greek text that rendered the passage as
"repent, for the Kingdom of God is at hand." For Luther, the words
penance and *repent* represented radically different spiritual worlds. His
great discovery was that believers are *made righteous by grace through
repentance and faith*, not through good works. Luther no longer saw
God as a severe, demanding judge but as a loving Father whose will
was to forgive the unrighteous. Righteousness is the undeserved gift
of divine grace which is to be received by faith alone.

> Through faith in Christ, therefore, Christ's righteousness becomes
> our righteousness and all that he has becomes ours; rather, he him-
> self becomes ours. Therefore the Apostle calls it 'the righteousness
> of God' in Rom. 1:[17] . . . This is an infinite righteousness, and
> one that swallows up all sins in a moment, for it is impossible that
> sin should exist in Christ. On the contrary, he who trusts in Christ
> exists in Christ; he is one with Christ, having the same righteousness
> as he. It is therefore impossible that sin should remain in him. . . .
> It is in this sense that we are to understand the prayer in Psalm
> 30: 'In thee, O Lord, do I seek refuge; let me never be put to
> shame; in thy righteousness deliver me!' It does not say 'in my' but
> 'in thy righteousness,' that is, in the righteousness of Christ my God
> which becomes ours through faith and by the grace and mercy of
> God.[2]

For Luther, any thought of persons meriting righteousness and salvation is utterly out of the question, indeed, it is a blasphemy. The
"merit-mongers," he says, "refuse to receive God's grace freely, which
is the glory of His divinity, but rather seek to deserve God's grace
by their own works." On the contrary, writes Luther:

> The Word of God cannot be received and cherished by any works
> whatever but only by faith. Therefore it is clear that, as the soul
> needs only the Word of God for its life and righteousness, so it is

The reformer Martin Luther's rediscovery that the
believer is saved through faith by God's grace alone
remains a bulwark of Protestant Christianity today.
(*Source*: Lucas Cranach, courtesy of Giraudon/Art
Resource.)

justified by faith alone and not by any works; for if it could be
justified by anything else, it would not need the Word, and con-
sequently it would not need faith. . . . So it is clear, then, that a
Christian has all that he needs in faith . . . and if he has no need
of works, he has no need of the law. . . . This is that Christian
liberty, our faith, which does not induce us to live in idleness or
wickedness but makes the law and works unnecessary for any man's
righteousness or salvation.[3]

While the law or good works, such as insuring public order and
justice, has its function in the maintenance of civil society, it has no
role whatsoever in our redemption. In fact, Luther sees works and
the law—that is, what is commanded—as the "hammer of God" breaking down human pride and self-reliance, that "rebellious, obstinate,
stiff-necked beast." God has need, writes Luther, "of a mighty hammer, that is to say, the law." God uses the law to teach us how
miserably we have failed and have "transgressed all the commandments

of God," and so the law only strikes a "a terror into the conscience so that it feeleth God to be offended and angry indeed, and itself to be guilty of eternal death."[4]

Luther's radical rejection of the way of works as a means of salvation might raise the questions of whether good works have any place in the religious life or what motivation there is in doing good works. According to Luther, these very questions show that we are still mired in our old egoistic perspective. The religious life remains motivated by thoughts of heavenly joy and the fear of hell, that is, by our own advantage. For Luther, to be blessed means only "to will the will of God and His glory and to desire nothing of one's own either here or hereafter." The pious do everything that may redound to God's glory alone. The Christian serves God for God's sake, simply because He *is* God. Otherwise, Luther believed, the Christian does not serve God but only himself or herself. In such a God-centered perspective, there is no consideration of meritorious action, for we are set free to pursue good works for their own sake.

Luther had experienced the contagious power of God's grace, his mercy and loving kindness freely bestowed. And so, in turn, the faithful, like Luther, are to seek to emulate God's love in their dealings with others. Luther put it briefly, "God and His children do good gratuitously"—that is, freely. To ask why the Christian, saved by grace through faith, should do good reveals a total miscomprehension of what it means to have the burden of our sin removed by God's grace.

> It is as absurd and stupid [Luther declares] to say: the righteous ought to do good works, as to say: God ought to do good, the sun ought to shine, the pear-tree ought to bear pears; . . . it follows without commandment or bidding of any law, naturally, willingly, uncompelled. . . . Just so, we do not have to tell the righteous that he ought to do good works, for he does so . . . without any commandment or compulsion, because he is a new creature and a good tree.[5]

Luther's joyous experience of being freed from the bondage of sin and condemnation and of being lovingly accepted by a gracious God has been duplicated in the lives of millions. The heart of the way of faith is the profound sense of blessedness, even ecstasy, that comes with the feeling of an awful burden removed, in spite of one's absolute inability to do anything on one's own behalf. It is expressed in the popular Protestant hymn, "Just as I Am":

> 1. Just as I am, without one plea
>   But that thy Blood was shed for me,
>   And that thou bidd'st me come to thee
>   O Lamb of God, I come, I come. . . .

3. Just as I am, though tossed about
   With many a conflict, many a doubt,
   Fightings and fears within, without,
       O Lamb of God, I come. . . .

5. Just as I am, thou wilt receive,
   Wilt welcome, pardon, cleanse, relieve;
   Because thy promise I believe,
       O Lamb of God, I come.

Shinran

It was mentioned earlier that the way of faith, while typical of Protestant Christianity, is also a popular way of liberation in Hinduism and Buddhism. It is especially typical of the Buddhist Pure Land sects in China and Japan. The description of Buddhist doctrine in Chapters 9 and 10 focused on the original teachings of Gautama the Buddha as they are found in the earliest Pali texts and interpreted by the elite Theravada monks. Theravada means the "Way of the Elders." Like Christianity, Buddhism experienced a celebrated split into two principal schools. Roughly about the beginning of the Christian era, popular devotional Hinduism (known as **bhakti**) began to influence Indian Buddhism in decisive ways. For example, the Buddha came to be represented as an image and to be worshipped. A revolutionary movement within Buddhism, called the Mahayana or the Greater Vehicle, was the result, in part, of this penetration of popular *bhakti*. Over the centuries, the Mahayana Buddhism of faith and devotion became the dominant form of Buddhism in China and Japan. Theravada remained the normative expression of Buddhism in Sri Lanka (Ceylon) and in Southeast Asia.

Theravada Buddhism centers on the highly disciplined, rather elite life of the monk who renounces life in the world. Conversely, Mahayana is a religion of laymen and teaches the universality of salvation. While Theravada Buddhism considers each person to be an individual who must work out his or her own salvation, Mahayana sees the fate of each individual as linked with that of all others. Associated with this belief was the development of *parināmanā*, the transfer of merit, whereby the meritorious action of those enlightened can assist those weaker beings enslaved to passion and attachment in this degenerate age. Note that such a transfer of merit runs counter to the strict Theravada doctrine regarding the pitiless workings of the law of *karma*. While Theravada stresses the original teaching of Buddha and considers him a great sage, a man among men, Mahayana focuses on the life of Buddha, especially on his selfless compassion (*karuna*), and looks to the Buddha as a savior of others. Mahayana removed the distinction between the ignorant laymen and the learned monk, between saint and sinner, and made salvation equally accessible to all. The ideal of Theravada remained the *arhant* (perfect being), the disciplined monk who, through concentrated meditation, seeks only his own enlightenment and Nirvana. The ideal type in Mahayana is the Bodhisattva (one whose essence [*sattva*] is wisdom [*bodhi*]), previous incarnations of the Buddha who, having achieved enlightenment and on the brink of Nirvana, return to the world to make salvation possible for others.

According to Mahayana, Gautama is a Bodhisattva, the last of many compassionate Buddha saviors. In later years, Mahayana came to teach that other Buddha saviors were yet to come, most notably Maitreya. As it developed, the world was seen as full of Bodhisattvas, each one an emanation of the Buddha-essence and each one seeking the liberation of other beings. However, the Pure Land sects of Mahayana taught that, while there were many emanations of the original Buddha-essence, the heavenly Buddha most concerned with earthly beings is Amitabha (Amida), the Buddha of Infinite Light who dwells in the Western Paradise, the Pure Land.

In medieval Japan, Pure Land or Amida Buddhism, as it is called, became the most popular and influential school. In a time of bewildering change and strife, it offered the weary soul hope for eternal bliss in the Western Paradise. Amida had vowed that all would be saved who simply called on his name, Namu Amida Butsu, with whole-hearted trust and devotion. This fervent repetition of Amida's name became known as Nembutsu. It originally signified the work of meditation on the name of Amida but took on the rather different connotation of radical reliance on the saving power of Amida alone.

It was Honen (1133–1212) who, more than any other Buddhist sage, called for mutual tolerance in the use of methods of achieving enlightenment and taught that rebirth in heaven is achieved by recitation of the Nembutsu while relying on the grace of Amida. It was Honen's disciple, Shinran (1173–1262 C.E.), however, who carried the logic of the way of faith to its conclusion. He came to believe that recitation of the Nembutsu was itself an act of merit and therefore self-assertion. He advanced a radical doctrine of salvation by grace through faith in Amida. His rejection of merit deepened his own sense of the ineradicable character of human sin and lostness to the point that he believed that wicked persons were more acceptable to Amida than righteous men and women, because the wicked were more aware of their need to throw themselves entirely on Amida's mercy.

With other Pure Land teachers, Shinran preached that humankind is living in the "degenerate age of the Dharma," a time of inescapable evil and degradation in the Buddhist world cycle. The age is so evil that no works of discipline can avail the individual. Shinran personally felt the full burden of radical evil and the futility of works and expressed this in his many confessions and laments:

> I am false and untrue
> And without the least purity of mind.
>
> We men in our outward forms
> Display wisdom, goodness and purity.
> Since greed, anger, evil and deceit are frequent,
> We are filled with naught but flattery.
>
> With our evil natures hard to subdue,
> Our minds are like asps and scorpions.
> As the practice of virtue is mixed poison,
> We call it false, vain practice.[6]

Shinran concluded that it was impossible for a person to do good works. All acts are tainted with self-centeredness. He saw no bridge between the holy, pure Amida and mankind's petty, egoistic deeds.

> However good a man may be, he is incapable, with all his deeds of goodness, of effecting his rebirth in Amida's Land of Recompense. Much less so with bad men. . . . Good deeds are of no effect and evil deeds of no hindrance as regards rebirth. Even the rebirth of good men is impossible without being helped by Amida's specific Vow issuing from his great love and compassion which are not at all of this world.[7]

Shinran taught that the way of faith, while seemingly easy, is the most difficult of all paths because human pride always tempts individuals to seek their own salvation, rather than to rely on the Buddha. For Shinran, all spiritual merit proceeds *from* the Buddha—including the gift of faith itself.

The experience of "acceptance," despite our being unacceptable, is central to the way of faith and is a pronounced feature of devotional hymns and literature in Protestantism, as well as in the True Pure Land sect. The sentiment is conveyed by the words of the hymn "Just as I Am," cited earlier. Because we are accepted by the mercy of God or by the compassion of Amida, we find rest and peace, a "nonchalance of faith," the taking of life as we find it, without fear or anxiety. The profound sense of release that accompanies Amida's "acceptance" wells up in expressions of joy and gratitude. In recounting the experience of his own conversion, Shinran describes his joy:

> O how happy I am. My mind is established on the Buddha land of the profound Vow . . . I have experienced the Tathagata's [Amida Buddha's] compassion deeply, and I sincerely cherish the kindness

of my teacher. Happiness abounds, reverence grows deeper. . . . I am only mindful of the depth of Buddha's grace, and I am not ashamed at the ridicule of men.[8]

As Luther was later to express it: Grace begets gratitude. The motivation for doing good works rests not in any effort to achieve merit or gain our personal salvation but in gratitude alone. For Shinran, as for Luther, all attempts to gain some practical benefit from religion must be rejected. True religion rests, finally, on a recognition of our own moral failure; on our nothingness; and on the infinite, unspeakable mercy of God or Buddha. It is this overflow of thankfulness and love that often is expressed in acts of devotion.

The Way of Devotion

The joy and feeling of exaltation that accompany the experience of divine grace impel the believer to acts of worship and witness. The response is expressed in the words of the Psalmist:

> Sing to the Lord and bless his name,
>   proclaim his triumph day by day.
> Declare his glory among the nations,
>   his marvelous deeds among all nations.
> *(Psalm 96)*

Acts of devotion are not, however, only grateful responses to divine mercy. They may be a *means*, a discipline, directed at achieving enlightenment, redemption, or even union with the divine. In this latter sense, devotion has more in common with the way of action or deeds. It is hardly distinguishable from either sympathetic magic or from the way of ritual action discussed in earlier chapters and observed, for example, in certain Hindu or Catholic sacramental practices. Devotion may also be an integral component of mystical insight, as in the case of the Hindu saint Ramakrishna, or the Catholic mystic St. Teresa of Avila. As such, it often is considered a distinct path and has been called *devotional mysticism*.[9]

The point that needs to be underlined here is that the way of devotion is found, more often than not, in company with the ways of faith, action, and insight, and is either an integral means or a natural outcome of those classic paths. The way of devotion is, then, an inclusive way of salvation. Nevertheless, it does have distinctive features that deserve brief analysis.

The intensity of devotional religion is often regarded with disfavor by those who follow the more-prosaic way of obligation and duty and by those who take the arduous path of wisdom and insight. An exam-

The emotional and ecstatic aspects of much religious devotionalism is
reflected in a revival meeting. The woman experiences the personal
presence and power of the Holy Spirit. (*Source*: Courtesy of Stock,
Boston, Inc.)

ple is the horror expressed by the temple priests on encountering
Ramakrishna's childish devotional excesses before the image of the
Divine Mother, the goddess Kali, or the revulsion of the sober and
inexcitable Protestant when confronted with the ecstatic shouting and
dancing of a Pentecostal revival. The first mark of devotionalism is
its deep feeling and emotion. It often reflects a dissatisfaction with
the formal, unfeeling character of traditional religion. Devotionalism
involves an effervescence of emotion that is often absent in older,
established churches.

Closely related to its emotional character is the deeply personal
quality of devotion. Here, again, it reflects a reaction against the
dispassion, even detachment, of much traditional religious practice.
Devotionalism expresses a deeply felt personal encounter with the
divine. God is felt as a profound presence, vividly experienced in a
revelatory encounter that leaves the devotee radically changed. In the
Bhagavad Gita, the way of devotion, of surrender to the god Krishna,
is regarded as the highest path. The song describes how the merciful
Krishna seeks out and reveals himself to the warrior Arjuna in a
glorious vision. Arjuna responds in loving devotion:

> O Eyes of God! O Head!
> My strength of soul is fled,
> Gone is heart's force, rebuked is mind's desire!

> When I behold Thee so,
>   With awful brows a-glow,
> With burning glance and lips lighted with fire. . . .
> Earth, Heaven! Ah me! I see no Earth and Heaven!
>
>   Thee, Lord of Lords! I see,
>   Thee only—only Thee!
> Ah! let Thy mercy unto me be given! . . .
>
>   Therefore, with body bent
>   And reverent intent,
> I praise, and serve, and seek Thee, asking grace.
>
>   As father to a son
>   As friend to friend, as one
> Who loveth to his lover, turn Thy face
> In gentleness on me![10]

On occasion, this direct, intense personal encounter with the divine issues in a rapture in which the devotee actually feels transported out of the body or to another spiritual plane. This is often the case with the great mystics, such as the Spanish nun St. Teresa of Avila (1515–1582). Ecstasy (from the Greek *ekstasis*) literally means being outside oneself. St. Teresa describes such a transport:

> In these raptures the soul seems no longer to animate the body, and thus the natural heat of the body is felt to be very sensibly diminished; it gradually becomes colder, though conscious of the greatest sweetness and delight. No means of resistance is possible. . . . Often it comes like a strong, swift impulse, before your thought can forewarn you of it or you can do anything to help yourself; you see and feel this cloud, or this powerful eagle, rising and bearing you up with it on its wings. . . .
>
> The majesty of Him who can do this is manifested in such a way that the hair stands on end, and there is produced a great fear of offending so great a God, but a fear overpowered by the deepest love, newly enkindled, for One Who, as we see, has so deep a love for so loathsome a worm that He seems not satisfied by literally drawing the soul to Himself, but will also have the body, mortal though it is.[11]

St. Teresa's frequent reference to the divine love is also characteristic of devotionalism. In fact, the divine–human encounter is often described in terms reserved for a lover's desire—words such as rapture, ecstasy, and thirst for union. Ramakrishna insisted that "extreme longing is the surest way to God-vision," and he often used the explicit language of passionate desire in expressing his encounters with the divine. This personal intimacy of devotionalism is pronounced in the ardent words of Muslim **Sufi** poet:

> A fever burns below my heart
> And ravages my every part;
> It hath destroyed my strength and stay,
> And smouldered all my soul away. . . .
>
> So passionate my love is, I do yearn
> To keep His memory constantly in mind;
> But O, the ecstasy with which I burn
> Sears out my thoughts, and strikes my memory blind.[12]

In the West—for example, in Catholicism or Islam—devotional mysticism occasionally will blur the distinction between the human devotee and God. Normally, however, Western devotion maintains the distinction and remains within the bounds of theistic orthodoxy. Only rarely does it reach the explicit eroticism of Hindu *bhakti*. The following is

The god Krishna (meaning "black" or "dark") in erotic play with the milkmaids, *gopis*. Krishna's amorous relations with the *gopis* symbolize the mutual loving devotion of god and devotee in popular Hindu *bhakti*. (*Source*: Courtesy of Ann & Bury Peerless Slide Resources and Picture Library.)

an excerpt from popular Bengali devotional lyrics offered to the god Krishna. He is depicted as a noble warrior and a divine lover, and the lyrics express the erotic longing of the beautiful young Radha as she waits for Krishna's return:

> When my beloved returns to my house
> I shall make my body a temple of gladness,
> I shall make my body the altar of joy
> and let down my hair to sweep it.
> My twisting necklace of pearls shall be the intricate
> sprinkled design on the altar
> my full breasts the water jars,
> my curved hips the plantain trees
> the twinkling bells at my waist the young
>   shoots of the mango.
> I shall use the arcane arts of fair women in
>   all lands
> to make my beauty outshine a thousand moons. . . .
>
> The moon has shown upon me,
> the face of my beloved.
> O night of joy![13]

The rapturous and erotic devotionalism of Hindu *bhakti* and some Sufi mysticism does appear occasionally, though more covertly, in Christian devotion. It is evident, for example, in some of the language used by devotees of the Roman Catholic cult of the Sacred Heart. One of the leaders of the cult, Mother Louise Margaret de la Touche (1868–1915), in her *Book of Infinite Love*, exhorts Catholics to adore the eucharistic Host, the wafer or bread, and to lovingly kiss the consecrated paten, or plate holding the wafer. Students of Protestant **revivalism** also have pointed to the veiled erotic imagery in some pentecostal sermons and hymns. However, Protestant devotionalism does not express so much erotic union as it does the warm personalism of friendship. God is spoken of in the intimacy of the man next door, a real human friend. The dominant feeling of Protestant devotionalism is expressed in the popular hymn "What a Friend We Have in Jesus":

> What a Friend we have in Jesus
> All our sins and griefs to bear!
> What a privilege to carry
> Everything to God in prayer.
>
> O what peace we often forfeit,
> O what needless pain we bear
> All because we do not carry
> Everything to God in prayer!

Can we find a friend so faithful
Who will all our sorrows share?
Jesus knows our every weakness
Take it to the Lord in prayer.

The Way of Action and Obligation

The human body and mind need to be active. This is a deep human compulsion. We are anxious and discontent when, involuntarily, we are inert and passive. It is no wonder, then, that activity is also central to the religious life of humankind. In fact, the way of action is the most universal and popular of the paths to salvation. Dramatic conversion experiences, mystical flights to the One, even devotional ecstasy are relatively infrequent events, the experiences of a religious elite. The vast majority of believers express their religious convictions and hopes through rather prosaic patterns of religious activities—rites, sacraments, and obligatory moral duties.

There are certain characteristic features of the way of action. First, it reflects a very *practical*, everyday, nondramatic approach to religion. It is the secular as sacred or, more accurately, the secular round of life punctuated by habitual religious duties. It is a deep, if unconscious conviction of the way of action that the cosmos or reality is sustained by a rehearsal of the "way of the fathers," the Grand Harmony, or what Eliade calls an eternal return *in illo tempore*. Without these actions, it is felt that the world will degenerate further and may even return to chaos.

A second feature of the way of action is its *patterned character*. What is striking about religious rite and duty—pointed out in Chapter 5—is the regular nature of this form of religious life—down-to-earth, ordered, and disciplined, usually lacking the ecstasy and effervescence of the devotional mystic. The way of action is typically conservative and institutional. This relates to a third feature, namely, the *traditional* character of religious action. It is the way not only of orthodoxy but also of *ortho-praxis*. Right duty or action means following the path established by the gods or the fathers "in the beginning." The way of action is suspicious of innovation; it demands a conformity of behavior as essential to community survival. The way of action is basically the only way found in primitive and archaic religion because the function of religious rite is to sustain social, even cosmic, order. It is natural that this way is also characteristic of the orthodox traditions in the historic religions: Orthodox Judaism and Islam, traditional Roman Catholicism, and caste Hinduism. Chapter 5 introduced the main features of the way of action as observed in the practice of religious ritual and sacrament. Here, we will concentrate on those aspects of religious action exhibited in the full range of obligatory duties expected of the faithful in Hinduism, Islam, and Judaism.

Hinduism

Orthodox caste Hinduism places great emphasis on the performance of duties associated with one's class and stage of life. These are formulated in ancient sacred codes of behavior, especially in a series of law books called the *Dharma Shastras*. The most ancient and authoritative of these texts is the *Manu Smriti*, or Code of Manu. The practice of duty — or *dharma*, as it is called — is the heart of orthodox Hinduism and, it is believed, will lead to a happy and moral life. Some also would see the fulfilling of *dharma* as leading to **moksha**, or liberation. In the Vedas, the word *dharma* stood for an eternally fixed moral law that underlies the universe. In the later law books, *dharma* came to refer specifically to the duties and obligations of social life. In the *Manu Smriti*, for example, these duties are elaborately formulated in terms of two social patterns: the four classes, or castes (**varnas**), and the four stages (**asramas**) of life.

Hinduism looks on social life as a complex and fragile organism. Complexity involves danger. It is possible that if there is a breakdown in one part of the organism, the whole social body will be endangered. Unless each strand of the social fabric is maintained and makes its proper contribution, the whole will unravel. And so Hinduism teaches that the functioning of the four classes — the Brahmans (priests), Kshatriyas (warriors), Vaishyas (farmers and producers), and Shudras (laborers) — is essential to the perfect ordering of society. So also is the right functioning of thousands of other caste groupings that are distinguished by occupation, family, geography, cult practices, and so on. Hinduism considers it entirely natural and realistic to recognize fundamental differences in sex, age, type, and status — and that to confuse the station and duties of various classes and stages of life is to invite chaos. The *Bhagavad-Gita* describes the consequence of such social confusion:

> When the religious laws of the family are destroyed, then lawlessness destroys the whole family. Because lawlessness prevails, the women of the family become corrupted, and when women are corrupt, intermingling of caste follows. Intermingling of caste leads to hell, both those who destroy the family as well as the family itself. The ancestors also fall into hell for they are deprived of the offerings of food made to them.[14]

The *Manu Smriti* describes in detail the *dharmas* of the four classes, including the sacraments (*samskaras*) appropriate for each stage (*asrama*) of life. It points out that "it is better to discharge one's own appointed

duty incompletely than to perform completely that of another,"[15] because to do otherwise is to introduce the confusion that results in
social chaos. Therefore, in the beginning the Lord

> for the sake of the prosperity of worlds, created the Brahman, the
> Kshatriya, the Vaishya, and the Shudra. . . .
> To Brahmans he assigned teaching and studying (the Veda), sac-
> rificing for their own benefit and for others, giving and accepting
> (of alms).
> The Kshatriya he commanded to protect the people, to bestow
> gifts, to offer sacrifices, to study (the Veda), and to abstain from
> attaching himself to sensual pleasures;
> The Vaishya to tend cattle, to bestow gifts, to offer sacrifices, to
> study (the Veda), to trade, to lend money, and to cultivate land.
> One occupation only the lord prescribed to the Shudra, to serve
> meekly even these (other) three castes.[16]

The *Dharma Shastras* describe the sacramental as well as the social
obligations that accompany each of the first three stages of life for
the males of the three "twice-born" classes. The *Gautama Dharma* alone
lists 40 sacraments, although there are 16 principal ones. Some of
these Hindu rites associated with birth were described in Chapter 5.
The numerous obligations and rites of the male of the "twice-born"
classes differ from stage to stage and therefore depend on the stage
in life he has reached.

The first stage—after a young man undergoes initiation, including
the investiture of the sacred cord—is that of a celibate student living
with his master, or **guru.** This *asrama* begins between the ages of 8
and 12 and lasts for 12 years, although today this first stage is not
as exacting as the one described, here in part, in the *Apastamba Dharma
Sutra*:

> Now follow the rules for the studentship.
> He shall obey his teacher, except when ordered to
> commit crimes which cause loss of caste.
> He shall do what is serviceable to his teacher,
> he shall not contradict him. . . .
> He shall not eat food offered at a sacrifice
> to the gods or the Manes,
> Nor pungent condiments, salt, honey, or meat. . . .
> He shall preserve his chastity. . . .
> Bringing all he obtains to his teacher, he shall
> go begging with a vessel in the morning and in the
> evening, and he may beg from everybody except low-caste
> people unfit for association with Aryas [Aryans].[17]

The second *asrama* begins with marriage, when a man's interests
are turned to family, occupation, and the wider community. Begetting

children, studying the Vedas, and performing the traditional rites, prayers, and sacrifices associated with the householder are especially important.

The third stage is that of retirement and retreat when the householder, "seeing his skin wrinkled and his hair white," takes to the forest as a **sadhu**, or ascetic, in search of self-control and spiritual insight. The *sadhu* spends his days fulfilling his new *dharma* through the study of sacred scripture and the performance of prescribed rituals:

> Taking with him the sacred fire and the implements required for domestic sacrifices, he may go forth from the villages into the forest and reside there, duly controlling his senses. . . .
> Let him offer those five great sacrifices according to the rule, with various kinds of pure food fit for ascetics, or with herbs, roots, and fruit.
> Let him wear a skin or tattered garment; let him bathe in the evening or in the morning; and let him always wear his hair in braids, the hair on his body, his beard, and his nails being unclipped. . . .
> He should live without a fire, without a house, a silent sage subsisting on roots and fruit. . . .[18]

The final stage of life is that of the homeless wanderer, the **sannyasin,** or recluse, who has no fixed abode, no possessions, and no obligations. He no longer performs sacrifices and other rites and has abandoned all attachments to this world. He shaves his head and beard and puts on the red-brown robe of the **mendicant**, or beggar. The *Manu Smriti* describes the renunciant:

> Delighting in what refers to the Soul, sitting in the postures prescribed by the Yoga, independent of external help, entirely abstaining from sensual enjoyments, with himself for his only companion, he shall live in this world, desiring the bliss of final liberation.[19]

It is only in this final stage of life that the orthodox Hindu finds himself freed of the obligatory duties that encompass his life from infancy to old age. However, all these actions and duties have but two purposes: knowledge of the soul and liberation from the rounds of births and deaths.

Islam

It is often remarked that the soul of Islam is to be found in its law rather than in its theology. The Muslim tradition is called *islām*, meaning "submission" or "surrender" to Allah, who guides the faithful "in the straight path" (*Qur'an* I, 6). Islam, like all the great historical religions, can point to Muslim saints and sages who epitomize the way of radical faith, the way of devotion, or the mystical path. However, the heart of normative Islamic religion is located in the daily obedience of the faithful to the commands of God.

The term used by Islam is *Sharī'ah;* it is the "way" or path of duty, both ethical and ritual. The *Sharī'ah* is law, morality, and religion; in Islam the three are not distinguished. The *Sharī'ah* is the sacred law given not only in the *Qur'an* but also in the *hadith*, or traditions, of the prophet Muhammad and the sayings of the Imams, and in the *ijmā*, or consensus, of the Muslim community. Islam's distinguishing mark is the law-abidingness of the Muslim in response to the commands of the *Sharī'ah*. The *Sharī'ah* is—like the Torah for Judaism—a complex of obligations governing personal, civil, political, and ritual activity.

Islam speaks both of things to be believed (*imān*, or faith) and things to be done or works (*islām*). It is clear, however, that for the faithful Muslim, things to be done take precedence over theology. A Muslim's obligations are principally expressed in five explicit duties or "Pillars of the Faith." The five "pillars" reflect the importance of the way of duty and action in a great religion.

SHAHĀDAH—CONFESSION   The first "pillar" of *islām* is bearing witness to the faith by saying the Confession: "There is no god but God and Muhammad is the Messenger (or Apostle) of God." The Confession must be said intentionally, thoughtfully, and with full understanding of its truth. The pious Muslim will recite the *Shahādah* several times a day in prayer.

SALĀT—PRAYER   In Islam, prayer is primarily something that must be *done*, must be ritually performed, although Muslims also engage in private devotional prayer (*du'ā, or wird*). There are five obligatory times of ritual prayer each day, each prayer having as its theme adoration and submission to God. The Muslim prays on arising, at midday, in the afternoon, immediately after sunset, and before retiring. The prayers vary in the number of ritual movements (*Rak'ah*) and appropriate recitations, but each begins and ends in an erect posture, with intervening bowings, prostrations, and recitations. The following is a description of some of the actions involved in the completion of one *Rak'ah*, so distinctive of *Salāt* in the Sunni tradition of Islam:

> Both hands are raised up to the ears in a standing position, with the face towards the *Qiblah* in Mecca, while the words *Allahu Akbar* [God is the greatest of all] are uttered. This is called the Takbir and is followed by a standing prayer and the recitation of the opening *surah* of the *Qur'an*. . . .

Then, saying *Allahu Akbar* the worshipper lowers his head down, so that the palms of the hands reach the knees. In this position, which is called *Rukū*, phrases expressive of the divine glory and majesty are repeated at least three times: 'Glory to my Lord the great.'

After this, the standing position is resumed, with the words: 'God accepts him who gives praise to Him, O our Lord, thine is the praise.'

Then the worshipper prostrates [the first *Sijdah* prostration] himself, the toes of both feet, both knees, both hands, and the forehead touching the ground, and the following words expressing the divine greatness are uttered at least three times: 'Glory to my Lord the most High.'[20]

The worshipper then sits in a reverential position, which is followed by a second prostration (as described above). This finishes one *Rak'ah*.

Noon prayer in the mosque—the place of prostration—on Friday is the time of congregational *Salāt*. The worshippers are called to prayer by a **muezzin**, usually from a tower or minaret. A sermon, often but not necessarily, by an *Imām*, or spiritual leader, usually in the form of an exhortation, precedes the *Salāt*. The *Imām* also leads in the timing of the congregational prayers.

There is something majestic and powerful in the corporate action of the faithful joining in their largely mental or subvocal recitations and ritual prostrations toward Mecca. The essence of *Salāt* is this personal sense of awareness and intention on the part of the faithful as they "remember" God in humility and reverent awe. *Salāt* involves this heightened response to God's mercy and "refuge" that discourages mere perfunctory, heedless gestures.

ZAKĀT—ALMSGIVING The third "pillar," *Zakāt* (or almsgiving), is derived from a root meaning "to purify." The *Qur'an* is full of appeals for charity to the poor and oppressed, and the practice of *Zakāt* has become the foundation of Islam's tradition of social responsibility.

The *Zakāt* is obligatory and—while technically not a civil function but a "pillar" of *islām*—in modern, complex society often is implemented by civil authority. Over the centuries, interpretations regarding the obligatory rate of alms tax on crops, cattle, camels, other possessions, and income has varied. As complex and legalistic as the administration of the *Zakāt* has become, its religious significance has remained foremost:

The doctrine is that property is validated as a private right and enjoyment, provided a portion of it is devoted to the common need, in token of the corporate awareness that should characterize all personal possession. This paid portion "purifies," that is, legitimatizes, what

Muslims performing their obligatory prayer (*salāt*) on
Friday at the mosque—one of the many duties set forth
in the *Sharī'ah*. (*Source*: Courtesy of Woodfin Camp &
Associates.)

is retained. Without this active conscience, retention and ownership
would be impure and disqualified. The community has not only a
stake in, but also a claim on, the individual's *amwal* or substance.[21]

SAWM—FASTING DURING RAMADAN   The duty of fasting during
the month of Ramadan (the ninth lunar month of the Islamic calendar)
is the fourth and most rigorous obligation of the Muslim's religious
life as set forth in the *Sharī'ah*. Like the other "pillars," the fast is a
physical, as well as spiritual, action or deed—a sacramental ritual. The
fast involves a total abstinence from food and drink during the day-
light hours for the 28 days of Ramadan. When the fast falls during
the heat of summer, the hardship of this obligation is intense.

Islam teaches that fasting nurtures self-discipline and compassion as
well as a sense of our own frailty and dependence on God:

The benefit of fasting is primarily in terms of character. The abstention from food and drink and the other material pleasures for the
long hours between dawn and dusk during the month of Ramadan
is an act of self-discipline by which an individual asserts his or her
ability to gain control over material pleasures and habits. This is a
triumph of mind over matter. The desire to quench thirst, to soften
the pangs of hunger, or to light a cigarette, are placed in their
proper perspective of things which can be postponed, and in some
cases given up entirely. . . . There is a social dimension of equal
importance. The community sense of those who fast and break their
fast together is greatly heightened and a necessary element for con-
certed social action is added. . . . One who can afford food and yet
abstains from it, is better able to understand the person who does
not have the food because he or she cannot afford it. . . . [22]

HAJJ—PILGRIMAGE TO MECCA   The fifth religious obligation is
pilgrimage to Mecca, the holiest shrine of Islam's faith. Every Muslim
who is physically and financially able is obliged to make this pilgrimage
at least once during his or her lifetime. The rites connected with the
pilgrimage bind the Muslim with his brothers and sisters from all
classes, nations, and races in a powerful sacrament of spiritual unity.
   The pilgrimage involves a series of rituals. First, the pilgrim must
undertake certain restraints, such as sexual abstinence. On approaching the city, the pilgrim greets Mecca with the cry, "Labbaika: 'Here
am I, Lord, here am I.' " There follows the sevenfold circuit of the
cube-shaped *Ka'bah* in the center of the mosque court. The pilgrim
must try to kiss, or at least to touch, the sacred stone that is mounted
on a corner of the *Ka'bah* and is the object of solemn reverence. The
climax of the pilgrimage comes between the eighth and tenth day
with a journey from Mecca through Mina to Arafat 12 miles away.
There, the pilgrim assembles with the others from noon to near sun-
down, a "standing in the presence of God." At sunset, the pilgrims
move on to Muzdalīfah for the night. The next day, a symbolic "ston-
ing" of Satan takes place at Mina. The 12-day pilgrimage ends with
a ritual sacrifice of animals at Mina and the return to Mecca for a
last circuit of the *Ka'bah*. The sense of excitement, of spiritual unity
and camaraderie is recalled by a convert to Islam, Malcolm X, on
returning from *Hajj*:

> We parked near the Great Mosque. We performed our ablution and
> entered. Pilgrims seemed to be on top of each other, there were so
> many, lying, sitting, sleeping, praying, walking. . . . Then I saw the
> *Ka'bah*, a huge block stone house in the middle of the Great Mosque.
> It was being circumambulated by thousands upon thousands of pray-
> ing pilgrims, both sexes, every size, shape, color, and race in the
> world. I knew the prayer to be uttered when the pilgrim's eyes first
> perceive the *Ka'bah*. . . .

Malcolm X then describes the indelible impression produced upon entering the Mosque:

> My feeling there in the House of God was a numbness. My *mutawwif* led me in the crowd of praying, chanting pilgrims moving seven times round the *Ka'bah*. Some were bent and wizened with age. It was a sight that stamped itself on the brain. I saw incapacitated pilgrims being carried by others. Faces were enraptured in their faith. The seventh time round, I prayed two *Rak'ahs*, prostrating myself. . . ."

At the conclusion of the pilgrimage, Malcolm X recalls the final rituals:

> Standing on Mount Arafat had concluded the essential rites of being a pilgrim to Mecca. . . . We cast the traditional seven stones at the devil. . . . I remember one night at Muzdalīfah with nothing but the sky overhead, I lay awake amid sleeping Muslim brothers and I learned that pilgrims from every land—every color and class and rank, high officials and beggars alike—all snored in the same language.[23]

The religious obligations of a pious Muslim do not end with the "Five Pillars." The faithful are expected to conform their daily lives to the entire Islamic *Sharī'ah*, which would include such things as prohibitions on drinking wine and eating pork; requirements of just actions in all commercial transactions; and even participation in holy war (*jihad*), the defensive war against the hostility of Islam's enemies.

Like the "twice-born" classes of orthodox Hinduism, the Muslim's life is encompassed by daily religious obligations that, far from being a burden, give life its dignity, its sense of purpose and communal unity, and its feeling of joy in conforming to a divine and sacred law.

Judaism

Christianity, at least until very recently, has placed great importance on belief and doctrine, on orthodoxy (*orthos*, meaning correct, and *doxa* meaning opinion). Judaism, on the other hand, has given greater attention to correct practice (*orthopraxis*). Judaism never established an official creed. Pious Jews differ widely on theological questions; what is central is a holy living as set forth in the Law, or Torah, and in the teachings of the biblical prophets. Judaism holds that an observant religious life prepares the way for the coming of the messianic age, God's kingdom on earth, when everything will be sanctified. It could be said that Judaism believes morality can be legislated, in the sense that habitual observance creates a complex of values and beliefs that, in turn, reinforces behavior.

The traditional path of life, or "way," prescribed for the religious Jew is set forth in what is called the *halakhah*—meaning walk—the tradition of legal decisions and prescriptive rules of the rabbis concerning every aspect of Jewish observance. *Halakhah* is the way the Jew shapes his or her daily routine into a pattern of sanctity. It is the way the Jew may achieve redemption. The hallowing of everyday activities—including eating, work, and sexual relations—means that for the Jew there can be no sharp separation of the sacred and the secular; the sacred impinges on every situation of life and under all circumstances. Since most activities are fenced by certain religious rules of observance, only a few examples can be mentioned here. Jews call their observance *mitzvah*, the pious response to God's command. Therefore, every act should, ideally, be preceded by the spoken intention that it be done "for the sake of Heaven."

The heart and soul of Jewish observance is the keeping of the Sabbath (*Shabbat*). On the Sabbath, a person must not work or engage in the usual mundane activities. It is a time of worship, rejoicing, and rest—a "taste of the world to come." Jacob Neusner describes the ritual of the *Shabbat* observance as follows:

> How does the pious Jew keep the Sabbath? All week long, he looks forward to it, and the anticipation enhances the ordinary days. By Friday afternoon, he has bathed, put on his Sabbath garments, and set aside the affairs of the week. At home, his wife will have cleaned, cooked, arranged her finest table. The Sabbath comes at sunset, and leaves when three stars appear Saturday night. After a brief service, the family comes together to enjoy its best meal of the week, a meal at which particular Sabbath foods are served. In the morning comes the Sabbath service, including a public reading from the Torah, the Five Books of Moses, and prophetic writings, and an additional service in memory of the Temple sacrifices on Sabbaths of old. Then home for lunch, and very commonly, a Sabbath nap, the sweetest part of the day. As the day wanes, the synagogue calls for a late afternoon service, and then comes a ceremony, *havdalah*, 'separation,' effected with spices, wine, and candlelight, between the holy time of the Sabbath and the ordinary time of the weekday.[24]

In addition to Sabbath observance, the traditional Jew also observes the several festivals that mark the seasons of the Jewish calendar year and commemorate significant events in Jewish history. The festivals mentioned here are the major holidays observed by Orthodox, Conservative, and Reform Judaism, the three principal twentieth-century movements.

Rosh Hashanah is the beginning of the year, New Year's Day, a fall festival originally associated with the harvest but now initiating a time of the Days of Awe, a week of remembrance, judgment, and penitence.

This period culminates in *Yom Kippur*, the Day of Atonement, the holiest day of the year, in which Jews confess their faults and ask for the forgiveness of God and their fellows (see Chapter 5). It is a 24-hour period of fasting and prayer, punctuated by confession. *Yom Kippur* is followed by *Sukkot*, a time of joy and thanksgiving, originally an autumn agricultural feast called the "festival of ingathering." God's preservation and shelter are symbolized by the construction of a booth or hut, covered with branches, fruits, and flowers, in which the family eats its meals. The hut now reminds the Jew that God made his people dwell in booths when he rescued them from Egypt and preserved them in their wanderings in the wilderness.

Two other principal festivals are *Pessah* (Passover) and *Shabuot*. Passover is a traditional spring festival celebrating the new life but also a festival of freedom commemorating the exodus of Israel from bondage in Egypt. The central ritual is the Passover *seder*, or family service, at table on the eve of the holiday. The father presides and, as he relates the story of deliverance, several symbols are present at the table as graphic reminders of both the renewal of life given by God (an egg and vegetable greens) and the suffering and cost of the exodus. The latter is represented by a dish of salt, symbolizing both the tears of slavery and the saltiness of the Red Sea; bitter herbs again remind those present of their earlier slavery; and *matzah* — or unleavened bread, baked like a cracker from flour and water — symbolizes the fact that the Israelites had to leave Egypt without preparation and had to take with them only unleavened bread.

The festival of *Shabuot*, or the Feast of Weeks (Pentecost), comes seven weeks after Passover and marks the end of the grain harvest and the sacrifice of first fruits. The rabbis later connected *Shabuot* with the giving of the commandments, or Torah, to Moses on Mount Sinai. Today, it is the day in which children are confirmed in a synagogue service to a life dedicated to the Torah.

Jewish life is also punctuated by a series of religious rites of passage—including the circumcision (*brit milah*) of the male child on the eighth day after birth and the advent of puberty, at which time the young boy undergoes the rite of *bar mitzvah* (*bar* means "son, or subject to," and *mitzvah* means God's commandment), a sign of allegiance to the Torah. Many congregations today have instituted a similar rite (*bat mitzvah*) for girls. In addition, there are, of course, rites prescribed for a traditional wedding as well as for sickness, funerals, and mourning. However, the observance that is perhaps most distinctive of Judaism, what can be called its "condensed symbol," is that associated with the *dietary laws*.

We know that most of the dietary observances followed today by traditional Jews have their origin in ancient taboos associated with hygiene. Yet they are also perceived by the devout as laws given by

God to sanctify life. Furthermore, they are an outward sign of a community of faith, an observance that helps bind the community around ancient practices. Observance of the dietary rules varies among modern practicing Jews. The Orthodox make every effort to observe these laws strictly, often at great personal inconvenience, indeed sacrifice. However, many Jews observe a *kosher* (fit and proper) table in their home but not when eating away from home. Others observe only some laws, such as the prohibition against eating pork, as a symbol of their participation in the community.

Strict adherence means a complex regimen involving the avoidance of certain prohibited foods and restrictions on foods that are permitted; this includes the proper preparation of meat and the uses of kitchen utensils and dishes. Permitted foods include all vegetables as well as animals that have "true hoofs, with clefts through the hoofs and that chews the cud" (Leviticus 11:3). This prohibits the eating of pigs and rabbits, for example. Also forbidden are a number of birds and fish that do not have fins and scales (Leviticus 11:9), for example, shellfish and eel. Permitted animals may not be eaten if they died on their own or were torn by other animals; blood and certain fats and sinews also may not be consumed. To be *kosher*, permitted animals must not be diseased and they must be slaughtered by a method approved by Jewish law. On the basis of the injunction "You shall not seethe the kid in his mother's milk" (Exodus, 23:19, 34:25; Deuteronomy 14:2), Jewish law prohibits eating meat and milk products together, cooking them together, or mixing them. Butter and milk cannot be served at a meal with meat. Moreover, different utensils and dishes must be used for milk and meat, which requires that a kosher family have two complete sets of kitchenware.

To the outsider, the meticulous following of the dietary laws, whose original meaning often is obscure, may well appear to be an obsolete irrelevance. However, to the observant Jew, these profuse requirements are meant to make God's presence known in one of life's fundamental activities. In carrying out this *mitzvah*, the Jew is made joyful in the knowledge that he or she is hallowing the day in following God's command. To be real, of course, commandment must be accompanied by faith and devotion. Commandment without devotion is dead.

The Way of Meditation and Insight

The three paths to salvation previously discussed are ways followed by millions of devout believers in all the major faiths. They are the *exoteric*, or common, means to salvation. The way of meditation and insight is an ancient path that also is open to all who are willing to follow its demanding discipline. However, just because of its rigorous conditions, it remains the *esoteric* way, that is, one pursued by a spiritual elite. Our Western word *meditation* does not adequately convey the meaning of the word in Hindu Sanskrit or Buddhist Pali. Meditation in these religions means a regimen of mental cultivation and development that proceeds, as we will see, through a series of moral and physical disciplines to the higher levels of mindfulness, concentration, and wisdom, or insight-enlightenment.

Those who follow this way believe that insight is absolutely crucial for the achievement of genuine spiritual freedom and release. But it is insight of a particular kind: enlightenment regarding the illusory division between subject and object, and between the self and the Ultimate. We select as examples two notable paths of meditation: (1) classical Yoga, expounded by the Indian sage Patañjali (second century B.C.E.) in his *Yoga Sutras* and, building on the techniques of Yoga, (2) the Eightfold Path of Theravada Buddhism.

The Yoga Techniques of Patañjali

Yoga (meaning "to yoke or join") is the physical and mental discipline, conjoined with certain philosophical principles, that constitutes one of the six orthodox philosophies of India. The yoga system was refined and combined with the Sankhya philosophy by Patañjali. Briefly, according to Sankhya (the oldest philosophy of India), the world is constituted by two uncreated eternal substances: *prakrti*, or indestructible matter, and *purusha*, or the infinite number of individual souls. The soul's entanglement in matter is the cause of its fall into misery and suffering due to its immersion in what is mutable or changing. Suffering, then, is due to a "want of discrimination," a failure to recognize the essential difference between soul and matter. Deliverance is the "discriminating knowledge" of the absolute difference between these eternal realities. Sankya describes the human situation and its "fall"; Yoga elaborates the techniques for the soul's release.

According to Patañjali, the soul's emancipation from illusion is achieved only through struggle, more particularly through **ascetic** techniques and meditation that alone can abolish our normal, illusory consciousness. Yoga begins then in action, ascetic practices, which lead on to concentration, meditation and, ultimately, wisdom. The point of departure is concentration on a single object, which can block or break the circuit or stream of the normal conscious and subconscious mind. However, concentration can be achieved only if the body is suitably prepared. Therefore, physiology plays a critical role in yoga. The body must be pure and without strain; the breathing must be rhythmical. The first four steps in the yogic technique prepare the body and mind for concentration. The first preliminary step involves the *yamas* ("restraints"), the five desire-killing vows: to abstain from killing living things (*ahimsa*), from lying, from stealing, from sensuality (unchastity), and from acquisitiveness. Along with these restraints, the yogi must practice *niyama*: a series of disciplines including physical cleanliness, ascetic mortifications, study, and devotion.

Yogic technique proper begins with the third step, *asana*, sitting in the proper posture. The **hathayoga** sutras describe innumerable possible *asanas*. The most famous of these postures is the *padmasana*, or lotus position, with the right foot on the left thigh and the left foot on the right thigh, with the chin resting on the chest and eyes focused on the nose. The purpose is to reduce physical effort and strain and to achieve a sense of physical weightlessness so that consciousness is no longer troubled by the presence of the body.

The fourth step is *pranayama*, the breathing discipline that eliminates respiratory effort and, again, reduces bodily activity to a few rhythmical processes. Now the yogi approaches the state of consciousness peculiar to sleep and the fifth step, *pratyahara*, the withdrawal of all senses from external objects. Mircea Eliade describes this withdrawal:

> Motionless, cadencing his respiration, fixing his eyes and his attention on a single point, the yogi experimentally steps outside the profane modality of existence. He begins to become autonomous in relation to the cosmos; he is no longer troubled by outer tensions; sensory activity no longer projects him outward toward the objects of the senses; the psychomental stream is no longer governed by distractions, automatisms, and memory: He is "concentrated," "unified." This withdrawal beyond the cosmos is accompanied by a plunge into the depths of himself ... [He] surrounds himself with increasingly powerful defences — in a word, he becomes invulnerable.[25]

The yogi no longer is distracted and troubled by sensory activity and now can concentrate (*dharana*) the mind, which is the beginning of the final, closely linked exercises leading to release. Concentration is fixation of *thought* on a single point with the help of an external object. It brings the mind to rest by emptying it of all else. It is called "conscious *samadhi*," or *samadhi* "with support." The mind is like the calm surface of a pond. The transition from concentration to meditation (*dhyana*) requires no new technique. *Dhyana* is the seventh step and is described by Patañjali as "a current of unified thought," free from all uncontrolled objects or associations. In meditation, a person is not conscious of consciousness; however, in *dhyana* the yogi can be interrupted by stimuli. In the eighth and final stage of *samadhi* "without supports," the yogi is invulnerable. The word *samadhi* means union, absorption, a full comprehension of being. It is spoken of as an unconscious trance, but this conveys too negative an impression. *Samadhi* is a state of superconsciousness. While it pre-

An Indian seated in motionless concentration in the lotus position. The senses are withdrawn from external distractions preparatory to *samadhi*, union or superconscious. (*Source*: Courtesy of Stock, Boston, Inc.)

supposes all the earlier disciplines and is not a gift of grace, it comes nevertheless without effort. It is like a rapture. Eliade describes it as follows:

> It would be wrong to regard this way of being of the spirit as a mere 'trance' in which consciousness was devoid of all content. [It] is not the 'absolute void.' . . . For, on the contrary, the consciousness is saturated at that moment by a direct and total intuition of being. . . . The yogi attains to deliverance: a 'death in life'. He is *jivanmukta*, 'the man delivered in life'. He no longer lives in time and under the control of time, but in an eternal present.[26]

The paradoxical nature of the release (*moksha*) achieved by *samadhi*, the "emptying" of being that at the same time is the "filling" of being in union or unity, is compared with other goals of salvation in Chapter 12. Suffice it to say here that it is one type of "rebirth" into a new, yet primordial sacred order.

Theravada Buddhism

We learned in Chapter 9 that in Theravada Buddhism, liberation from suffering (*dukkha*) comes through the cessation of craving (*tanha*), which is the cause of human unease and pain. The Fourth Noble

Truth preached by the Buddha was the way leading to cessation of suffering, what he called the Eightfold Path leading to Nirvana. This Middle Path (because it avoids the extremes of either pleasure-seeking or ascetic self-mortification) is a form of spiritual formation or therapy consisting of eight divisions:

1. Right understanding
2. Right aspiration
3. Right speech
4. Right action
5. Right livelihood
6. Right effort
7. Right mindfulness
8. Right concentration

The eight elements in the Buddha's path to enlightenment are not practiced in the above numerical order; rather, they are developed together, each assisting in the cultivation of the others. Together, they promote the three essentials of Buddhist discipline: *ethical conduct*, especially compassion (*karuna*); *mental discipline (samadhi)*; and *wisdom (prajna)*. Buddha insisted on the preliminary discipline of right association, since a person cannot expect to develop attitudes conducive to concentration and wisdom if he or she associates with others whose habits thwart spiritual progress.

Right understanding involves a deep or "penetrating" knowledge of the Four Noble Truths because these truths explain things as they really are, free of all illusion. Right aspiration involves a single-minded intention to be free of selfishness and desire, ill-will, and violence. Right speech, action, and livelihood are especially conducive to ethical conduct. Right speech includes abstention from (1) telling lies, (2) engaging in slander and backbiting, (3) using harsh and abusive language, and (4) indulging in idle speech and gossip. Disciples must become aware of how often they deviate from true and compassionate speech and why they do so. Right action involves a person's motives and intentions as well as outward behavior. Especially important is abstention from killing, stealing, and illegitimate sexual intercourse. A person's actions should be helpful and contribute to the welfare of others. Right livelihood reveals the radical character of Buddha's message. The disciple cannot expect to achieve liberation while engaging in a livelihood that brings harm and suffering to others. Five trades are specifically prohibited: trading in arms, in living beings, in flesh, in intoxicating drinks, and in poison. Neither may a person engage in military service or the work of a hunter. All permitted trades must be engaged in without deceit or usury. The moral conduct that is here called for is an indispensable basis for all further spiritual development.

Mental discipline is included in the final three categories of the Eightfold Path: Right effort, mindfulness, and concentration. Effort calls attention to the fact that liberation requires tremendous will-power and perseverance, especially in preventing and suppressing evil thoughts and actions and in nurturing and maintaining good thoughts and actions. But effort must not be hurried and fretful. It must be like the ox pulling itself out of deep mire; effort involves patience, a single-minded diligence without anxiety.

The Buddha admonished his disciples: "Be mindful!" Right-mindful-ness is not an occult mystical state. By mindfulness, the Buddha meant *attentiveness*, a diligent awareness regarding the activities of the body, the sensations, and the mind. To be mindful is to increase the intensity and quality of attention, to see things as they really are, purged of all false-hood. The numerous forms of mental discipline or meditation are dis-cussed in detail by the Buddha in the discourse entitled *Satipatthana-sutta* (*The Setting Up of Mindfulness*). It includes meditation on breathing and prescribes the yogic posture of sitting cross-legged. This and other yogic disciplines are proposed to develop concentration in preparation for the several stages of deep meditation (*dhyana*), necessary for achiev-ing "penetration" or liberating insight, including the realization of Nirvana. In the fourth stage of *dhyana*, all sensations have disappeared and the person rests in a state of equanimity and pure awareness. Illusion and craving are now overcome. With the extinction of desire (*tanha*) and attachment, the Absolute Truth, Nirvana, is realized: "deathlessness, peace, the unchanging state."

While the ways proposed by Patañjali and the Buddha are based on different and even conflicting metaphysical doctrines, they are one in insisting that the path to salvation is through the cultivation of the mind by meditation and in the achievement of insight or enlighten-ment. It is a strenuous discipline of self-help. During the last days of his life, the Buddha underlined this point:

> And whosoever, Ananda ... shall be an island unto themselves, a refuge unto themselves, shall betake themselves of no eternal refuge, but holding fast to the truth as their island and refuge. ... it is they, Ananda, who shall reach the very topmost height—but they must be anxious to learn.[27]

At the beginning of this chapter, we noted that the religions of the world offer a variety of "ways" or paths of deliverance from the suffering, the moral guilt, estrangement, and finitude that characterize human life. Furthermore, we noted that the great traditions include, in one form or another, all the classic ways—that is, of faith, devotion, disciplined action or duty, and meditation and spiritual insight. The "ways" are not exclusive, and the life of any single believer—especially the great saints and sages—may reflect all these patterns of religious experience and response. However, each way does often appeal to a quite different religious need and spiritual temperament and, therefore, it is quite natural that some persons and some cultural settings would regard a particular path or discipline as especially responsive to their religious requirements and their understanding of Ultimate Reality.

Having looked at several specific examples of these classic "ways," we are now prepared to examine the actual goals of salvation or enlightenment that are envisioned by the world's religions. We will describe, with examples, what is meant by such different concepts as Psychic Wholeness, the Messianic Age, Paradise, Immortality, Resurrection, *Samadhi*, and Nirvana.

Notes

1. Martin Luther, *A Commentary on St. Paul's Epistle to the Galatians.*
2. M. Luther, "Two Kinds of Righteousness." *Luther's Works* 31, ed. by Harold J. Grimm (Philadelphia, 1957), p. 298f.
3. M. Luther, "Freedom of a Christian." *Martin Luther: Selections from His Writings,* ed. John Dillenberger (New York, 1961), pp. 55, 58–59.
4. M. Luther, *Commentary on Galatians.* Dillenberger, *Selections,* p. 141.
5. M. Luther, *Commentary on Galatians.* Cited in Philip S. Watson, *Let God be God* (Philadelphia, 1947), pp. 47–48.
6. *Shinshu Shōgyō Zensho* II (Kyoto, 1953), p. 527. Cited in Alfred Bloom, *Shinran's Gospel of Pure Grace* (Tucson, 1965) p. 29. I am dependent on Bloom's excellent study for my exposition of Shinran's teaching.
7. Bloom, *Shinran's Gospel,* p. 32.
8. *Shinshu Shōgyō Zensho* II, pp. 202–3. Cited in Bloom, *Shinran's Gospel,* p. 66.
9. Winston King, *Introduction to Religion: A Phenomenological Approach* (New York, 1968), p. 337. King's analysis of the "discipline of devotion" has been helpful at this point.
10. *Bhagavad Gita* XI. Cited in Ainslie T. Embree, *The Hindu Tradition* (New York, 1966), pp. 127–28.
11. *The Complete Works of Saint Teresa* I, trans. and ed. by E. Allison Peers (New York, 1946), pp. 119f., 121.
12. A. J. Arberry, *Sufism* (New York, 1950), pp. 53ff., 62.
13. *In Praise of Krishna,* trans. by Edward C. Dimock, Jr. and Denise Levertov (New York, 1967), pp. 56f., 65f.
14. *Bhagavad Gita* I:40–42. Cited in Embree, *The Hindu Tradition,* pp. 83–84.
15. *Manu Smriti* X. Embree, *The Hindu Tradition,* p. 94.
16. *Manu Smriti* I and X. Embree, *The Hindu Tradition,* pp. 79–80.
17. I 1, 2, 3, 6. Embree, *The Hindu Tradition,* pp. 85–86.
18. *Manu Smriti* VI:2–8, 25. Embree, *The Hindu Tradition,* p. 91.
19. Embree, *The Hindu Tradition,* p. 93.
20. Sirdar Iqbal Ali Shah, *Lights of Asia* (London, 1934), p. 29f.
21. Kenneth Cragg, *The House of Islam* (Belmont, Ca., 1969), p. 48.

22. Kemal A. Faruki, *Islam, Today and Tomorrow* (Karachi, 1974), p. 264ff. Cited in Cragg, pp. 55–56.
23. Malcolm X, *The Autobiography of Malcolm X* (New York, 1965), pp. 327f., 341–42, 349.
24. Jacob Neusner, *The Way of Torah: An Introduction to Judaism* (Belmont, Ca., 1970), p. 27.
25. Mircea Eliade, *Patanjali and Yoga* (New York, 1975), pp. 81–82.
26. Eliade, *Patanjali*, pp. 113–14.
27. *Maha-parinbbana-sutta*. Cited in Nyanaponika Thera, *The Heart of Buddhist Meditation* (London, 1969), pp. 83–84.

Review Questions

1. Among the classic ways of liberation or salvation is the way of grace through faith. Describe the major features of Luther's experience of being liberated and "made righteous" by grace through faith. Include his understanding of the role of the law—that is, good works that are commanded of grace, and of the true motivation for doing good works.
2. While devotionalism is often a means or response to other ways of salvation, it does have its own distinct characteristics. Indicate the several features that characterize the way of devotion as described in this chapter.
3. The lives of the three "twice-born" castes of Hinduism are encompassed by numerous social and ceremonial duties, all of which are devoted to the knowledge and liberation of the soul. Describe the four classes, or castes, of Hinduism and the four stages of life that are elaborated in the Hindu Code of Manu.
4. The Islamic tradition includes all of the classic "ways" to salvation, but it is viewed as normatively a religion of *Shari'ah*, of ethical and ritual duty. Describe the five "pillars," or principal obligations, expected of the faithful Muslim.
5. In Judaism, redemption or the sanctifying of life is by means of *halakhah*, that is, those rules relating to all aspects of life, including the keeping of the Sabbath and the yearly festivals. Indicate the main features of some of the Jewish festivals and what they signify or commemorate.
6. The way of action or obligation is based, in part, on the insight that we humans are shaped by our daily or habitual gestures and activities. Would you agree that religious enlightenment or the sanctifying of life would be difficult, if not impossible, without the routine of holy obligation?
7. The way of meditation and insight is a difficult path requiring a series of physical and mental disciplines. Without having to refer to every single step (or the Sanskrit and Pali terms), describe the major practices or divisions of Patañjali's yoga technique to achieve *samadhi* or the Buddha's Fourth Noble Truth, that is, the Eightfold Path to Nirvana.

Suggestions for Further Reading

For general discussions of the classic ways of faith, devotion, obligation or duty, and insight, see the following:

KING, WINSTON, *Introduction to Religion* (New York: Harper & Row, 1968), Chs. 12–15.

STRENG, FREDERICK, *Understanding Religious Life* (Belmont, CA: Wadsworth Publishing Co., 1985), Chs. 2–5.

For the way of grace through faith, see the following:

BLOOM, ALFRED, *Shinran's Gospel of Pure Grace* (Tucson: University of Arizona Press, 1965).

DILLENBERGER, JOHN (ed.), *Martin Luther: Selections From His Writings* (New York: Doubleday, 1961). See, in particular, "Commentary on St. Paul's Epistle to the Galatians," "The Freedom of a Christian," and "Two Kinds of Righteousness."

JAMES, WILLIAM, *The Varieties of Religious Experience* (New York: Collier Books, 1961), Chs. 9–10.

For the way of devotion, see the following:

ARBERRY, A. J., *Sufism* (London: Allen and Unwin, 1950).

DATTA, A. K., *Bhaktiyoga* (Bombay: Bharatiya Vidya Bhavan, 1959).

EMBREE, A. T., *The Hindu Tradition* (New York: Random House, 1966), Part Four, "The Traditions and the People's Faith."

PADWICK, CONSTANCE E., *Muslim Devotions* (London: 1961).

TERESA, ST., *Complete Works* II (New York: Sheed, 1949), "Conceptions of the Love of God."

For the way of religious obligation and duty, see the following:

"The Dharmasastras," *The Cultural Heritage of India*, 2d ed. (Calcutta: Ramakrishna Mission, 1962).

MARTIN, RICHARD, *Islam: A Cultural Perspective* (Englewood Cliffs, N.J.: Prentice Hall, 1982).

TREPP, LEO, *Judaism: Development and Life* (Belmont, CA: Wadsworth Publishing Co., 1982). Part III, "Life as Mitzvah."

For the way of meditation and insight, see the following:

ELIADE, MIRCEA, *Patanjali and Yoga* (New York: Schocken Books, 1975).

JAMES, WILLIAM, *The Varieties of Religious Experience* (New York: Collier Books, 1961), Chs. 16–17.

THERA, NYANAPONIKA, *The Heart of Buddhist Meditation* (London: Rider, 1969).

SUZUKI, D. T., *Zen Buddhism* (New York: Doubleday, 1956).

Also see the Suggestions for Further Reading on comparative studies in mysticism, Chapter 12.

Goals of Liberation and Salvation

OVERVIEW

The word *salvation* comes from the Greek verb *sozein* (to save). In the Latin West, the word *salvus* was used to suggest that salvation is a process of healing, of making whole. However, the biblical Hebrew word that is most commonly translated as salvation implies a lack of constraint and conveys the sense of a deliverance or redemption. Salvation, then, is the process of being delivered, redeemed, or liberated from an enemy, danger, sin, pollution, finitude, or "the Devil's barter"—whatever is considered evil or threatening.

The phenomenologist van der Leeuw describes salvation as "Power experienced as Good." He points out that it implies a range of concepts such as "whole, complete, perfect, healthy, strong, vigorous, welfare, well-being, as contrasted with suffering and misery, and in some connections bliss, both earthly and heavenly."[1] The breadth of meaning conveyed by salvation is extraordinarily wide. In addition, the experience of salvation can be considered from a number of perspectives. Many religions understand it as both a personal and a cosmic process or event. Moreover, salvation is both a present reality and a future hope; it is described as involving the individual but also the community. Furthermore, it is a condition portrayed as both this-worldly and as a wholly transcendent, other-worldly state of affairs. These various modes of salvation are compared in the typology used for our analysis in this chapter.

Despite the numerous meanings that can be given to the word *salvation*, one thing stands out as certain. Salvation or liberation is the essential goal of religion. Religion is the means, the vehicle, or the process by which we are delivered from the profane world's disorder, meaninglessness, and evil. It is religion that redeems us from social

319

chaos and 'establishes our cosmos. On the personal level, it is the means by which we are freed from all those conditions that threaten and limit our very being. Salvation is so central to the nature of religion that one writer has defined religion simply as "a means to ultimate transformation."[2] Religion involves much more, of course, but personal and cosmic salvation is its fundamental purpose and goal.

Our analysis of salvation begins with entirely this-worldly, humanistic conceptions—for example, in the contemporary psychotherapeutic "cure of souls" and in some Eastern spiritual therapies, such as Zen Buddhism. A second form of salvation looks beyond personal psychic wholeness to a future but *this-worldly* liberation of the entire social order through the coming of a Utopian or Messianic Age. Here, we shall explore in some detail the development of biblical messianic eschatology since it has played a critical role in our Western consciousness of history and of the future. Chinese Marxism is proposed as an example of a modern secularization of certain features of biblical messianism.

A very different conception of salvation is found in those religions that look to salvation in a future *other-worldly* afterlife, conceived either as a rather insubstantial "shade" of the physical self, as a disembodied immortal soul, or as one or another form of resurrected body. We shall review these various ideas in ancient Egypt and Greece, as well as in Judaism and Christianity at the beginnings of the Christian movement. We shall also discuss the significant change that takes place in the medieval Christian view of salvation, involving the immediate translation of the individual to Heaven or to Hell at the time of death. Belief in a Heaven and a Hell are not, of course, uniquely Christian or even Western. We shall look at depictions of Paradise in Muslim and in Mahayana Buddhist scriptures, as well as in Christianity. The mystical, yet rather different concepts of the Beatific Vision and of Eternal Life as a present reality are also examined.

The last mode of salvation explored is that associated with various types of monism, for example, in Hindu Vedanta and in certain interpretations of Buddhist Nirvana. In both instances, meditation and concentration are seen as leading to the release or to the absorption of the self in union with Brahman or Nirvana—a state of perfect emptiness, of imperturbable and inexpressible bliss.

Psychic Wholeness and a Healthy Social Order

We begin with concepts of salvation that are radically this-worldly, nontheistic, and entirely humanistic. Many thoughtful contemporaries reject the belief that the amelioration of evil and human sorrow is dependent on powers or agents that are transcendent of human life itself. Nor do they believe that hope should be placed in a future, other-worldly salvation. The cosmos as such, they believe, is meaning-less—the accidental collocation of atoms—and all is finally destined to extinction. This view is expressed with feeling and force by Ber-trand Russell in his celebrated essay "A Free Man's Worship":

> No heroism, no intensity of thought and feeling, can preserve an individual life beyond the grave; that all the labours of the ages, all the devotion, all the inspiration, all the noonday brightness of human genius, are destined to extinction in the vast death of the solar system, and that the whole temple of man's achievement must inevitably be buried beneath the debris of a universe in ruins—all these things, if not quite beyond dispute, are yet so nearly certain, that no philosophy which rejects them can hope to stand.[3]

The cosmic pessimism of Russell's vision did not nor has not inevita-bly given rise to personal or even historical despair. On the contrary, it has shocked many persons into an acute need to shape their own meaning in life.

"I for one," writes the philosopher E. D. Klemke, "am *glad* that the universe has no meaning, for thereby is *man all the more glorious*. I willingly accept the fact that external meaning is non-existent... for this leaves me free to *forge my own meaning*."[4]

For Russell and Klemke, the amelioration of personal suffering and social conflict rests entirely on the application of human reason and creativity. However, it would be stretching the word to claim that Russell's humanistic creed is religious. His confidence in the improve-ment of individual life is cautious and his hope for society is equally guarded, if not altogether skeptical. Russell's convictions are thoroughly humanistic but hardly utopian.

There are humanists, however, who hold out a vision of the future for individuals and society that is both deeply spiritual and *utopian*. The last half century in the West has witnessed what Philip Rieff calls "the triumph of the therapeutic," the transference of the "cure of souls" from a priest to the psychotherapist and from the church to the "encounter group." The latter, like the former, offers oppor-tunities for confession, resistance to temptation ("ego strength"), heightened awareness, and reconciliation with our fellows. Psychologi-cal therapy appears to offer our scientific age a means of liberation and healing without the traditional theological constraints of dogma and church authority, or belief in a life after death. Salvation is here and is now! Erich Fromm refers to the religious dimensions of the psychoanalytic cure of souls as those that enable the individual "to gain the faculty to see the truth, to love, to become free and responsible . . . the wondering, the marveling, the becoming aware of life and of one's own existence."[5]

The religious character of the therapeutic movement is evident in organizations such as Transcendental Meditation, est, the Esalen institutes, "T" groups, Transactional analysis, Integrity therapy, Scientology, and numerous other forms of popular therapy. Closely related to these spiritual psychologies is the new interest in Eastern religions, especially Yoga, Taoism, and Zen. What they share in common is the romantic feeling of the pleasure to be found in the joys of the body and the earth, a confidence in the feelings, a positive attitude, an interest in the present, and a distrust of institutional religion and what they see as the inhibitions or "uptightness" of the Protestant work ethic. Among the gurus of the new therapeutic are Alan Watts (Zen), Fritz Perls (Gestalt therapy), Ida Rolf (massage therapy), Carl Rogers (sensitivity training), and Abraham Maslow ("peak experiences").

Maslow (1908–1970) is a leader of the movement known as "humanistic psychology." While he is critical of traditional religious supernaturalism, he recognizes that the human process of growth and "self-actualization" involves certain "peak experiences." These transcendent occasions that bring life new insight, joy, and creativity, are not unlike those experiences described by the great religious mystics. In fact, Maslow believes that the older reports of prophets and saints "phrased in terms of supernatural revelation, were, in fact perfectly natural human peak-experiences."[6] The mystic ecstasy of a St. Teresa and the "peak experience" of a mother flooded with joy as she holds her newborn infant, are essentially the same—what Maslow calls the "core-religious experience," or "transcendent experience." According to Maslow, most persons, but not all, experience peak or transcendent moments that are not simply "emotional highs" but genuinely cognitive, transformative events. These spiritual experiences are triggered, however, by entirely natural, even everyday occasions, such as engaging in an athletic contest, listening to waves crash against a rocky shore, watching a dance performance, or tending a flower garden. For Maslow, religion must be taken out of the narrow context of institutional churches, clergy, and dogma—a single department of life—and be recognized as a quality or state of mind achievable in almost any activity.

In his study of the peak experiences of a large number of individuals, Maslow discovered that they have many of the characteristics we associate with traditional religious experience. For example, "the whole universe is perceived as an integrated and unified whole . . . all of one piece and that one has a place in it . . . one belongs to it." This is accompanied by a new, total kind of visual concentration in which "things become equally important rather than ranged in a hierarchy from very important to quite important." The recognition of everything as equally valuable holds also for people: "the person is unique, the person is sacred, one person in principle is worth as much as any other person." This new cognition also "allows the individual to become more objective and detached, ego-transcending, self-forgetful, egoless, unselfish." Maslow furthermore has found that peak experiences change a person's sense of time and space. This person "may feel a day passing as if it were minutes or also a minute so intensely lived that it might feel like a day or a year or an eternity even."[7] The emotions of wonder, awe, humility, gratitude, creature feeling, and exaltation are often reported as the aftereffect of these unique occasions.

Maslow insists that genuine knowledge is attained in peak experiences. It is a new awareness that permanently affects a person's attitude toward life and death, "valuing reality in a different way, seeing things from a new perspective . . . the miraculous 'suchness' of things . . . which contrasts with what can only be called 'normal blindness.'" These natural peak experiences can therefore teach values and virtues previously thought to be the unique province of traditional religion: acceptance, unselfishness, seeing things under the aspect of eternity, reverence, love, and innocence.

Maslow believes that a psychologically healthy society is possible, and he envisions a utopia called Eupsychia. It will be brought about by a wide-scale application of psychotherapy since persons who have undergone therapy have greater self-knowledge, are "more perceptive, more spontaneous . . . come out a better citizen, a better husband, a better wife, certainly a better person."[8] Maslow again rejects the idea that these social values must be discovered outside the self, in God or in a sacred text.

> What I am doing is to explore the theory that you can find the values by which mankind must live . . . by digging into the best people in depth. I believe that I can find ultimate values which are right for mankind by observing the best of mankind. . . . I do not say we should look for goodness because we *ought* to, or because there is some principle outside of ourselves that tells us to. I am saying that if you examine human beings fairly, you will find that they themselves have innate knowledge of and yearning for goodness and beauty. . . . Our task is to create an environment where more and more of these innate instincts can find expression. This is what would characterize Eupsychia.[9]

A number of therapists have discovered an ally in Eastern spiritual techniques and meditation. Erich Fromm, for example, sees important resemblances between psychoanalysis and Zen Buddhism. The essence of Zen is *satori*, enlightenment or the acquiring of a new point of view. D. T. Suzuki, the foremost interpreter of Zen to the West, defines *satori* as "an intuitive looking into the nature of things in contradistinction to the analytical or logical understanding of it. . . . Or we may say that with *satori* our entire surroundings are viewed from quite an unexpected angle of perception."[10]

Satori is a flashing, momentary intuition, like an uncoerced discovery that, like Maslow's peak experiences, overcomes our normal dualistic perception of the world, transforming the entire personality. While not fully explicable, the instantaneous experience of *satori* is both authoritative and affirmative. It produces a sense of great release, joy, and exaltation that accompanies the breaking up of a person's dualistic, egocentric, acquisitive orientation. Suzuki describes the peculiar effect of *satori* as follows:

> All your mental activities will now be working in a different key, which will be more satisfying, more peaceful, more full of joy than anything you ever experienced before. The tone of life will be altered. . . . The spring flower will look prettier, and the mountain stream runs cooler and more transparent.[11]

Suzuki speaks of the aim of Zen enlightenment, in terms both religious and psychological, as "the way from bondage to freedom." He describes how Zen liberates a person's energies, normally cramped and distorted, so that they can find a creative channel for activity. The object of Zen, he says, is "to save us from going crazy or being crippled." This, he continues, is what "I mean by freedom, giving free play to all the creative and benevolent impulses inherently lying in our hearts."[12]

Struck by the similarities between Suzuki's description of Zen and psychoanalysis, Erich Fromm characterizes the psychic import of *satori* in the following terms:

> I would say that it is a state in which the person is completely tuned to the reality outside and inside of him, a state in which he is fully aware of it and fully grasps it. *He* is aware of it—that is, not his brain, nor any other part of his organism, but *he*, the whole man. He is aware of *it*; not as an object over there which he grasps with his thought, but *it*, the flower, the dog, the man, in its, or his, full reality. He who awakes is open and responsive to the world, and he can be open and responsive because he has given up holding on to himself as a thing, and thus has become empty and ready to receive. To be enlightened means 'the full awakening of the total personality to reality' . . . to have attained a fully 'productive orientation.'[13]

The goal of salvation proposed by Maslow, Fromm, and other therapists concerned with "self-actualization" is thoroughly humanistic and this-worldly. Salvation is achieved not by recourse to transcendent powers or a sacred code of behavior but by calling on a person's own innate rational and creative resources. For these spiritual therapies, the deepest level of human healing and liberation takes place in the unleashing of the human potential for goodness and community responsibility, all of which come with genuine self-knowledge.

A Messianic, or Utopian, Age

There are religious faiths, both traditional and secular, that look beyond the mere psychic healing of individuals to a future, this-worldly redemption of the social order itself through the coming of a Messianic, or Golden, Age. What these religions share is a view of salvation that is *future, this-worldly*, and *communal*. This salvational type was previously described in the discussion of revolutionary millenarianism—for example, see the Melanesian Cargo cults in Chapter 10. Two other examples will, therefore, suffice here: ancient Israelite eschatology and contemporary Marxism, a form of modern, secular eschatology.

Eschatology has to do with the end, or goal (the *telos*), of personal life or history and not simply with its temporal conclusion (*finis*). Since the eschaton is often depicted as occurring in the future, eschatological beliefs are frequently mythological, that is, imaginative visions derived from past experience and present convictions about the nature of God or Ultimate Reality, and about man and the historical process. Whether consciously or not, as self-transcendent beings we take some attitude toward the *telos* of life and history. In fact, the philosopher Nikolai Berdyaev ventured to claim that "it is only the future which gives human life meaning in the present." In any case, it is true that we do not decide *whether* we will have an eschatology; rather, we decide *which* convictions about life's goal we will embrace as most congruent with our experience and our deepest hopes.

Ancient Israel's Messianic Hope

It sometimes comes as a surprise to learn that the ancient Israelites did not hold a belief in individual life after physical death in the sense of personal self-awareness. They did, of course, believe in redemption, and it was a belief founded on certain religious convictions. Early Israel believed, first, that God had created the world for a purpose. The creation is essentially good but, because of Israel's "hardness of heart," it had forsworn God's purpose and his covenant commandments. Israel's God, Yahweh, had therefore afflicted Israel with "the rod" of his righteous anger: foreign oppression, even exile from the holy land of Palestine. Nevertheless, Yahweh's loving kindness and his covenant with Israel was not forsaken, for he had favored Israel as his chosen instrument, "a light unto the nations," to bring redemption and peace to the world. God's purpose for creation could not, therefore, be frustrated forever; God's redemption would come in some future time. While Israel's hope for a future, earthly kingdom of peace and prosperity was complex and various, it took two distinct forms in the period between the great prophets of the eighth century B.C.E. and the domination of Israel by the Persians, Greeks, and Romans after 500 B.C.E. The earliest expression of Israelite eschatology is basically *nationalistic*.

ISRAEL'S NATIONALISTIC HOPE   Israel's national hope was shaped by the belief in what was called the "day of Yahweh." Initially, it was conceived as a period of unbroken prosperity and glory inaugurated by Yahweh's victorious overthrow of Israel's enemies. It was Israel's duty to worship Yahweh and Yahweh's duty to protect Israel. In the eighth century, however, this rather simple idea gave way to the prophetic vision of a coming kingdom of God comprised only of an ethically regenerated Israelite nation, a community joined together by its devotion to the divine Commandments. Prophets such as Amos, Jeremiah, and Isaiah stood in the Temple and before the kings and rebuked the people for their unfaithfulness to the Covenant. They proclaimed that for Israel the "day of Yahweh" would not be light but darkness—a time of judgment on the nation. The land would be burned up; the people would be as fuel for a fire (Isaiah 9:19).

> And the haughtiness of man shall be humbled,
>   and the pride of men shall be brought low,
> And Yahweh alone will be exalted in that day.
> *(Isaiah 2:17)*

However, Yahweh's purpose was not simply destructive. Through the nation's suffering, Isaiah saw Yahweh purging the moral dross so that Jerusalem might become a place of true righteousness:

> I will turn my hand against you
>   and will smelt away your dross
>   as with lye
>   and remove all your alloy.
>
> And I will restore your judges as at
>   the first,
> and your counselors as at the beginning.
>
> Afterwards you shall be called the
>   city of righteousness,
> the faithful city.

> Zion shall be redeemed by justice,
> and those in her who repent, by
> righteousness.
>
> *(Isaiah 1:25–27)*

The prophet Zephaniah (628–22 B.C.E.) also prophesied that the immanent "day of Yahweh" would be "a day of wrath," "a day of darkness and gloom." He held out no hope for "the shameless nation" Israel. And yet, like Isaiah, he appealed to a righteous remnant:

> Seek Yahweh, all ye humble of the land,
> who do his commandments;
> seek righteousness, seek humility;
> perhaps you may be hidden
> on the day of the wrath of Yahweh.
>
> *(Zephaniah 2:3)*

Beyond the wrath of the day of Yahweh, the great pre-exilic prophets saw the dawn of a new era, inspired by the pious remnant of the nation Israel. They looked to God's agent, "the anointed one," a king who would come and restore the nation to its earlier glory under the great King David. The nations of the earth would beat their swords into ploughshares and the desert would blossom like a rose.

ISRAEL'S APOCALYPTIC HOPE   With the Exile of the Jews to Babylon (593 B.C.E.), a shift in Israel's eschatolgical hope began to take place. Israel's earlier "foes from the north" were now envisioned as the hosts of Gog, that is, the mysterious forces of cosmic evil. The warfare with evil now is perceived as the final battle of history. This new eschatology is evident, for example, in the prophecy of Zechariah (515 B.C.E.) who wrote at the time of the return of the Jewish exiles to Jerusalem. Zechariah envisions the restoration of the Jewish nation under the joint leadership of the High Priest and the messianic Davidic king. His oracles, couched in secret, symbolic language, speak of the coming consummation of history in a priestly utopia. Yahweh's foes will be destroyed and the kingdom established. Zechariah sees Zerubbabel, the Jewish governor, as Yahweh's Anointed One, the Davidic Messiah, "a shoot [branch] from the stump of Jesse." It is he who will rebuild the Temple.

> Thus says Yahweh of hosts: 'Behold the man whose name is the Branch, for he shall grow up in his place, and he shall build the temple of Yahweh. It is he who shall build the Temple of Yahweh, and shall bear royal honor, and shall sit and rule upon his throne. And there shall be a priest upon his throne, and peaceful understanding shall be between them both.'
>
> *(Zechariah 6:12–13)*

The prophetic oracles of Zechariah and later postexilic writers are call apocalyptic (from the Greek *apokalyptein*, meaning "to uncover or reveal"). They are a form of eschatological vision that is especially prominent during times of persecution and historical pessimism. The postexilic Jews had become increasingly doubtful about Israel's worldly glory as, again and again, Israel felt her hopes crushed by the Persians, then by the Greeks under the Seleucid kings, and finally by the Romans with Pompey's conquest of Jerusalem in 63 B.C.E. Under the influence of these historical disasters, Jewish writers began to modify Israel's earlier nationalistic, optimistic eschatology into a vast, imaginative, pessimistic vision of the end time.

According to these apocalyptic writers, who were influenced by Persian dualism (see Chapter 7), this earth or "the present age," the scene of so much misery and suffering, is now under the dominion of evil powers, with Satan at their head. The Powers of Darkness are successfully warring against Yahweh and the angels of light. However, this present, evil state of affairs will not continue forever; God will intervene and vindicate his kingly rule. But, humanly speaking, there is nothing that can be done; God alone is able to destroy the powers that rule this present, evil age. The apocalyptic prophets were certain that the turning point between this age and the new aeon was near at hand; this age was moving relentlessly toward its predetermined final encounter and the victory of God's kingdom. According to these writers, it was vitally important to recognize the signs of the approaching end. It would be heralded, for example, by a series of "messianic woes" when satanic evil would reach a climax in the coming of an anti-Messiah. Nature would run amuck; there would be fire on the earth; unnatural births, and cosmic disturbances (IV Ezra 5:4:12). Finally, the end would come when Satan is defeated and the faithful are rescued and exalted. *The Assumption of Moses*, a work contemporary with the New Testament, is a particularly good example of Jewish apocalyptic:

> And then his [God's] kingdom shall appear throughout all
>   his creation,
> And then Satan shall be no more.
> And sorrow shall depart with him.
> Then the hands of the angel shall be filled
> Who has been appointed chief,
> And he shall forthwith avenge them of their enemies.
> For the Heavenly One will arise from his royal throne,
> And he will go forth from his holy habitation
> With indignation and wrath on account of his sons.
> And the earth shall tremble: to its confines shall it
>   be shaken.
> And the high mountains shall be made low

And the hills shall be shaken and fall.
And the horns of the sun shall be broken and he
    shall be turned into darkness;
And the moon shall not give her light, and be turned
    wholly into blood. . . .
And the fountains of waters shall fail,
And the rivers shall dry up.
For the Most High will arise, the Eternal God alone,
And he will appear to punish the Gentiles,
And he will destroy all their idols.
Then thou, O Israel, shalt be happy. . . .
And God will exalt thee,
And he will cause thee to approach to the heaven of the stars,
In the place of their habitation.
And thou shalt look from on high and shalt see thy enemies
    in Gehenna,
And thou shalt recognize them and rejoice,
And thou shalt give thanks and confess thy Creator.

(10:1–10)

The final judgment is vividly portrayed in apocalyptic writings such as Daniel and IV Ezra. God comes forth as the "Ancient of Days," and he takes his seat on the throne, surrounded by his court of angels. The books that record the deeds of men are brought in and the judgment is given. The righteous are raised to participate in the eternal messianic kingdom. The writers portray the life of the righteous variously. In Daniel, the kingdom is on earth, but in other writers it is depicted as the New Jerusalem brought down from Heaven. In I Enoch, the abode of the righteous is entirely transcendent in Heaven above. The fate of the ungodly is also variously portrayed, but in each case no longer as a neutral abode of the departed but rather as a place of eternal punishment: Sheol, Gehenna, the Furnace, or Abyss of Fire.

The agent of salvation also takes on new forms. A new savior emerges, a heavenly, supernatural figure called the Son of Man (Enoch 46:1–6; 48:2–10 and IV Ezra 13), who comes to inaugurate the new age. In Daniel 7, the "one like unto a son of man" is a corporate figure symbolizing the "saints of the Most High," the righteous and faithful martyrs who bear witness that God is inaugurating his messianic kingdom in the end time.

We can see in these postexilic Jewish apocalyptic writings the appearance of themes—son of man, last judgment, resurrection, and Heaven and Hell—that are common to early Christian literature, for example, in the Gospels and the Book of Revelation. These concepts certainly reflect a more radically transcendent and cosmic Jewish eschatology than was present in Israel's earlier nationalistic hope. However, the record shows that many schools of thought struggled within Judaism in the century before the Christian era. This-worldly, political messianism competes with more-dualistic, cosmic visions, as is evident in the war of the Jewish **Maccabean** revolutionaries (168 B.C.E.) and the presence of the political **Zealot** party in Palestine in the first century of the Christian era. A psalm from the late Maccabean period reflects the continuing influence of Jewish political messianism:

> Behold, O Lord, and raise up unto
>   them their king, the son of David,
> All the time in which thou seest, O God, that he may
>   reign over Israel, thy servant.
> And gird him with strength, that he may
>   shatter unrighteous rulers,
> And that he may purge Jerusalem from nations
>   that trample her down to destruction.
>   *(Psalms of Solomon 15:21–25)*

At the dawn of the Christian era arose a Jewish party called the Pharisees that, like the earlier **Hasidim**, practiced a strict devotion to the Law—including the dietary rules—that separated the Jewish community from the Gentile world. The Pharisees believed that Moses had promulgated a body of oral law that was meant to guide the interpretation of the written Torah. This oral law, codified in the **Mishnah**, was later expanded into a vast library known as the **Talmud**. It was this Pharisaic or Talmudic Judaism that became the normative Judaism of the postbiblical era—and remains so today in Orthodoxy. Like the ancient Hasidim of Daniel's time, Talmudic Judaism looks with longing for the coming of the Messianic Age. However, Orthodoxy's devotion to the Torah has, on the whole, caused it to stand apart from radical forms of apocalypticism and political messianism. Furthermore, unlike certain movements within Christianity, Jewish belief in the resurrection of the body and a future life have not usually been thought of apart from participation in a redeemed messianic community. While the end time of history may look beyond the powers of history itself for the redemption inaugurated by the Messiah, the kingdom of God is essentially this-worldly. This is reflected in Israel's confidence that the coming Messianic Age will bring forth a new creation, a perfected world of redeemed men and women.

Chinese Marxism

Marxist criticism of religion is well known, as is the repression of religious practice in many communist countries. Karl Marx spoke of religion as "the opium of the people" and insisted that "to abolish religion as the illusory happiness of the people is to demand their real happiness"[14] through revolutionary socioeconomic change. Lenin believed that religion was a particularly potent weapon in the exploitation of the poor by the ruling class. "Religion," he wrote, "is one of the forms of spiritual oppression which everywhere weighs down heavily upon the masses of the people," for they "are taught by religion to be submissive and patient while here on earth, and to take comfort in the hope of a heavenly reward."[15]

Perhaps because Marxist opposition to religion is so commonplace, the religious dimensions of Marxist ideology and practice are not fully appreciated. Marx's prophecy of a new age of history in which human alienation would be abolished with the inauguration of a classless society can itself be viewed as an extraordinary visionary eschatology of secular redemption. The biblical analogies in Marx's apocalyptic prophecy are striking. Like biblical apocalypse, Marx sees history as driving relentlessly toward a grand crisis. He has his own conception of the *imago Dei* in human creativity and productivity, but also a Fall and expulsion from a mythical paradisical state with the appearance of egoistic acquisitiveness and alienation brought on by the division of labor, private property, and capitalism. Marx also sees the imperialist powers as the "rod" of God's (history's) anger—that is, instruments contributing to the final goal of history in the proletarian revolution. Marxist history moves through several ages, or "dispensations": ancient slavery, medieval feudalism, and modern capitalism in which evil estrangement grows apace. Marx's anti-Messiah is capitalism and his chosen elect, the "saving remnant," the bearer of the future age, is the proletariat. Marx saw the "solution" to the riddle of history as imminent and read the "signs of the times" as omens of the end time when the proletarian revolution would bring down the anti-Messiah (capitalism) and inaugurate the New Jerusalem, the classless society. Here, Marx believed, history would reach its *telos*, or end. Marx can be viewed quite legitimately as the prophet of a new secular religion.

In this century, the Chinese cult of Mao Tse-tung illustrates most dramatically the religious features of Marx's political ideology. Maoism was an authentic way of salvation for millions of Chinese, from peasants to intellectuals. Mao Tse-tung actually spoke of Chinese Marxism as "the religion of the people," so long, that is, as it remained faithful to its original revolutionary goals. "When we say," he wrote, " 'we are the Sons of the People,' China understands it as she understands the phrase 'son of Heaven.' The people have taken the place of the ancestors."[16] In Maoist ideology, the proletariat is the substitute for Heaven and is the *telos* of history.

In Chapter 9 on the human problem, we learned that in the Confucian tradition education occurs through the often unconscious imitation of models. It was believed that a virtuous person could change the behavior of large numbers of people. This older Chinese tradition was revived during the Maoist period, and Mao himself came to be treated as the chief model whose words and deeds were to be carefully studied and followed.

Mao's image and sayings appeared everywhere in China—on posters, in songs, and on lapel buttons; there were even Maoist "worship" services on trains. Since the Cultural Revolution of 1966, 30 million sets of Mao's four-volume *Selected Works* and many million copies of the "red book" of the *Sayings of Chairman Mao* have been distributed. For hosts of Chinese, the sayings of Mao became the "Way," a call to a transcendent purpose in life. Each day, members of the Peoples Liberation Army, the Red Guards, and masses of workers assembled in the public square in Peking and elsewhere throughout the country for morning and evening ceremonies (*Tien An Men*) to seek instruction from the spiritually present Mao and to report their ideological progress. A poet describes his feeling while waiting for the actual appearance of Chairman Mao at *Tien An Men*:

> Suddenly, like the eruption of a volcano,
> Like the crashing of thunder in spring,
> Before Tien An Men
> Joyful shouts burst from our throats:
> 'Long live Chairman Mao! Long, long life to him!'
> Chairman Mao has come!
> Chairman Mao has come!
> To the strains of 'The East is Red,'
> Chairman Mao and Vice-chairman Lin Piao
> Mount the Tien An Men rostrum—
> The highest peak in the world! . . .
> Chairman Mao, oh, Chairman Mao!
> You are the lighthouse by the misty sea,
> The bright lamp showing us the way;
> You are victory,
> You are light!
> We will follow you . . .[17]

Maoism incorporates most of the features of traditional religion: an object of "ultimate concern"; a charismatic, cultic leader; a faith; an ideology or system of belief; ritual and liturgical practices (including "a meal of bitter remembering"); and a canon of authoritative writings. Maoism also resembles religious orthodoxy in its concern to maintain the purity of doctrine, its intolerance of heresy, and its purges of liberal revisionists.

Of special note are the frequent instances of personal testimony, of young and old alike, relating experiences of conversion to Maoism. These testimonies follow a pattern long observed in accounts of religious converts. The psychologist Robert J. Lifton sees these Maoist confessions as quests for "revolutionary immortality." In place of the traditional Confucian immortality gained through the biological family, the Maoist revolutionary sacrifices him- or herself for the people, reaching back to the historical beginnings of the revolution and extending infinitely into the future.

There is an ancient Chinese fable called "The Foolish Old Man Who Removed the Mountain" that, in its retelling by Mao, makes the point about "a worthy death." It tells of an old man whose house faced two great mountain peaks that obstructed his view. He called on his sons to dig up the mountains.

> Another greybeard known as the Wise Old Man saw them and said derisively, 'How silly of you to do this! It is quite impossible for you few to dig up these two huge mountains.' The Foolish Old Man replied, 'When I die, my sons will carry on; when they die, there will be my grandsons, and then their sons and grandsons, and so on to infinity. High as they are, the mountains cannot grow any higher and with every bit we dig, they will be that much lower. Why can't we clear them away?' Having refuted the Wise Old Man's wrong view, he went on digging every day, unshaken in his conviction. God was moved by this, and he sent down two angels, who carried the mountains away on their backs. Today, two big mountains lie like a dead weight on the Chinese people. One is imperialism, the other is feudalism. The Chinese Communist Party has long made up its mind to dig them up. We must persevere and work unceasingly and, we too, will touch God's heart. Our God is none other than the masses of the Chinese people. If they stand up and dig together with us, why can't these two mountains be cleared away?[18]

In perceiving their work for the communist utopia as enduring for generations to come, the Chinese worker can achieve a sense of "objective immortality," a measure of transcendence over individual death, not unlike that offered by some religious traditions.

To this point, we have looked at examples of salvational goals—both theistic and radically secular—that hold in common an essentially this-worldly, historical conception of human liberation or redemption. Despite their considerable differences, each of these examples perceives human transformation as involving a self-transcending passage from an old self or an old aeon to a new and truer self or a new age, a Utopian or a Messianic Age—an enduring, ideal social order. We now turn to modes of salvation that may include this-worldly dimensions but that typically involve more-radical forms of transcendence of the finite order through *postmortem* survival of a personal soul or spiritual body in an afterlife in Sheol, Hades, Heaven, or Hell.

Resurrection, Immortality, and Eternal Life

We do not give the activity much thought, but a unique feature of
human life is the practice of burying the corpses of our own dead.
The practice suggests the special importance of death in human consciousness. Indeed, there is evidence from the caves near Peking that
a half-million years ago our prehominoid forbearers possessed some
sense of a life after death. Neanderthal and Cro-Magnon man placed
food and implements on their graves, and in the Neolithic Age, the
chieftain was often buried with his wives and slaves. These practices
show that our ancestors assumed some kind of afterlife. However, the
earliest forms of survival were not what we think of today as an
immortal soul or mind distinct from the body or a resurrected body.
What survived was a "shade," an insubstantial shadow image or double
of the body. The common prehistoric view is described as follows:

> The shade was assumed to continue after death, generally in a dim
> underworld beneath the level of the graves, which were sometimes
> thought of as entrances to the nether world. The dead were often
> thought of as potentially dangerous to the living and needing to be
> either placated or tricked into quiescence. Sometimes, however, a
> chief or leader was imagined to go to a distant part of the earth,
> or up into the sky, and was venerated and perhaps in due course
> worshipped as a god. Some tribes have believed in a happier hunting
> ground beyond the grave.... But the much more general belief
> was in a descent into the lower world in which the shade carried
> on a gradually fading life until eventually it passed out of memory
> and existence. This was not a conception of eternal life, or immor-
> tality, but of ghostly survival ... there was no thought of positive
> immortality.[19]

This lower world was called *Hades* or *Sheol*, a rather joyless under-
world where the shade lived a half-conscious, twilight existence. In
Homer's *Iliad*, the unhappy shade of Patroklos in Hades appears to
Achilleus who in sorrow describes Patroklos' sad state as a soul or
image with no real heart or life in it. All night long the phantom of
Patroklos stood over Achilleus lamentating and mourning. The Hebrew
Sheol was similarly a dark, underworld cavern or pit, so cheerless
and unwelcome that Job could cry:

> Let me alone, that I may find a little comfort
> before I go whence I shall not return,
> to the land of gloom and deep darkness,
> the land of gloom and chaos
> where light is as darkness.
>
> *(Job 10:20–22)*

The use of words like *lamentation* and *gloom* might give the impression that Hades and Sheol were places of divine judgment and punishment like Hell, but this is not the case. In early Greek and Hebrew writings, Hades and Sheol represent a neutral underworld where the shades of the dead persisted, regretfully, at least for a time. Generally speaking, there was little sense of an ethical judgment of the dead, one in which the wicked suffered retribution in Hell and the pious enjoyed the delights of a heavenly bliss. It was simply taken for granted that the self survives physical death. Since it was not a condition to which a person looked forward and had nothing to do with a person's moral rectitude or spiritual effort, existence in Hades or Sheol could hardly be regarded as a state of salvation or liberation, a genuine immortality or eternal life. Such a conception was present, however, in the Pyramid Texts in ancient Egypt as early as the third millennium B.C.E., long before Homer and the earliest Hebrew poets.

Immortality in Ancient Egypt and Greece

It was in Egypt that belief in a judgment of the dead and the related concepts of Heaven and Hell are first clearly recorded. The idea that a person's future life after death is conditioned by the person's present moral conduct is expressed in the Instruction for King Merikabe (Tenth Dynasty, ca. 2150–2060 B.C.E.), in a warning given by a father to his son:

> The judges who judge the sinner, thou knowest, that they are not mild in that day, when they judge the miserable one, in the hour when the decision is accomplished.... Trust not in the length of years: they look upon the duration of a life as but an hour. Man remains after death and his deeds will be laid before him.... But who comes to them, not having sinned, he will be there as a god, free-striding as the Lord of Eternity.[20]

The later *Book of the Dead* vividly portrays the judgment carried out by the god Osiris, in which a man's heart is weighed in a scale against the feather of Maat, symbolizing truth. The text includes an impressively long list of thirty-six "negative confessions" in which the man pleads his sinlessness:

> I have not committed evil against men ...
> I have not blasphemed a god ...
> I have not killed ...
> I have not defamed a slave to his superior ...
> I have not defiled myself ... [and so forth.][21]

A last judgment, "the weighing of the heart," from the Egyptian *Book of the Dead*. Behind the scales, the scribal god Thoth records the verdict. At the extreme right, "Devourness" waits to devour the unjust soul. (*Source*: Reproduced by Courtesy of the Trustees of the British Museum.)

The universal character of judgment and mention of the future abode of the righteous is described on a later tomb inscription of the priest Petosiris:

> The West is the abode of those without fault. Happy is he who arrives there! But none enters therein whose heart is not right in the deed of Maat. There is no distinction between rich and poor; he only counts who is found to be without fault when the balance and its burdens stand before the Lord of Eternity [the god Thoth].[22]

The Egyptian conception of life after death was a true immortality, but it was a future existence realistically conceived—that is, lifelike. The afterlife was not represented as a disembodied soul or mind, or as a resurrected spiritual body; rather, it was the survival as *ba*, an animated existence free from the human corpse but possessing the characteristics of real earthly life.

A quite different conception of an immortal soul emerged in Greece among the Eleusinian, Dionysian, and Orphic **mystery cults**, and within the philosophical schools. It reflects a radical dualism, both between the soul and its material body and between this earth and the soul's heavenly home. For example, the later Greek Orphic cults taught a belief not only in the soul's immortality but also of the soul's transmigration—its fall from Heaven into its earthly embodiment and its return to its heavenly home.

The Orphic philosopher Pythagoras (ca. 531 B.C.E.) taught that divine and immortal souls had fallen into material bodies in which they were now imprisoned. Salvation involved the cultic removal of the soul's taint, its rescue from its fallen state, and its return to its heavenly home. This Greek dualism had a significant influence on early Christianity (as did Jewish apocalyptic eschatology), but its influence was felt even earlier in the philosophy of Socrates and Plato. In his dialogue *Cratylus*, Plato writes:

> Some say that the body (*soma*) is the tomb (*sema*) of the soul, as if the soul in this present life were buried. . . . I think it most likely that the name was given by the followers of Orpheus, with the idea that the soul is undergoing whatever penalty it has incurred, and is enclosed in the body, as in a sort of prison-house, for safe-keeping . . . until the penalty it owes is discharged. . . .[23]

Plato's account of the soul's immortal, divine destiny is, however, divested of much of the earlier Orphic ritual and mystery. It is portrayed simply as life's most urgent moral challenge, namely, the perfecting of the human soul. According to Socrates and Plato, it is the philosopher's task—not that of an other-worldly savior—to free the soul from its bondage to the corruptible body and the world of mere appearances that it may enjoy its true and eternal destiny. In the *Phaedo*, Socrates points out the moral seriousness that is implied in a belief in the soul's immortality:

> But there is a further point, gentlemen, which deserves your attention. If the soul is immortal, it demands our care not only for that part of time which we call life, but for all time; and indeed it would seem now that it will be extremely dangerous to neglect it. If death were a release from everything, it would be a boon for the wicked, because by dying they would be released not only from the body but also from their own wickedness together with the soul; but as it is, since the soul is clearly immortal, it can have no escape or security from evil except by becoming as good and wise as it possibly can. For it takes nothing with it to the next world except its education and training.[24]

Postbiblical Judaism and Christianity

We have observed that in the postexilic period (sixth century B.C.E.), Judaism's hope for salvation shifted from a this-worldly nationalism to an other-worldly apocalypticism, with its attendant concepts of a resurrection, judgment, Heaven, and Hell. Especially significant was the emergence of the complex idea of resurrection. We noted that in the postexilic period, resurrection was conceived sometimes as the establishment of the community of the righteous in a kingdom on earth; sometimes as a wholly renewed earth, a New Jerusalem; and sometimes as a purely spiritual, angelic body raised directly to Heaven.

All these ideas were current in Judaism at the beginning of the Christian era, but prominent was the belief in the resurrection of a spiritual body. Jesus appears to have accepted this belief. It is reflected in his controversy with the Sadducees where he asserts that "when they rise from the dead, they neither marry nor are given in marriage, but are like angels in heaven" (Mark 12:25). St. Paul, too, makes a distinction between the natural, fleshly body and the resurrected spiritual body (*soma pneumatikon*):

> There are celestial bodies and there are terrestrial bodies; but the glory of the celestial is one, and the glory of the terrestrial is another. . . . So it is with the resurrection of the dead. What is sown is perishable, what is raised is imperishable. It is sown in dishonour, it is raised in glory. . . . It is sown a physical body, it is raised a spiritual body. If there is a physical body, there is also a spiritual body.
>
> *(I Corinthians 15:40–44)*

The New Testament texts that speak of the redeemed—the resurrected body—introduce two puzzles that the texts themselves do not easily resolve and that have produced an ongoing scholarly debate. The one issue is whether the spiritual resurrection involves a transformed body (both individual and corporate) here on earth—a new earth—or is to be understood as a heavenly body. The second question is whether the resurrection (and judgment) occurs immediately following the death of the individual or whether it is to come in some future time, at the "general resurrection" that precedes the Last Judgment. The New Testament passages reflect a tension between salvation (resurrection) conceived as present and as future. The tension is present in the teachings of Jesus. He clearly proclaims a future judgment and Kingdom, as when he speaks of the Son of man coming in his glory, and that "before him all the nations will be gathered and he shall separate them from one another, as a shepherd divides his sheep from the goats" (Matthew 25:31–32). On the other hand, Jesus proclaims God's Kingdom as already a present reality in his healing the sick, raising the dead, and casting out the devils (Matthew 11:3ff, 12:28; Luke 10:18; 11:20). In the parable of Dives and Lazarus, Jesus speaks of Lazarus, the righteous beggar, as immediately carried off by the angels "into Abraham's bosom," or Heaven, and the rich man dying and, in the torments of Hell, lifting up his eyes and seeing Lazarus in Heaven and crying for Abraham's mercy (Luke 16:22–23).

It appears that for Jesus and the early Christians salvation was understood in terms of the resurrection of the spiritual body and, furthermore, that they considered it as "already fulfilled" for those who were "in Christ"—that is, those who had died to the old self and were now raised to a life in Christ who had inaugurated the new age. Paul writes, "Behold *now* is the day of salvation" (II Corinthians 6:2); old things have passed away, those in Christ are "new creatures." The Fourth Gospel similarly speaks of the eschaton as realized, as a present reality. John records Jesus as proclaiming, "Verily, verily I say unto you, He that heareth my word, and believeth on him that sent me, hath everlasting life, and shall not come into condemnation; but is passed from death to life" (John 5:24).

This having been said, it is nevertheless true that the New Testament also envisions the Kingdom of God as a future event, as "not yet consummated." The Christian is thus living "between the times"—salvation is already present, but it is yet to be fulfilled on the Last Day. This tension between salvation as a present reality for those "in Christ" or "in Paradise" immediately on death and an entirely future salvation realized at the time of the Last Judgment has remained through the centuries.

After the second century C.E., however, interest in Christ's second advent and the coming of the general resurrection and final judgment faded in the popular consciousness. It was to be reawakened in times of social suffering and injustice, as we have seen, for example, in the preaching of Protestant millenarianists in the sixteenth century. However, by the early medieval period, the belief that each individual was judged at the time of death and the soul translated immediately to its eternal reward or punishment became the prevailing view.

Belief in a future life in Heaven or in Hell has been of decisive importance in shaping the Western moral imagination—at least until recently. The classic portrayals of Hell—in Dante's *Divine Comedy*, for example—describe the fate of the damned in the most vivid imagery. In fact, the portrayal of the suffering of the damned in some second-rate Christian literature is so graphic as to be morally offensive. In a literary master like Dante, however, the *Inferno* serves as a ghastly and horrific moral parable. Dante depicts Hell as a dark and frightening abyss: a steaming and stinking place, with howling winds, frightening cold, frenzied, tortured bodies, shrieking, and groaning. He portrays each sinner being punished in a manner appropriate to his or her sin.

In the Christian tradition, Heaven is not painted—with some exceptions—in quite the vivid colors as is Hell. In fact, with the decline of belief in a literal Hell in modern times, Christian discourse about a heavenly life has been quite reticent. In traditional devotional literature and in hymns, the picture of Heaven took two forms. One is the more-homely vision of the family of saints reunited in Paradise. It is a place of light, peace, and joy, with no more sorrow or pain, where the faithful join in worship before the Throne of God. Such representations of Heaven, or Paradise, are not unique to Christianity; they are common in all theistic religions, including Islam and Mahayana Buddhism. Islamic eschatology is similar in certain respects

"The Last Judgment" by Jan Van
Eyck, 1441. Christ appears as Judge,
accompanied by his saints. The dead
rise from their graves on earth, the
righteous ascending to Heaven and
the unrighteous descending to
eternal Hell. (*Source*: Courtesy of
The Metropolitan Museum of Art.)

to that in the Bible. It portrays a trumpeter announcing the Judgment
Day; the angels bringing forth the Throne of the Lord, and the
opening of the Book of Deeds. The unbelievers and the unrighteous
are cast into the eternal fire of Gehenna and the righteous are translated to Paradise, "the Gardens of Bliss." No subjects are mentioned
more frequently in the *Qur'an* than are the Day of Judgment,
Gehenna, and Paradise. And in Islamic literature, they are described
in the most vivid language, none more so than Paradise. The following
is a vision of Allah in Paradise. It describes in rich imagery Allah's
palace garden and the joys of the heavenly feast:

> This [Allah's palace] gate is of green emerald and over it are curtains
> of light of such brightness as almost to destroy the sight. . . . Its soil

is of finest musk and saffron and ambergris, its stones of jacinths and jewels, its little pebbles and rubble are of gold, while on its banks are trees whose limbs hang down, whose branches are low, whose fruits are within easy reach, whose birds sing sweetly, whose colours shine brightly, whose flowers blossom in splendour, and from which comes a breeze [so delightful] as to reduce to insignificance all other delights.

Then orders will be given that they [the righteous] be served the finest kinds of fruit such as they never before have seen, and they will eat of these fruits and enjoy thereof as much as they desire. . . . Then orders will be given for them to be clothed with garments [of honor] the like of which they have not seen even in Paradise; and of such splendour and beauty as they have never before had for their delight. . . . So they will fall down before their Lord in prostration and deep humility saying: 'Glory be to Thee, O our Lord. In Thy praise Thou art blessed and exalted, and blessed is Thy name.'[25]

We observed in Chapter 11 that the Mahayana Buddhist schools made provision for the fact that not all individuals are capable of achieving salvation by the difficult road of transcendental meditation and wisdom. The new path took the form of faith and devotion to personal Buddhas and Bodhisattva saviors. In the Pure Land schools of China and Japan, these saviors occupy numerous Paradises, or Pure Lands, where the faithful are reborn. The most famous is the Western Paradise of the Buddha Amitabha. A favorite subject of religious art, Amitabha is depicted seated on a lotus throne in the Western Heaven, flanked by his attendant Bodhisattvas, including Kuan-yin, the Goddess of Mercy. The following extract is from the popular Sanskrit *Description of the Happy Land* (second century C.E.):

15. This world Sukhavati [the Pure Land], Ananda, which is the world system of the Lord Amitabha, is rich and prosperous, comfortable, fertile, delightful and crowded with many Gods and men. And in this world system, Ananda, there are no hells, no animals, no ghosts, no Asuras, and none of the inauspicious places of rebirth. . . .
16. And that world system Sukhavati, Ananda, emits many fragrant odours, it is rich in a great variety of flowers and fruits, adorned with jewel trees, which are frequented by flocks of various birds and sweet voices. . . .
18. And nowhere in this world-system Sukhavati does one hear of anything unwholesome, nowhere of the hindrances, nowhere of the states of punishment, the states of woe and the bad destinies, nowhere of suffering. And that, Ananda, is the reason why this world-system is called the 'Happy Name.'[26]

A rather different and less-familial conception of the heavenly life is given in depictions of the Beatific Vision. It has played an important

Amida (Amitabha) descending from the Western
Paradise, accompanied by 25 protective Bodhisattvas.
Amida is embarked on a journey to assist the souls of
devotees. (*Source*: Courtesy of The Seattle Art Museum,
Eugene Fuller Memorial Collection, 34.117.)

role in Roman Catholic piety and is the image of paradise envisioned
by the great Christian mystics. As the words imply, the Beatific Vision
is the direct, unmediated vision of the Godhead. In traditional Catholic
spirituality, there are levels of sanctity as well as levels of punishment
and the direct vision of God is reserved for the highest purity. It is
the simultaneous intellectual perception of all things in God, an Eternal Present. It is not a vision of nature transfigured, as in Zen Buddhist *satori* or nature mysticism; rather, it is a direct vision of God,
of Infinite Love, face to face.

In the Beatific Vision, the self is united with God and yet is *not* God, in contrast to the isolation or extinction of the self in Vedanta and other forms of monistic liberation. The self dies to the old ego and is transformed into a new creature, "oned with God."

Practitioners of the contemplative life point out that a foretaste of the Beatific Vision is achievable here and now when the personal will becomes one with the divine will. When this occurs Eternal Life—or Paul's experience that "it is no longer I who live, but Christ who lives in me" (Galatians 2:20)—is not a condition of the soul translated to an other-worldly heaven but instead is a present, perfected or divinely transformed existence, wholly devoted to the divine will.

The contemplative does not leave the world but enters into it as a servant of the divine will. The test of a genuine contemplative vision, attested to by all theistic mystics, is a transformed, egoless life in the world, penetrated by the divine spirit. It is, writes the Catholic monk Thomas Merton (1915–1968),

> an experience of mystical renewal, an inner transformation brought about entirely by the power of God's merciful love, implying the 'death' of the self-centered and self-sufficient ego and the appearance of a new and liberated self who lives and acts 'in the Spirit.'[27]

To this point, we have surveyed a variety of representations of salvation that are common to theistic belief. It remains to describe the most radical form of self-transcendence. This is the monistic conception of liberation in which personal identity is extinguished or overcome in a state of nondualism—in which *atman* and Brahman are One. This is best illustrated in Hindu Advaita Vedanta philosophy and in some interpretations of Buddhist Nirvana.

Samadhi and Nirvana

In Chapter 7, we noted the movement in Indian religion from polytheism to pantheism and monism, especially in the *Upanishads*. In these texts, the unifying principle of the universe is called Brahman, the ultimate sacred power or world-ground. Since the power that works in everything cannot consist in parts or be subject to change, according to some Indian sages, it follows that everything is essentially Brahman, entire and indivisible. Ultimately, nothing exists other than Brahman, including the soul (*atman*) that *is* Brahman: Atman and Brahman are One. There is only the One, without a second. Vedanta philosophy expressed this monistic doctrine with utterances such as "I am Brahman" and "Thou are That."

Hindu Samadhi

As we have seen, the philosopher Śankara was the formative and most influential exponent of a thoroughgoing nondualism (*advaita*). He taught the nonexistence of the self as a separate entity. According to Śankara, belief in finite individuality is due to *avidya* (ignorance of reality) and the goal of Advaita Vedanta is release (*moksha*) from the illusion of a self or "I" and union with the Infinite without individual consciousness.

To achieve the self's *moksha*, Vedanta proposes a series of ascetic disciplines similar to those required in Sankhya-Yoga (see Chapter 11). Beginning with certain moral rules regarding such things as unselfishness and bodily cleanliness, it proceeds to disciplined postures of the body, to breathing exercises, to concentration, and to meditation. If successful, the candidate then progresses to the final goal of *samadhi*, or perfect absorption. The word *samadhi* means "to put together," "to unite," or "to compose." Vedanta, however, does distinguish two kinds of *samadhi*: (1) *savikalpa samadhi*, which is absorption with full consciousness of the duality of the perceiver and the perceived, and (2) *nirvikalpa samadhi*, perfect nondual absorption, which is totally devoid of any consciousness of a distinction between perceiver and perceived. In the first instance, the self remains aware of the blissful union with Brahman. As in the case of the Christian Beatific Vision, the subject enjoys the supreme ecstasy of union with the Infinite. However, this is not the highest goal in *nirvikalpa samadhi*, the One-without-a-second. Since it is the One without predicates, and therefore ineffable, it is the bliss of silence.

Four states of mind stand as obstacles to this highest form of *samadhi*. The first is the mind's misjudging the state of deep, dreamless sleep for *samadhi*. The second is the opposite: the distractions of normal wakefulness. The *Yoga-sutras* regard this as the major obstacle to spiritual progress and concentration. The third obstacle is attachment to worldly things, a paralysis of the mind due to the benumbing attractions of the world that engage our attention and our passions. The fourth obstacle is *savikalpa samadhi* itself—the ecstasy and bliss that the self enjoys in identifying *atman* and Brahman. It is called *rasa-asvada*: "the tasting or enjoying of the substantial sap or flavor of the Self." It is like the bliss of the Beatific Vision.

Nirvikalpa samadhi comes only when the mind is at complete rest, reposed in the changeless One: "As a lamp sheltered from the wind, that does not flicker." This final state, being without distinctions or predicates, is ineffable. And yet Vedanta uses many images to attempt to suggest it. One is the image of salt in water: "Just as when salt has been dissolved in water the salt is no longer perceived separately and the water alone remains, so likewise the mental state that has taken the form of Brahman, the one-without-a-second, is no longer perceived, only the Self remains."[28]

Unlike a dreamless sleep, a form of consciousness is present in *samadhi*.

> Undifferentiated [*samadhi*] is not the 'absolute void.' The 'state' and the 'knowledge' denoted by this term refer to the total absence of objects from consciousness and not at all to a consciousness emptied in an absolute fashion. It is the [*samadhi*] of total vacuity, without sensory content or intellectual structure, an unconditioned state that is no longer 'experience.' . . . The 'human' consciousness is eliminated; in other words, it no longer functions, its constituent elements having been re-absorbed into a primordial substance. The yogi . . . no longer lives in time and under the control of time, but in an eternal present. . . . [29]

The liberated person (the *jivanmukta*) would be entirely freed of the phenomenal world if it were not for the momentum of *karmic* actions that continue to carry him or her along. The *jivanmukta* therefore remains associated with a body, but in an imperturbable state of changeless serenity. Past, present, and future time are transcended; the person is indifferent to all actions, good or evil.

Being imperturbable, the liberated person sows no new *karma* and therefore the effects of the residual past *karma* slowly fade. When the vestigial shell of the body falls away in death, the liberated person achieves a supreme isolation (*kaivalya*), a "bodyless liberation." According to the *Vedantasara*, "then at last, when the remainder of *prarabdha-karma* has been exhausted . . . the life-breath (*prana*) dissolves into the Highest Brahman, which is inward Bliss."[30]

Buddhist Nirvana

The paths to liberation taken by the Indian yogi and the Buddhist *bhikkhu*, or monk, share certain family resemblances. Both emphasize the discipline of "sitting" or meditation. Both perceive liberation as a "release" or "extinction" of the illusory, phenomenal self. And yet for all these similarities, Buddhist Nirvana is described in what appears to be more-positive, world-affirming terms.

The goal of the Theravadin *arahant*, or fully enlightened one, is the Absolute Noble Truth of Nirvana. According to Buddhism, this Absolute Truth is that there is nothing absolute in the entire world. Everything is conditioned, changing, and impermanent, including the "self." To realize this truth without illusion involves the extinction of craving and the cessation of desire, which is Nirvana. The *Sanyutta-nikaya* speaks of Nirvana simply as "the stopping of becoming" and as "the getting rid of craving."

It would be incorrect, however, to think of Nirvana as the *result* of the extinction of craving. Nirvana is neither the cause nor the effect of anything. Nirvana *is*; it is unconditioned. This point is made by Buddha's disciple Nagasena in the famous dialogue *Questions of King Milinda*. It is possible to point out the path to the realization of Nirvana but, Nagasena insists, it is not possible to show a cause for its production:

'Could a man, who with his natural strength has crossed in a boat over the great ocean, get to the farther shore?' 'Yes, he could'—'But could that man with his natural strength bring the farther shore of the great ocean here?' 'No, he could not.'—'Just so one can point out the way to the realization of Nirvana, but one cannot show a cause for its production. And what is the reason for that? Because the dharma, Nirvana, is unconditioned . . . not made by anything.'[31]

Because it is unconditioned, Nirvana is beyond all conception and description. Buddha refused every request for a positive description, insisting that it was "incomprehensible, indescribable."

Because Nirvana is literally inconceivable and the Pali word for Nirvana (*Nibbana*) means "blowing out" or "extinction" (of a lamp), Nirvana is often thought of as a purely negative state, a nothingness. However, such a nihilistic view is a misconception, as is frequently pointed out by Theravadin scholars. While Nirvana is extinction, it is important to recognize that it is the negation of lust, hatred, illusion— the extinction of the finite self or ego consciousness. While often using negations to describe it, Buddha nevertheless speaks of Nirvana as a positive reality: "O bhikkhus, there is the unborn, ungrown, and unconditioned. Since there *is* the unborn, ungrown, and unconditioned, there *is* escape from the born, grown, and conditioned."[32] Similarly, the *Sanyutta-nikaya* describes Nirvana in a series of positive terms, including "the stable," "the excellent," "the blissful," "the security," "the cave of shelter," "the stronghold," and "the refuge."[33]

Since the *arahant* has purified the mind and no longer craves either becoming *or* extinction, he clings to nothing in the world; he knows that all is impermanent. He has realized Absolute Truth, Nirvana, in this life itself:

He who has realized the Truth, Nirvana, is the happiest being in the world. He is free from all 'complexes' and obsessions, the worries and troubles that torment others. His mental health is perfect. He does not repent the past, nor does he brood over the future. He lives fully in the present. . . . He is joyful, exultant . . . free from anxiety, serene, and peaceful. And he is free from selfish desire, hatred, ignorance, conceit, pride, and all such 'defilements. . . .' His service to others is of the purest, for he has no thought of self. He gains

> He gains nothing, accumulates nothing, not even anything spiritual,
> because he is free from the illusion of Self, and the 'thirst' for
> becoming.[34]

Theravadin schools do differ, however, in their view of what happens to the *arahant* after death. One view holds that the *arahant* has no re-existence, even in Nirvana, after death (*parinirvana*):

> The old craving exhausted, no fresh craving rises,
> Freed from the thought of future becoming
> They like barren seeds do not spring again,
> But are blown out just like a lamp.[35]

According to this interpretation, at death, the *arahant* is freed from the round of *samsara*, or rebirth, and is fully extinct. Nirvana, then, is a purely blissful psychological state of the living *arahant*. A person has realized Nirvana when he or she has extinguished the "self" of the Five Aggregates that cause craving and pain.

The alternative view denies that Nirvana is simply a psychological state of the living *arahant*; rather, it is the infinite supramundane Reality to which the *arahant* is joined or oned at death. In death, the "self" is dissolved, leaving only the "unborn," the "not-become," the "not-compounded." This conception is thoroughly monistic. It is the state of undifferentiated unity. It is deathlessness, perfect emptiness, and not the immortal soul's ecstatic Beatific Vision.

It is time to conclude. From this review of concepts of salvation or liberation, certain resemblances can be seen in the blissful sense of liberation and egolessness produced by "peak experiences," in Zen *satori*, in eternal "life in Christ," in Buddhist Nirvana, and in the Beatific Vision. And yet there are unbridgeable differences — not necessarily between Hinduism, Christianity, Buddhism, and Islam — but between the theist's conception of an immortal soul or resurrected body reunited with the divine through the loving action of a transcendent, personal God and the atheistic or monistic doctrines of liberation which hold that the soul and God are, finally, One and the same and all else is pure illusion. But, even here, are the doctrines irreconcilable? This directs us to our final subject: the new interreligious dialogue and the question of how or whether it is possible to judge or to reconcile seemingly contrary claims to religious truth.

Notes

1. Gerardus van der Leeuw, *Religion in Essence and Manifestation* I (New York, 1963), p. 101.
2. Frederick J. Streng, *Understanding Religious Life* (Belmont, Ca., 1985), p. 2.

3. Bertrand Russell, *Mysticism and Logic* (London, 1918), pp. 47–48.
4. E. D. Klemke, "Living Without Appeal," in E. D. Klemke, ed., *The Meaning of Life* (New York, 1981), p. 172.
5. Erich Fromm, *Psychoanalysis and Religion* (New Haven, 1950), pp. 93–94.
6. Abraham Maslow, *Religions, Values, and Peak Experiences* (Columbus, Ohio, 1964), p. 20.
7. Maslow, *Peak Experiences*, pp. 60–65.
8. Abraham H. Maslow, "Eupsychia—The Good Society," *Journal of Humanistic Psychology* I (Fall, 1961), p. 8.
9. Maslow, "Eupsychia," p. 6.
10. D. T. Suzuki, *Zen Buddhism* (New York, 1956), p. 84.
11. D. T. Suzuki, *Introduction to Zen Buddhism* (London, 1949), pp. 97–98.
12. Suzuki, *Zen Buddhism*, p. 3.
13. Erich Fromm and D. T. Suzuki, *Zen Buddhism and Psychoanalysis* (New York, 1960), pp. 115–16.
14. Karl Marx and Friedrich Engels, *Collected Works* 3 (London, 1975), pp. 175, 176.
15. V. I. Lenin, *Collected Works* 10 (Moscow, n.d.), pp. 175, 176.
16. André Malraux, *Anti-Mémoirs* (New York, 1970), p. 467.
17. *China Notes* (Summer, 1969). As cited in Donald E. MacInnis, *Religious Policy and Practice in Communist China* (New York, 1972), p. 336.
18. Wolfgang Bauer, *China and the Search for Happiness* (New York, 1976), pp. 410–11.
19. John Hick, *Death and Eternal Life* (New York, 1976), p. 56. Hick's study has been a valuable guide and resource for this segment.
20. S. G. F. Brandon, *Man and His Destiny in the Great Religions* (Toronto, 1962), p. 52.
21. Brandon, *Man and His Destiny*, p. 53.
22. Brandon, *Man and His Destiny*, p. 56.
23. *Cratylus* 400b; as cited in Brandon, *Man and His Destiny*, p. 186.
24. *Phaedo* 207c.
25. Arthur Jeffrey, *Islam: Muhammad and His Religion* (New York, 1958), pp. 98–103.
26. *Sukhavativyuka*, Chs. 15–18. Cited in Edward Conze, et al. *Buddhist Texts Through the Ages* (New York, 1964), pp. 202–04.
27. Thomas Merton, *Contemplative Prayer* (New York, 1969), p. 110.
28. *Vedantasara of Sadananda*. Cited in Heinrich Zimmer, *Philosophies of India* (New York, 1957), pp. 432.
29. M. Eliade, *Patanjali and Yoga*, pp. 113–14.
30. H. Zimmer, *Philosophies of India*, p. 446.
31. *Buddhist Scriptures*, ed. Edward Conze (Baltimore, 1968), pp. 158–59.
32. *Udana* 80. Cited in W. Rahula, *What the Buddha Taught*, p. 37.
33. *Sanyutta-Nikaya* IV. Cited in J. Hick, *Death and Eternal Life*, p. 435.
34. W. Rahula, *What the Buddha Taught*, p. 43.
35. *Sutta-Nipata* V. 235. Cited in J. Hick, *Death and Eternal Life*, p. 436.

Review Questions

1. What connections or analogies, if any, do you see between such "therapeutic" experiences as Maslow's "peak experiences" or Zen enlightenment and more-traditional religious experience?
2. Characterize Israel's early, this-worldly political hope. How does it differ from the apocalyptic motifs that began to appear in Israelite prophecy after the Babylonian exile?
3. Can you think of secular ideological commitments, other than the example of Chinese Maoism, that have some of the same religious features as Maoism?
4. Theistic religions have conceived of salvation in this-worldly terms, but also in terms of a postmortem life of a personal soul or a resurrected body. Contrast such concepts of survival as *ba*, the Greek immortality of the soul, the biblical resurrection of the body, and eternal life. How do earlier portrayals of Hades, or Sheol, differ from later depictions of Hell? How does the heavenly Beatific Vision differ from more familial portrayals of Paradise or Heaven in the Christian and Islamic traditions?
5. The highest goal of Hindu Vedantic liberation is *nirvikalpa samadhi*, or perfect, nondual absorption. Can you indicate how *samadhi* differs from either the Beatific Vision or a dreamless sleep or trance?
6. What is Nirvana? How is the term *extinction* to be understood in Theravada Buddhism?

Suggestions for Further Reading

For general accounts of salvation and life after death in the world's religions, see the following:

BRANDON, S. G. F., *The Judgment of the Dead* (New York: Scribner's, 1969).

———, *Man and His Destiny in the Great Religions* (Toronto: University of Toronto Press, 1962).

HICK, JOHN H., *Death and Eternal Life* (San Francisco: Harper & Row, 1976). This latter study is especially thorough and lucid and includes a valuable bibliography.

TOYNBEE, ARNOLD, et. al., *Man's Concern with Death* (London: Hodder & Stoughton, 1968).

For conceptions of eschatology, resurrection, immortality, and eternal life in the biblical religions, see the following:

CHARLES, R. H., *Eschatology: The Doctrine of the Future Life in Israel, Judaism, and Christianity* (New York: Schocken Books, 1963).

CULLMANN, OSCAR, *Immortality of the Soul or Resurrection of the Dead?* (New York: Macmillan, 1958).

DAHL, M. E., *The Resurrection of the Body* (London: SCM Press, 1962).

NICKELSBURG, GEORGE W. E., JR., *Resurrection, Immortality, and Eternal Life in Inter-testamental Judaism* (Cambridge: Harvard University Press, 1973).

RUSSELL, D. S., *The Method and Message of Jewish Apocalyptic* (Philadelphia: Westminster Press, 1964).

For conceptions of liberation in Hinduism and Buddhism, see the following:

ELIADE, MIRCEA, *Patanjali and Yoga* (New York: Schocken Books, 1975).

KAPLEAU, PHILIP, *The Three Pillars of Zen* (Boston: Beacon Press, 1967).

O'FLAHERTY, WENDY D., ed., *Karma and Rebirth in Classical Indian Traditions* (Berkeley: University of California Press, 1980).

RAHULA, WALPOLA, *Anatta and Nibbana* (Kandy, Ceylon: Buddhist Publication Society, 1971).

_____ , *What the Buddha Taught* (New York: Grove Press, 1959).

SUZUKI, D. T., *Zen Buddhism* (New York: Doubleday, 1956).

THERA, NYANAPONIKA, *The Heart of Buddhist Meditation* (London: Rider, 1969).

ZIMMER, HEINRICH, *Philosophies of India* (New York: Meridian Books, 1957).

For comparative studies of mysticism, see the following:

OTTO, RUDOLF, *Mysticism: East and West* (New York: Meridian Books, 1957).

SUZUKI, D. T., *Mysticism: Christian and Buddhist* (New York: Collier. 1962).

SUZUKI, D. T., E. FROMM, and R. DeMARTINO, *Zen Buddhism and Psychoanalysis* (New York: Grove Press, 1960).

UNDERHILL, EVELYN, *Mysticism* (New York: Dutton, 1961). First published in 1911.

ZAEHNER, R. C., *Mysticism: Sacred and Profane* (New York: Oxford University Press, 1961).

For nontraditional and secular ways to liberation or salvation, see the following:

LEONARD, G. B., *Education and Ecstasy* (New York: Delacorte Press, 1968).

LIFTON, ROBERT J., *Revolutionary Immortality: Mao Tse-tung and the Chinese Cultural Revolution* (New York: Alfred A. Knopf, 1968).

MASLOW, ABRAHAM H., *Religions, Values, and Peak Experiences* (Columbus, OH: Ohio State University Press, 1964).

MUNRO, DONALD J., *The Concept of Man in Contemporary China* (Ann Arbor: University of Michigan Press, 1977).

NEEDLEMAN, JACOB, *The New Religions* (New York: Crossroads, 1984).

CHAPTER 13

Religious Pluralism, Dialogue, and the Question of Religious Truth

OVERVIEW

Today, we are living in a time of unprecedented human hope and yet misgiving, even fear, for the future. Only recently have we become acutely conscious that we are living on a relatively tiny planet and that this fragile "space ship" earth is occupied by diverse, often discordant, even violently conflicting groups with opposing beliefs and ways of life. Religion is often the storm center of these tensions and quarrels. As the historian of religion Wilfred Cantwell Smith has written:

> Religious diversity poses a general human problem because it disrupts community. It does so with a new force in the modern world because divergent traditions that in the past did and could develop separately ... are today face to face.... Different civilizations have in the past either ignored each other or fought each other; very occasionally in tiny ways perhaps they met each other. Today they not only meet but interpenetrate; they meet not only each other, but jointly meet joint problems, and must jointly try to solve them. They must collaborate. Perhaps the single most important challenge that mankind faces in our day is the need to turn our nascent world society into a world community.[1]

351

The tragic consequences of Smith's remark that "religious diversity disrupts community" are all too apparent in Lebanon, in Pakistan, and in Northern Ireland, to name only a few of the world's trouble spots. We are living in a situation unprecedented in human history. Because of modern technology, we have instantaneous knowledge of events on the other side of the world. We travel to places and encounter foreign beliefs and practices about which our grandparents were wholly ignorant. Modern technology and the knowledge explosion have made us acutely aware of our differences, what can be called "the shock of diversity." On the other hand, the historical, phenomenological, and functional studies of the world's religions have forced us to acknowledge the striking parallels and similarities in humanity's religious heritage. We know that many religions have inspired scriptures, incarnations, baptisms, ritual sacrifices, salvation by faith alone, and heavens and hells. We also have experienced "the shock of similarity." Technology, travel, and education are slowly breaking down barriers of ignorance, fear, and suspicion between nations. Whether we like it or not, history compels us to a global perspective — to an urgent interest in and appreciation of faiths and practices other than our own.

This raises the perplexing question about how we are to understand the relationship between the world's religions. Does our new knowledge simply accentuate the differences and possible ongoing discord between the world's faiths? Or does it point to the essential, underlying similarities? Beneath the relative cultural variations, is there a fundamental unity? Are all religions basically one? Are there many different paths to the one truth or salvation? Or are we evolving toward a future, perhaps new, global faith? These questions have been much debated of late. At the center of this dialogue are the questions of how we are to understand the relationship between the world's religions and how we are to deal with their rival claims to truth. Here, we shall outline a variety of responses to these questions suggested by a number of distinguished contemporary historians, philosophers, and theologians. These questions and responses are not merely the ruminations of scholars; they involve the most serious social and political consequences. Indeed, in the long run the way in which these questions are resolved will, no doubt, be decisive in determining our human future.

One form of response we shall call *exclusivism*. As the word implies, this position asserts that the world's religions hold uniquely different beliefs about Ultimate Reality and the way and goal of salvation. Since truth is invariant and indivisible, one religion only can be *the* way and *the* truth. Modern apologists for Hinduism, and others, repudiate such exclusivism and champion one or another form of what we shall call *inclusivism*. This position maintains that the various religions represent different cultural paths to the one Ultimate Reality. What is called for is a world fellowship of faiths through which the many religions can share their experience and their wisdom. Inclusivism holds, however, that the many religions are ultimately only broken refractions, different aspects of the *one* Absolute. Some would argue, however, that the comparative study of religious experience and belief does not readily support the idea that the religions point to the same ultimate truth. Inclusivism contrasts with genuine *pluralism*, which insists that each religion is indeed *unique* and must be respected as *the* authentic way that "God's truth" is revealed to a particular culture at a particular time. We shall see that, while attractive for a number of reasons, pluralism also is not without its own problems and its critics.

Despite these issues, recent interreligious dialogue has produced quite unexpected agreements on what were thought to be irreconcilable matters. Some of these are briefly noted. Finally, we shall conclude with several possible responses that might be taken in the face of today's religious diversity. Living in a highly complex, pluralistic culture has its special perils but also its unique opportunities.

Exclusivism

Among other things, religions make certain factual claims about the nature of the human problem, about the way to salvation, and about the character of Ultimate Reality. Most persons commit themselves to a religion because they regard it as true—or at least as a more adequate expression of spiritual reality than the alternatives. Religion, Paul Tillich rightly contends, is a person's "ultimate concern." And individuals do not place their ultimate faith, hope, and loyalty in something that is here today and gone tomorrow, something transient and parochial. That is to say, religion has usually entailed a claim to exclusivity, to truth. To say that there is no self (*an-atta*), that Muhammad is the "seal" of the prophets, or that Christ is God incarnate is to stake a claim of very great importance, a claim to truth. It logically follows that the believer will regard as false whatever negates or denies these assertions. Because all religions make factual claims, which often are mutually exclusive, and because truth cannot be divided against itself, it would appear that religion is exclusive by its very nature and that the religions must stand against one another as truth stands against error.

This has, of course, been the position of most missionary religions— Christianity, Islam, and **Nicheren** Buddhism, for example—through the centuries. It certainly was the dominant position of the Christian Church until recently, and it is a position enshrined in the Roman Catholic doctrine *extra ecclesiam nulla salus* (No salvation outside the Church). The belief was officially declared by Pope Boniface VIII:

> We are required by faith to believe and hold that there is one holy,
> catholic, and apostolic Church; we firmly believe it and unreservedly
> confess it; outside it there is neither salvation nor remission of
> sins. . . .[2]

Because of its high doctrine of the Bible as the Word of God, Protestantism, through much of its history and today in many if not most of its branches, also has held an exclusive view of Christianity's relation to other faiths. Protestantism generally has assumed that there is only one true revelation of God and one way to salvation, and it finds ample support for this view in the New Testament. The words of the Apostle Peter are a case in point: "And there is salvation in no one else, for there is no other name under heaven given among men by which we must be saved" (Acts 4:12). Assuming certain presuppositions — for example, about the divine institution and authority of the Church and the Bible — the exclusivist position has a compelling logic and attraction. It is developed most systematically in the writings of the Christian missionary–theologian Henrik Kraemer, although the rational force of his position could be applied as well by non-Christian believers in defense of their faith.

Kraemer begins with the simple yet momentous conviction that Christianity possesses the only true divine revelation. All other sacred texts are mere "human creations." However, Kraemer rejects the idea that Christianity can tally up proofs or more-impressive evidences for its revelatory claim than can other great religions. As a historian, he considers all attempts to show the superiority of one religion — for example, Christianity — over others as futile. He insists that the study of the history of religions has not produced any readily acknowledged norms for settling claims to superiority or truth. Kraemer is therefore critical of theologians who try to demonstrate that Christianity "fulfills" or "crowns" other religions, such as the religion of Israel or Hinduism. This, he believes, can often mask the worst kind of arrogance and imperialism.

> The argument [that one religion is more valuable than another]
> does not coincide in any way whatever with that of truth. The
> non-Christian religions can just as well as Christianity show up an
> impressive record of psychological, cultural, and other values, and
> it is wholly dependent on one's fundamental axioms of life whether
> one considers these non-Christian achievements of higher value for
> mankind than the Christian.[3]

Kraemer insists that it is impossible to demonstrate the superiority or truth of a religion by religious or philosophical reasoning since there is no universally valid or agreed-on criterion to decide the question. For him, there is only one way out of the dilemma, "namely, to recognize the ultimate, inexplicable fact in human consciousness with which we are confronted is that . . . there is a primordial decision and act of faith which determines our religion or philosophy."[4]

A problem with Kraemer's exclusivism is that it would appear to rule out dialogue before it is even given a chance. While he may be correct about the absence of any universally valid or acceptable norms for judging religious truth-claims, Kraemer cuts off dialogue prematurely because there are undeniable parallels and resemblances in religious experience and belief. In any interreligious dialogue, the point may come, as Wittgenstein remarks, when "the shovel turns," that is, when the dialogue reaches bedrock, where differences are irreconcilable. But notable family likenesses and illuminating comparisons might be discovered long before that point is reached.

Kraemer assumes *a priori* that there are no analogies, no real points of contact. There is only contact by antithesis and, finally, by displacement or by conquest. This view continues to be held by conservative evangelical groups within Protestantism. It is implied, for example, in the following message delivered at a Congress on World Mission at Chicago in 1960: "In the years since the war, more than one billion souls have passed into eternity and more than half of these went to the torment of hellfire without ever hearing of Jesus Christ. . . ."[5] The assumption expressed here is that outside Christianity there is no salvation, no liberating religious truth.

While maintaining belief in the **normative** character of Christian revelation, the Roman Catholic Church and the major Protestant denominations have in recent years shown a new openness toward the non-Christian religions, seeing in them expressions of truth that necessarily must lead to genuine dialogue. This is reflected in the Second Vatican Council's *Declaration on the Relation of the Church to Non-Christian Religions*:

> The Catholic Church rejects nothing of what is true and holy in these religions. She has a high regard for the manner of life and conduct, the precepts and doctrines which, although differing in many ways from her own teaching, nevertheless often reflect a ray of that truth which enlightens all men.[6]

Inclusivism and Synthesis

If exclusivism has been characteristic of the Western religions until recently, a tolerance and inclusivism generally has marked Buddhism and, more especially, Hinduism. The latter opposes all exclusive claims and views the world's religions rather like a spiritual orchestra, each faith contributing to a grand religious symphony. Most apologists for the Hindu position hold in common what they call *Sanatana Dharma*, or Eternal Religion, that is, a fundamental metaphysical unity within the world's religious diversity. There exists, they maintain, a single spiritual Reality that "lends itself to being variously described: as the *Rig Veda* puts it, 'Reality is one: Sages call it by various names.' "[7]

Sanatana Dharma has been most effectively championed by Sarvepalli Radhakrishnan, the noted philosopher and one-time president of India. Hinduism, he writes, requires a respectful tolerance because all religions are so many paths to the One or Ultimate Reality. Exclusivism must be repudiated.

> Belief in exclusive claims and monopolies of religious truth has been a frequent source of pride, fanaticism, and strife. . . . Religious provincialism stands in the way of a unitary world culture which is the only enduring basis for a world community. To neglect the spiritual unity of the world and underline the religious diversity would be philosophically unjustifiable, morally indefensible, and socially dangerous.[8]

Since we all seek the same god under different banners, Radhakrishnan, quoting Ibn-ul-'Arabi, calls for a sharing, a fellowship of faiths:

> If the follower of any particular religion understood the saying of Junayd, 'The color of the water is the color of the vessel containing it,' he would not interfere with the beliefs of others, but would perceive God in every form and in every belief. Our aim should not be to make converts, Christians into Buddhists or Buddhists into Christians, but enable both Buddhists and Christians to rediscover the basic principles of their own religions and to live up to them.[9]

Radhakrishnan believes that such a fellowship of faiths, the evolutionary synthesis of all the higher forces of religion, is based on "the realization of the foundational character of man's religious experience" that, he perceives, is the monistic truth of Advaita Vedanta:

> The light of eternity would blind us if it came full in the face. It is broken into color so that our eyes can make something of it. The different religious traditions clothe the one Reality in various images and their visions could embrace and fertilize each other so as to give mankind a many-sided perfection, the spiritual radiance of Hinduism, the faithful obedience of Judaism, the life of beauty of Greek paganism, the noble compassion of Buddhism, the vision of divine love of Christianity, and the spirit of resignation to the sovereign lord of Islam. All these present different aspects of the inward spiritual life, projections on the intellectual plane of the ineffable experiences of the human spirit.[10]

On the basis of his monistic assumption, Radhakrishnan asserts that the diversity in the traditional formulations tends to diminish as we climb up the scale of spiritual perfection. All paths ultimately lead to the one mountain top, to the one thing signified by the diverse apparel of language and symbol—that is, the Absolute, "the One Spirit which takes us beyond the historical formulations."[11] Or, as the *Maitri Upanishad* says:

> Some contemplate one name and some another. Which of these is best? All are eminent clues to the transcendent, immortal, unembodied Brahman; these names are to be contemplated, lauded, and at last denied. For by them one rises higher and higher in these worlds; but where all comes to its end, there he attains to the Unity of the person.[12]

The inclusivism and synthesis advocated by Radhakrishnan is not, finally, a call for a continuing pluralism of religious paths. *Sanatana Dharma* precludes genuine pluralism in favor of what Radhakrishnan and Aldous Huxley call "the perennial philosophy," the One Spirit or immortal Brahman of which all the historical religions are merely "imperfect halting expressions." It could be argued that, in the final analysis, Radhakrishnan is no less exclusive than is Henrik Kraemer or Pope Boniface VIII. A genuine religious pluralism may be a more difficult, but more compelling, option.

Varieties of Pluralism

Various expressions of religious pluralism have attracted attention recently in the interreligious dialogue. Pluralism derives from two especially modern convictions, one theological and the other historical.

Toynbee and Troeltsch

The theological–moral conviction is well expressed by the historian Arnold Toynbee:

> If God loves mankind, He would have made a revelation to us among other people. But, on the same ground and in virtue of the same vision of what God's nature is, it would also seem unlikely that He would not have made other revelations to other people as well. And it would seem unlikely that He would not have given His revelation in different forms, with different facets, and to different degrees, according to the difference in the nature of individual souls and in the nature of the local tradition of civilization.[13]

The second, historical, conviction can be ascribed to the cumulative evidence of modern scholarship. Each religion is shaped by and therefore takes on the uniqueness and the individuality of its cultural context. This insight is forcefully stated by the historian and social theorist, Ernst Troeltsch:

> The universal law of history consists precisely in this, that history constantly manifests itself in always-new and always-peculiar individualizations—and hence that its tendency is not toward unity or universality [that is, Radhakrishnan] at all, but rather toward the fulfillment of the highest potentialities of each [separate] community.[14]

For Troeltsch, as well as for many historians of religion, this means that each religion is relative, is "indissolubly bound up" with the distinctive elements and needs of its own culture. Therefore, according to Troeltsch, Christianity is the religion of European culture, "it stands or falls with European civilization" just as Theravada Buddhism is inseparable from the culture of South Asia or Shinto from the historical conditions of Japan. Troeltsch asserts, however, that historical relativism does not invalidate claims to truth. "A truth which . . . is *a truth for us* does not cease, because of this, to be very truth and life."[15] Each religion

> is God's countenance as revealed to us; it is the way in which, being what we are, we receive, we react to, the revelation of God. It is binding upon us, and it brings us deliverance. It is final and unconditional for us, because we have nothing else, and because in what we have we can recognize the accents of the divine voice. But this does not preclude the possibility that other racial groups, living under entirely different cultural conditions, may experience their contact with the Divine Life in a quite different way.[16]

Scholars such as Toynbee and Troeltsch argue on both moral and historical grounds for a position of tolerance and genuine religious pluralism. Neither believes that this denies claims to religious truth or weakens religious conviction. This is the position that appears to be taken by most Buddhists. Although refusing to deny the distinctive tenets of their own religion and, while rejecting the notion that all religions lead to the same goal, Buddhists nevertheless rightly pride themselves on their long history of religious toleration. This toleration and cooperation is based on Gautama Buddha's original perception, not unlike that of Troeltsch, that all our human conceptions are culturally limited and relative, and on the moral implications of the Buddhist doctrines of *anatta* (no-self), *ahimsa* (noninjury), and *metta* (lovingkindness). This is conveyed in the following statement of Professor Nakamura of the University of Tokyo, one typical of the Buddhist position:

According to Gautama Buddha, the various views of other religions and philosophies are nothing but partial apprehensions of the whole absolute which lies beyond our area of cognition. The thought that in spiritual matters we are at best blind beggars fighting with each other in our native darkness is not conducive to a narrow and fanatical bigotry. We should respect each other. That is why Buddhism has been filled with the spirit of tolerance.[17]

Wilfred Cantwell Smith

Wilfred Cantwell Smith has served as Professor of World Religions and Director of the Center for the Study of World Religions at Harvard. He is a noted scholar of Islam and has been a major force in recent interfaith dialogue. His position is also quite distinct. Smith argues that the very concept of "religion" is a late Western idea and that it is quite wrong to initiate dialogue at the level of conflicting ideological or doctrinal truth-claims. First, the "cumulative traditions" we call "religions" are, like cultures, so complex and varied that it is impossible to consider a tradition such as Hinduism as a single religion. The same could be said for the complex of developments within Christianity or Buddhism. Therefore, Smith argues, it is pointless to ask if these multiform religions are "true." According to Smith, truth resides not in "religions" but in persons—in the integrity and faithfulness of persons. Religions are not in themselves true or false but may *become* true in the life of the believer. It is therefore

> dangerous and impious to suppose that Christianity [or Buddhism or Islam] is true, as an abstract system, something 'out there' impersonally subsisting. . . . Christianity, I would suggest is not true absolutely, impersonally, statically; rather it can *become* true, if and as you or I appropriate it to ourselves and interiorize it, insofar as we live it out from day to day.[18]

The so-called "religions," for Smith, are merely the historical–cultural contexts within which men and women have entered into a living relationship with God or Ultimate Reality:

> A devout person, whose sense of the presence of God is both vivid and sincere, and of his own unworthiness as he bows in that presence, may plead for God's mercy, and humbly know the quiet transport of its assurance because of his personal and living faith that God is indeed merciful. At that moment the truth of that man's religiousness is perhaps a different matter from the question of the earthly path by which he arrived at his awareness and his faith, or of the community of which he is a member.[19]

Smith's conception of truth as the integrity of personal faith has important implications for the process of interfaith dialogue. This

On his Far East journey, the Catholic Trappist monk
Thomas Merton met in dialogue with many Asian
religious leaders, including the Vietnamese Buddhist
monk Thich Nhat Hanh. (*Source*: Courtesy of Nancy and
Jim Forest.)

dialogue cannot be undertaken "externally" but only "from faith to
faith."

> The first great innovation in recent times has been the personaliza-
> tion of the faiths observed so that one finds . . . the situation is one
> of 'we' talking about 'they.' The next step is dialogue, where 'we'
> talk to 'you.' If there is listening and mutuality, this may become
> that 'we' talk *with* 'you.' The culmination of this process is when 'we
> all' are talking *with* each other about 'us.'[20]

Smith does not mean to imply that in interpersonal dialogue it will
be discovered that all faiths are, at bottom, equally true or adequate,
or that the movement of the future is convergence toward a single
world faith. He is uneasy about premature notions of unity. Yet he
believes that the various faiths are not so much "conflicting truth-
claims" as "divergent paths" that may, through dialogue, be "an invi-
tation to synthesis." In any case, genuine dialogue from "within" is

not predicated on converting the other person from error to truth but on understanding the other from "inside," which can deepen and enrich our own faith. The Muslim, Buddhist, or Christian remains faithful to his or her vision but also grows in awareness of what is shared and not shared with others. This is the crucial and imperative step toward greater mutual understanding, cooperation, and possibly even unexpected convergences.

If religious truth has to do with the Muslim's interiorizing of the teachings of the *Qur'an* or the Buddhist's appropriation of Buddha's *Dharma*, then, in Smith's view, there is empirical–historical evidence that the Muslim and Buddhist faiths are "true" in the sense that they are liberating or saving. By "saving," Smith means "saved from nihilism, from alienation, anomie, despair; from the bleak despondency of meaninglessness. Saved from unfreedom; from being the victim of one's whims within, or of pressures without; saved from being merely an organism reacting to its environment."[21]

If the "cumulative traditions" that we call "religions" were to see truth not in terms of abstract doctrines but in terms of personal liberation, then there is plenty of objective evidence that various faiths are true. "My submission would be this," Smith concludes,

> faith differs in form, but not in kind. This applies both within communities and from one community to another. My observation, as a historian of religion, would be put thus: in so far as he or she has been saved, the Muslim has been saved by Islamic faith (faith of an Islamic form, through Islamic patterns; faith mediated by an Islamic context); the Buddhist by Buddhist faith, the Jew by Jewish.[22]

Smith's insistence that interreligious dialogue must be an engagement from "within" in terms of personal encounter and not a debate about conflicting doctrines or concepts is an extremely valuable insight. But it has been widely criticized as valuable only as far as it goes, and for that reason it is deficient. When the Muslim or Christian truly commits himself or herself to the teachings of the *Qur'an* or the Bible, he or she does so because of a belief that these texts describe a reality that is true whether he or she as an individual appropriates it or not. In other words, existential truth presupposes a prior truth on which its faith rests. John Hick has summarized well the problem left unresolved by Smith's pluralism:

> The truth of Christianity [or Islam or Hinduism] does not consist without reminder in there being true Christians (or Muslims or Hindus). In addition to this it consists, presumably, in the reality, or authenticity, of the knowledge of God which occurs in Christianity, or Islam, or Hinduism. But in that case we still have with us the problem of the at least apparently conflicting truth-claims of differ-

ent religions. If Christianity cannot become (personalistically) true in a man's life unless it is (propositionally) true that God, as depicted in the New Testament, is real and that Jesus is God's love incarnate; and if, again, Islam cannot become (personalistically) true in a man's life unless it is (propositionally) true that God, as depicted in the Qur'an is real and that God does not become incarnate . . . then in order to affirm that these different faiths can become (personalistically) true in the lives of their sincere adherents it seems that we must be able to affirm that their essential (propositional) beliefs are true. But how can it be true . . . both that Christ is God incarnate, and that God does not become incarnate?[23]

While John Hick considers Smith's program of personal dialogue inadequate due to its failure to face head-on the thorny problem of clearly different doctrinal claims regarding the object of faith, he, too, remains committed to religious pluralism. Like Smith, he finds neither an exclusive claim to religious truth nor an appeal to Radhakrishnan's monistic unity as an adequate response to our new global awareness. We turn, then, to Hick's distinctive position.

John Hick

Like all pluralists, John Hick begins with the conviction that God, or the Ultimate, is savingly present, however conceived, in all the great religious traditions. He would insist that this can be maintained on rational — moral and theological — as well as on Smith's experiential–historical grounds. Hick suggests that we are undergoing a revolution in human thought. Just as human consciousness was transformed in the sixteenth century from a Ptolemaic to a Copernican vision of the cosmos, so in the late twentieth century we are undergoing a similar change from a Ptolemaic to a Copernican view of religion. Ptolemaic astronomy conceived of the earth as the center of the solar system and Ptolemaic religion holds that Christianity, Islam, or Buddhism is the center or the truth around which all other faiths revolve. One feature of Ptolemaic religion is that it depends, in large part, on where the believer happens to have been born and raised. Rather than being geocentric, it is ethnocentric. Hick suggests that the problem with both Ptolemaic cosmology and religion is that in the late twentieth century both fail to fit the observed facts. Copernicus rightly shifted the center from the earth to the sun, and a Copernican revolution in religion demands that we shift our religion — be it Christianity, Judaism, or Hinduism — from the center and acknowledge that it is God, the Ultimate, or the Eternal One who is at the center and around whom all the religions revolve.

There are good historical and philosophical reasons for recognizing the need for such a Copernican revolution. First, there are the obvious cultural factors. Because the Eternal only can be conceptualized by means of our experience, we cannot easily rise above our cultural categories in attempting to conceptualize the Infinite.

> Why should religious faith take a number of such different forms? Because, I would suggest, religious faith is not an isolated aspect of our lives but is closely bound up with human culture and human history, which are in turn bound up with basic geographical, climatic, and economic circumstance. It has been pointed out, for example, that 'in nomadic, pastoral, herd-keeping societies the male principle predominates; whereas among agricultural peoples, aware of the fertile earth which brings forth from itself and nourishes its progeny upon its broad bosom, it is the mother-principle which seems important. . . . Among Semitic peoples therefore, whose traditions are those of herdsmen, the sacred is thought of in male terms: God the father. Among Indian peoples whose tradition has been for many centuries, and even millennia, agricultural, it is in female terms that the sacred is understood: God the mother.' . . . We must, I think, distinguish between the Eternal One In Itself, in its eternal self-existent being beyond relationship to a creation and the Eternal One in relation to mankind and as perceived from within our different human cultural situations.[24]

The point can be made philosophically in terms of the philosopher Immanuel Kant's critique of human reason. Hick agrees with Kant that we cannot know *noumena*, things as they exist in themselves independent of our finite perception or cognitive apparatus. Thus, each divine image, or *persona*, "represents the Eternal One as experienced through the filter of a human religious tradition."[25] The world we perceive is real and not illusory, yet real *as humanly perceived*.

> We are real beings in a real environment; but we experience that environment selectively, in terms of our special cognitive equipment. Something similar has to be said about the human awareness of God. God as experienced by this or that individual group is real, not illusory; and yet is adapted to our human spiritual capacities.[26]

The hypothesis of an infinite divine reality experienced in a variety of historical images makes intelligible a religious pluralism while avoiding both exclusivism and religious relativism. There are *different* forms of human awareness of the one Ultimate Reality. We could compare this position to the knowledge of another person. The person *as such* is not fully known by any friend or relative, no matter how intimate the relationship. And yet that is not to say that Tom, Dick, and Harry do not have real, though differing, perceptions of their friend Richard.

To recognize these cultural and philosophical conditions may make religious pluralism intelligible, even compelling, but it does not constitute the end of dialogue. As Hick acknowledges, a huge task remains for future discussion, namely, the relative adequacy (truth?) of the various images of the Eternal One. By what criteria are such conceptions to be judged, and how are such criteria established or agreed on? These very real problems do not invalidate the genuine insights of pluralism. Nevertheless, we might be more skeptical than Hick regarding the purported common Reality underlying our diverse religious experience. Ninian Smart shares this misgiving, based on his own comparative analysis:

> The phenomenological judgment as to whether there is a basic common core of religious experience must be based on the facts and not determined *a priori* by theology. . . . From a phenomenological point of view it is not . . . reasonable to think that there is sufficient conceptual resemblance between God and nirvana (as conceived in Theravada Buddhism) to aver that the Theravadin and the Christian are worshipping the same God (for one thing, the Theravadin is not basically *worshipping*). Thus it is hard to justify the pluralistic solution. . . . In an important way, then, there is incompatibility (at present) between religious truth-claims.[27]

Despite such disagreements regarding the accomplishments and the prospects for interreligious dialogue, few would deny its real successes in overcoming suspicion, ignorance, and intolerance and in advancing real understanding of the genuine likenesses that do exist alongside the continuing differences. This not only has led to a furthering of dialogue on questions of doctrine but also has resulted in collaborative work on social and political problems and in efforts to build a world community. Perhaps the most significant outcome of dialogue for the participants is the deepening awareness of their own faith that, paradoxically, often results in a broadening of the base of that faith without distorting its essence. This has been the experience of many who have sought to understand other religions without assuming some *a priori* unity or without attempting a premature synthesis. The process is what the philosopher W. E. Hocking calls *reconception*.

According to Hocking, the world's religions are now brought for the first time into intimate contact and discourse. This has resulted in a broadening of understanding that leads, unconsciously perhaps, to a better grasp of our own beliefs and practices:

> For broadening necessarily stimulates the deepening process. One's conceptions have been inadequate; they have not anticipated these new vistas and motives: we require to understand our own religion better—we must *reconceive it*—then we shall see how new perspectives belong quite naturally to what has always been present in its nature, unnoticed and unappreciated by us.[28]

In recent years, the dialogues between Buddhists, Hindus, Muslims, Christians, and Jews have produced some remarkable openings toward possible accords on what were thought previously to be irreconcilable differences. One example is the Christian doctrine of the divine incarnation in Christ, which is offensive both to Judaic and to Islamic radical monotheism. New interpretations of the incarnation—for instance, the Islamicist Kenneth Cragg's concept of "divine sending"— has opened up new possibilities for reconceiving a central doctrinal conflict.[29] John Cobb has introduced new interpretations of the self, Nirvana, and God that may lead to quite unexpected convergences between Christianity and Buddhism.[30] John Hick has discerned important analogies between the Hindu belief in reincarnation and the Irenaean tradition in Christian (largely Catholic) eschatology, which may overcome what was thought to be a significant conflict in doctrine. Hick writes that

> there is a basic agreement between [Hindu and Catholic] about the principle of continued responsible life, in which the individual may learn and grow by interacting with human beings in a common environment or series of environments. They differ only as to *where* this continued life is to take place. . . . But this disagreement is relatively slight in comparison with the more fundamental agreement. Indeed the question whether man's continued life takes the form of progress through other spheres, or progress from incarnation to incarnation within this world, would seem to be a matter of probable judgement rather than of essential Christian or Hindu faith.[31]

The passing over into these and other converging insights should not, however, lead to easy expectations that there are, at bottom, few if any conflicting truth-claims. The real differences remain, and it would be a lazy tolerance to deny it. This is the conviction of Mahinda Palihawadana, Professor of Sanskrit at the University of Sri Lanka, who has studied the question of whether Theravada liberation is comparable with "grace" in the Christian tradition. At first, he thought he discerned what could be called "grace" in the movement from "delusion" to enlightenment or Nirvana. However, further exploration has convinced him that the "unwilled change" that comes with Theravadin liberation cannot, without distortion, be compared with Christian grace. Palihawadana points out that *magga*, the movement toward liberation, "can take place only when effort ceases to be, having exhausted its scope" and liberating contact with the uncaused ultimate reality, Nirvana, is made. Yet this reality is not envisaged as an active agent—God—moved by love. Despite this crucial difference, Palihawadana believes that a supreme truth is realized by both traditions, namely:

the redeeming change in a person takes place not ultimately by exercizing the will, but by its cessation, which is an indispensable factor for contact with supreme reality; it is the contact that truly renews and transforms the person.[32]

Other specific instances of creative dialogue could here be adduced, but we hope the points we want to exemplify are clear.

Conclusion

We conclude with some summary ideas that the reader can consider, question, and perhaps use as the basis for further dialogue.

Exclusivism is initially attractive because it does show a deep concern for what is true as against illusion and error. And yet exclusivism often asserts claims to truth dogmatically without recognizing the need to give compelling reasons for these claims. It rejects dialogue too quickly and often breeds an uneducated intolerance.

A complete religious relativism, while recognizing an element of truth in the cultural life of all religions, finally is not satisfactory since it ignores the importance of truth-claims in the religious life. If all religions are equally true, on what grounds does a person follow this rather than that religion? This is an especially important question in modern, pluralistic society. It simply is no longer true that we are fated to hold the religion or ideology into which we were born.

Syncretism, like relativism, often suffers from an easy toleration that does not reflect concern but, instead, indifference toward the questions of truth and error. In fact, toleration can reveal an insensitivity to and even contempt of the other person. As Goethe remarked, "To tolerate means to offend." The alternative to a slothful toleration is not intolerance. Syncretism is also questionable because it can mean the rather artificial joining of quite different religious beliefs and practices that together lack the necessary coherence and consistency. A religion must have a recognizable character of its own, an organic unity. It must be natural, substantial, and individual. A patchwork, concocted religion is in danger of glossing over the very real differences that do exist and of purchasing a spurious unity at too heavy a price—that is, artificiality and incoherence.

Another approach that appears questionable is to claim that any one religion is the fulfillment of another or others. There is, of course, a certain truth in the fact that Buddhism developed out of Hinduism, as Christianity emerged from Judaism, and that they carried forward certain teachings in these traditions and directed them along new, creative paths. But this is not the same thing as the claim that either religion "crowns" or "fulfils" the other. To make such an assertion involves a judgment about what constitutes the critical essence of religion. But this is exactly the matter in dispute and open, possibly, to further discussion. In any case, to picture other religions as mere preparations for our own can smack of arrogance and condescension — and, worse, can justify imperialistic actions.

Our current state of knowledge would seem to require that we recognize both a genuine religious pluralism and, at the same time, the need to avoid the pitfalls of relativism and syncretism. That means recognition of the genuine truths possessed by other religions while not neglecting the real differences and disagreements that do exist; it further means remaining attentive to the need for an ongoing reconception of our own faith in light of the continuing dialogue with others. That process could result in a number of possible outcomes.[33]

You might discover in the other religion a value or truth which you already find present in your own. So that at least at *that* level agreement or unity is already achieved. The fact that Jews and Christians or Hindus and Buddhists hold some central doctrines in common are cases in point.

You might find in the other religion beliefs and practices that you can neither accept as true nor dismiss as error. They may have spiritual value for others but do not seem necessary or even helpful to you. On the other hand, they may not conflict with your own tenets. These are what the theologians have called *adiaphora*, things neutral or indifferent. They might include numerous religious practices that reflect unique cultural circumstances.

You might find in other religions those central beliefs and practices that cannot be accepted as consistent with your own religious convictions. Here, real differences persist and, perhaps on some occasions, contention must be recognized as unavoidable.

You may discover in other religions *new* truths—some realities that you must make your own and that require a reconception of your previous religious belief or practice. You see in another religion crucial factors that are only latent or thoroughly undeveloped in your own, so that your own faith requires a broadening, which involves a process of deepening. However, what is taken in must be congruent with what is essential to your own religion. An example of this level of engagement is the profound influence that the aesthetic insights and meditation practices of Buddhism have had on Roman Catholic spiritual life as reflected in the writings of Thomas Merton, Heinrich Dumoulin, and others.

Another outcome that is becoming more common in our global society is conversion to another religion. Exposure to a different religion may lead to a deepening of your own, but it may, as we pointed out in Chapter 1, force you to a painful re-evaluation of your present religious convictions, with the possible result of a radical change of perspective and allegiance. This is part of the risk, as well as the opportunity, of living in a dynamic, open society. What is called for today is that difficult balance between commitment and real openness to what is new or foreign. This openness assumes commitment and rejects indifference in whatever form. Real dialogue does not mean listening with only one ear while you prepare for your next rebuttal; rather, it means engaging the other person in the lively expectation that you are about to learn something valuable and true.

Notes

1. Wilfred Cantwell Smith, "The Christian in a Religiously Plural World" in *Christianity and Other Religions*, ed. by John Hick and Brian Hebblethwaite (Philadelphia, 1980), pp. 94–95.
2. Densinger, 468–69. *The Church Teaches: Documents of the Church in English Translation* (St. Louis, 1955), pp. 153–54.
3. Henrik Kraemer, *The Christian Message in a Non-Christian World* (New York, 1938), p. 106.
4. H. Kraemer, *Religion and the Christian Faith* (London, 1956), pp. 85–86.
5. *Facing the Unfinished Task*, ed. by J. O. Percy (Grand Rapids, Mich., 1961), p. 9.
6. Austin Flannery, ed., *Vatican Council II. The Conciliar and Post-Conciliar Documents* (Dublin, 1975), p. 739.
7. Sri Anandashram Swamiji, in Moses Jung, et al. *Relations Among Religions Today* (Leiden, 1963), p. 75.
8. S. Radhakrishnan, "Religion and Religions" in M. Jung, *Religions Today*, p. 131–32.
9. Radhakrishnan, "Religion and Religions," pp. 132–33.
10. Radhakrishnan, "Religion and Religions," p. 134.
11. Radhakrishnan, "Religion and Religions," p. 135.
12. Radhakrishnan, "Religion and Religions," p. 135.
13. Arnold Toynbee, *Christianity Among the Religions of the World* (New York, 1957), p. 96.
14. Ernst Troeltsch, "The Place of Christianity Among the World Religions," in J. Hick and B. Hebblethwaite, *Christianity*, p. 17.
15. Troeltsch, "The Place of Christianity," p. 31.
16. Troeltsch, "The Place of Christianity," p. 25.
17. Najime Nakamura, "Buddhist Accommodation to Neighboring Religions," in M. Jung, *Religions Today*, p. 38. This volume contains similar statements by other noted Buddhist scholars, including D. T. Suzuki.
18. Wilfred Cantwell Smith, *Questions of Religious Truth* (New York, 1967), p. 68.
19. Smith, *Questions*, pp. 70–71.
20. W. C. Smith—in Kitagawa and Eliade, eds., *The History of Religions: Essays in Methodology* (Chicago, 1959), p. 34.
21. W. C. Smith, *Towards a World Theology* (Philadelphia, 1981), p. 168.

22. Smith, *World Theology*, p. 168.
23. John Hick, ed., *Truth and Dialogue in World Religions: Conflicting Truth Claims* (Philadelphia, 1974), p. 148.
24. John Hick, *God Has Many Names* (Philadelphia, 1982), pp. 51–52.
25. Hick, *God Has Many Names*, p. 84.
26. Hick, *God Has Many Names*, p. 106.
27. Ninian Smart, "Truth and Religions," in J. Hick, *Truth and Dialogue*, pp. 55–56.
28. William E. Hocking, *Living Religions and a World Faith* (New York, 1940), pp. 190–91.
29. Kenneth Cragg, "Islam and Incarnation," in J. Hick, *Truth and Dialogue*, pp. 126–139.
30. John B. Cobb, Jr., *Beyond Dialogue: Toward Mutual Transformation of Christianity and Buddhism* (Philadelphia, 1982).
31. J. Hick, *Truth and Dialogue*, p. 154. See also Hick's longer discussion in *Death and Eternal Life*.
32. Mahinda Palihawadana, "Is There a Theravada Buddhist Idea of Grace?" in Donald G. Dawe and John B. Carman, eds., *Christian Faith in a Religiously Plural World* (Maryknoll, N.Y., 1978), p. 101.
33. For this general scheme I am dependent on a similar one developed by E. L. Allen in *Christianity Among the Religions* (London, 1960).

Review Questions

1. Do you find the position of religious exclusivism reasonable or not? Why?
2. How do you respond to the Hindu philosopher Radhakrishnan's call for a unity and synthesis of all the religions? How might we criticize his view of the "One Spirit which takes us beyond the historical formulations"?
3. Describe Wilfred Cantwell Smith's view of religious truth and interreligious dialogue. According to John Hick, what is problematic in Smith's position?
4. Describe John Hick's call for a "Copernican revolution" in religion. What does Ninian Smart see as problematic in Hick's distinction between the Eternal One as independent of human perception and the Eternal One as perceived by different traditions?
5. Of the various approaches to the relation between the religions, which position do you find most compelling or appealing? Why?

Suggestions for Further Reading

For a variety of position statements on interreligious relations, see the following:

JUNG, MOSES, et al. (eds.), *Relations Among Religions Today* (Leiden: E. J. Brill, 1963).

HICK, JOHN, and BRIAN HEBBLETHWAITE (eds.), *Christianity and Other Religions* (Philadelphia: Fortress Press, 1980). While concentrating on Christianity, this latter work includes important statements by Troeltsch, Tillich, Vatican II, and so forth, as well as a valuable bibliography.

For extended statements of important writers on interreligious relations representing distinctive positions, see the following:

HICK, JOHN, *God Has Many Names* (Philadelphia: Westminster Press, 1982).

HOCKING, WILLIAM E., *Living Religions and a World Faith* (New York: Macmillan, 1940; reprint, New York, 1975).

KRAEMER, HENRIK, *The Christian Message in a Non-Christian World* (New York: Harper & Row, 1938).

RADHAKRISHNAN, SARVEPALLI, *The Hindu View of Life* (New York: Macmillan, 1927; reprint, London, 1980).

SMART, NINIAN, *Beyond Ideology* (New York: Harper & Row, 1979).

SMITH, WILFRED CANTWELL, *Towards a World Theology* (Philadelphia: Westminster Press, 1981).

SCHUON, FRITHJOF, *The Transcendent Unity of Religions* (New York: Harper & Row, 1975).

ZAEHNER, ROBERT, *Concordant Discord: Interdependence of Faiths* (Oxford: Oxford University Press, 1970).

For some examples of specific interreligious dialogue, see the following:

DAWE, DONALD G., and JOHN B. CARMEN (eds.), *Christian Faith in a Religiously Plural World* (Maryknoll, N.Y.: Orbis Books, 1978). Non-Christian scholars respond to a Christian position on interreligious relations.

INGRAM, PETER, and FREDERICK STRENG (eds.), *Buddhist-Christian Dialogue: Possibilities for Mutual Transformation* (Honolulu: University of Hawaii Press, 1984).

SAMARTHA, S. J., and J. B. TAYLOR (eds.), *Christian-Muslim Dialogue* (Geneva: World Council of Churches, 1973).

————, *Jewish-Christian Dialogue* (Geneva: World Council of Churches, 1975).

For discussions of the question of truth in interreligious dialogue, see the following:

HICK, JOHN (ed.), *Truth and Dialogue in World Religions: Conflicting Truth-Claims* (Philadelphia: Westminster Press, 1974).

WIEBE, DONALD, *Religion and Truth: Towards an Alternative Paradigm for the Study of Religion* (The Hague: Mouton Publishers, 1981).

Secularization and the Sacred— The Future of Religion

OVERVIEW

In Chapter 13, we considered the challenge posed by religious diversity in a rapidly contracting and interdependent world. Here, we are concerned with another, related, phenomenon: the process of modern secularization and its meaning for the future of religion. We begin with a discussion of what is meant by secularization and how it is defined. How we view secularization is largely determined by the way we interpret the causes or the indices of a secularization process at work in the modern world. On certain things, however, there is consensus. Since the seventeenth century in the West, we have witnessed an increasing differentiation and specialization of social institutions and functions. With this has emerged a competition of social authorities. Closely related to this phenomenon has been a growing social and religious pluralism, which has also meant intensive competition among a growing number of religious options and a loss of any religion's taken-for-granted character. A third factor contributing to secularization is the now-pervasive application of scientific thinking and technique to the solving of most human problems.

While these social processes are undisputed, there is disagreement as to their meaning. Some see these developments as signaling a clear decline in religious belief, practice, and influence, not only in the West but also in every society touched by modern science and industrialization where there is significant pluralism and specialization. These students of secularization are pessimistic about the future of religion, unless there were to occur a veritable revolution in human

371

consciousness and social organization—about which they are extremely dubious.

Others deny that secularization is taking place and point to the evidence of religious renewal in numerous modern, urban industrialized societies. A number of influential social theorists see secularization as essentially a process of social differentiation in which religion has been increasingly removed from other social institutions, such as government, education, and the economy. However, it is argued that this process does not imply a decline either of religion or its influence, but, rather, a change from older patterns of religious life to radically new, highly personal, and pluralistic forms of religious behavior.

We conclude this postscript with some thoughts on how the question of secularization and the future of religion may be viewed by reflecting again on what it means to be truly human, that is, on our ability to respond to existential predicaments through our capacity for self-transcendence.

Secularization: A Disputed Topic

During the past 200 years, a number of influential thinkers have prophesied that history signals an increasing process of secularization with an attendant decline of religion. By secularization, these thinkers refer to a series of social and intellectual changes by which vital sectors of modern society and culture have been and will continue to be removed from the domination of religious beliefs, institutions, and practices. Many of the *philosophes* of the eighteenth-century Enlightenment viewed this modern process of secularization as a liberation from the bondage of religious superstition, magic, and priestcraft. Secularization represented for them the unbinding of Prometheus, the freeing of Man to be master of his own fate.

Recently, social scientists, historians of religion, and theologians have expressed rather divergent views on the nature and meaning of secularization. Some theologians view secularization as *the* enemy, a fateful process. Other theologians and sociologists see secularization positively, as the purifying of true religion of magic and superstition. These radically different opinions have led to a renewed debate on the nature and significance of secularization for the future of religion.

What, for example, are the appropriate indices of secularization? Is it church attendance or the falling off of traditional religious practices? Is it the questioning of certain beliefs? Or is secularization a process that is more subtle, reflecting not the loss of religious belief and behavior but a momentous transformation of religiosity into new, quite unexpected patterns? In other words, is there a real waning of religion, or is it simply that religious values and behaviors are now expressed through often-hidden cultural forms?

Causes of Secularization

While there is considerable dispute over what constitutes true measures of secularization (and hence whether it is, indeed, a force leading to the real decline in religion), certain things are agreed on. These need to be taken into account in understanding religion in contemporary society and its future prospects. The word *secularization* came into use in the West at the time of the Peace of Westphalia in 1648. It referred to the process of transferring lands and possessions from ecclesiastical to civil control. That is a clue to one important index of the secularizing process at work at the beginning of the modern period: the structural *differentiation* and *specialization* of institutions and social roles in society. Since the middle of the seventeenth century in the West, there has been a growing differentiation between the realm of politics and government and religion. The same has occurred, gradually but relentlessly, in the spheres of economics, law, medicine, and education. Religion increasingly has become a single department in society alongside many others. Today, it is no longer *the* pervasive and determinant influence that it was in earlier centuries.

This differentiation and specialization of social institutions has inevitably resulted in competition and conflict among a variety of agencies (political, legal, economic, and so forth) for social and cultural authority. We see this today in the tensions between the church and the state, between the church and public education, and between the church and the economy. Related to this is a growing social and religious *pluralism*. In most Western societies today, citizens are confronted with multiple worldviews and value systems. The Catholic or Baptist can no longer take his or her religion for granted. The sociologist Peter Berger considers social and intellectual pluralism to be a powerful factor in the ever-increasing secularization of society.

In addition to institutional differentiation and a growing social pluralism, a third factor that has contributed to secularization is what Max Weber calls *rationalization*. By this term, Weber means the increasing application of scientific thinking to all activities of life in the modern world. Rationalization implies the prevalence of an empirical temper of mind, one that includes commitment to inquiry, observational detachment, and willingness to test alternative explanations and ways of doing things. This has enhanced our capacity, through science and technology, to harness nature and to organize society according to our own human designs and purposes. Our scientific ethos has, in turn, challenged supernatural explanations of the workings of nature and history and the proper ordering of society.

Whatever we think of secularization, the above factors are clear

signs of a contraction of religion from its dominant place in the
determination of social institutions and social action in at least many
Western societies today.

Meanings of Secularization

If we concede that the modern differentiation of social institutions,
the religious pluralism with its inevitable competition over beliefs and
values, and the scientific rationalization of human action are social
facts, one question remains: How has this altered religion? Do these
processes necessarily entail the decline or the ultimate eclipse of religion? Or, as indicated earlier, does secularization simply indicate a
significant shift in the patterns of religious belief and behavior? On
these issues there is much dispute.

Many writers contend that there is a very real decline in religious
belief and practice in the West and that there is evidence of a similar
process at work in other parts of the world where industrialization
and the rationalization of social life have taken hold—for example,
in China and Japan. The loss of social significance is an obvious
indication of the diminished role of religion in modern life. While
individuals may continue some traditional religious practices (churchgoing, baptism, marriage, and funerals), these activities are often
merely decorous. In any case, they have no influence on the real agencies
(government, education, and so forth) that propel the life of society.

Other students of religion see the so-called process of secularization
quite differently; indeed, some deny the concept altogether, while
others do not view it as the harbinger of religion's last hour. Rather,
they interpret secularization as a means of religious purification. As
they see it, one possible problem with the theory of religious decline is
the absence of any long-term comparative data. This makes it extremely
difficult to document a religious descent scientifically. We simply do not
have sufficient data from earlier historical epochs. Furthermore, the
evidence of even the past 200 years appears ambiguous.

There are, however, a number of studies that have shown not only
the persistence of but also the recent increase in religious activity,
even in highly urban, technocratic societies. This has led some to
propose an alternative interpretation of secularization, namely, that
what is occurring is not religious *decline* but, rather, a significant *change*
from historical patterns of behavior to radically new forms of religious
life. Here, it might be more accurate to speak of secularization as the
modern process in which religious life and institutions are progressively
differentiated from other parts of the social structure. This process has
enhanced personal religious consciousness and autonomy while con-
cealing religion's present, less visible but real public influence.

Clearly, social theorists are divided on whether secularization is a reality and, if it is, what it means for the future of religion. Theologians are also divided in their views on the subject. Many see the removal of religion from our public institutions and the "privatization" of religion as a dangerous threat to its future. They agree with Bryan Wilson: A religion devoid of a public role and sanction is an endangered species and perhaps faces a fate similar to that of the Etruscans or the Aztecs.

Some theologians are optimistic, perceiving secularization as a religious blessing. In fact, they see it as a process at work in the emergence of biblical faith itself, one that frees us from the worship of nature and which portrays God as turning the world over to human responsibility. While we can question such an optimistic view of secularization as a religiously purifying and liberating process, it does point up a striking feature of our human condition, about which we spoke in Chapter 1. We humans share a distinct form of self-consciousness which we called self-transcendence, that is, our human ability to stand clear of ourselves and to reflect on such questions as "What is the purpose of life?", "To whom or what do I owe my loyalty?", or "What endures?"

Some would claim that a total eclipse of our sense of the sacred would mean our dehumanization, for the sacred is intrinsic to our experience of genuine self-transcendence. Without attempting prophecy, we can perhaps conclude that the renewal of the sacred is presumable, since it has to do with our recognition of the mystery that lies deep in the ceaseless renewing of our existential questions concerning life's meaning, faith, evil, love, and hope.

Suggestions for Further Reading

BELL, DANIEL, "The Return of the Sacred," *The Winding Passage* (Cambridge, Mass.: ABT Books, 1980).

BELLAH, ROBERT, "Religious Evolution," *Beyond Belief* (New York: Harper & Row, 1970).

BERGER, PETER, *The Sacred Canopy* (New York: Doubleday, 1967).

COX, HARVEY, *The Secular City* (New York: Macmillan, 1965).

DOBBELAERE, KAREL, "Secularization: A Multi-Dimensional Concept," *Current Sociology* 29, no. 2 (Summer, 1981). A comprehensive overview and bibliography.

FENN, RICHARD, *Toward a Theory of Secularization* (Storrs, Conn.: Society for the Scientific Study of Religion, 1978).

HAMMOND, PHILLIP E., *The Sacred in a Secular Age* (Berkeley: University of California Press, 1985).

LUCKMANN, THOMAS, *The Invisible Religion* (New York: Macmillan, 1967).

MARTIN, DAVID, *A General Theory of Secularization* (New York: Harper & Row, 1978).

WILSON, BRYAN, *Contemporary Transformations of Religion* (London: Oxford University Press, 1976).

———, *Religion in Secular Society* (Baltimore: Penguin Books, 1966).

———, *Religion in Sociological Perspective* (Oxford: Oxford University Press, 1982).

Glossary

agnosticism   From the Greek *a* ("not") and the base of *gignoskein* ("to know"); applies to any proposition (but usually with respect to God) for which evidence for belief or dogmatic unbelief is insufficient.

analogy   A similarity between things otherwise unlike. Because religions often refer to things (gods, a future life, and so forth) that lie beyond finite experience, they must speak of these things by analogy. For example, the word *good* when applied to God is neither the same as nor entirely different from goodness when applied to humans. *Good* is here used analogously.

androgynous   From the Greek roots for male and female; denotes the joining of the physical characteristics and the natures of both sexes in one divine or human being.

animism   From the Latin *anima*, meaning "soul"; the belief that all things possess a soul or spirit—that is, all reality is animate. Introduced by E. B. Tylor to refer to what he conceived to be the earliest form of religion.

anomie   From the Greek *anomia*, meaning lawlessness; popularized in the study of religion by Emile Durkheim and has to do with a condition of the individual or society in which normal order is dissolving or absent, bringing a state of disorientation, anxiety, and chaos.

anthropomorphism   Meaning "of human form"; used for the attribution of human qualities to the divine or God. Often used critically as the conceiving of God or the gods in too-human form.

antinomian   From the Greek *anti*, against, and *nomos*, law; describes those religious groups or individuals who hold the doctrine that they are freed from and above the law that remains binding on others. Antinomian sects have threatened Christianity from time to time through the centuries.

apocalypse   From the Greek *apokalypsis*, meaning "revelation"; associated with a class of Jewish and Christian literature that purports to reveal, in highly symbolic language, what is to happen in the future.

archetypal   Original pattern, or model, from which other things—such as institutions, beliefs, and behavior—are patterned. In many religions, it is important to follow the model of behavior established by God or the gods "in the beginning."

ascetic   Generally refers to a person who lives an austere and self-denying life. In many religions, refers to a special group of devotees who lead a life of contemplation and self-denial, such as monks or hermits.

asrama   One of the four "stages of life" in Hinduism. The practice of withdrawal from the world in which one lives as a holy recluse; an ashram is a community dwelling place where those who have withdrawn can gather around a guru, or teacher, to study and meditate.

atonement   At-one-ment. Especially prominent in Judaism and Christianity; a representative sacrifice of the life of a victim (symbolized by its outpoured blood), to serve as an expiation (see p. 380) for an individual or a community to cover an offense to God or gods.

bar mitzvah   Means "Son of the Commandment"; applied to a Jewish boy on his thirteenth birthday when, in a synagogue ceremony, he takes on his religious responsibilities in the community. The boy thereafter has certain prerogatives, such as the reading of the Torah; is held accountable for his own sins, and is commanded to fast on the Day of Atonement.

bhakti   Sanskrit word meaning "devotion"; the path to God or liberation in Hinduism that stresses love and devotion to a deity rather than study or ritual obligation. The way of devotion is classically outlined in the *Bhagavad Gita*.

Calvinism   Expression of Protestant Christianity that traces its doctrines and practices to the teachings of the Reformer, John Calvin (1509–1564). These include the sovereignty of God, election or predestination, original sin, the irresistibility of grace, and a deep sense of calling in our secular occupation.

catharsis   Means a cleansing or a purging; in religion, one important function is the act of purification that is necessary if we are to be right with or in the presence of the sacred. Also serves to purge the emotions.

cosmogony Refers to those stories or theories that have to do with the birth or creation of the world or universe.

cosmological proof One of the classical proofs of the existence of God arguing that the world is not self-explanatory and requires an infinite (noncontingent) being, God, as its explanation. The contingency of the world requires a first cause, a necessary being.

cosmology Derived from the Greek words meaning "doctrine of the world"; has to do with the branch of philosophical or scientific speculation that deals with the origin and structure of the world.

Cro-Magnon Term that designates the first group of fully evolved representatives of *Homo sapiens*, who entered Europe from the Middle East between 42,000 and 30,000 B.C.E.

deism From the Latin *deus* (god); applies to a movement of thought in the seventeenth and eighteenth centuries in Europe that held a belief in one God who creates the world but who does not intervene directly in its ongoing functioning. God allows the world to operate by the natural laws he originally established. The deist God is a transcendent Creator but is not immanent in the world.

denomination A form of religious institution distinctive of Protestant Christianity and often contrasted with both state-established churches and religious sects; Common in pluralistic societies like the United States where no church is established by law or privileged by the state and each religious group receives equal treatment before the law. Resemble churches in that they are usually large and inclusive across socioeconomic lines, and their members are not alienated from the larger society.

dharma In the Hindu tradition, means "sacred law"; set forth in numerous texts, such as the Code of Manu, which has to do with caste duties and obligations. A caste member who does his *dharma* acquires good *karma*. In Buddhism, refers to the teachings of Buddha—for example, the Four Noble Truths.

epiphany From the Greek, meaning "manifestation" of a god or divine power. In Christianity, the feast of Epiphany, or Manifestation of Christ, is celebrated on January 6.

eschatology From the Greek *eschatos*, meaning the "last things"; the understanding of nature, of human life, and of history in terms of their goals or destinies. Often associated with beliefs concerning life after death, judgment, and Heaven and Hell. Some form is held, implicitly or explicitly, by all the religions.

ethnocentric Assumption that a person's own race or culture is normative or superior to others.

etiological Used in religion to designate those doctrines or myths that describe and explain the origin of some thing—for example, the world, human institutions, or beliefs.

Eucharist The chief sacrament of Christianity, derived from the Last Supper of Jesus and his disciples celebrated the evening before Jesus's crucifixion. Believers partake of the bread and wine in remembrance of Jesus Christ and his sacrifice.

evangelical Christians of any Protestant church or sect who place great importance on a conscious, personal conversion to Christ rather than on becoming a Christian through birth or baptism.

existential Those beliefs or actions that focus on personal existence in contrast to those matters that are impersonal or indifferent to the person. Existentialism is concerned with protesting against positions that view the person as an object of purely rational or scientific analysis. It emphasizes the "subjective"—things such as finitude, guilt, suffering, and death that cannot be approached in the manner of scientific problem solving—and the ambiguities of life that arise from our unique human freedom.

exorcist Priest or magician who practices exorcism or the expelling of evil spirits by the use of a special ritual or formula or the use of a holy name.

expiation Making right by some ritual act or offering for the injury or sin done to some other person or god; closely related to atonement (see p. 378) and propitiation (see p. 384) and involves an act of sacrifice to remove pollution or sin.

fetish Derived from the Portuguese *feitico*, meaning "skillfully made"; in religion, refers to various objects, either natural or artificial, that are endowed with supernatural magical power or virtue and are capable of averting evil or bringing good.

fideism From the Latin *fides*, meaning "faith"; associated with those who believe that faith must precede reason with regard to knowledge of God and that reason alone is incapable of producing genuine knowledge of God.

Functionalism Method applied to the study of religion that is not interested in the history or evolution of religions but rather focuses on how religion functions in a particular social structure or cultural context—for example, what role(s) a particular religious ritual plays in the social life of a tribe.

genetic fallacy   Logical error of judging the nature, value, or truth of a religion based on a description or analysis of its origin or earliest expression.

guru   In Hinduism, a spiritual teacher or guide who instructs his followers on the path to liberation.

Hasidim (or **Chasidim**)   From the Hebrew *hasid*, meaning "pietist"; a party among the Jews of Palestine who opposed the hellenizing of Judaism in the second century B.C.E. and were the backbone of Jewish resistance. In modern times, associated with an ultra-orthodox Jewish movement whose members refuse to wear modern Western clothing and dress as their ancestors in the ghettos of eastern Europe. Their piety is marked by a mystical joy and intensity.

hathayoga   One of the four types of yoga; stresses the discipline of the body as the means to liberation.

henotheism   From the Greek for "one" and "god"; ascribed to Max Müller, who used it to describe that form of religion in which one god is supreme but others exist; in contrast to monotheism, in which only one god exists.

hierophany   Proposed by Mircea Eliade to designate any act or manifestation of the sacred; literally means something sacred showing itself to us.

icon   From the Greek *eikon*, meaning "image" or "likeness"; a symbolic sacred image, usually painted on flat wood panels or canvas, that materially embodies a spiritual meaning and power. They are sacramental in that they make present the sacred or the divine and are venerated in Eastern Orthodox Christian churches.

incantation   Use of a verbal formula in the form of a spell or charm, either spoken or chanted, as part of a magical ritual.

Kaddish   Jewish public prayer that is characterized by the praise and glorification of God and by hope in the establishment of God's kingdom on earth; also used as a mourner's prayer and is recited at the graveside of close relatives and in the synagogue.

karma   In Sanskrit, literally means "action" or "deed"; the law governing deeds whereby our past and present actions determine our future condition both in this and in future lives; a foundation of the belief in reincarnation or rebirth.

legend   Story about the past that is popularly taken to be historical and that does have some historical basis but includes elements of the fictitious and even fabulous.

logos   In Greek, translated as "word", "speech", "discourse", or "reason"; used by the Stoics to refer to the divine Reason or God. The Jewish writer Philo identified the creative, divine word of the Hebrew scriptures with the logos of the Stoics. In the Gospel of John and in the early Church, was identified with the Son of the Christian Trinity.

Maccabees   Name given to patriotic Jewish warriors of the second century B.C.E., named after their leader, Judas Maccabeus, who resisted pagan (Greek) practices. The story is told in I Maccabees and is celebrated in the Jewish Festival of Hanukkah.

mandala   A symmetrical diagram, circular or square; symbolic representation of the universe, reality, or those energies depicted as deities, demons, Bodhisattvas, and the Buddha. Used in meditation practices in some schools of Buddhism.

mantra   A sacred sound of one syllable or more. In Hinduism, repeated during meditation in order to empty the mind in preparation for liberation; in Buddhism, expresses the essence of some transcendental power or being such as the Buddha or Bodhisattva. The most famous is the syllable OM.

masochism   Broadly associated with the feeling of pleasure that a person desires from being abused or dominated by another person or institution.

mendicant   A beggar; in many religions, such as Christianity and Buddhism, the act of begging for alms is (or was) a high form of the spiritual life and discipline.

metaphysics   From the Greek, meaning "after physics"; the branch of philosophy that investigates those first causes and essential principles of being—what it means to be. Concerned with such concepts as God, the soul, and freedom.

millenarianism   First appears in the New Testament book of Revelation (Ch. 20) in connection with the final struggle between God and Satan and the second coming of Christ in the immediate future, all of which precede the millennium— the 1,000-year reign of the Messiah. Used, however, to describe a large variety of Christian and non-Christian apocalyptic (see p. 378) movements that expect a redeemer to inaugurate a Utopian Age. Often used interchangeably with "messianism" or "messianic movements."

Mishnah From the Hebrew, meaning "to repeat"; the collection of oral Jewish law, in contrast to the written Law, or Torah, that was compiled by Rabbi Judah Ha-Nasi, circa 200 C.E. Six divisions of the Mishnah cover laws of agriculture, festivals, women, marriage, and so forth. Together with the Gemara, commentary on the Mishnah, it forms the bases of the Talmud (see p. 386).

moksha From Sanskrit, meaning "liberation" in Hinduism; liberation from the round of birth, death, and rebirth. Various classical schools of Hinduism define in different ways what constitutes liberation and the methods of achieving it.

monism From the Greek, meaning "one"; applied to those doctrines that teach that only one being exists, as differentiated from pantheism, which teaches that all beings are divine or that God is in everything. Especially associated with Indian nondualism or Advaita Vedanta.

monotheism Belief in one personal, transcendent Creator God as opposed to belief in many gods. Judaism, Islam, and Christianity are examples of monotheistic religions.

mudra A symbolic gesture or position of the hands in Hinduism and Buddhism; each mudra signifies a mood, virtue, or spiritual quality.

muezzin Official in Islamic countries who calls the summons to prayer; in large mosques, he speaks from a tower called a minaret.

mystery cults Associated especially with the secret religious cults of ancient Greece and Rome that practiced rites of initiation involving purification, the revealing of secret teachings and symbols, and a sacramental meal of communion with a person's fellows and with the divinity. The chief Greek cults were the Eleusinian and Orphic mysteries.

myth A narrative about gods or heroes, often a complex of stories, that may or may not refer to actual temporal events but that is regarded as true because it serves to explain how the world, creatures, and customs came to be; often represents a model or paradigm of aspects of the natural or human world.

Neanderthal A type of prehistoric man from the middle Paleolithic (see p. 384) age, whose remains were found in a cave in the Neanderthal Valley near Dusseldorf, Germany.

Neolithic The New Stone Age that began about 8000–7000 B.C.E.

in the Middle East and about 4000–3000 B.C.E. in Europe; was followed by the Bronze Age.

Nichiren   A Japanese Buddhist reformer (1222–1282 C.E.) and the sect named after him, which incorporates aspects of Buddhism and Shintoism, the indigenous national religion of Japan. Nichiren believed true Buddhism was found in the *Lotus Sutra* and that other forms of Buddhism were in error. A uniquely militant and zealous expression of Buddhism.

normative   The measure or standard by which other beliefs or practices are to be judged.

omnipotent   From the Latin *omni* (all) and *potens* (powerful), meaning all-powerful; traditionally ascribed to God in Western monotheism is his having unlimited power and authority.

omniscient   Having infinite knowledge; knowing all things is traditionally ascribed to God in the Western monotheistic religions.

ontological   The nature of being; the branch of philosophy that investigates the nature, the essential properties, and the relations of being.

Paleolithic   The Old Stone Age that began with the appearance of the earliest toolmakers and extended to about 10,000–8,000 B.C.E. It is characterized by the making of stone tools and weapons and by hunting and food-gathering.

pantheism   From the Greek *pan* (all) and *theos* (god); the doctrine that all that exists is God and God is all in all. God and nature are interchangeable terms.

pantheon   From the Greek, meaning "all the gods"; designates all the gods of a society taken collectively. Derives from the great Pantheon at Rome, a temple built in 27 B.C.E. and dedicated to all the gods.

polytheism   Recognition and worship of more than one god; conceives of sacred power as being manifested in diverse forms.

predestinarian   A person who holds the belief in predestination— the doctrine that God, from the beginning, has determined the ultimate destiny of every human being, some to salvation and others to damnation.

propitiation   Act of appeasing, pacifying, or making favorable, often through some form of sacrifice to a deity.

proselytize   Engaging in the effort of persuading or converting a person from one religion or opinion to another; a proselyte is one who has been converted from one religion to another.

rabbinic   Things that pertain to Jewish rabbis or teachers, their writings, opinions, and so forth.

reliquary   A small box, container, or shrine used to hold or exhibit a religious relic, such as the bones of a saint.

revivalism   A characteristic of certain religious groups, especially within Protestant Christianity, that emphasizes the importance of a personal, emotional conversion and commitment to Christ; effected through "revivals," evangelistic meetings, or even longer periods of religious fervor, in which a religious awakening and conversion of individuals is sought.

sadhu   In the Hindu tradition, a wandering holy man who is devoted fully to achieving *moksha*, or liberation.

saga   A heroic narrative about either a historical or legendary figure; classic sagas were those recorded in Ireland in the twelfth and thirteenth centuries.

sannyasin   In Hinduism, a person who has renounced the world and its possessions and has become an ascetic (see p. 378), seeking liberation through prayer and meditation.

shamans   A distinct class of religious specialists found among the Native Americans, Eskimos, and the tribes of South and Southeast Asia; undergo strenuous initiations by which they gain control over the spirits and are able to use them in healing and in flights to the spirit world.

Structuralism   A new method used in the study of religious myth and folktale that finds in the deep structure of these stories dualistic patterns of human relations and exchanges that require resolution.

Sufi   A Muslim mystic who teaches that salvation comes through a personal union with Allah and sometimes expresses views differing significantly from mainstream Islamic teachings; devotion often expressed in intense, passionate poetry.

superego   One of the three functional parts (with the id and ego) of the human personality as understood by Freud; originates in the child's identification with parents and others and serves as an internal censor of behavior. Embraces both the conscious and the unconscious conscience.

syncretism   In religion, the effort to bring together into a synthesis or harmony different beliefs or practices from several religious traditions to create a new union.

taboo   English form of the Polynesian word meaning "marked off" or "prohibited"; associated with a sacred—that is, dangerous—

object or person who is not to be touched or approached for fear of supernatural contagion.

Talmud   From Hebrew, meaning "learning" or "teaching"; an encyclopedic collection of the Jewish oral law consisting of the Mishnah (see p. 383) and Gemara. Compiled between the first century and the end of the fifth century C.E., and is the highest legal authority in Judaism after the five books of the written Torah.

theocratic   Of or under a theocracy—the rule of a state or a society by God or by priests or God's representatives who claim to rule by divine authority.

theodicy   From the Greek *theos* (god) and *dike* (justice); introduced by the philosopher Leibniz to designate the problem of justifying the goodness and power of God in view of the evil in the world. Used more broadly by social scientists to describe any legitimation of an ideology or world view in the face of the threat of chaos and meaninglessness.

theophany   The temporal and spatial manifestation of God or gods in some tangible, perceptual form; occurs in many religions, ancient and modern.

tonsure   The rite of clipping the hair or shaving the head to denote admission of a candidate to a religious order, often to a life of a monk.

totemism   Adopted from the Ojibwa Indian language for the widespread practice of associating human tribes or classes with animals or plants, from which the group is descended or has some close relationship. Some writers claim that the group worships the totem animal and that totemism is the earliest form of religion. These theories are now widely disputed.

Tripitaka   Sanskrit word used to designate the Buddhist sacred canon of writings.

typology   The study of types—for example, of religious phenomena such as forms of sacrifice and types of deity.

varna   Sanskrit word meaning "colors," or the four classes or divisions of society in Hinduism; the foundation of the caste system. The top three classes (Brahmans, Ksatriyas, Vaisyas) are the "twice-born" because they undergo initiations according to the sacred law.

Zealots   An ultranationalistic Jewish sect in Palestine who led the first war against Rome in 67–68 C.E.; disappeared after the fall of Jerusalem (70 C.E.).

Index

A

Action and salvation, 299–310
  Hinduism, 300–302
  Islam, 302–307
  Judaism, 307–310
Aggression, relationship to ritual, 123–124
Ahura Mazda and Ahriman, 178–179
Agnosticism, 35
Akitu festival, 117–119
al-Ghazālī, 272, 276
Allport, Gordon, 33–34
Almsgiving, Islam, 304
Alpert, Richard, 229
Amida Buddhism
  characteristics of, 292
  salvation, Shinran on, 292–293
An-atta, not-self doctrine, Theravada Buddhism, 241–242
Ancestor worship, 250
  natural religious communities and, 134–135
Androgyny, 201
Animism, 47, 51
Anomie, 89
Anthropology, 29–31
  functionalism, 29–30
    Nuer religion as example, 30–31
Anthropomorphism, 191
Anti-Christ, 261, 262
Antinomianism, 155, 262
Apocalypse, 178, 327–329
  apocalyptic writings, 327–328
  divergent schools of thought, 330
  final judgment, 329
  Marxist, 331

Aquinas, Thomas, 236
Archetypes, 10
  myth, Jungian view, 84–85
Aristotle, cosmological proof of God, 192–193
Asceity of God, 191
Ascetic methods, 311
Atonement
  doctrine of, 54
  and sacrifice, 121
    Yom Kippur as example, 122–123
Axis mundi, 56, 57, 60, 63

B

Babylonians
  Akitu festival, 117–119
  creation, concept of, 208–211
Bar/bat mitzvah, 309
Barbour, Ian, 91–92
Beatific Vision, 342–343
Berger, Peter, 254
Bhagavad Gita
  on caste, 300
  on devotionalism, 295–296
Bhakti, 291
Birth of the Gods, The (Swanson), 131
Birth rites, 108
  Hinduism as example, 108–109
Bodhisattva, 292
Book of the Dead, 335
Book of Infinite Love (de la Touche), 298
Book of Job, 270–273, 275–277
  suffering in
    and God's sovereignty, 275–276
    as result of sin, 270–271, 276